REGULATING ACCESS AND TRANSFER OF DATA

In theory, data is free, non-exclusive, and non-rivalrous. Yet data is off limits for business users of platforms in the data-driven economy. This book examines the infrastructure for collecting, storing, and distributing data to show how it is embedded behind technological barriers for the benefit of few large data-holders and to the detriment of business users and the economy as a whole. It proposes that the EU introduce an access and transfer right to data for users that can work in tandem with data protection rules and intellectual property law. Chapters explore the subject matter of this protection, potential rights holders and the scope of the protection, and exceptions and limitations under intellectual property law and competition law. Comprehensive and timely, *Regulating Access and Transfer of Data*, sets the foundations for a new legal system for our data-driven generation.

Björn Lundqvist is Professor of European Law with a focus on Competition Law at Stockholm University.

Global Competition Law and Economics Policy

This series publishes monographs highlighting the interdisciplinary and multijurisdictional nature of competition law, economics, and policy. Global in coverage, the series should appeal to competition and antitrust specialists working as scholars, practitioners, and judges.

Regulating Access and Transfer of Data

BJÖRN LUNDQVIST
Stockholm University

CAMBRIDGE
UNIVERSITY PRESS

CAMBRIDGE
UNIVERSITY PRESS

Shaftesbury Road, Cambridge CB2 8EA, United Kingdom

One Liberty Plaza, 20th Floor, New York, NY 10006, USA

477 Williamstown Road, Port Melbourne, VIC 3207, Australia

314–321, 3rd Floor, Plot 3, Splendor Forum, Jasola District Centre, New Delhi – 110025, India

103 Penang Road, #05–06/07, Visioncrest Commercial, Singapore 238467

Cambridge University Press is part of Cambridge University Press & Assessment, a department of the University of Cambridge.

We share the University's mission to contribute to society through the pursuit of education, learning and research at the highest international levels of excellence.

www.cambridge.org
Information on this title: www.cambridge.org/9781009335164

DOI: 10.1017/9781009335195

First published 2023

A catalogue record for this publication is available from the British Library.

ISBN 978-1-009-33516-4 Hardback

To my wife and daughters

Contents

1 **Introduction** 1

2 **The Data-Driven Economy** 6

2.1 Business Models 6
2.2 The Anticommons and Market Failures 22
2.3 More Economics for the Data-Driven Economy 34
2.4 What Is Data? 38
2.5 The Protection under Law for Data and Data-Driven Business Models 44
2.6 Technology Restrictions 46
2.7 Platform, Cloud, and IoT Contracts 51
2.8 The Bundle of Rights Identified as an Access and Transfer Right 56

3 **Competition Law** 68

3.1 General Competition Law 68
3.2 Abuse of Dominance 73
3.3 Anticompetitive Agreements 86
3.3.1 Data Pools 89
3.4 Procedural Challenges under Competition Law 92
3.5 Not Addressing the Issue of Accessing and Transferring Data? 93

4 **General and Sector-Specific Regulations** 95

4.1 Net Neutrality 95
4.2 Regulating Platforms and Data Holders 98
4.2.1 Platform-to-Business and Data Free Flow 99

4.2.2 The Data Act 102
4.2.3 The Digital Markets Act 108
4.2.4 A Competition Tool 123
4.3 Sector-Specific Regulations Targeting Access to Data 127
4.3.1 Open Data Directive 128
4.3.2 The Data Governance Act 130
4.3.3 The Digital Service Act and Directive on Payment Services II 134
4.4 Data Protection: GDPR 140
4.5 Not Addressing the Issue of Accessing and Transferring Data 144

5 **The Objectives of Regulating the Data-Driven Economy** 151
5.1 Introduction 151
5.2 Constitutional Aspects of the Enactment of an Access and Transfer Right 158
5.3 EU or the Member States 165

6 **The Intellectual Property Law System and Data** 167
6.1 Introduction 167
6.2 Rights and Exemptions in the Digital Economy 172
6.2.1 The New Copyright Directive: New Rights and Exemptions 172
6.2.2 Copyright Protection 176
6.2.3 Trade-Secret Protection and GDPR 190
6.2.4 The Interface 194
6.3 Exhaustion 196
6.3.1 Exhaustion and the Internet 196
6.3.2 Exhaustion and the Internet of Things 203

7 **An Access and Transfer Right to Data** 206
7.1 Introduction 206
7.2 Legal Definition of Data 211
7.3 GDPR for Individuals and ATR for Users 216
7.4 An Access and Transfer Right to Data for Business Users 219
7.5 A Property System or a Liability System? 223
7.6 Access and Transfer of Data for Complex IoT Systems 227
7.6.1 Complex Systems in Reference to Vehicles 230
7.7 A General Access and Transfer Right 234

8 **Conclusion** 239

Index 251

1

Introduction

The interface between digitalized information (Data), intellectual property, privacy regulations, and competition law in the 'Internet of Things' (IoT) scenario is currently triggering the interest of politicians, businessmen, the academic community, and, even, the general public. The groups are interested for different reasons; for example, businessmen see an opportunity for the creation of wealth; researchers see the possibility of gaining, analyzing, and distributing knowledge efficiently; and everyone acknowledges that the collection and distribution of data may raise several concerns in reference to private and public power, freedom, privacy, and data protection concerns.

The interface between the legal systems triggered by the creation, distribution, and consumption of data is difficult to grasp, and this book, therefore, tries to dissect this interface by the following information, that is, 'the data' from its sources, to users and reusers, and, ultimately, to its consumers.

The book starts with an attempt to identify the relevant problems from an economic and legal point of view. What are the major challenges? What legal systems are applicable in the process of creating and utilizing data? Which sector-specific regulations and intellectual property rights may be applicable when data is obtained from websites, platforms, and devices, and distributed to the Cloud, and, ultimately, when is it reused? Who 'owns' data, and do the current legislative efforts from the EU in reference to data create nascent property rules? The book will discuss when creators, holders, and users of raw or processed data, either private or public bodies, should benefit from the application of competition law, and whether competition law facilitates solutions for the needs that are identified.[1] The book specifically focuses on the application of competition law vis-à-vis the bodies that

1 See Ariel Ezrachi and Maurice E. Stucke, *Virtual Competition the Promise and Perils of the Algorithm-Driven Economy* (Harvard University Press 2016); and Maurice E. Stucke and Allen P. Grunes, *Big Data and Competition Policy* (Oxford University Press 2016).

collect or hold data focusing on the issue of whether competition law may be used to gain access to data, or the infrastructure around that data.[2] May competition law be used to create a level playing field between holders and nonholders of essential data?

The book will raise the issue of sector-specific regulation in the arena of data. Access to data is a disputed issue not only under 'general' competition law but also discussed in reference to general and sector-specific regulations in reference to data. Regulations such as the newly proposed Data Act,[3] Digital Markets Act,[4] Digital Service Act,[5] the Platform-to-Business (P2B),[6] Data Free Flow Regulation,[7] the Open Data Directive,[8] PSD2,[9] and the *eCall* Regulation[10] are discussed.[11] Indeed, it seems that rules regarding access of data are currently seeping into sector-specific

[2] In reference to Open Data, see Josef Drexl, 'The Competition Dimension of the European Regulation of Public Sector Information and the Concept of an Undertaking', in Josef Drexl and Vicente Bagnoli (eds), *State-Initiated Restraints of Competition* (ASCOLA Competition Law, Edward Elgar 2015), 64–100. See also Björn Lundqvist, '"Turning Government Data into Gold": The Interface between EU Competition Law and the Public Sector Information Directive – With Some Comments on the Compass Case' (2013) 44(1) IIC – International Review of Intellectual Property and Competition Law 79–95.

[3] 'Proposal for a Regulation of the European Parliament and of the Council on harmonised rules on fair access to and use of data (Data Act)', COM (2022) 68 final (23.2.2022).

[4] 'Proposal for a Regulation of the European Parliament and of the Council on contestable and fair markets in the digital sector (Digital Markets Act) Brussels', COM (2020) 842 final (15.12.2020).

[5] 'Proposal for a Regulation of the European Parliament and of the Council on a Single Market For Digital Services (Digital Services Act) and amending Directive 2000/31/EC', COM(2020) 825 final (15.12.2020).

[6] Regulation (EU) 2019/1150 of the European Parliament and of the Council of 20 June 2019 on promoting fairness and transparency for business users of online intermediation services.

[7] Regulation (EU) 2018/1807 of the European Parliament and of the Council of 14 November 2018 on a framework for the free flow of nonpersonal data in the European Union.

[8] The Directive on the reuse of public sector information Directive (EU) 2019/1024 of the European Parliament and of the Council of 20 June 2019 on open data and the reuse of public sector information, OJ L172, 26.6.2019, 56–83 (The old PSI directive: Directive 2003/98/EC, known as the 'PSI Directive') entered into force on 31 December 2003. It was revised by Directive 2013/37/EU, which entered into force on 17 July 2013.

[9] In order to accelerate retail banking innovation and simplify payments, the European Commission is mandating standardized API access across the EU. The initiative is part of the European Commission's update of the Directive on Payment Services(PSD). The revision to the Directive on Payment Services (PSD2) requires banks to provide access to third parties. See Directive (EU) 2015/2366 of the European Parliament and of the Council of 25 November 2015, on payment services in the internal market, amending Directives 2002/65/EC, 2009/110/EC, and 2013/36/EU and Regulation (EU) No 1093/2010, and repealing Directive 2007/64/EC (Text with EEA relevance). cf Commission, A Digital Single Market Strategy for Europe, COM (2015) 192 final <http://eur-lex.europa.eu/legal-content/EN/TXT/?uri=celex%3A52015DC0192> accessed 20 September 2016.

[10] Regulation (EU) 2015/758 of the European Parliament and of the Council of 29 April 2015, concerning type-approval requirements for the deployment of the eCall in-vehicle system based on the 112 service and amending Directive 2007/46/EC.

[11] There are several French national initiatives to open e-platforms for third-party competitors. See French Senate Report (20 March 2013).

regulations, implying an obligation either to share data or to grant open access to the device, which collects the data.[12]

The first part of the book concludes, first, that general competition law may not be readily applicable to access data, except for the situation where the dataset is indispensable to access an industry or a relevant market.[13] Even though general and sector-specific regulations seem to emerge as a tool for accessing data held by competitors or firms, in general, they fail to fulfill their aim to create competition and a leveled playing field.

In reference to the new obligations now being implemented vis-à-vis platforms, the use of a new competition tool for the benefit of use of the competition authorities is more beneficial than trying to obtain the same result through heavy and detailed sector-specific rules. Indeed, one takeaway of the first part of the book is that instead of having ex ante rules as prescribed in the Digital Markets Act, Data Act, and other sector-specific regulations, a more general Competition Tool should be enacted and used by national competition authorities.

The main challenge for the data industry, at its current development, is to create a leveled playing field by trying to facilitate the implementation of IoT. We will see IoT platforms developing by collecting, storing, and using data in competition with the incumbent industry firms. The utilization of data will increase competition and innovation in the industry to the benefit of consumers and society, and it is necessary to create the right balance or equilibrium in reference to access and utilization of data so as to generate innovation and competition. The second part, therefore, starts with a discussion of the relevant constitutional and market economy values and principles that is at stake for the future. Internet revolution 4.0 is discussed and dissected. Even though there is an emerging consensus today that big tech firms must be tamed, that has not always been the case. The hands-off policy choice both in the United States and in the EU throughout the twentieth century was to treat the Internet as a new legal dimension and that information society services should be nonregulated.[14] The choice was to subject it to significantly less regulation than

[12] Alex Chisholm and Nelson Jung, 'Platform Regulation – Ex-Ante versus Ex-Post Intervention: Evolving Our Antitrust Tools and Practices to Meet the Challenges of a Digital Economy' (Spring–Autumn 2015) 11(1) Competition Policy International 7–21.

[13] cf C-170/13 – Huawei Technologies ECLI:EU:C:2015:477.

[14] According to Savin, in 1997, then-US President Bill Clinton's senior policy advisor Ira Magaziner played a decisive role in outlining the scope of regulatory reach toward information society services, thus defining the shape of the modern Internet. Magaziner's main contribution was a 'hands-off' approach to regulating the content layer of the Internet. The policy principles that Magaziner introduced were deceptively simple. The Internet is a medium with enormous potential for 'promoting individual freedom and individual empowerment'. In order to preserve this, where possible, the rules that govern it 'should be set by private, non-profit, stakeholder-based groups'. Governments should refrain from intervening unless absolutely necessary. This approach resulted in a firm policy based on a simple idea: The private sector should lead and, where regulation is needed, it should be kept to a minimum and should foster a 'predictable, consistent, and simple legal environment'. This created a completely different

either telecommunications networks and services or broadcasting media with editorial control.[15] The magnitude of this policy choice should not escape us, indeed while cables and radio waves used to convey the Internet were heavily regulated to disperse power, the content layer largely remained free. The issue is then whether to start regulating the content layer, that is, the data-driven businesses, or whether there is still a compelling reason for not introducing heavy behavioral regulations.

The thesis put forward in the book is that neither heavy sector-specific regulation of the data-driven economy should be introduced nor strict principles of net neutrality, while instead a new form of right to access and transfer data should be enacted for the benefit of the business users of platforms and users and data generators of IoT devices. The solution could diminish market power and alleviate signs of unfairness and market failures, while keeping the data-driven economy and competition 'free' from excessive ex ante regulation. It will infuse competition by promoting the users, often small- to medium-sized enterprises (SMEs), to equal access and utilization of data in the digital economy. This issue is explored in Chapters 4–7, while dissecting the Digital Markets Act and the Data Act.

In the end, it will be argued that the regulation of the data-driven economy could be limited in ambit, while being amended or supplemented with a right for accessing and transferring the data that is collected and stored by data holders. Such an access and transfer right should be drafted as a 'countervailing' right with inspiration from the exemptions for data mining and reverse engineering and would allow users to circumvent the data holders' right to protection under technical protection measures (TPMs), database rights, and trade-secret legislation to gain access to the data generated by themselves and to utilize said data. Such a limited access and transfer right (ATR) could be included in the Data Act or be included in an updated database directive.

Moreover, the right to access and transfer for users should also be aligned with the General Data Protection Regulation (GDPR), giving a user the right to access and transfer personal data when the user can provide equal protection under the GDPR as the original data-holder.

The ATR could be supplemented in an updated version of the database directive, for the benefit of users. The database directive could moreover go further and grant a more elaborated right when users have invested time and/or effort to create useful data to the level that the user would gain a database right in its own right

regulatory pattern on the content layer than the one seen in many other networked industries. cf Andrej Savin, 'New Directions in EU Policymaking on the Content Layer: Disruption and Law' (29 April 2020) Copenhagen Business School, CBS LAW Research Paper No 20-05 <https://ssrn.com/abstract=3588387>. See also Ira C. Magaziner, 'Creating a Framework for Global Electronic Commerce' (July 1999) Future Insight, Release 6.1 n <www.pff.org/issues-pubs/futureinsights/fi6.1globaleconomiccommerce.html>; and Jonathan Nuechterlein and Philip Weiser, *Digital Crossroads: Telecommunications Law and Policy in the Internet Age* (2nd ed., MIT Press 2013).

[15] Nuechterlein and Weiser (n 14).

In reference to the sensors or the systems that will collect the data from IoT devices, the book argues that the Data Act should be revised and – more clearly – take its starting point in the principle or doctrine that the holder of the property right to the device and the sensor should also hold the right to extract data from the sensor and device. The legal point of departure should, thus, be based on the legal consequences of trade in goods and services, and the doctrine of exhaustion. A property holder should have the right to license access to the sensor to third parties. Often that would imply giving access to a platform or tech giants. Yet, the user of IoT devices with sensors should have equal right to access and transfer the user-generated data, including such inferred data originating from the sensor. Indeed, the right proposed in the book (the ATR) should be granted to the user, and it will create a level playing field between users, property holders, and platforms, while protecting and honoring the business model of data-driven platforms as well as business models of the incumbents of the old industry, and ultimately of the users.

2

The Data-Driven Economy

2.1 BUSINESS MODELS

Data is vital to the internet-based economy and will become even more important in the old economy as the Internet of Things (IoT) gains ground. The competitiveness of firms will increasingly depend on timely access to relevant data and the ability to use that data to develop new, innovative applications and products. In consumer-oriented businesses, the relevant data is often personal information; although this data is becoming increasingly collectable, only a few firms have access to larger amounts of it.[1]

Consumers' access to digital services is offered to a significant degree in exchange for the sharing of personal data.[2] However, this data-for-service concept applies to most of the large platforms, which collect personal and nonpersonal data from individuals and firms that are compelled to provide data when they want to be active on the Internet.

[1] See generally Ariel Ezrachi, *Virtual Competition: The Promise and Perils of the Algorithm-Driven Economy* (Harvard University Press 2017); Shoshana Zuboff, *The Age of Surveillance Capitalism: The Fight for a Human Future at the New Frontier of Power* (Profile Books 2019); Nick Srnicek, *Platform Capitalism* (John Wiley & Sons 2017); Jonathan E. Nuechterlein and Philip J. Weiser, *Digital Crossroads* (MIT Press 2005); José van Dijck, Martijn de Waal, and Thomas Poell, *The Platform Society: Public Values in a Connective World* (Oxford University Press 2018); Inge Graef, *EU Competition Law, Data Protection and Online Platforms: Data as Essential Facility* (Kluwer Law International, International Competition Law Series, vol 68, 2016); Orla Lynskey, *The Foundations of EU Data Protection Law* (Oxford University Press 2015).

[2] This applies to about 30 percent of antivirus and navigation software and cloud storage services, 77 percent of streaming services, and more than 50 percent of movies, video, TV content, e-books, and games. See Stefan Larsson, på uppdrag av Konkurrensverket, Dataekonomier: Om plattformar, tredjepartsaktörer och behovet av transparens på digitala marknader [2020] Uppdragsforskningsrapport 4 34.

A major gateway for business users of platforms is the application programming interface (API). An API is software that allows a program to access and interact with another program to share data and functionality. Application programming interfaces provide a standardized way to integrate different businesses, optimizing their level of interoperability and reducing barriers to enable more agile and interconnected ecosystems. Platforms, therefore, use thousands of APIs to allow third-party developers and service providers to use and interact with these platforms. Application programming interfaces can presumably be protected by copyright in some jurisdictions,[3] while platforms may technically use APIs to exclude third-party developers and third-party service providers or to deprecate the services that these third parties provide on the platforms.[4] Indeed, APIs are the gateways, while platforms are the gatekeepers controlling the APIs. Inside is the so-called 'walled garden'.

The notion of the walled garden[5] is often used to describe ecosystems, such as Google's and Facebook's respective systems, which exclusively collect the data and

3 See however *Google v Oracle*, where the US Supreme Court indicated that access and use of APIs fall under the US fair-use exemption. For the background of the case, see J. Ciani, 'A Competition-Law-Oriented Look at the Application of Data Protection and IP Law to the Internet of Things: Towards a Wider "Holistic Approach"' in Mor Bakhoum, B. Conde Gallego, Mark-Oliver Mackenrodt, and Giantre Surblytė-Namavičienė (eds), *Personal Data in Competition, Consumer Protection and Intellectual Property Law* (MPI Studies on Intellectual Property and Competition Law, vol 28, Springer 2018), explaining that the CAFC reversed the ruling by Judge William Alsup of the Northern District of California that APIs are not subject to copyright. The CAFC treated patents and copyrights as providing overlapping protection for computer program innovations. The US Supreme Court decision not to review the CAFC ruling left this finding intact. However, the case returned to Judge Alsup's district court for a jury trial focused on Google's fair-use defense. In May 2016, the jury unanimously agreed that Google's use of the Java APIs 'constitutes a fair use under the Copyright Act', cf. *Google, Inc. v Oracle America, Inc.*, 135 S.Ct. 2887 (2015). Oracle appealed the retrial. On 27 March 2018, the US Court of Appeals for the Federal Circuit reversed the retrial's decision, concluding that Google's use of the Java API packages was not fair and violated Oracle's copyrights. Google's commercial use of the API packages weighed against a finding of fair use. Google merely copied the material and moved it from one platform to another without alteration, not a transformative use. The court remanded for a trial on damages, but Google may still appeal to the Supreme Court. See *Oracle America, Inc. v Google, Inc.*, No 17-1118 (Fed. Cir. 2018). For an interesting paper discussing APIs, see Jörg Hoffmann and Begoña Gonzalez Otero, 'Demystifying the Role of Data Interoperability in the Access and Sharing Debate' (29 September 2020) Max Planck Institute for Innovation & Competition Research Paper No. 2016 <https://ssrn.com/abstract=3705217> or <http://dx.doi.org/10.2139/ssrn.3705217>.

4 According to Appendix J of the Competition and Markets Authority (2020), Online platforms and digital advertising: Market study final report (hereinafter CMA Final Report), on a number of occasions Facebook has excluded or deprecated third-party business users of the Facebook platform with the use of APIs.

5 'Walled gardens' are closed ecosystems in which a platform provides a complete, end-to-end technical solution for advertisers and publishers, and advertisers and publishers are restricted in their ability to choose other technical solutions. These ecosystems can be very large; Google's system includes Android and Chrome operating systems, YouTube, Gmail, and Google Maps.

where individual-level data remains under the control of these platforms and is generally not shared with other market participants.[6]

It should be acknowledged that platforms – specifically Google and Facebook – do not collect data solely from their own respective ecosystems or walled gardens. Data is also provided by third parties: the business users of platforms, for example, advertisers and publishers, including news and other content providers. They provide data voluntarily to the platforms while also indirectly giving access to their websites so that Google and Facebook can collect data. As stated in a final report from July 2020, the Competition and Markets Authority (CMA) claims that for platforms in reference to digital advertisement, there are two broad sources to use for collecting data: (1) data gathered from the platforms' own walled garden (or, as CMA defines it, their 'consumer-facing services and products') and (2) data collected from third parties, notably those that use the platforms' services and technology on their own websites.[7]

In reference to their own ecosystems, platforms collect data regarding each individual user when that user browses or logs on to a platform. Everything is collected, from web and search history, the hardware used, uploaded or written information on the web, and clicks to information that the user's mouse has hovered over. Generally, information regarding all individual activities in the ecosystems and background information regarding the users is collected, categorized, and stored as data. It should also be noted that while Google has an unprecedented fifty-three consumer-facing services, where data may be harvested directly, Google's and Facebook's substantial ability to collect data from third-party websites and apps sets them apart from other platforms.

Competition and Markets Authority has found that Google is the leader in terms of coverage of third-party websites and holds even more of a lead if one considers the platform's popularity. Google tags that collect data are found on over 80 percent of the world's most popular websites, and Google has provided software development kits that collect observed and volunteered data to 85 percent of the most popular apps in the Play Store.[8] Google also collects data from its publishing service and ad exchange. Oracle Moat claims that it is impossible to use the Internet without providing data to Google and that approximately 75 percent of the top 100,000 websites on the Internet use Google Analytics.[9] This is also supported by earlier

Facebook's ecosystem includes WhatsApp, Instagram, Messenger, and Marketplace. CMA Final Report 4.24 fn 225.

6 See CMA Final Report 4.24. Platforms share aggregate-level data to some extent with other market participants.

7 CMA Final Report Appendix F.

8 Ibid.

9 Ibid. The research by Elena Maris, Timothy Libert, and Jennifer R Henrichsen, 'The Tracked Society: Interdisciplinary Approaches on Online Tracking' (2020) 22(11) New Media & Society 2018–2038 should also be mentioned. Their analysis of 22,484 pornography websites indicated that 93 percent leak user data to a third party, and tracking on these sites is highly concentrated

research. Engelhardt and Narayanan's detailed measurement of online tracking in 2016, based on a crawl of the top 1 million websites, shows that Google tracked activities on 85 percent of the sites.[10] All of the top five third-party trackers belonged to the Google ecosystem, and twelve of the top twenty were Google-owned domains.[11]

Facebook holds second place regarding the prevalence of tags, covering 40 to 50 percent of the most popular websites, and providing software development kits that collect observed and volunteered data to 40 percent of the most popular apps on the Play Store. Facebook thus tracks users on websites without advertisements. Such tracking can provide additional insights into individuals' habits, and online advertising companies such as Facebook and Google offer web developers a range of 'free' nonadvertising services that are subsidized when developers allow Facebook and Google to track users. For example, a developer may include the Facebook 'Like' button on a website to facilitate sharing content, which allows Facebook to track the activities of all visitors – irrespective of whether these visitors are Facebook users.[12]

The Australian Competition Authority (ACCC) reached similar findings in its Digital Platforms Inquiry. According to the ACCC, the breadth and depth of user data collected by the incumbent digital platforms provide them with a strong competitive advantage, creating barriers to rivals' entry and expansion in relevant markets, and allowing the incumbent digital platforms to move into adjacent markets. Although there is no shortage of user data, and a large number of businesses track consumers' digital footprints, no other businesses come close to achieving the level of tracking undertaken by Google and Facebook. The ACCC estimates that more than 70 percent of websites have a Google tracker and more than 20 percent of websites have a Facebook tracker. It is also estimated that of the apps available on the Google Play Store, 88 percent send user data back to Google and 43 percent send user data back to Facebook. The multiple touch points that Google and Facebook each have with their users enable them to collect more user data, improve their services, and attract more users and advertisers, creating a virtuous feedback loop.[13] The required data is the fabric used to develop and create new services.

to a handful of major companies. Google was by far the top third-party tracker, monitoring 74 percent of the pages in the analysis. According to the researchers, the primary reason for tracking pornographic websites was to identify sexual preference. CMA Final Report Appendix F; Commission, 'Enter the Data Economy: EU Policies for a Thriving Data Ecosystem' 21 EPSC Strategic Notes, 11 January 2017, 1.

10 Steven Englehardt and Arvind Narayanan, 'Online Tracking: A 1-Million-Site Measurement and Analysis' (2016) ACM Conference on Computer and Communications Security Section 5, FPF Privacy Papers for Policy Makers Award. See also T. Libert, 'Exposing the Invisible Web: An Analysis of Third-Party Http Requests on 1 Million Websites' (2015) 9 International Journal of Communication 3544–3561.

11 Englehardt and Narayanan (n 10).

12 Maris et al. (n 9).

13 Australian Competition & Consumer Commission (ACCC), Digital Platforms Inquiry, Final Report, part 1, p. 11.

Given the business strategy of data-driven businesses and the reach of Google and Facebook, individuals as well as firms using these and other services on the Internet are de facto forced to yield data.[14] Several of the services provided on the Internet are indispensable to proper and normal function in society, and accessing these services requires the user's consent under the General Data Protection Regulation (GDPR) for platforms to collect data. Even if the provider of the specific internet-based service in question does not collect the data, this data can still be generated – and may benefit the large platforms because they provide third-party technology and services to the website in question and have acquired broad consents from users.[15] Moreover, several of the necessary services provided on the Internet today also force users to agree to allow the provider to store and to be able to analyze the data created by user activities on the platform.[16]

It should be noted that Facebook and Google are active on a global, internet-based advertising market, where access to individuals and knowledge of their conduct is core business practice. Globally, spending on digital ads was expected to reach $333.25 billion in 2019, representing half of global spending on advertising. According to CNBC and emarket, Google and Facebook now represent a global duopoly that accounts for at least half of this market, followed by China's Alibaba and then Amazon. Rounding out the top six are two other Chinese companies, Baidu and Tencent.[17] Together, Google and Facebook account for 70 percent of the US market for digital ads.[18] Studies conducted by the ACCC provide clear indications that commercial media, and in particular traditional print media (now print/online media), suffered a significant reduction in advertising revenue owing to the unbundling of classified advertisements from newspapers and increasing competition from internet-based platforms. A considerable drop in the print advertising revenue of commercial Australian media publishers has been accompanied by a rise in spending on online advertising. The authority concluded that digital platforms have clearly taken an increasing share of advertising expenditure, with a significant portion of the increase in online advertising revenue from 2014 to 2018 going to Google and Facebook.[19]

[14] It seems very difficult to de facto refuse or withdraw consent to access data, see discussion in Chapter 6. cf Eugenia Politou, Efthimios Alepis, and Constantinos Patsakis, 'Forgetting Personal Data and Revoking Consent under the GDPR: Challenges and Proposed Solutions' (2018) 4 Journal of Cybersecurity 1 tyy001 <https://doi.org/10.1093/cybsec/tyy001>.

[15] See discussion in Chapter 6.

[16] For an early reference regarding data, see Ezrachi (n 1) [Elektronisk resurs].

[17] Megan Graham, 'Earnings This Week Show Snap, Amazon and Twitter are Cutting into the Google-Facebook Ad Duopoly' (CNBC, 27 July 2019) <www.cnbc.com/2019/07/27/snap-twitter-and-amazon-are-cutting-into-google-facebook-duopoly.html?source=twitter%7Cmain>.

[18] Associated Press, 'Plummeting Digital ad Market May Complicate Life for Google, Facebook' (MarketWatch, 28 April 2020) <www.marketwatch.com/story/as-demand-for-digital-advertising-plummets-google-and-facebook-could-have-shrinking-revenues-2020-04-28>.

[19] ACCC, Digital Platforms Inquiry, Final Report, part 1, p. 17 et seq.

Google and Facebook are not the only players collecting data. According to some estimates, Amazon captures 46 percent of online shopping, selling around 90 percent of all e-books in the United States,[20] and more than 70 percent of online shoppers use Amazon to compare products found on a brand's website. Amazon collects data from these activities on its own platform and nearby ecosystem and also receives information from third-party publisher sites, where publishers monetize their ad inventory through Amazon Publisher Services or Amazon Ad Exchange.[21] Amazon also collects cookie IDs when customers use a web browser as well as mobile advertising IDs when users link to sites on mobile devices.[22] Amazon seems to collect vast amounts of data from purchasers and users of the platforms, but Amazon also has access and the right to use suppliers' or business users' data. Access and the right to use that data would, under certain circumstances, give Amazon considerable leverage in terms of knowledge.

It should be noted that several authorities are investigating whether Amazon uses business customers' data to promote its own private label. The German *Bundeskartelamt* has concluded such an investigation.[23] The European Commission has informed Amazon of its preliminary view in its Statement of Objection, charging that the company has breached EU antitrust rules by distorting competition in online retail markets. The Commission took issue with Amazon's systematic reliance on nonpublic business data from independent suppliers who sell in Amazon's marketplace, to the benefit of Amazon's own retail business, which directly competes with those third-party sellers.[24] The Commission's preliminary findings show that very large quantities of nonpublic seller data were available to

[20] Lina Khan, 'Amazon's Antitrust Paradox' (2017) 126 Yale Law Journal 712 et seq; Olivia LaVecchia and Stacy Mitchell, 'Amazon's Stranglehold: How the Company's Tightening Grip Is Stifling Competition, Eroding Jobs, and Threatening Communities' [2016] Institute for Local Self-Reliance 10 <https://ilsr.org/wp-content/uploads/2020/04/ILSR_AmazonReport_final.pdf>.

[21] From a review of Amazon's privacy policies, it appears that the company probably does not sell personally identifiable Echo data to third parties such as music streaming services, though the policy is not clear in this respect; there does not appear to be any limitation on the transfer of aggregated data, and Amazon may change these policies at any time. It is not evident from Amazon's privacy policies that there are limits on the company's ability to purchase data from a third party such as Fitbit, to aggregate that database with Amazon's own data, and then to identify particular kinds of consumers (e.g., long-distance runners) on that basis. See Stigler Final Report 232. For a critical analysis of other firms' collection and mining of data, see W. Christl, 'Corporate Surveillance in Everyday Life: How Companies Collect, Combine, Analyze, Trade, and Use Personal Data on Billions' (Cracked Labs 2017) 6.

[22] CMA Final Report Appendix F.

[23] For the Bundeskartelamt investigation, see <www.bundeskartellamt.de/SharedDocs/Meldung/EN/Pressemitteilungen/2019/17_07_2019_Amazon.html>. These investigations are discussed in Björn Lundqvist, 'Regulating Competition in the Digital Economy with a Special Focus on Platforms' in Björn Lundqvist and Michal Gal (eds), *Competition Law for the Digital Economy* (ASCOLA Competition Law Series, Edward Elgar 2019).

[24] The EU Commission is looking into the standard agreements between Amazon and marketplace sellers, which allow Amazon's retail business to analyze and use third-party seller data. In

employees of Amazon's retail business; this data were transferred directly into the automated systems of that business, and these systems aggregate the data and used it to calibrate Amazon's retail offers and strategic business decisions – to the detriment of the other marketplace sellers. For example, the data allowed Amazon to focus its offers for the bestselling products across product categories and to adjust its offers based on nonpublic data of competing sellers. The Commission's preliminary view, outlined in its Statement of Objections, was that the use of nonpublic marketplace seller data allowed Amazon to avoid the normal risks of retail competition and leverage its dominance in the market for the provision of marketplace services in France and Germany – Amazon's biggest EU markets. The case has now been settled.[25]

The US House Antitrust Subcommittee is also looking into Amazon's behavior. In response to questions for the record from House Antitrust Subcommittee Chairman David Cicilline (D-RI), Amazon claimed not using individual data, and that it only uses aggregated data to develop with its own line of products. Amazon's use of private data to shape and promote its own branded goods seems to be a key question for lawmakers and regulators probing the company's competitive practices.[26] Nevertheless, Amazon still seems to be the leading transaction platform globally, collecting vast amounts of data about customers, the business users of its marketplace, and the products and services being purchased. The company has an exclusive, bird's eye view of several markets, including the data representing the sales and purchasing activities of possibly all firms and customers active in these markets – on an individual level – and may thus understand purchasing and supply patterns that enable Amazon to enter the market vertically and successfully with its private label.[27]

However, in terms of advertising business, Google and Facebook are the clear leaders. These firms are vertically integrated, in the sense that they sell their own public ad inventory, that is, ads on their platforms and websites[28] to publishers, while

particular, the Commission will focus on whether and how the use of accumulated marketplace seller data by Amazon as a retailer affects competition. The EU Commission will also examine the role of data in the selection of the winners of the 'Buy Box' and the impact of Amazon's potential use of competitively sensitive marketplace seller information on that selection. The Buy Box is displayed prominently on Amazon and allows customers to add items from a specific retailer directly into their shopping carts. Winning the Buy Box seems key for marketplace sellers, as a vast majority of transactions are conducted through it. See <https://ec.europa.eu/commission/presscorner/detail/en/IP_19_4291>.

25 See discussion infra in chapter 3 European Commission, 'Antitrust: Commission Sends Statement of Objections to Amazon for the Use of Non-public Independent Seller Data and Opens Second Investigation into Its E-Commerce Business Practices' (10 November 2020) <https://ec.europa.eu/commission/presscorner/detail/en/ip_20_2077>.

26 Lauren Feiner, 'Amazon Admits to Congress That It Uses "Aggregated" Data from Third-Party Sellers to Come up with Its Own Products' (CNBC, 19 November 2019) <www.cnbc.com/2019/11/19/amazon-uses-aggregated-data-from-sellers-to-build-its-own-products.html>.

27 Björn Lundqvist, 'Cloud Service as the Ultimate Gate(Keeper)' (2019) 7(2) The Journal of Antitrust Enforcement 220.

28 Google controls websites such YouTube; Facebook controls Instagram and WhatsApp.

also providing their own respective ad exchanges or platforms where they sell publishers' ad inventory to third parties. Interestingly, these companies also are active on the other side of the ad market, where they both offer demand-side platforms providing purchasers with advertising inventory.[29] According to CMA, Google is dominant in both the respective ad exchanges or platforms and the demand-side platforms.[30] A CMA report also notes that Google has been able to use its market power in search technology and its wider ecosystem to build its ad inventory business and, in addition, its position as a demand-side platform.[31] To do so, Google has leveraged its user data and large base of advertisers (from Google Ads, its ad inventory business) to favor its demand-side platform, and by tying access to YouTube, to allow use of its demand-side platform services. Google, Facebook, and Amazon thus collect huge amounts of information horizontally regarding individuals and who they are while also collecting data vertically regarding the products and firms utilizing the platforms' services

Google and Facebook possess a competitive advantage in terms of having such a broad network among third-party service providers that collect data for them. Moreover, these platforms can carry out attribution accurately for campaigns that advertisers run, at least in part, on their own 'walled garden' platforms. The ability to attribute, that is, to track users to see whether the advertisement or promotion was successful, sets Google and Facebook apart from the rest of the platforms, which are not ad-focused to the same degree. Amazon has access to detailed, high-quality data about consumers' activities and other types of data originating from Amazon's own platform, but Amazon's reach does not extend widely to the rest of the Internet (or to the physical (IRL) world, for that matter).

There is some evidence suggesting that Google may face competition from Amazon on Google's search queries that relate to retail.[32] Amazon is likely to have important competitive advantages owing to its broader role as an e-commerce channel. Some survey evidence suggests that Amazon is sometimes the preferred

[29] CMA Final Report 19 et seq.

[30] Their analysis of 22,484 pornography websites indicated that 93 percent leak user data to a third party. Tracking on these sites is highly concentrated to a handful of major companies, which were identified. We successfully extracted privacy policies for 3,856 sites, 17 percent of the total. The policies were written so that one would likely need at least a two-year college education to understand them. Our content analysis of the sample's domains indicated that 44.97 percent of them expose or suggest a specific gender/sexual identity or interest likely to be linked to the user. We identified three core implications of the quantitative results: (1) the unique/elevated risks of porn data leakage versus other types of data, (2) the particular risks/impact for 'vulnerable' populations, and (3) the complications of providing consent for porn-site users and the need for affirmative consent in these online sexual interactions.

[31] This is also supported by research conducted on the behalf of the Swedish Competition Authority, where out of the media website analyzed, all news media and 28/39 websites used Google Ad Works, and Google was tracking 90 of the analyzed 116 sites. See Larsson (n 2) 67.

[32] BloomReach Survey, 'State of Amazon 2016' (23 September 2016) found that Amazon is the preferred starting point for product search.

consumer starting point for product search, while other survey evidence seems to imply the opposite; the latter indicates that the percentage of shoppers starting their shopping journey on Amazon is significantly lower than the percentage of shoppers starting on Google.[33]

Content providers noted that Google's and Facebook's attribution tool allows advertisers to track views of their ads and then link this to behavior on the advertiser's site and stores. The content providers claim that these kinds of tools place the digital giants at a commercial advantage because they can collect and analyze viewing data from content providers but then do not provide this data on an individual level to the content provider.[34]

'Walled garden' platforms can thus combine the ability to accurately monitor conversions with the ability to track users across different devices and sessions, resulting in more accurate attribution of consumers' actions. In the case of Google, the platform can track users across more than fifty-three consumer-facing services under its control. However, Google's access to mobile data from Android also gives it some ability to monitor the actions of consumers offline (IRL), for example, by identifying store visits. Google can thereby conclude quite accurately whether a marketing activity on its platform has been successful. Did indeed the target purchaser – the individual exposed to the ad – purchase the marketed goods by physically transferring themselves to the store in question within a certain time after being exposed to the ad? At the same time, the broader effects generated by the content provided on the platform can be monitored. Given the enormous penetration of Google and other platforms, the ability to monitor effects originating from specific events or behavior, both globally and on an individual level, is unprecedented in history.[35]

It should be mentioned that platforms also try to restrict other firms from acquiring the muscle needed to monitor and attribute. In 2018, Google restricted access to its User IDs (the DoubleClick ID) by removing the DoubleClick ID from its Campaign Manager and demand-side platforms (DSPs) log files, and curtailed the availability of user-level exposure data from ad campaigns. This meant that ad buyers could no longer extract data from the DoubleClick Campaign Manager for reporting on ad performance and ad attribution. Google indicated that the DoubleClick ID could be tied to sensitive information such as user search histories and could thus violate the strict data privacy requirements of GDPR.[36] However, it seems clear that Google could still access individual data – or at least extract the same information from other parts of its ecosystem.

33 Ibid.

34 CMA Final Report Appendix F.

35 Ibid.

36 Ibid.

Stakeholders on the buyer side suggested that stripping out the DoubleClick ID removed visibility about user activity within the DoubleClick ecosystem, making it almost impossible to compare the performance of ads purchased through the Google AdTech stack to ads purchased through other intermediaries. It was also suggested that the change made independent ad attribution much more difficult.[37]

The strategy of restricting data access for competitors and potential competitors is particularly relevant, for example, to understand the impact of Google's recent announcement that Chrome browsers will stop support for third-party cookies in the future, thus restricting the ability of publishers to sell personalized advertising.[38]

It seems clear the platform providers can become the masters of their respective data ecosystems, or walled gardens, and inside these gardens they can indeed hoard data. Generally, they do not trade or share the individual-based data originating from the platform, or more precisely, the walled garden.[39] It seems much more profitable to provide sophisticated and refined services based on collected data than to sell the raw data as a commodity.[40] Other platforms have more limited access to data in terms of quantity and/or quality of analytics data coming from Google's and Facebook's walled gardens; on the other hand, these platforms have a general reach that allows them to mine data across the entire Internet, and this constitutes a barrier to entry and expansion.[41] The advantage held by Google, Facebook, and (to some extent) Amazon is that they are vertically integrated into the digital advertising business.

Competition and Markets Authority claims in its report that publishers in particular complain about the extent of vertical integration that has taken place in the open display market. While vertical integration can allow intermediaries to realize

37 Ibid.; Damien Geradin, 'Online Platforms and Digital Advertising Market Study: Observations on the Statement of Scope' (13 February 2020) <https://ssrn.com/abstract=3537856> or <http://dx.doi.org/10.2139/ssrn.3537856>.

38 CMA Final Report Appendix F; Damien Geradin, Katsifis Dimitrios, and Theano Karanikioti, 'Google as a De Facto Privacy Regulator: Analyzing Chrome's Removal of Third-Party Cookies from an Antitrust Perspective' (26 November 2020) <https://papers.ssrn.com/sol3/papers.cfm?abstract_id=3738107>; Damien Geradin and Dimitrios Katsifis, 'Taking a Dive into Google's Chrome Cookie Ban' (19 February 2020). <https://ssrn.com/abstract=3541170> or <http://dx.doi.org/10.2139/ssrn.3541170>; Damien Geradin and Dimitrios Katsifis, 'Trust Me, I'm Fair': Analysing Google's Latest Practices in Ad Tech from the Perspective of EU Competition Law' (7 October 2019) TILEC Discussion Paper No DP 2019-029 <https://ssrn.com/abstract=3465780> or <http://dx.doi.org/10.2139/ssrn.3465780>.

39 As mentioned earlier in this book, neither Google nor Facebook trades personal data to third parties. cf <https://safety.google/privacy/ads-and-data/> and Kurt Wagner, 'This Is How Facebook Uses Your Data for Ad Targeting. You've Got Questions. We've Got Answers' *Vox* (11 April 2018). See also Lundqvist (n 27) 220 and CMA Final Report Appendix F.

40 Regarding value chains, see M. E. Porter, 'Clusters and the New Economics of Competition' (1998) 76(6) Harvard Business Review 77–90. See generally regarding profit margins for data-driven value chains: Roberto Moro Visconti, Alberto Larocca, and Michele Marconi, 'Big Data-Driven Value Chains and Digital Platforms: From Value Co-Creation to Monetization' (18 January 2017) <https://ssrn.com/abstract=2903799> or <http://dx.doi.org/10.2139/ssrn.2903799>

41 CMA Final Report Appendix F.

technical efficiencies, it can also give rise to conflicts of interest and permit companies with market power at one stage of the value chain to use that power to undermine competition at other stages. The concerns that CMA noted focus on the role of Google, which has a very strong position in advertising intermediation in the UK, controlling a share of 90–100 percent of the publisher ad server segment, 80–90 percent of the advertiser ad server segment, 50–60 percent in supply-side platforms (SSPs), and 50–60 percent in demand-side platforms (DSPs).[42] In their joint complaint from December 2020, a number of Republican state attorneys in the United States claim that Google has monopoly positions in the United States on the ad server market, ad exchange market, and display ad exchange and network markets.[43]

Competition and Markets Authority states:

> Google has market power in the open display market stemming from three main sources: its inventory of search and display advertising and associated large base of advertisers; its data on users; and its strong position in intermediation, particularly as the largest publisher ad server, initially through the acquisition of DoubleClick and other intermediary businesses.
>
> We have identified two main concerns. First, Google has been able to use its market power in search and its wider ecosystem to build its position as a DSP. This has involved leveraging its user data and large base of advertisers (from Google Ads) to favor its DSP, and tying access to YouTube to use of its DSP services.
>
> Second, Google's strong position at each level of the intermediation value chain creates clear conflicts of interest, as it has the ability and incentive to exploit its position on both sides of a transaction to favor its own sources of supply and demand. While some other intermediaries are also vertically integrated, Google's market power gives it the ability to exploit these conflicts by self-preferencing its own activities, and thereby further reinforcing its market power.
>
> Parties have expressed to us a wide variety of specific concerns regarding Google's self-preferencing behavior in intermediation. These relate to, for example, restrictions on publishers' ability to access the bid data required to compare the performance of Google's SSP with rivals and the imposition of restrictions on publishers' ability to set differential price floors. In some of the cases we have discussed, Google has highlighted a potential efficiency justification for the practice in question. In others, Google has stated that it has changed its behavior in response to concerns, although we note that the lack of transparency of auction mechanisms makes it difficult for publishers and advertisers to verify whether this is the case.
>
> Overall, the fact that Google has a very strong position as: a publisher ad server, with influence over which ads are served and at which price; an SSP, which sells

[42] CMA Final Report 20 et seq.

[43] Russell Brandom, 'Texas Attorney General Announces Ad Tech Antitrust Probe against Google: "This Goliath of a Company Is Using Its Power to Manipulate the Market"' *The Verge* (16 December 2020) <www.theverge.com/2020/12/16/22178988/google-antitrust-ad-tech-lawsuit-texas-attorney-general-paxton>.

inventory on behalf of publishers; and a DSP, which buys inventory on behalf of advertisers, raises clear conflicts of interest. Google has been able to exploit these conflicts in the past and retains the ability and incentive to continue to do so.[44]

It seems that Facebook and Amazon have similar vertical set-ups connected to their walled garden and ecosystem as Google, although these two platforms have not gained the same leading market position – or as much data – as Google. In reference to vertical integration, it should also be mentioned that Amazon, as discussed above, is being investigated regarding use of business customers' data to promote its own private label. Facebook, Google, and Amazon have a data advantage and do not trade in data, but there are data brokers that can provide the information but not the services provided by the platforms.[45]

In addition, as the Internet of Things gains momentum, matters such as access, use, and portability of data will become a concern. In terms of the vehicle industry, John Deere's data-driven 'precision agriculture' business model may best depict the future for connected vehicles.[46] John Deere produces farm machinery, holding by some estimates the largest market share in the world and approximately 30 percent of the global tractor market;[47] today, these products are part of the IoT for precision agriculture, in which John Deere, farmers, and third parties may access the John Deere platform. Data, including agronomic (crop management) data and machine operation data (e.g., fuel level, location, machine hours, engine RPM), is collected primarily from sensors embedded in both the machines and soil of the fields but is also extracted from external sources (e.g., weather prediction data, commodity pricing). Through telematics, the data is automatically uploaded into the cloud

44 CMA Final Report 20 et seq.

45 Federal Trade Commission, 'Data Brokers: A Call for Transparency and Accountability: A Report of the Federal Trade Commission' (May 2014) <www.ftc.gov/reports/data-brokers-call-transparency-accountability-report-federal-trade-commission-may-2014>. According to the FTC, data brokers collect and store a vast amount of data on almost every US household and commercial transaction. Of the nine data brokers, one data broker's database has information on 1.4 billion consumer transactions and over 700 billion aggregated data elements; another data broker's database covers 1 trillion dollars in consumer transactions; and yet another data broker adds 3 billion new records each month to its databases. Most importantly, data brokers hold a vast array of information on individual consumers. For example, one of the nine data brokers has 3,000 data segments for nearly every US consumer.

46 It should be noted that the first investigation of the European Commission (Commission) regarding the digital agriculture sector was conducted in the Bayer/Monsanto merger decision, which according to Atik provides a great overview on the major players in the sector and their positions. It is stated that the traditional input (seeds, pesticides, insecticides, fertilizers, etc.) production conglomerates have more incentives to initiate downstream digital agriculture operations (ATPs) because 'Smart Farming' such as precision agriculture threatens their traditional business with targeted solutions that reduce unnecessary input usage. See an Can Atik, 'Data Act: Legal Implications for the Digital Agriculture Sector' (23 June 2022) <https://ssrn.com/abstract=4144737>.

47 See, for example, statistics from Farmer Insight, <www.fginsight.com/news/news/tractor-sales-breakdown-john-deere-still-out-in-front-but-kubota-is-charging-up-the-outside-18529>.

via cellular networks, WiFi, or Bluetooth. Farmers access and manage the data through the cloud software platform. Through the Operation Centre app on this platform, farmers – and John Deere – can monitor activity in real time, analyze performance, determine how best to utilize equipment, and collaborate with partners for insights and 'prescriptions' using algorithms that help the farmer decide what to plant, where, and when with optimized conditions. John Deere runs an open data platform, where farmers are encouraged to share their data with third parties. Software providers access the data through John Deere's APIs. The more data that is collected, the more valuable the platform becomes to all stakeholders. For example, farmers can benefit from analyzing data collected over time and from other farmers' data to inform their business decisions, and software developers gain more insights, paving the way for development of new value-added products and services. Nevertheless, John Deere will be the holder of the platform, controlling much of the data, and perhaps will not be so keen on sharing that data. John Deere can also share the data with input suppliers (seeds, fertilizer, chemicals), and the information can be connected to trigger automatic ordering from the same firms.[48] What John Deere is trying to create with the data-driven business model is network effects, where John Deere, its platform, and its machines will be the hub in the system. Indeed, it can be a strategy to try to become a monopolist: The platform services, multifaceted features, and inherent network effects will tip the market to John Deere's favor, elevating the company to a monopoly, because John Deere will exclusively control the data generated by the vehicle – and in essence the data covering the whole farming sequence.[49]

The transformation that occurs under data-driven business models in the vehicle industry will have large consequences also for regular purchasers of cars. Today, sensors, applications, and monitors inside the car collect data from new vehicles and drivers, but data is also collected by various parts of the car and by the interaction between the vehicle, road, and other vehicles. The sensors included in parts may originate not from the vehicle manufacturer, but the parts manufacturer, that is, the subcontractors to the vehicle manufacturer. The data collected by the vehicle as it is being driven, including the data originating from the driver or other passengers, is collected by car manufacturers because these car manufacturers have designed the data architecture to allow collection of data only from vehicles of their respective brands. It seems that carmakers have been able to exclude external platforms from collecting in-vehicle data, while other platforms such as Google might still be able to breach the architecture by being downloaded to the vehicle or by being invited by

[48] See C. Williams, 'Farm to Data Table: John Deere and Data in Precision Agriculture' (12 November 2019) <https://digital.hbs.edu/platform-digit/submission/farm-to-data-table-john-deere-and-data-in-precision-agriculture/>. See also M. Ryan, 'Agricultural Big Data Analytics and the Ethics of Power' (2020) 33 Journal of Agricultural Environmental Ethics 49–69 <https://doi.org/10.1007/s10806–019-09812-0>.

[49] Network effect and tipping are discussed in Section 2.3.

individual vehicle manufacturers to provide software.[50] It seems that the most far-reaching implementation of a data-driven business model in the vehicle industry thus far is the one implemented by John Deere and its precision agriculture business, yet also exists in the personal car industry.[51] Indeed, as Andreas Wiebe discusses regarding the networked car, a car is today equipped with a lot of sensors and an average of eighty steering devices. These collect data on the state of the car, the behavior of the driver, heartbeat, alcohol and traffic, and environmental conditions. Different parties could be interested in this data:

- Owner of the car
- User of the car (data input)
- Navigation and TC services
- Insurance companies ('pay as you drive')
- Internet service provider, ISP (distribution channel, data collection for advertising, growth potential EUR 80 billion 2015–2020)
- government (traffic control, eCall, toll system, crime prevention)

Given the number of interested parties, several different conflicts may emerge:

- May the owner prohibit data collection in the car by producer?
- May the owner allow third-party access against the will of the producer?
- May the producer forward data to third parties?

Notwithstanding this, it seems clear that today the car manufacturer controls the data. The paradigm shift resulting from the huge amounts of data now being collected may compel the car industry to become data-driven; in this case, the firm holding most and 'best' data with the best tools for analytics may understand how to produce the 'best' vehicle; however, depending on which firm holds the data, the successful firm in this regard may not be one of the incumbent car manufacturers.[52] Indeed, several new carmakers appear to be entering the industry, and these companies are focusing on inter alia data collection.[53]

A further example of the paradigm shift that data and data-driven business models are bringing to established industries is the health sector. In this industry, several firms hold different forms of data. Clinical (patient) data is normally held by

[50] Damien Geradin, 'Access to In-Vehicle Data by Third-Party Service Providers: Is There a Market Failure and, If So, How Should It Be Addressed?' (28 February 2020) <https://ssrn.com/abstract=3545817> or <http://dx.doi.org/10.2139/ssrn.3545817>.

[51] See Williams (n 48).

[52] Michele Bertoncello et al., 'Monetizing Car Data New Service Business Opportunities to Create New Customer Benefits' (September 2016) Advanced Industries, McKinsey Report <www.mckinsey.com/~/media/McKinsey/Industries/Automotive%20and%20Assembly/Our%20Insights/Monetizing%20car%20data/Monetizing-car-data.ashx> accessed 23 July 2018.

[53] See, for example, Google's Waymo self-driving car project, <www.google.com/selfdrivingcar/> accessed 24 July 2018. See also Huawei's new line of vehicle components <www.huawei.com/en/news/2019/4/huawei-enable-car-oems-build-better-vehicles>.

physicians and hospitals, and clinical trial data is held by pharmaceutical firms, which also hold early R&D data. Public health authorities, insurance companies, and specific health data firms (e.g., IMS Health) hold data regarding cost and consumption of pharmaceuticals. Now, digital intermediates such as Google or specific vertical medical internet service providers hold considerable quantities of data about patient behaviors, fears, and conduct. They collect that information from the search inquiries made by the individuals. However, as the IoT continues to gain ground, clothes, watches, bathrooms, and more will collect health data from individuals. This will boost the amount and quality of the collected data; device manufacturers will collect the data and store it in the cloud. The health data could be used to invent health solutions for the future – and these solutions do not necessarily have to be drug based. While producing drugs can also be personalized through personal data, health can be monitored and controlled through data collection.[54] Indeed, given the introduction of the IoT, there will be multiple firms holding health data, but it is obvious that health solutions would benefit from this data being pooled under one roof to achieve the best data analytics.[55] Nonetheless, in the end, one firm, for example, an internet intermediate and cloud provider, may obtain more and better health data and would be able to use this quality edge to enter the general market of inventing or creating personalized health solutions for the future. It is even possible that with network effects, the company could tip the market and gain monopoly power.[56]

It is difficult to generalize regarding data trading and markets. The trade in data appears to be increasing, but not in the same manner as data collection. Indeed, it seems that commercial providers are hoarding data and are not marketing the data

54 Kevin Cyr, 'Forecasting the Future of Personalized Medicine' <https://medium.com/healthfurther/forecasting-the-future-of-personalized-medicine-c88bc55bb668> accessed 25 May 2018.

55 The General Data Protection Regulation (GDPR) may restrict possibilities for pooling personal data, especially high-risk data such as patient data, and firms should be cautious with what they may pool in these circumstances. Council Regulation (EU) 2016/679 on the protection of natural persons with regard to the processing of personal data and on the free movement of such data [2016] 1–88.

56 Perhaps this seems unrealistic now, but pooling all that knowledge into one platform could provide many benefits as well as risks. If the pharmaceutical firms or the intermediates could pool collected data instead and place it in a data commons, doing so could prove very useful in the fight against all kind of diseases. It may substantially decrease the time required to identify outbreaks of diseases, develop new drugs, and understand the impact of new drugs, side-effects, etc. Indeed, data-driven business models may be very successful in the pharma/biotech sector, and this success would be predicated on the need for and benefits of pooling large quantities of data from many sources. See, for example, Peter Groves et al, 'The "Big Data" Revolution in Healthcare' (McKinsey & Co January 2013) <www.mckinsey.com/~/media/mckinsey/industries/healthcare%20systems%20and%20services/our%20insights/the%20big%20data%20revolution%20in%20us%20health%20care/the_big_data_revolution_in_healthcare.ashx> accessed 15 April 2018. See also David Champagne, Amy Hung, and Olivier Leclerc, 'The Road to Digital Success in Pharma' (McKinsey & Co August 2015) <www.mckinsey.com/industries/pharmaceuticals-and-medical-products/our-insights/the-road-to-digital-success-in-pharma> accessed 15 April 2018.

they collect. In its new data strategy, the EU Commission acknowledges this problem and states that there is little incentive to share data.[57] The vehicle industry and the health sector also seem to verify this development.[58] It would seem that the difficulty here is that platforms and other private and commercial providers of web-based services are trading current – 'nowcasted' – data, which can be used for 24/7 connected services.

Moreover, as discussed below, very few individuals use their GDPR-assured right to port data. They do not seem to see the benefits of porting data to new platforms and clouds. Even if porting is on the rise, data portability under the GDPR is unlikely to remedy market tipping or, in general, create a market for data.[59]

Indeed, it seems clear that a legal system must be created to distribute and disseminate data more generally throughout the economy, allowing firms to realize the necessity of accessing and porting data. Could this be accomplished under the contractual legal system?

The above presentations of Google, Facebook, Amazon, and John Deere show that platforms are 'walled gardens' and networks for collecting data, where the center of gravity is the hubs – the platforms. Receiving all data from the ecosystems, these platforms have technical and legal systems that allow them to prevent sharing the data and limit interoperability of data. The business strategy is based on the notion of collecting, analyzing, and using services based on data, while not giving access to data. Data is the key to this set-up, and the data comes from other sources than the actions of the platforms. Instead, the data is generated by the parties on either side of the platforms – consumers or business users. The platforms represent data hubs, R&D collaborations, data pools, and standard-setting organizations for the control and general benefit of the platforms and their systems management, while denying access to the rest. Indeed, they become monopolies with data-based business strategies that in turn create competitive advantages that become great barriers to entry.

57 The EU Commission Data Strategy from February 2020 states 'Sharing and use of privately-held data by other companies (business-to-business – B2B – data-sharing)'. Despite the economic potential, data sharing between companies has not taken off at sufficient scale. This is due to a lack of economic incentives (including the fear of losing a competitive edge), lack of trust between economic operators regarding whether the data will be used in line with contractual agreements, imbalances in negotiating power, fear of misappropriation of the data by third parties, and a lack of legal clarity regarding who can do what with the data (e.g., in the case of cocreated data, in particular IoT data). Commission, 'A European Strategy for Data (Communication)' COM (2020) 66 final, 19 February 2020, 8.

58 Ibid. See also Wolfgang Kerber, 'Data Sharing in IOT Ecosystems and Competition Law: The Example of Connected Cars' (2019) 15(4) Journal of Competition Law & Economics 381–426 <https://doi.org/10.1093/joclec/nhz018>.

59 Inge Graef and Jens Prüfer, 'Mandated Data Sharing Is a Necessity in Specific Sectors' (2018) 103(4763) Economisch Statistische Berichten 298–301.

2.2 THE ANTICOMMONS AND MARKET FAILURES

It is a law of history, he wrote, 'that contemporaries are denied a recognition of the early beginnings of the great movements which determine their times.'

—Stefan Zweig

A general reflection here is that we are facing a paradigm shift. The revolutionary step, with major and sudden impact on society and human endeavor as we know it and in reference to the new infrastructure made up of 5G telecom technology, the Internet, server interfaces, the Internet of Things, and the industrial internet, is the possibility to monitor, collect, analyze, and store huge amounts of information. As numerous studies have shown, data is becoming the lifeblood of the global economy.[60] In essence, the new technology makes it possible to monitor, collect, and efficiently analyze data from all human and machine activities. Data is the new raw material; the consequences of this statement should not be underestimated.[61] The new paradigm may make it possible, in theory and practice, to monitor all global activities and transform them into collectable data. However, what we did not know when embarking on this journey is that this data would come to be owned and controlled by one, or possibly two to three firms: Google, Facebook, and Amazon.

Information and knowledge are easily available for large platforms; it is transparent, searchable, and transferable. These platforms will see and understand connections between different events and situations in society that we did not grasp before. They may also predict the future because we will be able to understand the structures and fibers in the fabric of what is to come. Indeed, being able to monitor, collect, analyze, and store huge amounts of information will decrease cost of search, access, and knowledge and the cost of predicting events, even on an individual level. The drawback is that data and data flows can be controlled by technical means, and when a few platforms limit access to individual data, they hold a de facto monopoly over the data. Indeed, de facto exclusive control over much of the data generated, which they acquire without compensation.[62] The set-up represents a market failure restricting the efficient use of the data collected.[63]

[60] Commission (n 9) 1.

[61] Commission, 'Towards a Common European Data Space (Communication)' COM (2018) 232 final, 25 April 2018, 2. See also OECD, 'Data-Driven Innovation: Big Data for Growth and Well-Being' (2015) 7.

[62] Nicholas Economides and Ioannis Lianos, 'Restrictions on Privacy and Exploitation in the Digital Economy: A Market Failure Perspective' (27 January 2021) Journal of Competition Law and Economics, Forthcoming, NET Institute Working Paper No #20-05, NYU Stern School of Business Forthcoming <https://ssrn.com/abstract=3686785> or <http://dx.doi.org/10.2139/ssrn.3686785>.

[63] Ibid. See also Wolfgang Kerber, 'Specifying and Assigning "Bundles of Rights" on Data: An Economic Perspective' (26 April 2021) <https://ssrn.com/abstract=3847620> or <http://dx.doi.org/10.2139/ssrn.3847620>. For an overview, see OECD, 'Enhancing Access to and Sharing of

Interestingly, using terms from economic and biology research, the notion of the 'commons' and 'anticommons' may be used to describe the market failures represented by the collection of data currently happening in the platform economy and what may be accelerated due to the IoT development. The technology has made it possible to digitalize all internet-connected activities into data. This is an enormous achievement creating a pool or common of digitalized information that could be efficiently utilized to create new knowledge, ideas, and innovations. The notion that this potential pool of data represents a 'common' is derived from the belief that information as such is often considered a public good.[64] However, large platforms may today hold-up access to the pool of information currently being constantly collected in their various ecosystems. This may cause the problem of the so-called anticommons.[65] As discussed below, the problem of anticommons may be described as the result when entities may exclude or hold-up access to a valuable source of income, with the effect that the source will not be efficiently utilized.

The paradigm shift of the Internet of Things that will usher in the possibility to collect, store, and control data assumes some fundamental changes. First, the future is within grasp for less money than before. Predicting industry and market development will become cheaper, easier, and much more stable.[66] Indeed, traditional innovation processes such as divisions between product development and sales may be a thing of the past: Large datasets connected to data analytics may offer better and less costly understanding of the business strategies, models, and products that will be successful. Current 'nowcasted' information and knowledge can be collected and stored in datasets.[67] Data, collected in real time and reflecting peoples' knowledge

Data: Reconciling Risks and Benefits for Data Re-use across Societies' (2019). The economics of data is discussed infra under Sections 2.3 and 2.7.

64 Garrett Hardin, 'The Tragedy of the Commons' (1968) 162(3859) Science 1243–1248; Michael Heller, 'The Tragedy of the Anticommons: Property in the Transition from Marx to Markets' (1998) 111(3) Harvard Law Review 621; Michael Heller and Rebecca Eisenberg, 'Can Patents Deter Innovation? The Anticommons in Biomedical Research' (1998) 280 Science 698, 698 et seq. According to some disputed research, the problem of anticommons do not exist, cf John Walsh et al., 'Research Tool Patenting and Licensing and Biomedical Innovation' in Wesley M. Cohen and Stephen A. Merrill (eds), *Patents in Knowledge-Based Economy* (2002) 285 et seq. The Walsh study has been criticized by, inter alia, Professor Paul David as unfounded. cf Michael Mireles, 'An Examination of Patents, Licensing, Research Tools, and the Tragedy of the Anticommons in Biotechnology Innovation' (Fall 2004) 38(1) University of Michigan Journal of Law Reform 141, 185 et seq., with references.

65 See (n 64).

66 See, for example, The Council of Economic Advisers, Executive Office of the President, Big Data and Differential Pricing (2015). See also Iain M. Cockburn, Rebecca Henderson, and Scott Stern, 'The Impact of Artificial Intelligence on Innovation: An Exploratory Analysis' in Joshua Gans, Ajay Agrawal and Avi Goldfarb (eds), *The Economics of Artificial Intelligence: An Agenda* (University of Chicago Press 2019); Ajay Agrawal, Joshua Gans, and Avi Goldfarb, *Prediction Machines: The Simple Economics of Artificial Intelligence* (Harvard Business Review Press 2018).

67 cf Imanol Arrieta Ibarra, Leonard Goff, Diego Jiménez Hernández, Jaron Lanier, and Eric Glen Weyl, 'Should We Treat Data as Labor? Moving beyond "Free"' (2017) 1 American

and actions, can be stored and will become a discrete, productive resource apart from land, labor, and capital.[68]

Indeed, the second main purpose of data in data-driven business models, for example, in digital advertising and in terms of evaluating platform conduct, in general, is to provide verification, attribution, and measurement of effectiveness. From a platform or systems management perspective, it implies that research development may be conducted differently. The research can be conducted upfront on e-commerce sites or through sensors inside the products that collect relevant data for R&D, that is, in the sale and use of products produced and services rendered. The relevant information for developing new products and services will be identified when data is collected – that is, at the marketing stage, not in the back-office R&D centers. This would imply that R&D will be conducted continuously, and not as separate projects with a beginning and an end.[69] The control of data makes it possible to connect specific individual data points (a piece of information) in reference to products and services to an individual and follow that piece of information to all corners of the Internet. This implies that firms can monitor in real time whether a new product, service, or marketing campaign is truly successful and understand what is needed to make it more successful. This could also enable firms to personalize products to reflect our personal data.[70]

Before discussing whether the EU should implement a new right with respect to data, or whether the fundamental problems facing the data-driven economy may be

Economic Association Papers & Proceedings 1, forthcoming <https://ssrn.com/abstract=3093683>

68 For the classical resources of production, see, for example, Adam Smith, *The Wealth of Nations* (1776) Book I chapter 6 and Karl Marx, *Das Kapital* (1867) chapter 7, section 1.

69 Cockburn et al. (n 66), also discussed in Chapter 3.

70 A great example of this vision is depicted in the 'Yellow Book', produced by Google's Sidewalk Labs for its service of making Toronto a smart city. According to the document, personalization of services and products, and in fact the whole smart city, would increase as users contributed more data, leading to 'more complete or personalized services from Project Sidewalk in return'. An example states that people choosing to share 'in-home fire safety sensor' data could receive advice on health and safety related to air quality, or provide additional information to first responders in case of an emergency. The document also describes reputation tools that would lead to a 'new currency for community cooperation', effectively establishing a social credit system. Sidewalk could use these tools to 'hold people or businesses accountable' while rewarding good behavior, for example by rewarding a business's good customer service with an easier or cheaper renewal process on its license. This 'accountability system based on personal identity' could also be used to make financial decisions. 'A borrower's stellar record of past consumer behaviour could make a lender, for instance, more likely to back a risky transaction, perhaps with the interest rates influenced by digital reputation ratings.' Those choosing to remain anonymous would not be able to access all of the area's services, the book warns: automated taxi services would not be available to anonymous users, and some merchants might be unable to accept cash. Tom Cardoso and Josh O'Kane Small, 'Sidewalk Labs Document Reveals Company's Early Vision for Data Collection, Tax Powers, Criminal Justice' (The Globe and Mail 30 October 2019) <www.theglobeandmail.com/business/article-sidewalk-labs-document-reveals-companys-early-plans-for-data>.

addressed under competition law or by sector-specific regulations, certain relevant characteristics of the data-driven economy and its regulation need to be presented. First, it is essential to introduce the current legal landscape for data; second, the factual circumstances in reference to data should be explored. The relevant factual characteristics are difficult to distinguish and are fast-moving targets. In addition, as with all paradigm shifts in history, the consequences of the current changes are difficult to predict. Indeed, the characteristics discussed in the chapter are based to a certain degree on assumptions or even hypotheses to the extent that these can be defined as such. At any rate, because the development of the data-driven economy is moving so rapidly, there seems to be a consensus that legislative effort is sorely needed in this area. Researchers and legislators, therefore, need to assume certain characteristics and, based on intuition, predict developments in their effort to suggest and dismiss new regulations.

The new paradigm lies at the heart of the fourth industrial revolution, and the importance of data causes great controversies. How should data be regulated? Information, or knowledge – the archetype of intangible public good – in an internet setting has become similar to a tangible unit, which is collectable and tradable. Should data, therefore, belong to someone, or something?[71]

Industrial revolutions have become springboards for important changes to the regulation of relevant productive resources. The first, second, and third industrial revolutions led to the regulation of labor, limited firms and securities, and competition but also to the regulation, revision, and general realization of intellectual property law.[72] Intellectual property law was introduced in several European countries in parallel with the first industrialization, which coincided with the shift from a guild-based regulated society to an open (or at least to a less regulated) free-market economy.[73] Intellectual property law developed further around the beginning of the twentieth century and onward, despite the backlashes of a more regulatory nature in the 1930s. Nascent competition rules and the unfair competition legal systems had existed in Europe since the beginning of industrialization, but developed later, especially with the emergence and expansion of the European Union.

The development of the intellectual property legal system from the mid-1860s and onward, as a property system, has contrasted with the general trend in civil and public law of increased consideration for social and public policy concerns, which in turn was reflected by the increase in unfair competition rules and labor law development.[74] Intellectual property law is different in that it reflects a private,

[71] Zuboff (n 1).

[72] Ulf Bernitz, *Marknadsrätt - en komparativ studie av marknadslagstiftningens utveckling och huvudlinjer* (Jurist- och samhällsvetareförbundet 1969) 89 et seq.; Joel Mokyr, 'Intellectual Property Rights, the Industrial Revolution, and the Beginnings of Modern Economic Growth' (2009) 99(2) The American Economic Review 349–355 <www.jstor.org/stable/25592423>.

[73] Bernitz (n 72) et seq.

[74] Ibid., esp 177.

decentralized legal system based on personal rights, while the legal development in other areas, instead of applying a property solution, has implemented liability rules or public prohibitions governed by expert authorities.[75]

The major reason for the structural changes to economic regulation in the past three revolutions was a de facto change in the underlying fundamentals of conducting business and to exert power, for example, to shift from a guild-regulated business society to a market economy and from expertise-driven artisans to low-skilled, labor-intensive mass production. The issue facing us now is whether a similar change of fundamental basic conditions for conducting business will also take place in the fourth revolution.

As we have already witnessed, the fourth revolution has caused major changes in several aspects. The increased network effects and the tipping of markets to the benefit of monopolists reflect the fact that the Internet and Internet of Things are network or infrastructural services, similar to telecommunications, but which have been allowed to develop without any sector-specific regulation. The content provided on the Internet is often media, broadcasted without editorial control. Nevertheless, the true fundamental shift in the fourth revolution is the ability of monopolists (gatekeepers) to control data and data flows – an effect that will profoundly change the equilibrium in private or market power on which the current economic legal system is built. As will be discussed in this book, this shift will require changes to market or economic law, or more specifically to the legal systems governing competition, including intellectual property law and anticompetition and unfair competition rules.

In a civil society that includes a market economy and a property-owning democracy[76] with a functioning legal system,[77] state intervention should be minimized and

75 Bernitz (n 72) 79 and 177. See also Guido Calabresi and A. Douglas Melamed, 'Property Rules, Liability Rules, and Inalienability: One View of the Cathedral' (1972) 85(6) Harvard Law Review 1089. See also Mark A. Lemley and Phil Weiser, 'Should Property or Liability Rules Govern Information?' (2007) 85(4) Texas Law Review 783; Stanford Law and Economics Olin Working Paper No 341; University of Colorado Law Legal Studies Research Paper No 07-18 <https://ssrn.com/abstract=977778>.

76 See also John Rawls, *Justice as Fairness: A Restatement* (Harvard University Press 2001). Rawls derives two principles of justice from the original position. The first of these is the Liberty Principle, which establishes equal basic liberties for all citizens. 'Basic' liberty entails the freedoms (familiar in the liberal tradition) of conscience, association, and expression, as well as democratic rights; Rawls also includes a *personal property* right, but this is defended in terms of moral capacities and self-respect, rather than an appeal to a natural right of self-ownership. (This distinguishes Rawls's account from the classical liberalism of John Locke and the libertarianism of Robert Nozick.) See also Karl Popper, *The Open Society and Its Enemies* (editions 1 and 2 Routledge 1995).

77 See Herbert Lionel Adolphus (H L A) Hart, The Concept of Law (Oxford University Press 1961) 113.

property rights respected.[78] Often the market reacts and counter-reacts, and barriers may very well be opportunities to overcome problems without the need for the state to intervene. Still, the new paradigm presents barriers and challenges that cause the market economy and even civil societies to work less efficiently.[79] The possibility to tame information and shape it into data implies that societies are facing challenges and multiple market failures, where data advantages may cause the balance of markets to tip into the hands of a few platforms. It can therefore be assumed that in the data economy, information – despite its inherent status as a public good – will become less available.[80] As will be discussed below, information as such is now being technically and contractually protected, and only a few have access to the relevant data that many others need to conduct business.[81] The problems associated with data and a data-driven economy will be discussed, and how resultant market failures need to be identified and corrected.

First, controlling or holding large datasets that are not freely available implies market power, even monopoly power.[82] Second, even though data collection is increasing exponentially, this collection does not seem to lead to more trade in data.[83] On the contrary, it seems that data is rarely shared or traded on a large scale through multilateral platforms.[84] Large platform monopolies may also lessen multi-homing because monopolizing data collection and storing industry or 'space' for a

78 Ibid. Hart's work in relationship to property has been heavily analyzed; see, for example, Michael Payne, 'Hart's Concept of a Legal System' (1976) 18 William & Mary Law Review 287 <https://scholarship.law.wm.edu/wmlr/vol18/iss2/4>.

79 Michal Gal and Oshrit Aviv, 'The Competitive Effects of the GDPR' (2020) Journal of Competition Law and Economics 22 et seq. and 30 et seq. <https://ssrn.com/abstract=3548444>; See also Cockburn et al. (n 66) 115, 125–128, 139–143.

80 Wolfgang Kerber, 'Rights on Data: The EU Communication "Building a European Data Economy" from an Economic Perspective' in Sebastian Lohsse, Reiner Schulze, and Dirk Staudenmayer (eds), *Trading Data in the Digital Economy: Legal Concepts and Tools* (Nomos 2017) 109, 120; Bertin Martens et al., 'Business-to-Business Data Sharing: An Economic and Legal Analysis', JRC Digital Economy Working Paper 2020-05; Christian Reimsbach-Kounatze, 'Enhancing Access to and Sharing of Data: Striking the Balance between Openness and Control over Data' in *Data Access, Consumer Interests and Public Welfare* (Nomos 2021) 27, 39–49.

81 It should be noted that when technology is able to restrict use and limit accesses to a public good, governments should generally step in and create a property system – indeed, because the good that was considered public is not public anymore.

82 Discussed in Chapter 3, with several sources.

83 European Commission, 'Building a European Data Economy' COM (2017) 9 final, 8; European Commission, 'Staff Working Document to the Communication "Building a European Data Economy"' SWD (2017) 2 final, 12 et seq. See also Pantelis Koutroumpis, Aija Leiponen, and Llewellyn D. W. Thomas, 'The (Unfulfilled) Potential of Data Marketplaces' (29 September 2017) ETLA Working Papers No 53 <http://pub.etla.fi/ETLA-Working-Papers-53.pdf>.

84 Koutroumpis, Leiponen, and Thomas (n 83). The problem could be due to insufficient demand for data (insufficient awareness of the value of data), interoperability problems and insufficient standards, problems in regard to the pricing of data, the lack of open platforms for data sharing, and an insufficient number of skilled data workers.

given market imply that fewer firms will collect and store such data. Third, reducing the trade in data and minimizing the establishment of data markets cement the dominance of a few platforms, while lessening creativity and innovation output – not only in the markets for the platforms but also in the connected and downstream markets from which the data was collected in the first place. Fourth, the fact that information may be technically protected, and is not traded, may cause scarcities of relevant information for relevant markets, industries, or 'spaces'. Indeed, if the data economy is to thrive the large data collectors, for example, platforms or system leaders in closed data architected silos must be obligated by law to disclose data.[85] Every area of the economy is increasingly integrated with a digital layer; therefore, owning the infrastructure that is necessary for every other industry to function is an immensely powerful and profitable position.[86]

From an economic point of view, the network effect works here because as the numbers of platform users increase, the more data that is generated; the more data, the better the service, implying that even more users are drawn to the platform. When it comes to data, 'the bigger the better' is obvious.[87]

While the precise characteristics of each platform vary from market to market, they tend to share a set of general features that collectively support a 'winner takes most' dynamic:[88]

- Online platforms typically have very low marginal costs and significant economies of scale in delivering the core service.

[85] The EU Commission data strategy from February 2020 states:

> *Imbalances in market power:* Beside the high concentration in the provision of cloud services and data infrastructures, there are also market imbalances in relation to access to and use of data, for example when it comes to access to data by SMEs. A case in point comes from large online platforms, where a small number of players may accumulate large amounts of data, gathering important insights and competitive advantages from the richness and variety of the data they hold. This can affect, in turn, the contestability of markets in specific cases – not only the market for such platform services, but also the various specific markets for goods and services served by the platform, in particular if the platform is itself active on such related markets. The high degree of market power resulting from the 'data advantage' can enable large players to set the rules on the platform and unilaterally impose conditions for access and use of data or, indeed, allow leveraging of such 'power advantage' when developing new services and expanding towards new markets. Imbalances may also arise in other situations, such as with regard to access to co-generated IoT data from industrial and consumer devices.

Commission, 'A European Strategy for Data, Brussels' COM (2020) 66 final, 19 February 2020, 8.

[86] Srnicek (n 1) 63.

[87] See Carl Shapiro and Hal R. Varian, *Information Rules: A Strategic Guide to the Network Economy* (Harvard Business Press 1998) for early research pointing to the importance of network effect in the digital economy.

[88] See generally CMA Interim Report (2019), Furman Review (2019), Unlocking digital competition. Stigler Center (2019), Committee on Digital Platforms Final Report.

- Network effects mean that the value of a service to existing users of a platform increases as the total number of users increases. The nature of network effects can vary significantly between platforms.
- The fact that consumers do not pay directly for the platform's services limits consumers' incentives to switch and means that new entrants must attract users through demonstrably better quality or innovative features, rather than being able to undercut on price.
- The data-driven business strategies employed by these platforms feed on data and require a constant influx of fresh, nowcasted data.

The problem described above indicates that market failures may already be present in the data-driven economy. Leading internet intermediates collect vast amounts of data on their platforms and have access and the right to use data generated by firms' activities on their platforms, while are neither giving remuneration for the data nor trading or sharing the data.[89] In certain situations, access and the right to use this data would give the leading internet intermediates considerable information leverage against the firms that are active on their platforms.[90] It can be assumed that with the implementation of the IoT, this development will also migrate to old, economy oligopoly markets. The structures inherent in data-driven business models will be transferred to the B2B platforms and will transform the brick-and-mortar industry. Markets will tip in favor of platforms and dominance, and monopoly positions will be created. Indeed, this reflects a market failure.[91] However, more fundamentally, the issue is whether the new data paradigm also implies that a new structural

[89] In reference to the discussion regarding data capitalism and data as capital, see Sarah Meyers West, 'Data Capitalism: Redefining the Logics of Surveillance and Privacy'(2019) 58(1) Business & Society 20–41; Jathan Sadowski, 'When Data Is Capital: Datafication, Accumulation, and Extraction' (2019) 6(1) Big Data & Society; Marion Fourcade and Kieran Healy, 'Seeing Like a Market' (2017) 15(1) Socio-Economic Review 9–29; Economides and Lianos (n 62).

[90] Discussed in detail in Section 2.4. However, as stated in the CMA's Interim Report from 18 December 2019,

> Google and Facebook have a competitive advantage because they collect a large amount and variety of data types from their widely used consumer-facing services and their broad coverage of third-party sites and apps. Rival platforms such as Microsoft and Amazon have access to some detailed high-quality data about users and other types of data, but we understand this is largely limited to their own services or does not extend widely to the rest of the internet. In order to compete, these platforms as well as intermediaries in the open display market can supplement their own data with data from other market participants, such as data management platforms. However, this requires rival platforms and intermediaries to extensively share data between one another and match different identifiers in order to compile rich user profiles. This process is less precise than the matching that takes place uniquely within closed ecosystems and we have heard that it also gives rise to privacy concerns caused by data flows.
>
> (See <https://assets.publishing.service.gov.uk/media/5df9ecc040f0b609402e2838/Appendix_E_The_role_of_data.pdf>)

[91] As Kerber puts it,

solution needs to be implemented. Transparency of the new data being collected is necessary to maintain research and to develop innovations. Access to data collected by platforms must be distributed so that firms can use the information that resides in the collected data. Still, there is more to consider.

The economic notion of theory of the tragedy of the anticommons may easily manifest in reference to the data-driven economy. The problem of anticommons may be described as the result when entities may exclude or hold-up access to a valuable source of income, with the effect that the source will not be efficiently utilized.[92] In reference to the development where data from all social interactions on the Internet and IoT will be collected and exclusively used by only a few platforms, this may in fact create the tragedy of the anticommons. Indeed, the pools of public good, that is, the information – not protected by property rights – but technically kept away from being efficiently utilized by the platforms may create such a tragedy.

> Although markets for these data can emerge, it cannot be assumed that this will lead to an optimal allocation of the options to use these data in the data economy, because these markets suffer from serious market failure problems. Particularly important is that the data holders often have distorted incentives for making these data available to others. One important example are the options to use the control over these data for getting or defending posi-tions of market or gatekeeper power, leading to the above-mentioned competition problems. Another problem is that, e.g., data-holding platforms can use the ensuing information asymmetry vis-a-vis consumers for informational manipulation, e.g. with respect to search rankings [footnotes omitted].
>
> (Kerber n 63)

In addition, in its preliminary conclusion of its sector inquiry, the Swedish Competition Authority states that

> Digital platforms restrict companies' access to customer data. When consumers shop on a platform, they generate a number of data points, such as which options they select between, the sites they previously visited, and contact details. Exactly what data is collected depends on the platform and whether the consumer consented to data collection. According to companies using these platforms to distribute their products, customer data is important and necessary to develop and improve their offerings, to sell to repeat customers and to target marketing to new customers. Customer data is also valuable to the platform, allowing it to develop its own services and offering. However, companies feel that customer data tends to be retained by the platforms and not shared with the companies using them. This has a negative impact on companies as it limits their ability to develop, get repeat sales and market themselves, which in turn may result in entry barriers. Some respondents also indicated that as a consequence, the customer relationship is handled by the platform rather than the selling company.
>
> (See <www.konkurrensverket.se/globalassets/english/competition/19-0627_sammanfattning_sektorsundersokning-digitala-marknader_februari2020_english.pdf>)

The Furman Report and the observations regarding the CMA Interim Report also indicate that data mobility was a problem and that pursuing personal data mobility and systems with open standards will deliver greater competition and innovation. See <https://assets.publishing.service.gov.uk/government/uploads/system/uploads/attachment_data/file/785547/unlocking_digital_competition_furman_review_web.pdf>.

92 Heller (n 64); Heller and Eisenberg (n 64). According to some disputed research, the problem of anticommons do not exist; cf Walsh (n 64). The Walsh study has been criticized by, inter alia, Professor Paul David as unfounded. cf Mireles (n 64).

Indeed, that business users and other users are not able to access and use the data they generate but collected by the platforms so as to efficiently use these new pools or commons for wealth creation should be considered a market failure. Indeed, to some extent the users are locked in with the incumbent services due to nonaccess to the generated data.[93] The data-driven markets of the future seem to swiftly migrate toward monopolies that, as discussed in the Section 2.3, present unavoidable classical market failures, which implies that intellectual property and competition law must adapt to this new reality.

This book presents the following line of argument: The general solution to this market failure is that the data created by the business users or its product on a platform, or which is generated by a sensor included in that product, should generally be made available to the product creator – because the lack of access and control of this data reflect the precise and significant market failure of the data-driven economy. This data is called the business user's 'data' in this book, that is, the data generated by the activities of respective business users on platforms, be it B2C or B2B platforms, and Internet of Things systems.[94] Indeed, the idea is that this data 'belongs' to and should be controlled by the brick-and-mortar firm in question. A right to access and port such data should be included in the bundle of rights held by the brick-and-mortar firms. The embryo for such a right exists in the Digital Markets Act, where data is defined as 'any digital representation of acts, facts or information and any compilation of such acts, facts or information, including in the form of sound, visual or audio-visual recording'.

It is increasingly acknowledged that data collection is key in the ability of firms to gain and hold market power in industries where data-driven business models are being applied.[95] The market power obtained through access to or control and

93 B. Engels, 'Data Portability among Online Platforms' (2016) 5 Internet Policy Review 2 et seq. <https://doi.org/10.14763/2016.2.408>.

94 It is thus either consumer or company data directly relating to the effort that the business user has invested in the platform, that is, when consumers or officers of companies shop on a platform, they generate a number of data points, such as the options from which they can select, the sites they visited previously, and contact details. In reference to Internet of Things platforms, this can be data picked up by sensors included in the devices or parts sold by firms to system managers (platforms) or directedly to the end customer. I also refrain from using concepts here such as inferred, observed, and contributed data, as these definitions are overlapping. Business user's data as defined above may include, as far as the author understands, all these data, however, business user's data should legally be distinguished vis-à-vis the databases held by the platform providers that contain aggregated and analyzed data, while the platform's databases will include the business user's data.

95 The German Competition Law has been amended so that data should be taken into consideration when establishing dominance, see discussion in this book. See, for example, Geoffrey Parker, Georgios Petropoulos, and Marshall W. Van Alstyne, 'Digital Platforms and Antitrust' (22 May 2020) <https://ssrn.com/abstract=3608397> or <http://dx.doi.org/10.2139/ssrn.360839>. Wolfgang Kerber, 'Digital Markets, Data, and Privacy: Competition Law, Consumer Law, and Data Protection', MAGKS, Joint Discussion Paper Series in Economics (No 14-2016) <http://ssrn.com/abstract=2770479> or <http://dx.doi.org/10.2139/ssrn.2770479>

holding of vast amounts of data,[96] connected to software for predictive modeling, creates barriers to entry for second movers. Further, the markets for providing services or products where data-driven business models are successful may tip and be monopolized due to network effects resulting from the data-driven business strategy of the leading firm on the market.[97] The amount of data collected increase knowledge of the users and their understanding of what they want, and this increases the quality of the service or product marketed by the leading firm, which in turn attracts more users.[98] More users imply more data that will lead to better knowledge, quality, personalization, etc. The German Competition Act was recently amended to reflect this and now stated that 'access to relevant data is a potential source of market power'.[99]

3 Wt seq. Several authors claim that holding big data does not equate to holding market power. Generally, they argue that big data does not create a significant barrier to entry and they base their claims, inter alia, on the nonexclusive and nonrivalrous nature of data and a claimed ease of collecting it, while disregarding many potential entry barriers. Other scholars argue that the harm created by big data pertains mainly to privacy. Yet these conclusions are based on the limited existing economic studies on big data, which often focus on one specific market (most commonly on search engines or personal data markets). Daniel L. Rubinfeld and Michal Gal, 'Access Barriers to Big Data' (2017) 59 Arizona Law Review 339 <https://ssrn.com/abstract=2830586> or <http://dx.doi.org/10.2139/ssrn.2830586> accessed 12 December 2017. See, for example, Darren S. Tucker and Hill Wellford, 'Big Mistakes Regarding Big Data', (2014) 6 *Antitrust Source*. See also Maureen K. Ohlhausen and Alexander P. Okuliar, 'Competition, Consumer Protection, and the Right [Approach] to Privacy' (2015) 80 Antitrust Law Journal 121; James C. Cooper, 'Privacy and Antitrust: Underpants Gnomes, the First Amendment, and Subjectivity' (2013) 20 George Mason Law Review 1129.

96 There is a discussion regarding the definition of 'data': does it encompass syntactic information, semantic information, or both, and where should one draw the line in reference to protecting 'data'? See Josef Drexl, 'Designing Competitive Markets for Industrial Data: Between Propertisation and Access' (31 October 2016) Max Planck Institute for Innovation & Competition Research Paper No 16-13 12 et seq. <https://ssrn.com/abstract=2862975> or <http://dx.doi.org/10.2139/ssrn.2862975> accessed 2 December 2017. See also Andreas Wiebe, 'Protection of Industrial Data – A New Property Right for the Digital Economy?' (2017) 12(1) Journal of Intellectual Property Law & Practice 62–71, 67 <https://doi.org/10.1093/jiplp/jpw175> accessed 2 December 2017.

97 Ibid. See also OECD, 'Big Data – Bringing Competition Policy to the Digital Era' (2016) <www.oecd.org/daf/competition/big-data-bringing-competition-policy-to-the-digital-era.htm> accessed 2 December 2017, Autorité de la concurrence and Bundeskartellamt (2016), Competition Law and Data 7, 10 et seq. <www.autoritedelaconcurrence.fr/doc/reportcompetitionlawanddatafinal.pdf> accessed 2 December 2017.

98 Rubinfeld and Gal (n 95) 356 et seq. with references.

99 Section 18 paragraph 2(a) of the ARC now clarifies that 'market' – in so far as this term is used within competition law – can also exist where products and/or services are provided free of charge. This clarification follows an initiative by the FCO to better understand and tackle competition issues in digital markets, which led to the publication of a Working Paper on 'Market Power of Platforms and Networks' in June 2016. Consequently, Section 18 paragraph 3 (a) of the ARC now provides certain specifications on the assessment of market power with respect to multisided markets and networks, listing, among other things, network effects and access to market relevant data. Norton Rose, Fulbright, German Competition Law update: New revised act against restraints of competition entered into force, <www.nortonrosefulbright

Moreover, predictive modeling needs to work rapidly to identify current and future trends in 'nowcasting' – the capacity of a company to use the velocity at which a dataset grows to discern trends before others do so. The technique enables a firm not only to track trends in users' conduct in real time but also to monitor trends in (potential) competitors' conduct, and to respond more quickly, which helps the firm push or nudge the market.[100] Indeed, to function well as a right, access to data must include the right to 24/7 instant access. Otherwise, the right to access may very well have no substance. Data as information goods is nonrivalrous and may be collected from various sources (multihoming), but in industries where nowcasting is important for the business model, these features are not strong enough to create competition. The need for fast delivery of current data to the business model may imply that certain data holders do hold market power, even though similar data is available but lags in time. When markets have tipped and there is a system leader controlling the data flows, there is less possibility to multi-home the relevant data to compete with the system leader.

Leading internet intermediates collect vast amounts of data and may have access and the right to use other firms' data. In certain situations, access and the right to use that data would give these firms significant leverage in terms of knowledge. Based on the advantage in data, the companies can presumably act, in reference to both the data market and the connected product or service market, independently and with self-assurance, knowing that they hold an advantage in knowledge in relation to competitors, customers, and consumers.[101] This would apply at least in a situation where the platform provider has access to the data collected by all firms on a market, while the firms active on the market have access only to their own data. It should be noted that the issue of whether Amazon uses business customers' data to promote its own private label is under investigation by several authorities. As discussed above, the EU Commission is currently investigating Amazon's use of data, and the German *Bundeskartelamt* recently concluded such an investigation.[102] The US

.com/knowledge/publications/155186/german-competition-law-update-new-revised-act-against-restraints-of-competition-entered-into-force> accessed 31 December 2017.

[100] Rubinfeld and Gal (n 95).

[101] 'The dominant position thus referred to by Article [82] relates to a position of economic strength enjoyed by an undertaking which enables it to prevent effective competition being maintained on the relevant market by affording it the power to behave to an appreciable extent independently of its competitors, customers and ultimately of its consumers.' *United Brands Company and United Brands Continental BV v Commission of the European Communities* (Case 27/76) ECLI:EU:C:1978:22 para 38.

[102] The EU Commission investigated standard agreements between Amazon and marketplace sellers, which allowed Amazon's retail business to analyze and use third-party seller data. In particular, the Commission focused on whether and how the use of accumulated marketplace seller data by Amazon as a retailer affects competition. The EU Commission also examined the role of data in the selection of the 'Buy Box' winners and Amazon's potential use of competitively sensitive marketplace seller information. The Amazon investigation and settlement are dicussed in chapter 3 infra.

House Antitrust Subcommittee is also looking into the matter. In response to questions for the record from House Antitrust Subcommittee Chairman David Cicilline (D-RI), Amazon said it does not use personal data, only aggregated data to come up with its own products. At any rate, Amazon's use of private data to shape and promote its own branded goods seems to be a key question for lawmakers and regulators probing the company's competitive practices.[103]

The collection of market-relevant data could possibly cause the platform or cloud provider to be considered a competitor in the relevant product market. However, could it imply something more? Given the importance of aggregated data and information for the data market, and upstream in relation to the product market, is it possible that the platform providers – if no contractual or legal restrictions are available – could be monopolizing this upstream 'data market'? Moreover, it seems logical that when downstream product markets have been monopolized, for example, the market for general search, multi-homing will decrease because there will be only one firm providing the relevant service.[104]

2.3 MORE ECONOMICS FOR THE DATA-DRIVEN ECONOMY

Online platforms typically seek to attract consumers by offering their core services for free. Once they have attracted a critical mass of consumers, they seek to make money from business users on another side of the platform. In transaction-based platforms, such as Amazon Marketplace or Apple's App Store, this is done predominantly through the commission that is charged to retailers or app developers, respectively.

For other platform services, such as search engines and social media services, monetization results predominantly from serving ads. Google and Facebook are by far the largest two companies operating according to this business model.[105]

Although consumers do not pay money for these services, they can be considered to pay for them by giving the platform their attention, as well as data about themselves.[106] Advertising-funded platforms are able to combine the attention of

[103] Feiner (n 26).

[104] It is still very difficult to measure such dominance, while there are famous competition law cases where the ECJ have identified upstream markets for licensing intellectual property rights, and hence, dominant position for the rights holders. Such line of reasoning may be used in analogy for identifying data markets. 1 *RTE, ITP & BBC v Commission* (C-241/91 and C-242/9) ECLI:EU:C:1995:98 and *IMS Health v NDC Health* (C-418/01) ECLI:EU:C:2004:257.

[105] CMA 2020 Final Report.

[106] Tim Wu, 'Blind Spot: The Attention Economy and the Law' (2017) 82(3) Antitrust Law Journal 771. See also David S. Evans, 'Attention Platforms, the Value of Content, and Public Policy' (2019) 54(4) Review of Industrial Organization 775–792.

their users with contextual or personal information they have about them to serve highly targeted adverts, for which advertisers have high demand. Research published in 2018 demonstrated that consumers place great value on a range of online services and that values of multiple thousands of dollars are assigned to search engines and digital maps. Generally, video streaming services such as YouTube and social media received lower valuations, but these valuations by far exceed the price that is paid by the consumers, which is normally zero.[107]

Search engines give us instant access to information, news, directions to destinations, and other websites with minimal effort. Social media services let us connect with friends and family around the world, make new friends, keep up with the news or current trends, and share creative content with one another.[108]

The system leaders are regulators of their respective ecosystems. They have certain technology preferences and require users to accept these, mainly by using the relevant gateways – the APIs. These leaders also use their system of contracts to control the ecosystems and to exclude the use and importance of intellectual property rights (IPR). The platform or data holders contractually secure – for example, with the platform or cloud user – the right not only to store the data but also to analyze it, and make use of it for the platform or data holder's own benefit, and for others in the ecosystem, on all connected markets. The platform providers can become the masters of their respective data ecosystems and indeed hoard the data; generally, they do not trade or share the data.[109] The economists Prüfer and Schottmüller have identified in a recent well-received paper[110] that

[107] Erik Brynjolfsson, Felix Eggers, and Avinash Gannamaneni, 'Using Massive Online Choice Experiments to Measure Changes in Well-being' (2018) National Bureau of Economic Research Working Paper 24514.

[108] According to the CMA Report, in terms of reach, around 95 percent of UK Internet users access at least one Google site each month. Facebook's reach is around 85 percent. Of the total time spent by users online, just over a third of this time is spent on sites owned by either Google (including YouTube) or Facebook (including Instagram and WhatsApp). The success of Google and Facebook in attracting consumers' attention is illustrated when consumer time spent on the top 1,000 properties is measured. Consumers spend around 86 percent of their total time online on these top 1,000 properties, with the remaining 14 percent distributed over an extremely long 'tail' in excess of 16,000 websites.

[109] As mentioned earlier in this book, neither Google nor Facebook trades personal data to third parties. cf <https://safety.google/privacy/ads-and-data/> and Wagner (n 39). See also Lundqvist (n 27) 220–248.

[110] Jens Prüfer and Christoph Schottmüller, 'Competing with Big Data' (CentER Discussion Paper; vol 2017-007), Tilburg: CentER, Center for Economic Research. See also the *Google Search (Shopping)* (Case AT.39740 27/06/2017 and European Commission, Commission Staff Working Document Impact Assessment, Accompanying the document Proposal for a Regulation of the European Parliament and of the Council on a framework for the free flow of nonpersonal data in the European Union, SWD/2017/0304 final, 2017/0228 (COD), 13 September 2017 (Impact Assessment); Commission, 'Staff Working Document on the Free Flow of Data and Emerging Issues of the European Data Economy', COM (2017) 9 final, 10 January 2017.

data-driven markets tend to tip as a result of even slight differences in the amount and quality of data, and when such a market tips, there is no remedy to reestablish competition except by granting access to data. Moreover, the economists also showed that superiority in data on one market may be leveraged to create market dominance on neighboring markets, should a data-driven business model be implemented.[111]

Several economists point to the fact that direct and indirect network effects have become relevant because of recent progress in data storage and data analytics technologies.[112] In contrast to direct network effects and dynamic economies of scale (learning curve effects), data-driven indirect network effects cannot be easily copied by competitors or eliminated by innovation or new technology.[113] With initial differences in amount and quality of data, a market plagued by indirect network effects will eventually tip, and one firm will dominate the market. An important feature of a tipped market is that there are very few incentives for either the dominant firm or the ousted firms to invest further in innovation. The reason is that in the stable, steady state where one firm has virtually no demand and the other firm has virtually full demand, the ousted firm knows that the dominant firm both offers consumers a significantly higher quality level and has significantly lower marginal costs of innovation.[114] When a market has tipped due to data-driven indirect network effects, new firms are deterred from entry, even if they have developed revolutionary technology, that is, a disruptive innovation.[115] Indeed, when this has occurred and a firm holds a monopoly or quasi-monopoly position, it could be declared that the market or the industry is failing.[116] The market itself cannot create competition. This, in turn, according to several economists, could imply that competition law should be applicable and used to facilitate a functional market.[117]

[111] Ibid.

[112] See ibid. but also for example Parker, Petropoulos, and van Alstyne (n 95). See also Monopolkommission, 'Competition Policy: The Challenge of Digital Markets, Special Report No. 68' (2015). Lianos and Motchenkova show that a dominant monopoly platform results in both higher prices and underinvestment in quality-improving innovations by a search engine, relative to what would be optimal for society. More generally, they also show that a monopoly is sub-optimal because of harm caused to advertisers in the form of high prices, harm to users in the form of reduced quality in search results, and harm to society in the form of lower innovation rates in the industry. Ioannis Lianos and Evgenia Motchenkova, 'Market Dominance and Search Quality in Search Engine Market' (2013) 9(2) Journal of Competition Law & Economics 419–455, 419, 451.

[113] Prüfer and Schottmüller (n 110).

[114] Ibid.

[115] Ibid.

[116] Wolfgang Kerber and Jonas Frank, 'Data Governance Regimes in the Digital Economy: The Example of Connected Cars' (3 November 2017) <https://ssrn.com/abstract=3064794> or <http://dx.doi.org/10.2139/ssrn.3064794> accessed 2 January 2018.

[117] Ibid.

In addition, Padilla and Condorelli agree that a strategy whereby large platforms request consumers to grant their consent to combine consumers' data in both origin and target markets could cause anticompetitive effects. This may allow the large platforms to fund the services offered to all sides of the target market by monetizing data in the origin market, monopolizing the target market, and entrenching its dominant position in the origin market.[118] Indeed, other economists also argue that value creation is reinforced through a recursive data-capture and data-deployment feedback loop enabled by machine learning technologies, and suggest a regulatory intervention that facilitates data sharing mechanisms.[119] According to these scholars, the notion that data will provide value not only to market leaders but also to their competitors, to the benefit of consumers, is crucial for creating more competitive and innovative digital markets.[120] However, this would imply using legal tools early in the competitive process also for IoT markets, before the market has tipped, to create competitive functional markets.

An issue could be raised on whether the strong network effects displayed in the platform economy may arise in the IoT sector. The IoT industry is still in making, and the effect of the ability of manufacturers of IoT products to unilaterally exclude the accessibility and, hence, usability of the data by third persons based on the product design is still uncertain. Is this position in the market different from the position held by large platform operators of the internet economy that are identified as 'gatekeepers'?

As provided by the economist discussed above, the datafication of the IoT industry will most likely lead to network effects. Manufacturers of IoT products will benefit from network effects that considerably reduce the contestability of their position in the primary market. Early examples, such as the auto industry, where vehicles of the same brand exchange data and communicate, may increase the quality of the services (e.g., safety features) for the users, and the more users using the system, the better the services (e.g., safety features) will work. Certain software appliances which collect data and create the best heat environment for the process for large metallurgic (iron) plants can work better when more plants join the IoT systems. Indeed, IoT system will not only have an exclusionary effect vertically, the hold-up and lock-in effects will also prevent contestability of IoT product producers that through network effect will gain the position as gatekeepers.[121]

118 Daniele Condorelli and Jorge Padilla, 'Data-Driven Predatory Entry with Privacy-Policy Tying' (13 May 2020) <https://ssrn.com/abstract=3600725> or <http://dx.doi.org/10.2139/ssrn.3600725> and Daniele Condorelli and Jorge Padilla, 'Harnessing Platform Envelopment in the Digital World' (14 December 2019) <https://ssrn.com/abstract=3504025> or <http://dx.doi.org/10.2139/ssrn.3504025>.

119 Parker, Petropoulos, and van Alstyne (n 95).

120 Ibid.

121 Compare Josef Drexl et al., Position Statement of the Max Planck Institute for Innovation and Competition of 25 May 2022 on the Commission's Proposal of 23 February 2022 for a Regulation on harmonized rules on fair access to and use of data (Data Act), 15 et seq.

Going a step further, economists also argue that a dominant position in one data-driven market could be used to gain a dominant position in another market that was not (initially) data-driven. If market entry costs are not prohibitive, a firm that manages to find a 'data-driven' business model can dominate virtually any market in the long term. Consequently, if internet intermediates realize that the data they hold constitutes a key input to the production of quality on a market, they will most likely enter that market and continue to enter neighboring markets, even if these are old economy device markets.[122] The IoT and the infusion of data-driven business models will transform such markets into network-driven ones that are likely to tip in favor of one firm. This suggests a domino effect: A first mover in data can leverage its competitive edge to a dominant position in the market. This can lead to tipping of connected markets, even when these markets are already served by traditional brick-and-mortar firms. Indeed, it shows that in the end and in theory, the platform with the most data can take over any market as long as a data-driven business strategy can be utilized. This is clearly a paradigm shift and should be viewed as something even more transformative than a market failure; indeed, this is the essence of a new industry revolution.

2.4 WHAT IS DATA?

In reference to the discussion above regarding data-driven business strategies employed by platforms, several issues arise. The first question is: 'what is data'? Second, is it the data or the information provided in the data that is of importance? What data or information is causing the problem in the digital economy? These issues will be introduced below.

According to Wikipedia, data is units of information, often numeric, that are collected through observation.[123] In a more technical sense, data is a set of values of qualitative or quantitative variables about one or more persons or objects, while a datum (singular of *data*) is a single value of a single variable.[124]

Although the terms 'data' and 'information' are often used interchangeably, these terms have distinct meanings. Data as a general concept refers to the fact that some existing information or knowledge is represented or coded in some form (e.g., 1s and 0s). Data is often represented and coded in such a way that the information contained in the data cannot be acquired without a process making the data into information.[125]

[122] Prüfer and Schottmüller (n 110).

[123] <https://en.wikipedia.org/wiki/Data>.

[124] Ibid.

[125] Data can be defined as 'putative fact[s] regarding some difference or lack of uniformity within some context'. Luciano Floridi, 'Semantic Conceptions of Information' in Edward N. Zalta (principle ed), *The Stanford Encyclopedia of Philosophy* (Spring 2017 edition) <https://plato.stanford.edu/archives/spr2017/entries/information-semantic>.

The difference between, on the one hand, data and, on the other, information is important when addressing the issue of regulating data and of regulating information. As purported by Janeček, when discussing the issue of control and ownership of data, the difference between sematic and syntactic information also becomes important.[126] Semantic information (i.e., information per se) can never be protected by the law because it would violate free access to information. Yet, information can be protected under intellectual property law, however, only when the information as a whole meets the thresholds contained in the applicable intellectual property regime representing a work.

When discussing the free flow of data, the Commission implies that a new right to data covering syntactic information could be enacted.[127] The Commission discusses that the right should be protected only at the syntactic level and not at the semantic level. Therefore, the protection would extend only over the code and not the ideas or information. The idea behind this is to grant a right over some manifestations of data but to avoid information monopolies and the overextension of the right. Several authors still purport, however, that by creating protection of syntactic information, that is, individual data points, such protection would severally affect access to information on the level of semantics and pragmatics. Thus, protection of individual data points, implying that protection of the level of syntactics (i.e., 0s and 1s), could have a strong chilling effect of access and use of information for creating works, design, know-how, innovations, etc.[128]

In comparison, copyright does not protect information as such, but only the creative elements of a song or painting. Copyright refers only to certain aspects of information. If individual data points would be the subject matter for an exclusive data right, it has the potential of a basic paradigm shift from the principle of free use of information to a principle of protection of information. In addition, 'if we search for the right balance in reference to intellectual property protection, our focus should be on the information/semantics level, and under this perspective the introduction of a broad data right on the syntactic level would have serious consequences.'[129]

Indeed, exclusive right to or ownership of individual data points – at least in reference to the syntactic level – should be avoided.[130] Otherwise, significant hold-up problems may appear. However, that does not preclude firms or individuals from having a right to datasets or, as already granted in the EU, to databases, while still the

[126] Václav Janeček, 'Ownership of Personal Data in the Internet of Things' (2018) 34(5) Computer Law & Security Review 1039–1052 <https://doi.org/10.1016/j.clsr.2018.04.007>.

[127] Commission (n 110) 33 et seq.

[128] See, for example, Josef Drexl, 'Data Access and Control in the Era of Connected Devices', Study on behalf of the European Consumer Association BEUC (2018) discussing this at 33.

[129] Wiebe (n 96).

[130] Drexl (n 96) 17 et seq. See also Herbert Zech, 'A Legal Framework for a Data Economy in the European Digital Single Market: Rights to Use Data' (2016) 11 Journal of Intellectual Property Law & Practice 460–470, 462 et seq.

information contained in the dataset or database is not foreclosed. Indeed, it is only the dataset or database structure that is being protected against substantial extractions of data.[131] In other words, the large academic discussion regarding semantic and syntactic data, and what can be included under some form of property right,[132] could be disregarded if the right created is not exclusive.[133] Indeed, if the right to data only covers access and portability to data, while such a right does not give exclusive control, data can still be defined as information, which is the most common form under intellectual property law.[134]

There is no comprehensive legal definition of data that matches the discussion in academia regarding the delineation of the meaning of data. In reference to the Public Sector Information (PSI) Directive and other data access regimes, the focus is rather on the subject matter of the access tool. Data should, for example, according to Article 5 of the Open Data Directive be made available in preexisting format or language and, where possible and appropriate, by electronic means, in formats that

[131] The scope of the sui generis database right is discussed in Section 5.3.4.

[132] See, for example, Commission (n 83) 9–10, 13; Commission, 'On the Free Flow of Data and Emerging Issues of the European Data Economy', accompanying COM (2017) 9 final (Commission Staff Working Document) SWD (2017) 2 final, esp. 23, 33–38; Osborne Clarke LLP, 'Legal Study on Ownership and Access to Data' (European Commission 2016) <https://bookshop.europa.eu/en/legal-study-on-ownership-and-access-to-data-pbKK0416811/> or <https://perma.cc/82D8-9787>; Nestor Duch-Brown, Bertin Martens, and Frank Mueller-Langer, 'The Economics of Ownership, Access and Trade in Digital Data' (European Commission 2017) JRC Digital Economy Working Paper 2017-01; Anette Gärtner and Kate Brimsted, 'Let's Talk About Data Ownership' (2017) 39(8) EIPR 461; Sjef van Erp, 'Ownership of Data: The Numerus Clausus of Legal Objects' (2017) 6 Brigham-Kanner Property Rights Conference Journal 235; Herbert Zech, 'Information as a Tradable Commodity', in Alberto De Franceschi Ferrara (ed), *European Contract Law and the Digital Single Market* (2016) 51–79; Josef Drexl et al., 'On the Current Debate on Exclusive Rights and Access Rights to Data at the European Level' in Max Planck Institute for Innovation and Competition Position Statement (16 August 2016) 12; Wolfgang Kerber, 'A New (Intellectual) Property Right for Non-Personal Data? An Economic Analysis' (2016) 11 GRUR International 989.

[133] For a similar discussion, see Kerber (n 63).

[134] The EU Commission also envisioned something similar. Instead of creating the data producer right as a right in rem, the Commission purports that it could be conceived of as a set of purely defensive rights. This option would follow the choice made in the design of the protection given to know-how by the Trade Secrets Protection Directive. Its objective would be to enhance the sharing of data by giving at least the defensive elements of an in rem right, that is, the capacity for the de facto data holder to sue third parties in case of illicit misappropriation of data. This approach thus equates to a protection of a de facto 'possession,' rather than to the concept of 'ownership'. According to the Commission, a number of civil law remedies could be introduced such as:

(i) the right to seek injunctions preventing further use of data by third parties who have no right to use the data,
(ii) the right to have products built on the basis of misappropriated data excluded from market commercialization, and
(iii) the possibility to claim damages for unauthorized use of data.

cf Commission (n 110) 33 et seq. See also Kerber (n 132).

are open, machine-readable, accessible, findable, and reusable, together with their metadata, preferably through an API,[135] while in the field of transport and financial services[136] and in other legislative initiatives,[137] the definition or rather the subject matter of the access rule for data can be focused on semantics.

The Database Directive does contain something akin to a legal definition of data. According to Article 1(2) of the Database Directive, 'database' shall mean 'a collection of independent works, *data* or other materials. . .'. The word 'data' was included so to enable the definition to be in line with the Trade-Related Aspects of Intellectual Property Rights (TRIPS) agreement.[138] Data can imply both information and syntactic, yet it seems that the legislator implied that data should be understood as information. The term 'information' is used in several places in the preamble synonymously to data.[139] Syntactic data that is not yet information, since it cannot be perceived as information by humans, should not be understood as 'data' in the meaning of the directive.[140] This is supported by the Advocate General Stix-

135 The Directive on the reuse of public sector information Directive (EU) 2019/1024 of the European Parliament and of the Council of 20 June 2019 on open data and the reuse of public sector information, OJ L172, 26 June 2019, 56–83 (The old PSI directive: Directive 2003/98/EC, known as the 'PSI Directive') entered into force on 31 December 2003. It was revised by Directive 2013/37/EU, which entered into force on 17 July 2013.

136 In order to accelerate retail banking innovation and simplify payments, the European Commission is mandating standardized API access across the EU. The initiative is part of the European Commission's update of the Directive on Payment Services (PSD). The revision to the Directive on Payment Services (PSD2) requires banks to provide access to third parties. See Directive (EU) 2015/2366 of the European Parliament and of the Council of 25 November 2015 on payment services in the internal market, amending Directives 2002/65/EC, 2009/110/EC and 2013/36/EU and Regulation (EU) No 1093/2010, and repealing Directive 2007/64/EC (Text with EEA relevance). cf EU Commission, 'A Digital Single Market Strategy for Europe', COM (2015) 192 final.

137 Several regulatory initiatives are discussed below. However, for access data regimes, see also the REACHRegulation, Article 25 Regulation (EC) No 1907/2006 of the European Parliament and of the Council of 18 December 2006 concerning the Registration, Evaluation, Authorisation and Restriction of Chemicals (REACH), establishing a European Chemicals Agency, amending Directive 1999/45/EC and repealing Council Regulation (EEC) No 793/93 and Commission Regulation (EC) No 1488/94 as well as Council Directive 76/769/EEC and Commission Directives 91/155/EEC, 93/67/EEC, 93/105/EC and 2000/21/EC. See furthermore Article 16 of the new Digital Content and Digital Services Directive making reference to GDPR discussed in Z. Efroni, *Gaps and Opportunities: The Rudimentary Protection to 'Data-Paying Consumers' under New EU Consumer Protection Law* (Weizenbaum Series, 4, Weizenbaum Institute for the Networked Society – The German Internet Institute 2020) <https://doi.org/10.34669/wi.ws/4>. See also the new Electricity Directive of June 2019, which imposes the sharing of consumer data, including metering and consumption data, as well as data, required for customer switching, demand response, and other services. In order to stimulate competition and innovation among electricity suppliers, Article 23(2) of the Directives provides that porting of data should be required. Finally, the Clinical Trials Regulation 536/2014 sets out requirements for clinical trials on medicinal products for human use, and repeals Directive 2001/20/EC.

138 Johan Axhamn, *Databasskydd* (Stockholms universitet 2017) 96.

139 See, for example, preambles 3, 9, 10 and 12.

140 Axham (n 138).

Hakl in *Oy Veikkaus*: '[t]he question whether the main proceedings concern data or materials need not be considered in greater depth, because in practice they concern either data, in the sense of combinations of signs representing facts, that is to say, elementary statements with potentially informative content, or materials as recognizable entities.'[141]

The issue is also the requirement of *independent* data or material. It seems that data and also the notion of *material* need to have independent meanings to be recognized by the directive, that is, that individual data points should contain information that can be understood by an individual (possibly using a machine). They should have independent meanings. In *OPAP*, concerning whether football team schedules could be protected under the directive, the EU Court states that '... the date and the time of and the identity of the two teams playing in both home and away matches are covered by the concept of independent materials within the meaning of Article 1(2) of the directive in that they have autonomous informative value.'[142] The EU Court has even found in a separate case that an individual point on a map can constitute a relevant element.[143] Individual pieces of information in combination can also constitute independent material.[144]

The definition of data, independent material, and that individual pieces of information can in combination constitute 'independent material', within the meaning of Article 1(2) of Directive, point to the fact that 'data' should be viewed as information rather than syntactic figures or numbers.[145] On the whole, it seems that the database directive does focus on datasets that contain comprehensible information, yet it should be acknowledged that the scope can be limited.[146] Indeed, a map can be considered a database.[147] Independent data is information.

Although the definition of data in Article 2 of the Digital Markets Act is vague, it is similar to the one found in the Database Directive: 'data means any digital

[141] *Oy Veikkaus* (Case C 46/02) 33. The AG continues, stating on page 36, that the criterion of 'independent' should be understood as meaning that the data or materials must not be linked or must at least be capable of being separated without losing their informative content: this is why sound or pictures from a film are not covered. One possible approach to interpretation is to focus not only on the mutual independence of the materials from one another but on their independence within a collection.

[142] *OPAP* (Case 444/02) ECLI:EU:C:2004:697 33.

[143] *Verlag Esterbauer* (Case C-490/14) ECLI:EU:C:2015:73520 et seq.

[144] Ibid. See Wiebe (n 96).

[145] It should be acknowledged, however, that the Database Directive definition of data is uncertain, and some developments have occurred in which basic information or 'raw data' could be seen as being covered by the directive; cf. discussion earlier in this book regarding *OPAP Verlag Esterbauer*. The First evaluation of the Database Directive by the EU Commission states '[h]owever, as evidenced by the ECJ's differentiation between the 'creation' of data and its collection demonstrate, the 'sui generis' right comes precariously close to protecting basic information.' See also Drexl (n 128).

[146] Axham (n 138) 98. See *Fixtures Marketing* (C-444/02) ECLI:EU:C:2004:697 para 35, and *Football Dataco and Others* (C-604/10) ECLI:EU:C:2012:115 para 26.

[147] *Verlag Esterbauer* 20 et seq.

representation of acts, facts or information and any compilation of such acts, facts or information, including in the form of sound, visual or audio-visual recording.' The notion of data should also be considered including 'raw data, inferred data' and meta data, even though there is no clear definition of either term.

Moreover, only the data that is provided for or generated in the context of the use of the relevant core platform services by those business users and the end users engaging with the products or services provided by those business users are encompassed by the obligation for the platform providers in the Digital Markets Act to share data.

In reference to the definition above, the issue is however how to delineate the business users' data from the data generated by the business of the platform. As will be discussed below, blockchain technology could define the limits of which data will originate from which entities, that is, pinpoint data 'provided for or generated in the context of the use of the relevant core platform services by those business users and the end users engaging with the products or services provided by those business user...' However, referred data can actually have several sources.

It is proposed in this book that the subject matter of an access and portability right should thus be information. Though vague, the definition in the Digital Markets Act captures the gist of what needs to be included: data representing 'any digital representation of acts, facts or information and any compilation of such acts, facts or information, including in the form of sound, visual or audio-visual recording'. Indeed, interesting data is the data of the platform referring to the data created due to activities or contributed data of the business user, or in an IoT setting, data collected by sensor.[148] It is the business user's data, that is, 'any digital representation of acts, facts or information and any compilation of such acts, facts or information, including in the form of sound, visual or audio-visual recording' created by the business user's commercial activities on the platform (hereinafter business user's data).

As developed in Chapter 6, the data should be provided by the platform in a similar fashion as public entities often need to provide public sector information to reusers under the Open Data Directive, that is, aggregated or nonaggregated data, in preexisting format or language and, in real time by electronic means, in formats that are open, machine-readable, accessible, findable, and reusable, together with its metadata, preferably through an API.[149] Nevertheless, an access and portability right could also include a right to enter the platform by reengineering and data mining to gain access to the data, or require the platform to open an API or set up a blockchain

[148] As discussed below, the aggregated data should be controlled by the platform provider.

[149] The Directive on the reuse of public sector information (EU) 2019/1024 of the European Parliament and of the Council of 20 June 2019 on open data and the reuse of public sector information, OJ L172, 26 June 2019, 56–83 (The old PSI directive: Directive 2003/98/EC, known as the PSI Directive) entered into force on 31 December 2003. It was revised by Directive 2013/37/EU, which entered into force on 17 July 2013.

of data, thus giving business users access to certain blocks representing the users' data.

A further issue is whether each and every data point should fall under an access and portability right or whether there should be a threshold requirement. A business user should only have the right to access and port data when such data have reached a certain volume reflecting that the business users have made use of the platform to such extent that the data created actually possess knowledge and are valuable.

Interestingly, the obligation in Article 6 (2) compared to the obligations in (9) and (10) in the Digital Markets Act does reflect that the business users have an indirect bilateral 'countervailing' right to the data generated, vis-á-vis the platform provider, indeed, a preferential right to data, as defined above. An interesting consequence of having the right to focus only on data generated by the business user is that information obtained will not contain, or it is very unlikely it would contain, works covered by third-party intellectual property rights.[150] Moreover, by focusing on the data generated by the actions of the business user or provider only, that is, directly collected on inferred through the action of ends users and business users, it still preserves the general picture of inferred data from the actions of several users, industries, and markets connected to the platform and hence protects the platform providers general business model.

2.5 THE PROTECTION UNDER LAW FOR DATA AND DATA-DRIVEN BUSINESS MODELS

It should be clear that Article 6 paragraphs (1), (9), and (10) in the Digital Markets Act, read in combination, stipulate an obligation for gatekeepers to give access and transfer data to their business users and end user, to a level that could be regarded as an access and transfer right for business users (with some help from end users) vis-à-vis gatekeepers (an ATR). A right that business users could presumably go to court to claim. It stipulates that gatekeepers are de facto not allowed to use the data generated by the business users, and their end users, on the platforms, in competition with the business users, while the obligation in Article 6 (9) and (10) reflects that the business users have some sort of right to gain access, port, and reuse the data generated by their action on the platforms. Indeed, a right to receive a steady stream of data from the platforms, a stream that can also be transferred to third parties.

Similarly, Articles 3, 4, and 5 of the Data Act create a similar – yet not the same – access and transfer right to users vis-à-vis data holders of data generated by users of IoT devices. The ATR according to the Data Act is narrower in reference to the data

[150] For the problems in reference to third-party rights when porting data. see Barbara van der Auwermeulen, 'How to Attribute the Right to Data Portability in Europe: A Comparative Analysis of Legislations' (2017) 33 Computer Law & Security Review 57, 60 et seq.

generated, the transfer possibilities less, while the access obligation and right are wide.

This could be a game changer. The combination of Article 6 paragraphs (1), (9), and (10) in the DMA and Articles 3, 4, and 5 of the Data Act, respectively, creates a compulsory access and transfer regime, stopping just short of a property right, to the data generated by the business user and its end users on the platform. It is – not under central European doctrine a property right to data since there is no exclusive right to the data generated. The platform and the data holder according to the DMA and the Data Act respectively have access – and even more access – to the data generated.

However, as discussed in Chapters 4 and 6, the issue is whether these gateways for users to access and transfer data are in fact such a revolutionary tool for creating interoperability, or whether the intellectual property legal system or GDPR will in the end, de facto, prevent data access, reuse, and portability. It seems obvious that the gatekeepers will try to claim that the obligation to give access and for the business users to reuse the data generated on their platforms should not be enforced because the data are walled in by intellectual property rights or reflect personal data.

Data as such is not covered by any property right irrespective of how valuable or personal it is. Yet, data can still be protected for the benefit of platform providers. As discussed in Chapter 6, technical protection measures (TPMs), cf. Article 6 InfoSoc, can prevent access to copyright-protected content and unfortunately also unprotected data. 'Hacking' or breaching technical measures to gain access to unprotected data can be a violation of Article 6 InfoSoc. Moreover, the gates to platforms (the APIs) may be copyright protected, restricting access. However, perhaps the biggest hurdle to gain access to the data is that the platform providers when storing the data in databases or in private-centralized blockchains could most likely hold sui generis database protection under the 1996 directive.[151]

The application of these rules in reference to the obligation in the Digital Markets Act and Data Act can perhaps be denied – that, in the end, there is no infringement inherent in the access and reuse of the data by business users. Nevertheless, the rights described above, together with the right to trade secrets and the notion that personal data is off-limits, seem to create so much uncertainty that gatekeepers and data holders may choose to deny the obligation to grant access to data, because such access and reuse could allegedly infringe the rights of the gatekeepers and data holders.

It is true that the users also have tools for accessing data under the intellectual property law system. The new data-mining regulation in the (new) Software Directive, used in conjunction with the proposed Data Act and Digital Markets Act, could perhaps – with help of a creative CJEU – bend open the gates so as to access the keepers' data. The reverse-engineering doctrine in the Software Directive

[151] See further discussion in Chapter 6.

could perhaps also be used together with the proposed Data Act and Digital Markets Act, in analogy breaching the keepers' gates. However, the application of these exemptions is uncertain at best.

Generally, a right to access and port or transfer data should be enacted for the benefit of users of platforms. It needs to be clarified whether the proposed Data Act and Digital Markets Act are capable of creating access and transfer of data unilaterally or in combination with the rights of data mining and reverse engineering in the area of copyright (discussed infra under Chapter 6). And, if not, the regulations should be amended accordingly, with inspiration from reverse-engineering and data-mining principles. Should, for example, the Digital Markets Act be viewed as creating an obligation for the gatekeepers to allow access also to intellectual property law or trade secret protected subject matters (held by the platform or third party)? Is the Digital Markets Act a developed reverse engineering – data mining – tool, for business users and end users to apply? Is it a development of the reverse-engineering right inherent in copyright law, cf. the EU Software Directive, paralleling the data-mining exemption under the new Copyright Directive?

As discussed in Chapter 6, the proposal for an access and transfer Rrght to business user's data provided in this book would in essence trump the potential legal obstacles created by the intellectual property law system, the GDPR, and the trade secret directive and allow users to access and transfer data from platforms and IoT devices.

2.6 TECHNOLOGY RESTRICTIONS

As stated above, a major gateway for business users of platforms is application programming interfaces (APIs). They are the gates to the platforms. Application programming interfaces are software that allows a program to access and interact with another program, sharing data and functionality. Application programming interfaces provide a standardized way to access and port data. Platforms therefore use thousands of APIs to enable third-party developers and service providers to make use and interact with the platforms. Indeed, access and portability of data can be conducted through APIs, yet they are controlled by the platforms. However, that implies that one API technology becomes standardized and that such standardization leads to interoperability between platforms and Clouds. A global standardized API technology can play a desirable global rule-setting function in controlling access and use.

Continuous data transfers would require some degree of interoperability between the transmitting and receiving platform or in-house server. It would also presumably be of much more use in rapidly evolving markets for data-intensive services, relative to a one-off transfer of data that could become obsolete. An equivalent measure to continuous data portability could be providing third parties with the rights to run algorithms or programs directly on the data located on a data controller's (or platform's) server.[152]

Application programming interfaces and other standards to enable interoperability can thus either be closed, meaning they are unique to each platform, or can be based on open standards.[153] Open standards allow third-party service providers to build their systems around a standard that would be interoperable with multiple platforms, helping to manage costs and increasing their viability and attractiveness to users. However, as discussed in Chapter 3, access to APIs for digital platforms will often be subject to restrictions if there are privacy, security, or technical limits that must be placed to prevent misuse or degradation of the platform's functionality.[154] Moreover, there can be restrictions and limitations inserted in the APIs with the aim to exclude competitors.[155]

In Europe, the Software Directive (2009/24/EC) clarifies that ideas and principles underlying any element of a computer program, including – presumably – those underlying its interfaces, for example, APIs, are not protected by copyright.[156] The Court of Justice has already ruled in a case referred by the UK (SAS *Institute Inc. v World Programming Ltd*) that copyright of a program cannot be infringed, where the lawful acquirer of the license merely studied, observed, and/or tested the program in order to reproduce its functionality in a second program. Although the Court did not address specifically the question of whether or not copyright attaches to APIs, it did state that 'neither the functionality of a computer program nor the programming language and the format of data files used in a computer program in order to exploit certain of its functions constitute a form of expression of that program'. Although not specifically addressing the issue, the judgment has been recognized as stating that

[152] OECD, 'Data Portability, Interoperability and Digital Platform Competition', OECD Competition Committee Discussion Paper (2021) 11 et seq. <http://oe.cd/dpic>.

[153] OECD, 'Financial Markets, Insurance and Private Pensions: Digitalisation and Finance' (2018) <www.oecd.org/finance/private-pensions/Financial-markets-insurance-pensions-digitalisation-and-finance.pdf>.

[154] C. Riley, 'Unpacking Interoperability in Competition' (2020) 5(1) Journal of Cyber Policy 99 et seq. <https://doi.org/10.1080/23738871.2020.1740754>.

[155] Ibid.

[156] According to Band, 'the Software Directive does not directly address the protectability of interface specifications. Rather, Article 1(2) provides that '[i]deas and principles which underlie any element of a computer program, including those which underlie its interfaces, are not protected by copyright. . . .' Commentators interpreted this provision to mean interface information necessary to achieve interoperability must fall on the idea side of the idea/expression dichotomy; otherwise, the detailed decompilation provision in Article 6 would have little utility.' Jonathan Band, 'The Global API Copyright Conflict' (2018) 31 Harvard Journal of Law & Technology 615. See also Kemp IT Law, 'APIs and Copyright: Who Owns the Glue that Sticks the Digital World Together?' <www.lexology.com/library/detail.aspx?g=a124eb8e-d92c-4729-a2a2-8fbef75806c0>; Komal Shemar (Legal Consultant @ Gerrish Legal), 'Reverse Engineering: When Can Users Lawfully Decompile Software?' (2020) <www.gerrishlegal.com/legal-blog/2020/4/7/reverse-engineering-when-can-users-lawfully-decompile-software>.

the accepted EU position appears to be that APIs are not protected by copyright because they are functional in nature.[157]

However, this can change should APIs be protected in other jurisdictions. A protection of APIs should also have large implications for accessing data and platforms for business users and would clearly imply that business users would need an overriding right to access data, going beyond what the Digital Markets Act now is stipulating.

The new paradigm implies that data – to a greater extent than ever before – can be collected and stored. Technically, data will be stored on servers in datasets or in databases, regardless of whether the data is stored in-house by an undertaking or in the cloud. However, databases or datasets can be set up differently, utilizing single servers and multiple servers, or even excess drive and network capacity on PCs, which can be geographically divided, for storing data.

The precise nature of interoperability schemes and measures will vary according to the markets involved. In the CMA Final Report from 2020, the authority considered 'content interoperability', which allows users to 'post, view and engage with content across platforms without having to switch service'.[158] This definition has parallels with the type of interoperability envisaged in the UK Open Banking reforms, which seek to allow users to access multiple bank accounts and services through a single application. It is also how platforms and content providers interact in the online gambling industry. However, the main goal should be that data seemingly flow from platform to platform and cloud to cloud for the benefit of users, which requires full data portability or even interoperability – something that a global standardized API could possibly achieve or, at least, common data schema will need to be developed. This could be accomplished with the use of intermediaries to produce a schema mapping that enables interoperability. Alternatively, data portability could be facilitated through the use of intermediary data controllers (i.e., third parties accessing the data and passing it on), through the private services of Personal Information Management Systems (PIMS),[159] possibly connected to data pools as discussed in Chapter 3. However, could the technology of blockchain be used?

The term 'blockchain' derives from a concept where transactions and information are recorded continuously and irreversibly in an ever-growing chain of cryptographically linked and time-stamped data blocks, stored primarily in a decentralized

[157] Komal Shemar (Legal Consultant @ Gerrish Legal), 'Reverse Engineering: When Can Users Lawfully Decompile Software?' (2020) <www.gerrishlegal.com/legal-blog/2020/4/7/reverse-engineering-when-can-users-lawfully-decompile-software>.

[158] CMA Final Report 372.

[159] J. Krämer, P. Senellart, and A. de Streel, 'Making Data Portability More Effective for The Digital Economy' (2020) 8 et seq. <https://cerre.eu/publications/report-making-data-portability-more-effective-digital-economy/>.

manner.[160] Blockchain is thus a technology that facilitates the storage and exchange of data in a secure and decentralized fashion, without the need for an intermediary or centralized hub. The primary component of blockchain is a distributed ledger containing a record of all digital transfers, for example, business data (i.e., the digital transfers that are part of the blockchain's 'domain'); members of the blockchain determine the data that will be kept in the ledger. This digital ledger or blockchain is encrypted, thus protecting this ledger from being 'minded', or tampered with, and distributed and stored through the sharing of excess drive and network capacity on the participants' computers and in data centers (servers).[161]

Blockchain is in essence a database, where data is continuously arranged and stored in blocks of data,[162] and where the members have decided on rules for who can add blocks, access blocks, and port the data included in the blockchain. Different users (nodes) may have different types of authority to add blocks and to use and access the data stored in the blockchain. The blockchains can be roughly divided into open (public) and closed (private) blockchains. Public blockchains are open for anyone to use, while private blockchains have been created for use within a business, a government agency, or consortium of companies, where permission from the network creator (a custodian) or existing members is required to participate. These public blockchains are often decentralized in the sense that all members have the same rights and privileges, for example, to add or view blocks of data. They technically and jointly determine the blocks that will be added to the blockchain.[163]

[160] T. Schrepel, *Blockchain + Antitrust* (Edward Elgar 2021) <www.elgaronline.com/view/9781800885523.xml> accessed 19 May 2022.

[161] Jeremy Clark and Alexander Essex, 'Commitcoin: Carbon Dating Commitments with Bitcoin' in Angelos D. Keromytis (ed), *International Conference on Financial Cryptography and Data Security* (Springer 2012) 390–398. Interestingly, from an intellectual property law perspective, encrypted blockchain technology could be viewed as technical protection measures (TPMs) (cf Article 6 InfoSoc Directive); to prevent access to the copyright-protected content, the data could be copyright protected. In addition, under the InfoSoc Directive, not only is a breach of these technical protection measures considered a copyright infringement; the manufacturing and sale of devices whose primary purpose or effect is to enable such circumvention may be a copyright infringement in itself. Indeed, blockchain may solve the problem of the legal obstacles associated with legal ownership and the problem of system leaders.

[162] The size of the block differs but averages approximately 1 MB of data per block. cf <www.blockchain.com/charts/avg-block-size>.

[163] The exact difference between a centralized and decentralized blockchain is not entirely clear. Compare, for example, Praveen Jayachandran, 'The Difference between Public and Private Blockchain', Blockchain Pulse: IBM Blockchain Blog (2017) <www.ibm.com/blogs/blockchain/2017/05/the-difference-between-public-and-private-blockchain/>, claiming that the sole distinction between public and private blockchain is related to who is allowed to participate in the network, execute the *consensus* protocol, and maintain the shared ledger. A public blockchain network is completely open, and anyone can join and participate in the network. cf ibid. with Pontus Lindblom, 'Blockkedjeteknik utifrån ett konkurrensperspektiv' (2019) Uppdragsforskningsrapport 4 43 <www.konkurrensverket.se/globalassets/publikationer/uppdragsforskning/forsk-rapport_2019-4.pdf>.

One of the main features of public, decentralized, blockchain-based applications, therefore, is that the users have technical control, 'ownership', of their assets (i.e., submitted data blocks) without requiring a custodian (e.g., a platform system leader, online intermediaries, or cloud provider) that controls the chain.[164]

Transaction platforms are an area where decentralized blockchain could be an alternative. Instead of centralized platforms such as Amazon Marketplace or eBay, where a hub firm controls all transactions and collects all data, platforms using a decentralized blockchain could organize transactions between business users and individuals, so that the data generated by these transactions would be available, free to use, and stored for in perpetuity for the business users and the platform providers.[165]

A public, decentralized blockchain would even enable individuals and firms to maintain technical control over all data generated by individuals or business activities or when 'transactions' take place on a platform. However, a centralized, closed blockchain is not very different from a database for which a system leader or custodian stores and controls all data collected on a platform.

The question is how solid the 'blockchain dream' is, and whether this innovation is a blessing or a curse. The essence of the 'dream' is that the decentralization and disintermediation that blockchain enables will challenge the current centralized architecture for collecting data on the Internet and will fulfill the expectations of the original vision of Internet as a borderless and radically democratic space. The internet era gave rise to online intermediaries and digital platforms that control and orchestrate value-generating e-ecosystems, offering not only products and online services but also the infrastructure and tools on which other platform businesses are built. In contrast, blockchain technology has been widely perceived as promising a decentralized and largely disintermediated organizational model for the digital economy – a model that would dispense with intermediaries and thus the risk of monopolistic bottlenecks.[166]

While in the digital platform model, only the centralized online platform collects information about past transactions, blockchain offers a distributed, decentralized ledger that keeps a complete record of all past transactions on the network. This enables all participants to access information about previous transactions related to a platform, for example, and thus ensures that no participant in the network enjoys the superior bargaining power produced by informational asymmetries. This guarantee is strengthened by the transparency of the process: Each new transaction is broadcast

[164] The main drawback of a public blockchain is the substantial amount of computational power that is necessary to maintain a distributed ledger at a large scale. More specifically, to achieve consensus, each node in a network must solve a complex, resource-intensive cryptographic problem called a proof of work to ensure all are in sync. See Jayachandran (n 163).

[165] An example of this is OpenBazaar, a peer-to-peer software solution with open-source code. See Lindbom (n 163).

[166] Ioannis Lianos, 'Blockchain Competition' in Philip Hacker, Ioannis Lianos, Georgios Dimitropoulos, and Stefan Eich, *Regulating Blockchain: Political and Legal Challenges* (Oxford University Press 2019) forthcoming <https://ssrn.com/abstract=3257307>.

to the entire network, and each participant has the power to determine the transaction's authenticity. This breaks with the centralized data-silo model of the platform economy, where only certain actors have access to information – because all interactions between the network participants happen through these actors – and these few actors can accumulate data to increase their bargaining power and erect barriers to entry.[167]

However, blockchain technology also provides possibilities to control data when blockchain is implemented in a closed (private), centralized manner rather than in a decentralized manner. Indeed, private blockchain resembles a regular database, where a system leader controls the content, access, and possibilities to port the data.

Nevertheless, and of importance for the discussion in this book, a decentralized flavor of blockchain technology could be a solution for the legislator that is crafting regulations for access and right to portability, or for the creation of common data spaces or pools in certain areas, such as transaction or transport platforms, or IoT platforms for sectors such as the vehicle industry or healthcare. Indeed, the original internet dream for a borderless and radically democratic space implied that property systems should also be limited. For example, in the original ideal scenario, platforms would have only limited liability for content found in infringement of copyright.[168] The blockchain movement still clings to this dream, but the technology also contains the possibility to identify and systematize data blocks and assign a controlling party, making blockchain ideal for implementing a property regime for a future Internet and IoT that is borderless, democratic, and, to the extent that is possible, 'just'.

2.7 PLATFORM, CLOUD, AND IOT CONTRACTS

Guaranteeing functioning and competitive markets is the very purpose of economic regulation, with the contract law system, intellectual property law, and competition law as its key legal components. These components need to find an equilibrium that also takes into consideration the distribution of market power and negotiation power. It should be acknowledged that with respect to platforms and cloud services, there is an unequal distribution of negotiating power. The business users of transaction platforms or cloud services seem to face difficulties when purchasing these services. They cannot negotiate individual contracts that take into consideration the individual needs of business users.[169]

It should be pointed out from the start that platform and cloud computing services are still emerging market(s); the basic economic effects in reference to network externalities and tipping are the driving forces, while access to the relevant technology steers platform users to accept that certain solutions are necessary. Nonetheless,

[167] Ibid.

[168] See discussion in Chapters 5 and 6.

[169] The EU Commission investigation of Amazon discussed in Section 2.1 focuses on Amazon's use of standard contracts.

the services provided and the terms and conditions for these services are also evolving and can be used to trigger and protect the network effects.

When preparing the platform-to-business regulation (P2B), the EU Commission identified several problems that businesses faced in reference to platforms.[170] For example, platforms controlled the contract and could make changes, suddenly and without explanation, to the Terms and Conditions. The problem was especially acute regarding data; platforms had unclear policies for accessing data generated through online intermediation services. Thirty-three percent of the heavy users of transaction platforms considered the platforms' data policies to be a problem. The problem was related to the fact that platforms tended to promote and give benefit to their own services, while downgrade competing services.

Cloud computing services may overlap, but they can be defined as three main services: Infrastructure as a Service (IaaS), Platform as a Service (PaaS), and Software as a Service (SaaS). These services are more or less complex, and the degrees of complexity and intertwined collaborations between the cloud provider and the user imply a corresponding level of how much access the cloud provider requires to user-provided data. The increased complexity may thus have consequences for data ownership and user rights. According to the Commission, it is often easier, for example, for a user to switch cloud service providers in the IaaS context, where the services rendered are only for data storage.[171] Moving into more complex services such as PaaS and especially SaaS increases the difficulties of switching providers. Therefore, can cloud service users in the IoT be the actors that create and uphold competition? Can they create competition by efficiently choosing between different cloud service providers? Unfortunately, this does not seem to be the case.

According to the Commission, vendor lock-in actions by cloud service providers are common and constitute a form of data localization restriction imposed by the private sector, specifically targeting data mobility across the cloud or IT systems. Problems may arise when users of data storage or processing services try to switch cloud service providers.[172]

[170] Commission, 'Online Platforms: New Rules to Increase Transparency and Fairness' (14 February 2019) <https://ec.europa.eu/digital-single-market/en/news/online-platforms-new-rules-increase-transparency-and-fairness>.

[171] Commission, 'Commission Staff Working Document accompanying the Document Proposal for a Regulation of the European Parliament and of the Council on a Framework for the Free Flow of Non-personal Data in the European Union' SWD/2017/0304 final, 2017/0228 (COD 13 September 2017) (herein after Impact Assessment) 11 et seq.

[172] Ibid. Other studies seem to indicate some degree of lock-in effects, while also indicating that these may differ – especially between user-paid services and free services. See, for example, Simon Bradshaw, Christopher Millard, and Ian Walden, 'Contracts for Clouds: Comparison and Analysis of the Terms and Conditions of Cloud Computing Services' Queen Mary School of Law Legal Studies Research Paper No 63/2010, 15 <https://ssrn.com/abstract=1662374> or <http://dx.doi.org/10.2139/ssrn.1662374> accessed 24 July 2018, listing among others Google Docs as a Cloud. SSRN, 15 et seq. Chris Reed and Alan Cunningham, 'Ownership of Information in Clouds' in Christopher Millard (ed), *Cloud Computing Law* (Oxford University Press 2013) 151 et seq. See also Ian Walden and Laise Bornico, 'Ensuring

Cloud switching or platform switching can be very costly for customers (especially small- to medium-sized enterprises (SMEs), including fees for data transport and licenses, downtime, and the need to use concurrent services during a transition period, as well as the costs of network use. According to the Commission, costs may vary depending on the complexity of each switching scenario, but in one example the cost amounted to EUR 2,700,000. Some cloud customers have reported instances where cloud service providers gave no information regarding how to exit the cloud or switch cloud service providers. The report also notes cases where the costs for entering the cloud were much lower than those for customers wanting to exit and port data. Thus, the cloud providers attract customers by offering low thresholds for entry, but 'lock them in' by making switching difficult and costly. This may be a practical consequence, however, when the user and the provider have engaged in a more complex collaboration, for example, a SaaS contract, while exiting may be easier under an IaaS contract.[173]

One less altruistic or practical reason for lock-ins could be to guarantee the flow of user-created data to the cloud provider. This becomes apparent when analyzing 'free' clouds, when some cloud providers grant access to cloud space for free, as long as the providers are given full access and rights to use any and all data in the cloud.[174] These agreements can be difficult for cloud customers to exit.[175]

Competition in the Clouds: The Role of Competition Law?' (2011) 12 ERA Forum 282 et seq., indicating lock-in effects as a potential competition law problem.

[173] According to the Commission, it is often easier to switch cloud service providers in the Infrastructure as a Service (IaaS) context, where the services rendered are only for data storage. For more complex services such as Platform as a Service (PaaS) and especially Software as a Service (SaaS), the difficulties of switching increase. IaaS and PaaS standards can be defined using simple interfaces, but this is often not the case with SaaS standards, which require more complex interfaces to retrieve data. Commission, 'Commission Staff Working Document Impact Accompanying the document Proposal for a Regulation of the European Parliament and of the Council on a framework for the free flow of non-personal data in the European Union SWD/2017/0304 final – 2017/0228 (COD) 13 September 2017 (Impact Assessment) 11 et seq.

[174] Bradshaw, Millard, and Walden (n 172). See also the critique against Google for a contract clause giving Google the right to use the user's data for the Google Drive/Docs cloud service, catering mainly to individuals and SMEs. For example, Zack Whittaker, 'Who Owns Your Files on Google Drive? Google Drive's Terms of Service Do Indeed Allow You to Own Your Own Files, But Grant the Company a License to Do as It Wants with Your Uploaded Content' (CNET 24 April 2012). *The clause read: 'Your Content in our Services: When you upload or otherwise submit content to our Services, you give Google (and those we work with) a worldwide licence to use, host, store, reproduce, modify, create derivative works (such as those resulting from translations, adaptations or other changes that we make so that your content works better with our Services), communicate, publish, publicly perform, publicly display and distribute such content. The rights that you grant in this licence are for the limited purpose of operating, promoting and improving our Services, and to develop new ones. This licence continues even if you stop using our Services (for example, for a business listing that you have added to Google Maps).'*

[175] Michael R. Overly, 'Crossroads of Cybersecurity and the Law' (2017) <www.csoonline.com/article/3217724/cloud-security/what-can-my-cloud-provider-do-with-my-data.html> accessed 14 April 2018. Indeed, an appropriate best-practice clause would be: *'During the term of this*

One of the main issues identified so far by the Commission is that providers impose data localization restrictions, both contractually and technically.[176] For firms that have provided data to the cloud, exiting may be difficult.[177] To a certain extent, business users lack access to and/or the ability to transmit or port certain types of data, of both a personal and nonpersonal character. This concerns not only sophisticated product preference and customer data. For example, in certain circumstances, specific cloud service or platform users such as Uber drivers may not have access to the contact details of the customers that they serve via platforms.[178] As a result, they are unable to interact with their customers outside of the platform, for example, for targeted marketing initiatives or to move their customer base to another platform. Some cloud service or platform users (cf. Uber drivers) are contractually limited in their ability to use data generated through a specific platform to improve their activities on other platforms. In these circumstances, data protection rules may further limit the cloud user from competing with the cloud provider.

Firms, especially SMEs, may have major difficulties engaging platform providers in negotiating the terms of service agreements and resolving the issues and problems they face when utilizing cloud services. The fact that these agreements may be skewed in favor of the cloud/platform providers can cause problems.

Moreover, intermediate service customers are often less knowledgeable than their providers and, according to the Commission, this creates a certain imbalance in bargaining power, causing friction and enabling unfair behavior on the part of internet intermediates.[179] It seems that wide nonassert clauses, which are not limited to the service given by the cloud service provider, together with nontampering and non-reverse-engineering clauses, are (or at least until recently were) used in cloud

Agreement, Customer grants Vendor a non-transferable, non-exclusive, terminable at-will license to use the Customer Data solely for purposes of performing the Services for Customer's benefit.' That licence should be based on the database right held by the device producer, that is, the collector of data, who merely stores the data with the cloud service provider. It seems that several of the larger cloud providers, for example, Amazon and Google, state that they will access customer data only to develop the specified service.

[176] Several cloud contracts, see, for example, Amazon and Google, give the user the right to select location. Regarding the technical side, that is, technical standards, interoperability, and the IoT, see Björn Lundqvist, 'Standardization for the Digital Economy: The Issue of Interoperability and Access under Competition Law' (2017) 62(4) Antitrust Bulletin 710–725.

[177] Commission, 'Commission Staff Working Document Accompanying the document Proposal for a Regulation of the European Parliament and of the Council on a framework for the free flow of non-personal data in the European Union, SWD/2017/0304 final – 2017/0228 (COD) 13 September 2017 11 et seq.

[178] Web-based taxi services such as Uber and hotel websites may have strict rules on access to customer data.

[179] Commission, 'Fairness in platform-to-business relations' Ref. Ares(2017)5222469 – 25/10/2017 <https://ec.europa.eu/info/law/better-regulation/initiatives/ares-2017-5222469_en> accessed 28 May 2018.

service agreements.[180] Regarding nonassert clauses, the cloud users have been required to agree not to utilize their intellectual property portfolio vis-à-vis the cloud provider and the e-platform ecosystem as a whole. All firms connected to the e-ecosystem in question would be encompassed by the nonassert clause. This is quite intrusive, as it might enable the system leaders or other firms in the ecosystem to use data collected in the cloud to leverage downstream onto markets relevant for brick-and-mortar firms, without risking infringement suits. Indeed, these practices may facilitate the conduct that Prüfer and Schottmüller warned about in their paper. Cloud users, active downstream, cannot bring their intellectual property rights to bear against the cloud provider when the cloud provider uses data to acquire the cloud users' market-based knowledge. As discussed below, nonassert covenants may be considered anticompetitive when used for leveraging under Article 102 TFEU; however, the Commission is also trying to address some of these issues with sector-specific regulations.

In conclusion, it seems that large internet intermediates (platform providers), often doubling as cloud providers, have been able to become the data-transfer nodes in their e-ecosystems through contracts with their business users. Both the data architecture in IoT settings and the contracts are skewed to direct all data to the gatekeepers, while the business users of their e-ecosystems encounter great difficulties when trying to exit these agreements; at best, these business users have access only to their own generated data. Moreover, the contracts seem to pave the way for the gatekeepers to enter the markets of their business users and to benefit from their own services downstream.

Enabling functioning and competitive markets is the very purpose of the economic legal system in liberal economies, and it seems that the legal system must develop to deal with the realities of the data-driven economy. The new paradigm

[180] iam-media, 'Beware the IP Non-assert Clause in AWS Cloud Service Agreement, Warns Ex-Microsoft Patent Chief' (12 July 2015) <www.iam-media.com/blog/detail.aspx?g=16404f83-82a0-4a0f-bc79-38ba53ceaf2d> accessed 10 May 2018. See also Jaydip Sen, 'Security and Privacy Issues in Cloud Computing in Fernando Pereniguez Garcia' in Rafael Marin-Lopez, Antonio Ruiz-Martinez (eds), *Architectures and Protocols for Secure Information Technology Infrastructure* (IGI-Global 2013) 16 et seq., discussing the Amazon cloud service contracts, where the non-assert clause required the customer to refrain from asserting, on its own or through others, any IP claims regarding the AWS services the customer had used. The clause was applied, without any time limit, after the agreement had ended, and could be said to amount to a patent no-challenge clause; see also Tom Krazit, 'Amazon Web Services Adds IP Protection While Dropping Controversial Patent Clause from User Agreement' (14 July 2017). It seems that the non-assert clause has been dropped, but the indemnification (Section 9.2 of the cloud service contract, cf <https://aws.amazon.com/agreement/>) could still be interpreted as shielding Amazon and others in its ecosystem from infringement damages suits; see <www.geekwire.com/2017/amazon-web-services-added-ip-protection-dropping-controversial-patent-clause-user-agreement/> accessed 10 May 2018. See also Richard Kempe, 'Growing Patent Claim Risks in Cloud Computing' (9 June 2017) <www.kempitlaw.com/growing-patent-claim-risks-in-cloud-computing/>. For the Google cloud service agreement, see <https://console.cloud.google.com/tos?id=cloud&pli=1>.

that enables data to be monitored, collected, analyzed, and stored also enables intermediates to control and privatize huge amounts of information. Contractually, the relevant parties are not able to create functioning and competitive markets, and therefore, appropriate competition law, sector-specific regulations, and intellectual property legislation must be put in place to protect markets and the liberal economy.

2.8 THE BUNDLE OF RIGHTS IDENTIFIED AS AN ACCESS AND TRANSFER RIGHT

The data-driven economy clearly faces challenges. Monopolies are being created based on data advantages, and it is easy to imagine that with the implementation of the Internet of Things, this development will also migrate to old economy oligopoly markets. The structures inherent in data-driven business models will be transferred to B2B ecosystems and may transform the old – nonconnected – economy. It is possible that the B2B transaction and social information-sharing platforms will not span all industries of the world and will instead become more industry specific, such as the John Deere platform that is being developed for interested parties in the farming business or industry. Economists are telling us that monopolies will be created[181] – monopolies based on the platform's ability to exclusively collect and control data that is created by others, users, and business users.[182]

As indicated above, vertical cloud and platforms contracts do not mitigate these circumstances, and the parties to the digital economy cannot deal with inherent data economy developments through contractual arrangements with platforms. Indeed, power is being concentrated in the hands of a few in the data-driven industries, owing to their advantages and ability to use data-driven economies of scope and scale. The data that is collected enables platforms to enter new areas, and the variable cost of developing new products will be decreased. By adding network effects and the fact that markets are multisided to this equation, it is easy to understand how monopolistic platforms are created.[183] The subsequent antitrust harm would be excessive prices, reduced quality, and decreased incentive to innovate.[184] It seems clear that this data collection creates and enhances barriers to entry, deters the creation of economy of scope, and intensifies network effects.

Against this backdrop, an important debate has emerged according to the Commission, regarding whether – and if so, under which conditions and on which legal basis – public intervention is needed to ensure sufficient and timely access to

[181] Kerber discussed the response to data-driven business models inherent in IoT in reference to in-vehicle data, and where the incumbent car manufacturers seem to have jointly understood the benefits of not giving access to a single, shared platform. cf Kerber (n 58).

[182] See Section 2.3.

[183] Parker, Petropoulos, and van Alstyne (n 95).

[184] Ibid.

data, even personal data on an individual level, to competitors of the platforms, third-party users, and even to the public.[185]

Data and information are very broad, fuzzy terms that are difficult to grasp and precisely describe.[186] However, some things are known. Data, the information (as such), is a public good. Data is generally not covered by property rights, regardless of how private and valuable it is.[187] No one owns personal data, although under the GDPR, individuals as 'data subjects' in the EU retain some rights with respect to their data.[188] This notwithstanding, if an individual piece of data or a general dataset (personal or nonpersonal) fulfills the requirement for intellectual property rights or for status as a trade secret, it can be protected. For instance, content uploaded on a platform, for example, a YouTube clip, can be covered by third-party copyright.[189] However, the data generated on platforms due to the third-party content being used, or data generated when products are sold on Amazon Marketplace, for example, or the data generated by sensors in 'things' is normally not covered by any economic

185 Jacques Crémer, Yves-Alexandre de Montjoye, and Heike Schweitzer, *Competition Policy for the Digital Era* (Publications Office of the European Union 2019) 73.

186 Lennart Chrobak, 'Proprietary Rights in Digital Data? Normative Perspectives and Principles of Civil Law' in M. Bakhoum, B. Conde Gallego, M. O. Mackenrodt, and G. Surblytė-Namavičienė (eds), *Personal Data in Competition, Consumer Protection and Intellectual Property Law* (28 MPI Studies on Intellectual Property and Competition Law, Springer 2018) 254 et seq.

187 Some authors propose the recognition of ownership rights for consumers to the data they produce, for example, Chris Jay Hoofnagle and Jan Whittington, 'Free: Accounting for the Costs of the Internet's Most Popular Price' [2014] 61(3) UCLA Law Review 606–670. Moreover, there is a discussion regarding how to conceptualize privacy, sphere theory, data category theory, ownership theory, empirical theory, and what seems to be relevant 'decisional autonomy'. cf Stanley Greenstein, *Our Humanity Exposed* (Doctoral thesis, Stockholm University 2017) 187 et seq.

188 There are some rights connected to personal data in Articles 18–20 of the General Data Protection Regulation, such as the right to have data corrected, the 'right to be forgotten,' and the right to data portability, which are akin to economic and even property rights. In reference to data portability, the right is limited, making it less attractive for consumers to switch social websites. There is a discussion about whether to develop the GDPR to become a property regime. Louisa Specht, 'Property Rights Concerning Personal Data' (2017) 9(3) Zeitschrift für Geistiges Eigentum 411 (arguing against the need of such an extension). See also Christian Berger, 'Property Rights to Personal Data? An Exploration of Commercial Data Law' (2017) 9(3) Zeitschrift für Geistiges Eigentum 340–355. For GDPR, cf Regulation (EU) 2016/679 of the European Parliament and of the Council of 27 April 2016 on the protection of natural persons with regard to the processing of personal data and on the free movement of such data, and repealing Directive 95/46/EC (General Data Protection Regulation) (Text with EEA relevance) OJ L119, 4 May 2016, 1–88.

189 Moreover, the firms providing the e-ecosystem or infrastructure of the IoT will have the infrastructure covered by patents and copyright and, technically, can also prevent access to the data. Traditionally, copyright owners resort to technical protection measures (TPMs), cf Art 6 InfoSoc, to prevent access to the copyright-protected content. Interestingly, InfoSoc finds that not only a breach of this technical protection constitutes copyright infringement; the manufacturing and sale of devices whose primary purpose or effect is to enable such circumvention may be a copyright infringement in itself. In the case of datasets including copyright-protected data, Article 6 InfoSoc would still be applicable. See the interesting conference paper by Ciani (n 3).

rights. Indeed, all that data is generally being collected – exclusively – by the system leaders of respective dominant platforms. In addition, other forms of data, such as 'metadata', that is, data about user data, and 'derived data', that is, new data generated through the analysis of user data or metadata, need to be considered.[190]

However, if the data is generally free, nonexclusive, and nonrivalrous, how can platforms control the data? The reason is that the infrastructure for collecting, storing, and distributing data is normally embedded behind technology barriers, and there are legal and contractual barriers to refusing access but also to gaining access.

Traditionally, copyright owners regularly resort to technical protection measures (TPMs), cf. Article 6 InfoSoc,[191] to prevent access to copyright-protected content.[192] Interestingly, InfoSoc finds that not only a breach of these technical protection measures is a copyright infringement; the manufacturing and sale of devices whose primary purpose or effect is to enable such circumvention may be a copyright infringement in itself.[193] Breaching technical measures to gain access to data can be a violation of Article 6 InfoSoc. Thus, Article 6 InfoSoc also protects the platforms from being 'hacked' to gain access to data.[194] Possibly, restricting the use of APIs by a gatekeeper may also prevent access of data held by the same.[195]

Other legal systems can protect the system leaders that control platforms and data. The system leaders would most likely hold some intellectual property rights, such as *sui generis* database protection, for the data generated on the platforms and when storing the data in databases or in private, centralized blockchains.[196] Moreover, system leaders can claim that the datasets they collect are trade secrets under the new EU Directive,[197] or in the case of personal data, the data might be off-limits under the GDPR.

Interestingly, and as will be discussed below, it seems clear that GDPR may empower large platforms in several instances. It can be presumed that the burden of

[190] Chrobak (n 186) 255 et seq.

[191] According to Article 6 (3) Directive 2001/29/EC on the harmonization of certain aspects of copyright and copyright related rights in the information society of 22 May 2001 (OJEU 2001 L 167, 10; 'InfoSoc Dir.'), technical protection measures enjoy legal protection because they serve to prevent acts infringing copyright.

[192] See Ciani (n 3).

[193] Ibid.

[194] Hanns Ullrich, 'Technology Protection and Competition Policy for the Information Economy. From Property Rights for Competition to Competition without Proper Rights?' (12 August 2019) Max Planck Institute for Innovation & Competition Research Paper No 19-12 20 et seq. <https://ssrn.com/abstract=3437177> or <http://dx.doi.org/10.2139/ssrn.3437177>.

[195] See discussion in this chapter and in Chapter 6.

[196] Matthias Leistner, 'Big Data and the EU Database Directive 96/9/EC: Current Law and Potential for Reform' (7 September 2018) <https://ssrn.com/abstract=3245937> or <http://dx.doi.org/10.2139/ssrn.3245937>. As discussed below, a private, centralized blockchain should be regarded as a database.

[197] Directive 2016/943/EU of 8 June 2016 on the protection of trade secrets.

GDPR increases as the size of the business and managed data increases. However, it seems that, de facto, the system works the other way around. Large players use broad consent covenants to circumvent the GDPR. They use data-driven business models in a multitude of services and markets without being tamed by data protection authorities. For example, with Google search, Google Maps, and the other Google services within the Google ecosystem, Google can deal with the GDPR requirements better than smaller players.[198] Large, well-known platforms easily obtain broad and detailed consent statements from individuals, thus acquiring permission to use the data over various services, but these platforms often use the data in ways that go beyond the scope of users' consent. Faced with the sheer magnitude of platforms' activity, data protection authorities may find it difficult to identify incidents where data is processed without the necessary consent.

Even though these legal rights and barriers exist, platforms appear to be using technology primarily to 'wall off' their respective ecosystems. A major gateway to platforms is the application programming interface (API). Application programming interfaces are software solutions that allow a computer program to access and interact with another program, sharing data and functionality. Application programming interfaces provide a standardized method for integrating different businesses, thus optimizing interoperability and reducing barriers to enable more agile and interconnected ecosystems. Platforms use thousands of APIs to enable third-party developers and service providers to use and interact with the platforms. Application programming interfaces can be protected by copyright,[199] and platforms can technically use APIs to exclude third-party developers and third-party service providers or to deprecate third-party services provided on the platforms.[200] Indeed, APIs are the gateways, while platforms are the gatekeepers that control the APIs; inside is the 'walled garden'.[201]

198 Ibid, 77 et seq. See also Gal and Aviv (n 79). Also, to some extent, Michal Gal and Daniel L. Rubinfeld, 'Data Standardization' (2019) 94 NYU Law Review forthcoming; NYU Law and Economics Research Paper No 19-17 <https://ssrn.com/abstract=3326377> or <http://dx.doi.org/10.2139/ssrn.3326377>.

199 See *Google v Oracle*, currently being argued at the US Supreme Court. For an interesting paper discussing APIs, see Hoffmann and Otero (n 3).

200 According to Appendix J of the CMA Final Report, Facebook has used APIs on a number of occasions to exclude or deprecate third-party business users of the Facebook platform.

201 Facebook has been accused of using APIs to exclude competitors. According to the article Attorney General James Leads Multistate Lawsuit Seeking to End Facebook's Illegal Monopoly, Facebook's strategy is based partially on the claim that Facebook was imposing anticompetitive conditions on access to its APIs – or as the state lawsuit puts it, deploying an open-first, closed-later strategy. See also <https://theplatformlaw.blog/2020/12/14/ftc-us-states-file-antitrust-lawsuit-against-facebook-to-challenge-its-buy-or-bury-open-first-closed-later-strategies/>, explaining that Facebook launched Facebook Platform in 2007, encouraging third-party developers to write apps that interoperate with Facebook Blue. In 2010, Facebook provided third-party apps access to APIs such as the Find Friends APIs, which allowed users of third-party apps to invite their Facebook friends to use the app. In 2010, Facebook launched the Open Graph API, allowing third-party apps and websites to add social plug-ins to their

The breadth and depth of data collection, mainly by Google and Facebook but also by Amazon, and the possible amount of data being collected by system leaders such as John Deere in a more industrial internet setting (Internet of Things) indicate that in general, regulation of the digital economy cannot withstand these powerhouses. These major players are also de facto protected by the legal system as it is set up today.

On the different sides of the platforms, consumers, private users and business users, and suppliers are de facto forced to yield data to the hubs in these machines, which force all data generated by the ecosystems to the center of the hubs. Indeed, as discussed in Section 2.1, the consumers and suppliers cannot avoid being on the Internet; nor can they deny that data is collected by platforms – primarily Google, Amazon, and Facebook. It seems clear that the attitude of the public in reference to the monitoring, surveillance, and collection of data is one of resignation. The individual is compelled to accept these activities and the fact that the data collected in each individual action is of little or no value. A growing body of research has identified feelings of futility regarding companies' respect for consumer privacy by suggesting a link between these feelings and the activities of the companies they benefit.[202] The researchers conceptualize 'digital resignation' as a rational response to consumer surveillance. Draper and Turov argue that routine corporate practices encourage this sense of helplessness, thus illuminating the dynamics of this sociopolitical phenomenon that reflect and shape uneven power relationships between companies and society in the digital age.[203] However, as will be discussed throughout this book, the value of the collected data is enormous, and should individuals or business users be allowed to control, use, and benefit from their data, the individual as well as groups of individuals or business users

websites and apps (e.g., Like or Share button). This looked like a win-win for apps/websites and Facebook: Third-party developers had a new distribution channel, while Facebook expanded its data foothold by tracking the off-site activities of its users. The problem seems to be that for many apps, access to Facebook APIs became critically important for their growth; losing access to such APIs would place them to survival mode. Facebook used this power to adopt conditional dealing policies that limited how third-party apps could use Facebook Platform. Between 2011 and 2018, Facebook made access to its Platform available only on the condition that third-party apps neither competed with Facebook nor promoted competitors. Among others, developers were prohibited from exporting user data to competing social networks. Any apps found in breach of such policies were punished by losing access to such APIs. This is said to have altered the incentives of app developers, discouraging them from trying to compete against Facebook.

202 Joseph Turow, Michael Hennessy, and Nora Draper, 'The Trade-off Fallacy: How Marketers Are Misrepresenting American Consumers and Opening Them up to Exploitation' (2015) <https://papers.ssrn.com/sol3/papers.cfm?abstract_id=2820060> and Nora Draper, 'From Privacy Pragmatist to Privacy Resigned: Challenging Narratives of Rational Choice in Digital Privacy Debates' (2017) 9(2) Policy & Internet 232–251.

203 Nora Draper and Joseph Turow, 'The Corporate Cultivation of Digital Resignation' (2019) 21 (8) New Media & Society 1824–1839 <https://doi.org/10.1177/1461444819833331>.

would be empowered to demonstrate proper care and cultivate their data for new innovations and uses. In short, we lack incentives for individuals and users to develop their own data into wealth.

As they are set up today, legal systems offer the center of the systems the possibility to refuse to give any or all of its collaborating parties access to data. As will be developed below, the GDPR and the intellectual property legal systems enable platforms to refuse to give access to data. The TPMs stipulated in the InfoSoc Directive prevent reverse engineering,[204] trade secret, and database protection rules 'properties' data, and all make it possible for the platforms to preempt interoperability and access to data. Indeed, the ecosystems being set up on the Internet today transform data and information into de facto private goods. This most public of public domains – information and knowledge – is at risk of becoming private; platforms thus hold knowledge and information under technical barriers, which must be viewed as technical and semi-legal property rights. The collected data represents the fabric of innovation and progress. Indeed, it is input to R&D processes from which new products and services are developed. This, of course, is a source of power.

If power is being concentrated, either as a reflection of market power (as argued in cases currently being brought by competition authorities around the globe vis-à-vis Google, Facebook, and Amazon) or by the fact that these firms are holding data representing all or much of current information that is available, the issue is how to regulate this power. Power can be regulated through various means, by property regimes, liability rules, or something in between, such as public prohibitions.[205] Depending on the viewpoint, the issue is when to intervene in the market, and with what kind of regulation. What would be the relevant and effective regulation?

In Europe, the consensus in academia and among the public seems to be that platforms should be regulated because they are too powerful in too many areas of society. However, should regulation take place through a rights system, a property regime, liability rules – or through some other mechanism? This is the heart of the

[204] See, however, Article 5 of the Software Directive and the data-mining exception in the new Copyright Directive (Articles 3 and 4).

[205] There are several academic works discussing this based on different approaches, for example, law and economics, ordoliberal. See an example for the law and economics viewpoint in Calabresi and Melamed (n 75). The article begins by discussing the crucial concept of 'entitlements', which are defined as the rights established and protected by law, and whose absence would result in a 'might makes right' world, where either the strongest or shrewdest emerges victorious in any conflict. Thus, as the authors point out, the fundamental thing that law (the setting of entitlements) does is to decide which of the conflicting parties will be entitled to prevail based on justice considerations. See also Lemley and Weiser (n 75). See also Nadezhda Purtova, 'Do Property Rights in Personal Data Make Sense after the Big Data Turn? Individual Control and Transparency' (2017) 10 Journal of Law and Economic Regulation 2; Tilburg Law School Research Paper No 2017/21 <https://ssrn.com/abstract=3070228>.

controversy, and a matter that has given rise to research in several EU member states,[206] while also spurring the interest of European politicians.[207]

The first notion that springs to mind is that in liberal economies, power can be distributed through property regimes.[208] Indeed, the property legal system is an allocation of a regime that distributes and disseminates power. This allocation of power can be based on various factors: as a reward for labor or from an investment, as an expression of personality, as a basis for economic freedom, or in terms of economic utility (efficiency based).[209] In several aspects, there are several different sorts of justice considerations for altering the paradigm that in an unregulated scenario, the strong and the powerful will prevail over the weak.[210] From this viewpoint, the economic rights inherent in property are not an end in themselves but a means to protect something else – often the investment in capital or time required to create tangible goods or intangible information, which on a grander scale implies that property protects the distribution of opportunities and the function of the market economy as such.[211] In essence, property rights protect the liberal economy from degenerating into a heavily regulated, feudalistic society with a few strong players, yet without property rights for innovators and competitors.

Also, in microeconomics, private property has been seen as a main institutional precondition for a market economy, because property and contracts ensure the decentralized character of decision making by firms and individuals. The freedom of the economic actors to make economic decisions is key to a thriving and innovative economy.[212]

206 There is primarily a vibrant German discussion on this matter. Drexl (n 96) 12 et seq. See also Wiebe (n 96). See also Zech (n 132). Thomas Hoeren, 'Big Data and the Ownership in Data: Recent Developments in Europe' (2014) 7 European Intellectual Property Review 751–754; A. de Franceschi and M. Lehmann, 'Data as Tradable Commodity and New Measures for their Protection' (2015) 1 Italian Law Journal 51–72; Zech (n 130). See also Zeitschrift für geistiges Eigentum (ZGE) Jahrgang 9 (2017) / Heft 3 317–330 (14) with several contributions in English.

207 In March 2017, ahead of CeBIT, the world's biggest information technology trade fair, German Chancellor Angela Merkel used a podcast to call for rules for data ownership. See Jeffrey Ritter and Anna Mayer, 'Regulating Data as Property: A New Construct for Moving Forward' (2018)16 Duke Law & Technology Review 220–277, 228. For EU politicians stand in reference to data ownership cf Infra Chapter 5.

208 Rawls has the honor of having formulated the notion of property-based democracies. See Rawls (n 76).

209 For a similar list, see Heike Richter, 'The Power Paradigm in Private Law' in Mor Bakhoum, Beatriz Conde Gallego, Mark-Oliver Mackenrodt, and Gintare Surblytė-Namavičienė (eds), *Personal Data in Competition, Consumer Protection and Intellectual Property Law* (28 MPI Studies on Intellectual Property and Competition Law Springer 2018) 552 et seq.

210 Calabresi and Melamed (n 75) 1093.

211 Bernitz (n 72) 54 f.

212 Friedrich Hayek, 'The Use of Knowledge in Society' (1945) 35 American Economic Review 519.

The most important contribution of this microeconomics-based property rights theory is the methodological approach to analyze 'property' by deconstructing it into a 'bundle of rights' that the owner holds regarding a good or a resource.[213]

The question, then, is do we need a property right for data, and what rights should be bundled for such property in data? While regulation of power is the underlying issue in why property should be created, and distribution of power hinges on various justice issues, the main issue to address should be the identified market failure(s). Indeed, the data collected and controlled by platforms is not dispersed in a decentralized manner, causing the data not to be efficiently used.[214]

The important economic rights in the bundle of rights identified as property or ownership are the right to use a good (including transforming it), the right to earn income from the good (e.g., by renting or licensing it), and also the right to sell the good to others, that is, enabling the trading of resources (transferability of property rights).[215] An important consequence of the notion of bundle of rights is that different persons and firms can be the holders of different rights of the bundle, as well as also that several persons or firms can be the joint owners of a resource.[216] Given the special feature of data being nonrivalrous, it implies that all right holders to data can in theory actually use the property without excluding each other. Indeed, most important when discussing a property right to data, the microeconomics-based property rights theory about bundle of rights implies that rights to data do not need to be and should not be exclusive. This is indeed of major importance and essential for creating an access and transfer right system proposed in this book. An ATR would not be considered a property right under central European civil law doctrine because it is not an exclusive right, while still lending several attributes from the property or more specific intellectual property legal system. That is why it is interesting to discuss the function of property and intellectual property in the economy in general and in the data-driven economy especially.

The debate regarding whether we should have a data property right seems more confined to the principles for establishing rights under intellectual property law.[217] These three principles are explored below.

First, intellectual property rights can be necessary, working as an inventive force for producing or developing new knowledge. If new knowledge was instantly copied, leaving its creator no means to benefit from it, the creator would hardly want to

[213] See discussion in Kerber (n 63) making reference to inter alia Ronald Coase, 'The Problem of Social Costs' (1960) 3(1) Journal of Law and Economics; Eirik G. Furubotn and Svetozar Pejovich, 'Property Rights and Economic Theory: A Survey of Recent Literature' (1972) 10 Journal of Economic Literature 1137; Harold Demsetz, 'Property Rights' (2002) 3 *Palgrave Dictionary of Law and Economics* 144; Thrainn Eggertson, *Economic Behavior and Institutions* (Cambridge University Press 1989).

[214] Kerber (n 63).

[215] Ibid.

[216] Eggertson (n 213) 34.

[217] See, for example, Wiebe (n 96), Zech (n 130) 460, 468 and Drexl (n 128).

spend time and resources to come up with the new knowledge. However, competition also works as an incentive. From an economic welfare policy viewpoint, the collection of data, be it personal or nonpersonal, is a sign of developing, competing firms and the creation of more efficient markets, providing goods that consumers are willing to buy. As several commentators have acknowledged, competition works well as an incentive for firms to collect data. Incumbent internet service providers (ISPs), platforms, and brick-and-mortar firms collect data and will continue to do so under the IoT paradigm. A property right is not needed for firms to monitor and collect data. Both business with data-driven business strategies and regular brick-and-mortar firms collect data in the current setting.[218]

However, second, and as will be discussed further in Chapter 5, another reason for creating property regimes is that property may help to create markets (for goods and innovation).[219] The third principle is to make the protected information transparent, so that others (i.e., third parties and not the right-holder) may access the information and pursue further research or effort to collect and create more information. The property right creates transparency that leads to competition in innovation.

Unregulated competition as an incentive structure does not seem to work well in creating functioning data-driven markets. On the contrary, they seem to tip easily and become failing markets in the hands of strong monopolies. Competition does not seem to work well to boost creativity or benefit innovation in reference to the markets where the data is harvested (collected). Moreover, we are also lacking data markets here. The collected data does not seem to be traded or disseminated. Instead, generally, this information is used by platforms and system leaders to pursue more developed services. The knowledge contained in the data is thus not transferred to the undertakings that could use it to pursue R&D and innovation. Indeed, platforms that collect massive amounts of business-relevant data use that data to compete with connected brick-and-mortar firms.[220] The platforms' advantage in data disincentives brick-and-mortar firms to conduct R&D. The brick-and-mortar firms rather subdue and become subcontractors to system leaders controlling the relevant platforms.

The problem seems to be that competition creates incentives for large platform providers to make access to data difficult: to keep data confidential, within the limits of the law. When being obligated to give access, platforms tend to provide only information required by law, in a format that is difficult to process (cf. the information provided under the access rule in GDPR, discussed later in this book).

[218] See, for example, Wiebe (n 96). See also Drexl (n 128).

[219] Hanns Ullrich, 'Intellectual Property: Exclusive Rights for a Purpose' in *Problemy Polskiego e Europejskiego Prawa Prywatnego: Ksiega Pamiatkowa Profesora Mariana Kępińskiego* (LEX Warszawa 2012) 425–459.

[220] For the investigation of Amazon, see discussion in Section 2.1.

They provide services based on the collected data and are not the platforms that are necessary for creating markets for trading or competing with data. Data is concentrated on a few platforms or system leaders, turning these forms into bottlenecks for the data-driven economy. Indeed, the current system creates a few gatekeepers that hold market, industry, and public power. Property rights, given to entities other than the platforms, may create functioning markets.

Property creates markets where property is traded. For creating competition, markets are of vital importance; without property regimes, markets become dysfunctional. Intellectual property rights inherently create markets and transparency by transferring public goods (information or knowledge) and making these goods private and tradable. Then trade can be conducted, and markets can be formed – starting the cycle again. The most straightforward example is patents. Patents and competition are not inconsistent notions; instead, they are complementary. Patents are a foundation of competition.[221] Competition is based on the basic concept of a market where trade is taking place. Patents create markets by limiting information (knowledge) and by commercializing it, thus giving the inventor certain specific rights to this information.[222] This enables trade because it generates rivalry by limiting the free supply of that specific knowledge for the purpose of commercial use.[223] The intellectual property system, by defining what becomes a product, constitutes the framework for markets.[224]

Competition law should respect the creation of the intellectual property law system. Patents and other intellectual property – as property – must not be dealt with differently from any other property.[225] Hence, intellectual property rights create

[221] Hanns Ullrich, 'Legal Protection of Innovative Technologies: Property or Policy?" in O. Granstrand (ed), *Economics, Law and Intellectual Property* (Kluwer Academic Publishers 2003) 439, 447 et seq.

[222] According to some scholars, Kenneth Arrow was the first to conclude that patents and other intellectual property rights concern the markets for information. cf Kenneth Arrow, 'Economic Welfare and the Allocation of Resources for Invention' in H. Groves (ed), *The Rate and Direction of Inventive Activity: Economic and Social Factors* (Natl Bureau of Economic Research 1962) 609, 609 et seq. The rights included within a patent are, for example, a distribution right (including a rental right), a manufacturing right, and a user right.

[223] Ullrich (n 221) 448 et seq. Participants in the FTC hearing regarding the interaction between competition law and intellectual property law support the idea that granting a patent marks the beginning of commerce. When the US Supreme Court granted a patent in *Diamond v Chakrabarty* 447 U.S. 303 (1980) for a live, human-made microorganism, the fundamentals for the genetic engineering industry as such were created. See FTC, *To Promote Innovation: The Proper Balance of Competition and Patent Law and Policy* (FTC 2003) 21 with references.

[224] Ullrich (n 221) 450.

[225] See Ullrich (n 221) et seq.; see also the Department of Justice and the Federal Trade Commission, Antitrust Guidelines for the Licensing of Intellectual Property (1995), Appendix D, which regard IP as basically similar to other property. Nevertheless, in the United States there are still valid precedents stipulating that a patent confers a presumable monopoly position; see *United States v Lowe's Inc.* 371 U.S 38, 83 S. Ct. 97, 9 L. Ed.2d 11 (1962); *Jefferson Parish Hospital Dist. No. 2 v Hyde* 466 U.S. 2, 104 S. Ct. 1551, 80 L.Ed.2d 2 (1984). Nevertheless, these precedents seem to be challenged in *In dep. Ink. Inc. v Illinois* 396 3d 1342

a new layer or dimension to competition. Competition will take place on the level of intellectual property rights.[226] In fact, where there is no property regime, and no functional market, competition law works less well. The notion and failed example of innovation markets demonstrate the limits of competition law when there is no property. Nevertheless, this does not imply that it should be impossible to eliminate or limit invalid or overly broad patents within the context of competition law that is interpreted in the light of intellectual property law.[227]

Intangible objects are the domain of thoughts, where freedom reigns.[228] Under freedom of expression, there is a right to receive and impart information and ideas without interference, and such messages cannot and should not be controlled.[229] The question is whether the dichotomy between tangibles and intangibles is still fruitful. It depends on perception. In real life, data is intangible, while in the virtual world the smallest data point is tangible. Interestingly, under the new paradigm, information – even individual words or letters – is no longer intangible, at least not in the virtual world. Data is in one sense tangible due to new innovations in digitalization, data collection, and storage. However, were the data to contain an intellectual object, that intellectual object would still be intangible and should be recognized as *corpus mysticum*, even when it consists of tangible words and letters. While datasets or databases are also intangibles, from an IRL perspective, this is not the case in the virtual world. One could imagine that data and datasets do not need to be covered by a property regime because they can be traded without a property regime. However, as the discussion above shows, this is a misconception. On the contrary, under the new paradigm intangible information consists of entities that can be collected, stored, and controlled; to uphold general access to information and prevent monopolistic tendencies, a property regime needs to be implemented. Indeed, private ownership might be needed to create publicly available information, akin to a public good.

However, we are dealing with a new paradigm, and perhaps the property system as such is a function of the past; other forms of bundles of rights should be envisioned for data-driven industries.

Fed. Cir. 2005 *cert. granted*, 125 S Ct 2937 (2005), which has been granted certiorari to the Supreme Court.

226 Cf Hanns Ullrich, 'Intellectual Property, Access to Information, and Antitrust: Harmony, Disharmony, and International Harmonization' in Rochelle Dreyfuss et al. (eds), *Expanding Boundaries of Intellectual Property* (Oxford University Press 2001) 365, 368 et seq.

227 For a US case regarding the validity of patents and competition law, see *Schering-Plough Corp. v Federal Trade Commission* 402 F.3d 1056 (11th Cir. 2005), stating that it is impossible to measure a patent settlement's effect on competition without deciding on the issue of validity of the relevant patent.

228 Eric Tjong Tjin Tai, 'Data Ownership and Consumer Protection' (2018) 7(4) Journal of European Consumer and Market Law 136–140 <https://ssrn.com/abstract=3172725> or <http://dx.doi.org/10.2139/ssrn.3172725>.

229 Article 10 ECHR.

It seems clear that semi-property solutions to the new paradigm are currently being pursued in several European capitals (including Brussels). Liability rules or other forms of legal systems providing private-public prohibitions, obligations, and 'rights' are being created to address the problems of the data-driven economy that have been generally presented in this chapter. These solutions have several merits in terms of creating competition, yet they seem to be off target. Even the *ex ante* rules and legal systems now being developed by the EU Commission fail to address the intellectual property perspective and will not work to create healthy interoperability and transparency for data. The Digital Markets Act includes a right for business users vis-à-vis platforms to access the users' data, yet it seems that platforms can refuse access by claiming intellectual property law protection or GDPR's applicability. Indeed, in terms of creating, accessing, trading in, and porting data, the proposed solution could be a dead end.

Below, the EU's efforts in this area will be scrutinized. The liability route to regulating platforms and creating markets and innovation will be investigated first. Can gatekeepers be regulated by competition law or sector-specific regulations (unfair competition rules) with the purpose of establishing markets? After concluding that this is not possible and that sector-specific regulation for data access benefits the dominant platforms instead of diminishing their gatekeeping status, the 'property' route is investigated. In the end, a transformative concept is presented: An access and transfer rights regime based on available data-server interface technologies, such as blockchain.

3

Competition Law

3.1 GENERAL COMPETITION LAW

Generally, it might seem that the problem of a few system leaders hoarding data should be addressed by competition law. Market power and monopolizations generally trigger competition-law remedies. However, as will be discussed below, when it comes to accessing data, and especially when access to data should be granted as a continuing service, competition law is generally the wrong platform to use. Access or forced collaboration is difficult to establish under competition law. The case law of the Court of Justice of the European Union (CJEU) makes it difficult to succeed in arguing that a refusal to grant access to data is an abuse of market dominance under Article 102 TFEU. Proving market dominance in data-related markets is a challenging undertaking and is highly case specific. Similarly, the very stringent requirements defining abuse were developed for different situations and may need to be adapted to circumstances of the data-driven economy. More importantly, only undertakings would be able to rely on a right to access data under Article 102 TFEU, which would generally exclude access claims of consumers. Finally, the enforcement system of competition law does not seem to be sufficiently effective to guarantee competitive markets for the mass phenomenon of data lock-ins caused by connected devices.[1]

With the Internet of Things (IoT) and industrial internet, data will be collected and stored with the leading firm in the relevant ecosystem; the systems leader will have designed the data architecture, and de jure or de facto entered into vertical agreements with business users in their respective ecosystems. The ecosystems are thus made up of agreements that can be addressed under Article 101 TFEU. The aim of these vertical agreements may vary, but is generally benign, while an ancillary

[1] Josef Drexl, 'Data Access and Control in the Era of Connected Devices' Study on behalf of the European Consumer Association BEUC (2018) 34 et seq.

restraint may be out in place: The data and traffic produced by the business users (or their products or parts) in the system are shared or even exclusively belong to the system leader.[2] Moreover, it seems that the system leader often gives access to the data but only to a few firms in the ecosystem, thus granting user-data access arbitrarily to affiliated firms or third parties.[3] However, the Article 101 TFEU route is difficult. Few, if any, cases have or will be successfully argued in court, and it is very difficult to develop a coherent doctrine that could compel firms to conduct themselves accordingly.

Interestingly, in this scenario, the system leader then becomes the hub for data in its ecosystem – a very advantageous position in an IoT or Industrial internet setting.[4] The system leader will have instant access to the generated data and can control the flow of data. Indeed, as discussed above, 'nowcasted data',[5] a term which implies that data needs to be very fresh and crisp, is the privilege of the system leader; the system leader has the prerogative to decide how to get access. Therefore, multihoming (where the same data can be managed by various sources) generally will not preserve competition, because the time needed to access data from a second source may cause the data to become obsolete.

Being the hub implies market power inside the ecosystem because the platform has instant access to the data created in the ecosystem – data to which the business users of the platforms are generally denied access. The ability to collect and control vast amounts of data implies both private (market) and public (political) power. It also enables the dominant firm to conduct self-preferencing, that is, to allow only themselves the benefits of accessing the data.

[2] Bertin Martens and Frank Mueller-Langer, 'Access to Digital Car Data and Competition in Aftersales Services' EUR – Scientific and Technical Research Reports (September 2018) <https://ec.europa.eu/jrc/sites/jrcsh/files/jrc112634.pdf>.

[3] Björn Lundqvist, 'Cloud Service as the Ultimate Gate(keeper)' (2019) 7(2) Journal of Antitrust Enforcement 220.

[4] As discussed above, the EU Commission data strategy from February 2020 states '*Imbalances in market power*: Beside the high concentration in the provision of cloud services and data infrastructures, there are also market imbalances in relation to access to and use of data, for example when it comes to access to data by SMEs. A case in point comes from large online platforms, where a small number of players may accumulate large amounts of data, gathering important insights and competitive advantages from the richness and variety of the data they hold.... The high degree of market power resulting from the 'data advantage' can enable large players to set the rules on the platform and unilaterally impose conditions for access and use of data or, indeed, allow leveraging of such 'power advantage' when developing new services and expanding towards new markets. Imbalances may also arise in other situations, such as with regard to access to co-generated IoT data from industrial and consumer devices.' Commission, 'A European Strategy for Data' COM (2020) 66 final, 19 February 2020, 8.

[5] Nowcasting is the capacity of a company to use the velocity at which a dataset grows to discern trends before others do. Nowcasting enables a firm not only to track trends in users' conduct in real time but also to monitor trends in (potential) competitors' conduct, and to respond more quickly, which helps the company push or nudge the market. Daniel L. Rubinfeld and Michal Gal, 'Access Barriers to Big Data' (2017) 59(2) Arizona Law Review 339 <https://ssrn.com/abstract=2830586> or <http://dx.doi.org/10.2139/ssrn.2830586> accessed 12 December 2017.

Moreover, the conduct of platform providers regarding data should be analyzed. 'Tipping' platform markets into monopoly is not necessarily a 'natural' market outcome; instead, it can be actively promoted or induced by certain practices of relevant market actors. These practices include unilateral behavior, such as strategic obstruction of multihoming, access to data, or data porting, or preventing business users from switching ecosystems. Under existing competition law, such unilateral behavior can be addressed only if the respective undertaking possesses a degree of market power that is relevant under competition law (i.e., a dominant position under Article 102 TFEU). We are not yet sure what test to use for these forms of conduct. Moreover, it is uncertain that such conduct would fall outside the notion of competition on the merits as such or trigger the as efficient competitor test.[6]

Ecosystems of this kind may be more common in the IoT scenario, and we also can see the trend in reference to recognized tech giants. It is not unusual for Amazon, Google, and other gatekeepers to have access to all data in their respective ecosystems, even though business users in each ecosystem have – at best – access only to their own data.[7] Entertainment platforms such as Netflix and other platforms also appear to deny content providers (i.e., producers of films and series) access to user data and want to maintain this situation to develop their own content. Indeed,

[6] Heike Schweitzer, Justus Haucap, and Wolfgang Kerber, 'Modernizing the Law on Abuse of Market Power in the Digital Age: A Summary of the Report for the German Ministry for Economic Affairs and Energy' (18 December 2019) <www.competitionpolicyinternational.com/modernizing-the-law-on-abuse-of-market-power-in-the-digital-age-a-summary-of-the-report-for-the-german-ministry-for-economic-affairs-and-energy/>.

[7] See the EU Commission data strategy from February 2020, which states '[t]he high degree of market power resulting from the "data advantage" can enable large players to set the rules on the platform and unilaterally impose conditions for access and use of data or, indeed, allow leveraging of such 'power advantage' when developing new services and expanding towards new markets. Imbalances may also arise in other situations, such as with regard to access to co-generated IoT data from industrial and consumer devices.' See Commission (n 4). The EU Commission also found that Google required third-party publishers in *Google Adsense* to use Google exclusively and not transfer advertisements to other providers; this implies that these other providers would not get access to data generated by the publishers' ads. cf 'Antitrust: Commission Fines Google €1.49 Billion for Abusive Practices in Online Advertising' (Case AT.40411) 20 March 2019 <https://ec.europa.eu/competition/elojade/isef/case_details.cfm?proc_code=1_40411>.

The European Commission has begun investigations based on European competition law into Amazon's European marketplaces and, in particular, Amazon's collection and (exclusive) use of transaction data originating from business users. In addition, the German Competition Authority has initiated an investigation into Amazon's conduct. Bundeskartellamt, 'Bundeskartellamt Initiates Abuse Proceeding against Amazon' (29 November 2018) <www.bundeskartellamt.de/SharedDocs/Publikation/EN/Pressemitteilungen/2018/29_11_2018_Verfahrenseinleitung_Amazon.pdf?_blob=publicationFile&v=2 > accessed 4 December 2018. See also Adam Satariano, 'Amazon Faces E.U. Inquiry Over Data from Independent Sellers' *New York Times* (17 July 2019) <www.nytimes.com/2019/07/17/technology/amazon-eu.html>.

See also Nathan Newman, Search, 'Antitrust and the Economics of the Control of User Data' (2013) 30(3) Yale Journal on Regulation 2014 <https://ssrn.com/abstract=2309547> or <http://dx.doi.org/10.2139/ssrn.2309547>.

this seems to be a common problem.[8] Moreover, Uber and some other ecosystems have a business idea where the system leader exclusively collects the data generated by their users' business (the drivers), while the drivers, should they wish to leave the Uber system, do not have a right to port the data from their customers.[9]

Several expert reports were published in 2019, in which the anticompetitive effects of platforms and the digital economy were analyzed.[10] The boundaries for the prohibition on abuse of dominance were explored in detail. Interestingly, the reports seem to reach a consensus: Competition law, in general, and the prohibition on abuse of dominance, specifically, should be more readily available to the digital economy, especially in cases of leveraging or self-preferencing through data use. The reports, in varying scope, all propose sector-specific regulations in certain areas, with particular focus on the regulation of data.[11]

The EU has already recognized the problems of platforms in the platform to business regulation (P2B). This regulation stipulates that a platform provider must be transparent regarding the data it collects from its business users, and if the platform provider intends to limit access to business users and give access to that

8 See generally Commission (n 4) and Lina M. Khan, 'Amazon's Antitrust Paradox' (2016) 126 Yale Law Journal.

9 Commission (n 4).

10 ACCC, 'Digital Platforms Inquiry', Final Report (2019); BRICS Competition Law and Policy Centre, 'Digital Era Competition: A BRICS View' (2019); Committee for the Study of Digital Platforms, 'Final Report by the Market Structure and Antitrust Subcommittee', George J. Stigler Center for the Study of the Economy and the State (2019); Jacques Crémer, Yves-Alexandre de Montjoye and Heike Schweitzer, *Competition Policy for the Digital Era* (Publications Office of the European Union 2019); Federal Ministry for Economic Affairs and Energy, 'A New Competition Framework for the Digital Economy', Report by the Commission 'Competition Law 4.0' (2019); Furman Report: HM Treasury, 'Unlocking Digital Competition', Report of the Digital Competition Expert Panel (2019).

11 Examples of sector-specific rules suggested in expert reports as potential measures to open up the search market include access to click and query data and limiting Google's automatic selection as the default search engine on devices and browsers, requiring Facebook to connect more seamlessly with rival social networking sites, measures to address the conflicts of interest and lack of transparency in digital advertising, and requiring platforms to allow users to turn off personalized advertising.

The Stigler researchers believe the standard tools of competition policy – for evaluating whether mergers can proceed and whether antitrust action is warranted to remedy abuses by companies – could play a role in helping to promote competition and the associated improved outcomes for consumers and innovation. Accordingly, competition policy will need to be updated to address the novel challenges posed by the digital economy. Some of these updates could take place within current powers, but legal changes are important to ensure that this job can be done effectively. The biggest gains, however, will come from going beyond these tools to focus on policies that actively promote competition, foster entry of new competitors, and benefit consumers. This will entail a code of conduct for the most significant digital platforms, measures to promote data mobility, and systems with open standards, as well as expanding data openness. By working with businesses and other stakeholders to set up predictable rules in advance, a regime can be created that allows competition and innovation to thrive.

data to its business users in a discriminating fashion, it needs to inform its business users, and be transparent, about its business intentions.[12]

What the Commission seemed to allude to when proposing the P2B regulation was that through their positions as ecosystem hubs, system leaders may hold the knowledge of entire markets and industries, and with this advantage in data, these system leaders could eventually dominate their ecosystem or customers' markets, even by entering these markets and integrating downstream.[13] Indeed, we see platforms such as Google, Netflix, HBO, and Amazon that use their data advantage to leverage neighboring markets. However, the P2B regulation sets out rules regarding only transparency and does not assure rights for business users or prohibitions for platforms.

It was anticipated that the European Commission would soon thereafter propose a specific European (unfair) competition regulation for platforms that offer infrastructure-type services or that can be deemed as having 'strategic market status'[14] or 'undertakings with paramount significance for competition across markets'.[15] In December 2020, this platform regulation – the Digital Markets Act – was proposed under 114 TFEU, and does indeed address both classical antitrust harm situations and new forms of unfair conduct. In July 2022, it was finally enacted. Issues such as self-preferencing or leveraging, data interoperability, and porting data are addressed, ex ante. Under the Regulation, the EU Commission would also be allowed to decide whether certain platforms would benefit from undergoing heightened scrutiny.[16]

[12] Commission, 'Fairness in Platform-to-Business Relations' Ref. Ares (2017)5222469, 25 October 2017.

[13] Martens and Mueller-Langer (n 2).

[14] Furman Report: HM Treasury (n 10).

[15] The German Commission of Experts on Competition Law 4.0 presents final report to Minister Altmaier: A New Competition Framework for the Digital Economy seems to propose a European Platform Regulation; cf <www.bmwi.de/Redaktion/EN/Pressemitteilungen/2019/20190909-commission-of-experts-on-competition-law-40-presents-final-report-to-minister-altmaier.html>.

[16] The proposed new EU rules may have been drawn up based on some inspiration from a German bill for amending the unfair competition rules with rules regarding platforms; this bill is currently before the German Parliament. Once the *Bundeskartellamt* has identified a platform with 'paramount cross-market relevance', the authority can issue an order prohibiting this undertaking from any of the following (exhaustive) practices:

1. **Self-favouring**: treating the offers of competitors differently from its own offers when providing access to supply and sales markets;
2. **Impeding competitors by leveraging market power**: directly or indirectly impeding competitors on a market in which the respective undertaking can rapidly expand its position even without being dominant, provided that the impediment is likely to significantly obstruct the competitive process;
3. **Using third-party data to create barriers to entry**: creating or raising barriers to market entry, or impeding other undertakings in another way by using data relevant for competition that has been collected from the other side on a dominated market, also in combination

Given the above, the consensus seems to be that there is a need for sector-specific regulation or general legislation to address inter alia the issue of data and the collection and aggregation of data to specific hubs or platforms, so that the data exclusively reaches only the system leaders in ecosystems. Regular competition law is not sufficient for addressing these problems.

3.2 ABUSE OF DOMINANCE

The use of general competition-law doctrines, such as refusal to provide access to datasets, may be somewhat problematic.[17] Is the data holder dominant on a relevant market? How should the relevant market be identified? Are there double or multi-sided markets, and would such definitions of the relevant market facilitate the

with other data relevant for competition from sources beyond the dominated market, or demanding terms and conditions that permit such use;

4. **Hindering interoperability and data portability:** making the interoperability of products or services or data portability more difficult and thereby impeding competition; and
5. **Insufficient information about performance of customers:** informing other undertakings insufficiently of the scope, the quality or the success of the performance they provide or commission, or making it difficult in other ways for them to assess the value of such performance.

According to item 5 above, some data information could be made available up front for these firms. The German bill also includes a broadening of the possibility to access data under the rules addressing firms with relative market power vis-à-vis dependent companies. In addition, firms with little bargaining power may be exposed to unfair impediment if they have not been granted access to data. However, as with general competition law, it will be difficult to enforce these rules, and much litigation will be needed to ensure that firms are obligated to give access to data. Moreover, the firms should be remunerated for the data they transfer. See Thomas Höppner, 'Digital Upgrade of German Antitrust Law – Blueprint for Regulating Systemic Platforms in Europe and Beyond?' <www.hausfeld.com/news-press/digital-upgrade-of-german-antitrust-law-blueprint-for-regulating-systemic-platforms-in-europe-and-beyond>.

17 In reference to public sector bodies, the issue has been whether they can be regarded as undertakings. First, the data holder's activities with the data must be analyzed to establish whether the holder is an undertaking according to Article 102 TFEU. Is the activity under scrutiny an economic activity, that is, a commercial activity, conducted on a market? This may be established only if the end market, where the undertaking is facing its 'customers', is scrutinized. Of course, when dealing with private entities such as Google and Facebook, establishing whether they are undertakings may not cause concern. However, when dealing with public sector bodies, problems could arise. See the *Compass* case, where according to CJEU, an activity consisting of the maintenance of and furnishing of thus collected data to the public, whether through a simple search or hard-copy print-outs, in accordance with the applicable national legislation, does not constitute an economic activity, because the maintenance of a database containing data and making that data available to the public are activities that cannot be separated from the activity of collection of the data. *Compass-Datenbank* (Case C-138/11) ECLI:EU:C:2012:449, discussed in Björn Lundqvist, 'Turning Government Data into Gold: The Interface between EU Competition Law and the Public Sector Information Directive – With Some Comments on the *Compass* Case' (2013) 44(1) International Review of Intellectual Property and Competition Law 79–95.

competition-law analysis?[18] Moreover, in reference to the exceptional circumstance doctrine, is accessing data or the relevant gateway, for example, application programming interface (API) or data schema, an exception that requires the application of competition law? If so, is there a second (downstream) market that the undertaking is reserving for itself? Is there an elimination of competition and prevention of the appearance of a new product according to the case law of *Magill*, *IMS Health*, and *Microsoft*? Finally, is the data or API an indispensable input or even an essential facility under the same and similar line of case law? In a scenario where a competitor wants access to specific, unique datasets, which are indispensable for conducting business, competition law has an applicability; however, perhaps that scenario is not very common. Indeed, the essential facility or exceptional circumstance doctrine is difficult to apply and is very case specific, making it difficult to develop a general doctrine for the data-driven economy.

Notwithstanding the above, the *Magill*[19] 'logic' – at first glance – works well in a data scenario: Entities (in the *Magill* case, the publicly owned BBC and RTE et al.), engaging in their primary market or (public) task (producing and distributing TV programs), create information (in the form of TV listings) that might be copyright protected. Under the rules of abuse of dominance, and due to the information's indispensability and the fact that a refusal would be unjust, these entities are required to give access to this information (the TV listings) to an undertaking that will create a new product (TV guides). Thus, in the *Magill* case, the appellants were not allowed to reserve a secondary market for themselves. However, this is a very special case, because it is not generally applicable to creation of general doctrine.[20] The *Magill* case dealt with unique data, in the sense that TV listings could not be obtained from any other sources. *Magill* may be used to argue for access to certain, specific kinds of datasets under the exceptional circumstance doctrine; however, perhaps – and especially after the introduction of IoT – general data that users generate and voluntarily provide will not be indispensable. This will trigger application of the doctrine. Indeed, in the future, certain devices (e.g., cars, refrigerators, mobile phones) may be able to collect the same or similar personal data from us.[21]

18 For an interesting analysis of how e-platforms are not multisided markets, see Nathan Newman, 'Search, Antitrust and the Economics of the Control of User Data' (2014) 30 Yale Journal on Regulation 3 <http://ssrn.com/abstract=2309547> or <http://dx.doi.org/10.2139/ssrn.2309547>.

19 *RTE, ITP & BBC v Commission* (Joined Cases C-241/91 and C-242/91)1995 ECR. II-485.

20 Moreover, as Drexl points out, the *Magill* case can no longer arise as a matter of harmonized copyright law. According to the case law of the CJEU on the concept of a copyrightable work, the mere listings of TV programs, which are defined by the programming schedule, can no longer be considered as protected by copyright. See Drexl (n 1) 32 referring to inter alia *Football Association Premier League* and *Murphy* (Joined Cases C-403/08 and C-428/08) ECLI:EU:C:2011:631 paras 96–98 (holding that football matches are not protected by copyright).

21 An issue discussed in this book is whether general competition law (and more specifically, the exceptional circumstance doctrine) will be applicable to access of general personal data, that is, the personal information that people generate when using the Internet; this matter has not yet been conclusively scrutinized by any competition law court. Nonetheless, one can question

In reference to the EU doctrine, the European Court found in *Télémarketing* that the dominant firm's practices on neighboring markets may constitute a stand-alone abuse of competition law that could fall under Article 102 TFEU.[22] The CJEU concluded that, notwithstanding the presence of a refusal to deal, an abuse of a dominant position was committed, where[23]

> without any objective necessity an undertaking holding a dominant position on a particular market reserves to itself or to an undertaking belonging to the same group an ancillary activity which might be carried out by another undertaking as part of its activities on a neighboring but separate market, with the possibility of eliminating all competition from such undertaking.[24]

The broad approach of the CJEU may be explained by the specificities of the case. The dominant position of the undertaking in question, RTL, was not due to the activities of the undertaking itself, but because provisions laid down by law stipulate that no competition or only very limited competition can be present on the market.[25]

The European Commission's Expert Panel on Competition Policy for the Digital Era opined that the competition-law approach, seemingly focused on the refusal to supply or exception circumstance doctrine, should be reserved for situations in which data transfer arrangements or APIs can be standardized, according to stable conditions.[26] When this is not the case, the report suggests that a regulatory approach be taken. However, competition-law enforcement remedies may also have the advantage of flexibility, in particular through measures that are time-limited and subject to reassessment as the market evolves.[27]

In relation to access to the API, for example, the *Microsoft* case,[28] where Microsoft was considered (super) dominant on the client PC operating systems market and the

whether a court would find the exceptional circumstance doctrine applicable in these circumstances. The doctrine may be applicable in a few cases, depending on the dataset that is collected. Applicability will also depend on the actual size and magnitude of the data collected. No one really knows the extent of the personal data that is collected by current e-platforms and e-ecosystems.

22 *Centre belge d'études de marché – Télémarketing (CBEM) v Compagnie luxembourgeoise de télédiffusion SA (CLT) & Information publicité Benelux SA* (Case C-311/84) [1985] ECR 3261.

23 Bjorn Lundqvist, Ioannis Lianos, Wang Xianlin, Matt Strader with Igor Nikolic and the BRICS teams, 'Exclusionary and Unfair Unilateral Practices in Reference to Platforms', Digital Era Competition' BRICS Report <http://bricscompetition.org/upload/iblock/6a1/brics%20book%20full.pdf>.

24 *Centre belge d'études de marché – Télémarketing (CBEM) v Compagnie luxembourgeoise de télédiffusion SA (CLT) & Information publicité Benelux SA* (Case C-311/84) [1985] ECR 3261 para 27.

25 Lundqvist et al. (n 23).

26 Crémer, de Montjoye and Schweitzer (n 10) 107.

27 OECD, 'Data Portability, Interoperability and Digital Platform Competition', OECD Competition Committee Discussion Paper (2021), 28 et seq.

28 Case T-201/04 *Microsoft v EU Commission* [2007] ECR II-3601.

workgroup server operating systems (WGOS) market, and used that dominant position to exclude competitors. Microsoft did not give access to the interface (API) to its PC client operating system, which, according to the Commission and EU Courts, excluded competition on the WGOS market. In the 2004 decision, the Commission found Microsoft had abused its dominant position by refusing to supply this technical information. The decision ordered Microsoft to provide complete and accurate specifications for the protocols used by Windows work group servers, and that this information be provided in a timely manner subject to reasonable and nondiscriminatory terms. The decision specifies that any remuneration charged for access to this information should not reflect 'strategic value' stemming from Microsoft's market power, should not restrain innovation or create disincentives to compete with Microsoft, and should be sufficiently predictable to enable investments. The arrangements brought forward by Microsoft to comply with this order were market tested, and their implementation was overseen by a monitoring trustee selected by the Commission.[29]

However, more recently, the leverage theory has also inspired the recent *Google Search* (Shopping) case regarding practices of self-referencing.[30] A system leader may not generally give better access to its own service, while leveraging the power of the platform downstream onto the market for the service provided in competition with other service providers. The EU *Google Shopping* case presents an example of this conduct. Discrimination on behalf of the system leaders, in relation to the

[29] OECD (n 27); European Commission, Case COMP/C-3/37.792 Microsoft, Commission Decision, 24 March 2004 <https://ec.europa.eu/competition/antitrust/cases/dec_docs/37792/37792_4177_3.pdf>; European Commission, Press Release: Competition: Commission to market test new proposals from Microsoft on interoperability, 6 June 2006 <https://ec.europa.eu/commission/presscorner/detail/en/IP_05_673>; European Commission, Press Release: Commission appoints Trustee. In the US *Microsoft* case, the US District Court also noted that Microsoft delayed providing a crucial API to Netscape, although interoperability limitations were not a major theme of the Department of Justice complaint. In a settlement approved by the Court in a final judgment in 2002 (and later renewed with modifications), Microsoft agreed to a range of conditions regarding business practices and technical arrangements. With respect to interoperability, Microsoft agreed to disclose to manufacturers, software, and hardware vendors as well as internet service providers, the APIs and related documentation needed to interoperate with Windows. Sources: US V. Microsoft Corp., Civil Action No 98-1232 (Antitrust), Complaint, 18 May 1998 <www.justice.gov/atr/complaint-us-v-microsoft-corp>; US V. Microsoft Corp., Civil Action No 98-1232, United States District Court for the District of Columbia, Findings of Fact, 5 November 1999, www.justice.gov/atr/us-v-microsoft-courts-findings-fact#vb/. US V. Microsoft Corp., Civil Action No 98-1232, United States District Court for the District of Columbia, Final Judgment, 12 November 2002 <www.justice.gov/atr/case-document/final-judgment-133>.

[30] *Google Search (Shopping)* (Case AT.39740) Commission Decision, C(2017) 4444 final (27 June 2017) para 339.

platform or the data collected, enables a system leader to leverage onto the market of a business user.[31]

The dual role of Google, as a digital platform but also a competitor of vertical websites, may also be addressed by applying principles deriving out of network neutrality regulation. Network neutrality is an important principle of internet technology operation, that is, the network provider does not treat the content it transmits differently, and its application in the big data environment is reflected collectively as 'search neutrality' and 'algorithmic neutrality'.[32]

It is worth noting, notwithstanding the fact that the Commission relied on the argument that the loss of traffic from Google's general search results pages represents a large proportion of competing comparison shopping services' traffic that could not effectively be replaced, that the Commission framed this case under a leverage theory of harm in combination with discrimination, rather than the more challenging refusal to supply access to an essential facility. Indeed, the Commission relied on *TeliaSonera* to argue that it is sufficient to establish that Google's conduct could make it more difficult (i.e., just short of impossible) for competing comparison shopping services to access their separate but adjacent markets. This bar is clearly lower than a requirement to prove that access to Google's general search pages is indispensable; this would have been necessary, had Google's conduct qualified as a vertical foreclosure case akin to a refusal to supply (the *Oscar Bronner* conditions).[33]

In the appeal, the General Court agreed with the Commission that, by favoring its own comparison shopping service on its general results pages through more favorable display and positioning, while relegating the results from competing

[31] The platform provider would collect and give access to data or the result of predictive modelling to a specific firm, while refusing access to others, to enable that firm to leverage the data advantage against existing competitors, could be viewed as secondary line discrimination. There are some similar French cases: The French Competition Authority imposed an interim measure to GDF, ordering the gas supplier to grant its competitors an access to some of the consumer data, in particular consumption data, that it collected as a provider of regulated offers (on the gas market). The aim of this interim measure was to allow all suppliers to have the same level of relevant data to make competitive offers to consumers for gas and electricity (no public information or third-party private database existed for households subscribing to gas contracts). French Competition Authority, Decision 14-MC-02 of 9 September 2014. Due to privacy laws, the transmission of GDF data to competitors was conditioned on an approval by consumers. A significant share of the consumers did refuse to allow their data be transferred from GDF to competing operators. The case is discussed in The German and French Competition Authorities joint paper 'Competition Law and Data' (n 1) 20. French Competition Authority, Decision n°13-D-20 of 17 December 2013, confirmed on that point by the court of appeal on 21 May 2015; a similar reasoning has also been used in some merger cases, for instance, in the EDF-Dalkia merger decision. Commission, *EDF/Dalkia en France* (Case COMP/M.7137) 25 June 2014. 68 French Competition Authority, Decision n° 14-D-06 08 July 2014, relative à des pratiques mises en œuvre par la société Cegedim dans le secteur des bases de données d'informations médicales. This decision has been confirmed on appeal but is still pending before the Cour de Cassation (the French Supreme Court).

[32] Lundqvist et al. (n 23).

[33] Ibid.

comparison services in those pages by means of ranking algorithms, Google departed from competition on the merits. On account of three specific circumstances, namely (1) the importance of the traffic generated by Google's general search engine for comparison shopping services; (2) the behavior of users, who typically concentrate on the first few results; and (3) the large proportion of 'diverted' traffic in the traffic of comparison shopping services and the fact that it cannot be effectively replaced, the practice at issue was liable to lead to a weakening of competition on the market.[34]

The probe by the EU Commission of Amazon should also be mentioned as an example of the development of a new form of abuse in reference to self-preferencing utilizing data catering to the digital economy. DG Comp opened a probe in 2019 into Amazon's use of data generated by its third-party merchants. The idea was to assess the dual role of Amazon, given that it hosts but also competes against these other merchants. There are concerns that Amazon could be using data about its competitors' products to its own advantage.[35] It seems that Amazon uses data it collects from its competitors' business transactions on Amazon to set up or intensify its own service or product line, in competition with the business users of its marketplace.[36]

Moreover, business users seem to be at a disadvantage in the Amazon ecosystem. The Commission will look into issues regarding the use of marketplace data and Buy Box. The subject of examinations conducted by the European Commission will be the standard agreements between Amazon and marketplace sellers, which allow Amazon's retail business to analyze and use third-party seller data. In particular, the Commission will focus on whether and how the use of accumulated marketplace seller data by Amazon as a retailer affects competition. Moreover, the role of data in the selection of the winners of the Buy Box and the impact of Amazon's potential use of competitively sensitive marketplace seller information on that selection. The Buy Box is displayed prominently on Amazon and allows customers to add items from a specific retailer directly into their shopping carts. Winning the Buy Box seems key for marketplace sellers as a vast majority of transactions are done through it.[37]

On Amazon Marketplace customers can also find many reviews of sellers by other customers (so-called seller ratings) and of products (so-called product reviews or customer reviews). Business users (sellers) consider themselves at a disadvantage in

[34] *Google and Alphabet v Commission (Google Shopping)* (Case Case T 617/17) ECLI:EU:T:2021:763 paras 169–185.

[35] Ibid. See the German Competition Authorities press release: <www.bundeskartellamt.de/SharedDocs/Meldung/EN/Pressemitteilungen/2018/29_11_2018_Verfahrenseinleitung_Amazon.html?nn=3591568>.

[36] Lundqvist et al. (n 23).

[37] Commission, 'Antitrust: Commission Opens Investigation into Possible Anti-competitive Conduct of Amazon' (Press Release 17 July 2019) <https://ec.europa.eu/commission/presscorner/detail/en/ip_19_4291>.

respect of seller ratings because Amazon is not rated as a seller itself. They complain that they face disadvantageous consequences from negative seller ratings (in the presentation of their offers on the website and in the ranking list and the Buy Box), whereas no seller rating is requested after a purchase transaction from Amazon Retail. However, Amazon has asserted that it does not prioritize its own retail business over third-party sellers. The question as to whether reviews can influence the ranking of sellers, including the Buy Box, may possibly also be addressed by the EU Commission's current inquiry against Amazon.[38]

The requirements for finding abuse under the monopoly leveraging – self-preferencing – concept would then need a finding for two separate markets (the data market and device market). The dominant intermediate must adopt a business strategy outside the notion of competition on the merits, for example, lock-in, nonaccess to data, nonassert requirement, discrimination in access to data, or other

[38] Interestingly, to address the Commission's competition concerns in relation to the investigations, Amazon shortly after the final text of the Digital Markets Act was decided offered the following commitments:

- With respect to the marketplace seller data, Amazon commits to refrain from using non-public data relating to, or derived from, the activities of independent sellers on its marketplace, for its retail business that competes with those sellers. This would apply to both Amazon's automated tools and employees that could cross-use the data from Amazon Marketplace, for the purposes of retail decisions. The relevant data would cover both individual and aggregate data, such as sales terms, revenues, shipments, inventory related information, consumer visit data or seller performance on the platform. Amazon commits not to use such data for the purposes of selling branded goods as well as its private label products.
- In relation to the Buy Box Amazon commits: to apply equal treatment to all sellers when ranking their offers for the purposes of the selection of the winner of the Buy Box; and in addition, to display a second competing offer to the Buy Box winner if there is a second offer that is sufficiently differentiated from the first one on price and/or delivery. Both offers will display the same descriptive information and provide for the same purchasing experience. This will enhance consumer choice.
- Lastly, regarding Prime Amazon commits: to set non-discriminatory conditions and criteria for the qualification of marketplace sellers and offers to Prime; to allow Prime sellers to freely choose any carrier for their logistics and delivery services and negotiate terms directly with the carrier of their choice; not to use any information obtained through Prime about the terms and performance of third-party carriers, for its own logistics services. This is to ensure that carriers' data is not flowing directly to Amazon's competing logistics services.

The offered commitments cover all Amazon's current and future marketplaces in the European Economic Area. They exclude Italy for the commitments related to Buy Box and Prime in view of the decision of 30 November 2021 of the Italian competition authority which already imposed remedies on Amazon with regard to the Italian market.

The commitments would remain in force for five years. Their implementation would be monitored by a monitoring trustee who would report regularly to the Commission.

Ibid. German Competition Authority, 'Amazon Amends Its Terms of Business Worldwide for Sellers on Its Marketplaces – Bundeskartellamt Closes Abuse Proceedings' (Case Summary) Sector: Online sales Ref: B2 – 88/18 Date of Decision: 17 July 2019 <www.bundeskartellamt.de/SharedDocs/Entscheidung/EN/Fallberichte/Missbrauchsaufsicht/2019/B2-88-18.pdf?__blob=publicationFile&v=4>.

forms of self-favoring, on the primary data market. It must subsequently cause an exclusionary effect on the (competitive) secondary market. Lastly, the dominant intermediate must have no objective justification for not giving access to the data.[39]

Notwithstanding the above, some inspiration can also be found in the marginal squeeze doctrine, or even discrimination doctrine.[40] One potential approach could be to consider degradations in data portability to be a margin squeeze strategy when they affect downstream competition. For example, a digital platform may seek to make the continuous porting of data to downstream rivals, while giving full access to in-house downstream entities. This approach implies that the digital platform has market power or at least bargaining power over the supply of data used as an input on the downstream market. The doctrine could apply if alternative data sources are not available, or if the data is not an important input for the feasibility and attractiveness of the service.[41]

The *Google Android* case seems to have been somewhat different, with a rather more straightforward theory of tying as the antitrust harm compared to the *Google Shopping* case. The Commission states:

> When Google develops a new version of Android it publishes the source code online. This in principle allows third parties to download and modify this code to create Android forks. The openly accessible Android source code covers basic features of a smart mobile operating system but not Google's proprietary Android apps and services. Device manufacturers who wish to obtain Google's proprietary Android apps and services need to enter into contracts with Google, as part of which Google imposes a number of restrictions. Google also entered into contracts and applied some of these restrictions to certain large mobile network operators, who can also determine which apps and services are installed on devices sold to end users.[42]

The Commission Android decision concerned three specific types of contractual restrictions that Google has imposed on device manufacturers and mobile network operators, which seem to show a general exclusionary business strategy amounting to an exclusionary tying abuse. The restrictions have enabled, according to the Commission, Google to use Android as a vehicle to cement the dominance of its search engine. Thus, the Android operating system was provided with the requirement to install Google Search app (and Chrome browser app). In other words, the Commission decision does not question the open source model of the Android operating system as such, however, the contractual restrictions Google imposed. The Commission decision also addressed that Google made payments to certain large manufacturers and mobile network operators on condition that they exclusively preinstalled the Google Search app on their devices, and that Google has prevented manufacturers wishing to preinstall Google apps from selling even a single smart

[39] Ibid.

[40] See discussion above regarding the use of TeliaSonera in the *Google Shopping* case.

[41] OECD (n 27).

[42] Press release regarding the Commission decision of 18 July 2018 in Case AT.40099 – Google Android <http://europa.eu/rapid/press-release_IP-18-4581_en.htm>.

mobile device running on alternative versions of Android that were not approved by Google (so-called Android forks).[43] The EU *Google Android* case seems to resemble the classical tying and exclusionary covenants cases such as the *Microsoft* case.[44]

The EU Commission's *Google AdSense* case should also be mentioned here. According to the Commission, Google used exclusivity or relaxed exclusivity clauses to exclude competitors such as Microsoft or Yahoo from third-party platforms. Websites such as newspaper websites, blogs, or travel sites aggregators often have a search function embedded. When a user uses this search function, the website delivers both search results and search adverts, which appear alongside the search result. Through AdSense for Search, Google provides these search adverts to owners of 'publisher' websites. Google is thus an intermediary, like an advertising broker, between advertisers and website owners that want to profit from the space around their search results pages. Therefore, AdSense, which is by far the largest firm on the relevant market, works as an online search advertising intermediation platform.[45]

The German probe into Google shopping supplemented the EU Commission probe, and the German Competition Authority analyzed Amazon's terms of business and related practices. The Authority looked into several terms and covenants: liability provisions to the disadvantage of business users, the combination with choice of law and jurisdiction clauses that restricted business users to filing complaints against Amazon only in the court of law in Luxembourg, the rules on product reviews that discriminated against business users vis-à-vis Amazon retail business, the rule giving Amazon the right to withhold or delay making payment, etc.[46] Amazon seemed to have contractually limited its liability vis-à-vis business users in reference to intellectual property infringements, and the standard contract also stipulated a far-reaching right to terminate business users' accounts.[47] Moreover,

43 Commission decision of 18 July 2018 in *Google Android* (Case AT.40099).

44 The General Court largely confirmed the Commission's decision that Google imposed unlawful restrictions on manufacturers of Android mobile devices and mobile network operators in order to consolidate the dominant position of its search engine. In essence, it confirmed the Commission in reference to the tying allegation and the restrictions on Android forks, while the General Court did not agree that the evidence supported the finding of an abuse in reference to the revenue-sharing agreement under the as-efficient competitor test. Case T-604/18 Google and Alphabet v Commission ECLI:EU:T:2022:541 (Google Android).

45 Google was by far the strongest player in online search advertising intermediation in the European Economic Area (EEA), with a market share above 70 percent from 2006 to 2016. In 2016, Google also held market shares generally above 90 percent in the national markets for general search and above 75 percent in most of the national markets for online search advertising, where it is present with its flagship product, the Google search engine, which provides search results to consumers.

46 German Competition Authority, 'Bundeskartellamt Initiates Abuse Proceeding against Amazon' (29 November 2018) <www.bundeskartellamt.de/SharedDocs/Meldung/EN/Pressemitteilungen/2018/29_11_2018_Verfahrenseinleitung_Amazon.html?nn=3591568>.

47 In 2018, Amazon permanently blocked more than 250,000 seller accounts on its German Marketplace and temporarily blocked over 30,000 accounts. German Competition Authority, 'Amazon amends its terms of business worldwide for sellers on its marketplaces –

the standard contract included clauses assigning rights to use the information material, which a seller has to provide with regard to the products offered to an extent that business users may not provide a qualitatively better package of product information on their own websites, 'quality parity clause'. This will enable manufacturers and sellers to make their own websites more attractive in terms of quality (e.g., images, content) and prevent a potentially stronger pull effect to Amazon Marketplace due to a standardized product description across sales channels. In particular, possibilities are to be kept open to enter into effective competition with large internet platforms on price and quality. The German Competition Authority also referred to its 2013 proceedings to abolish price parity on Amazon Marketplace in and against the best-price clauses of hotel portals (see HRS and booking.com cases), which already served this purpose.[48]

Amazon agreed, however, to change the terms and conditions, and the German Competition Authority closed the investigation, referring to the upcoming platform to business regulation (cf. Chapter 4) and that the standard contract by Amazon must be amended due to the implementation of said regulation. Indeed, the decision by the German Competition Authority lies in the interface between competition rules and the regulation of unfair contract terms, in reference to business-to-platform relations, and the Authority seems to be using both interchangeably.[49]

App store contracts, platform agreements, in general, and cloud service agreements may contain potentially anticompetitive clauses. Moreover, several jurisdictions have legal systems that include rules addressing unfair competition. French, German, and Japanese competition law, and even the United States with Section 5 of the FTC Act, may be used to address unfair commercial terms. One advantage from the viewpoint of the enforcer is that often unfair competition-law stipulates less stringent rules regarding the need to establish dominance and also in reference to what clauses violate competition law.

In reference to app stores, there are court cases and investigations regarding Apple charging a 30 percent commission on app purchases, both in the United States and in the EU.[50] The cases in the United States currently deal mainly with the issue of standing for purchasers of apps, while the main focus in the cases is whether Apple can require all apps to be downloaded in the iTunes App Store, with an associated fee of 30 percent. App Store providers give priority treatment to their app stores vis-à-vis potential rivals by requiring phone manufacturers to exclusively use their app stores, or

Bundeskartellamt closes abuse proceedings' (Case summary) Sector: Online sales Ref: B2 – 88/18 Date of Decision: 17 July 2019 <www.bundeskartellamt.de/SharedDocs/Entscheidung/EN/Fallberichte/Missbrauchsaufsicht/2019/B2-88-18.pdf?__blob=publicationFile&v=4>.

48 Ibid., 4.

49 Lundqvist et al. (n 23).

50 The EU investigation concerning Spotify, whether Apple is not granting access to the Spotify app/service on certain platforms, and whether Apple charges exorbitant fees to gain access to the Apple Store. See 'Spotify Complaint to the European Commission regarding "the Apple tax"' <https://techcrunch.com/2019/03/13/spotify-files-a-complaint-against-apple-with-the-european-commission-over-apple-tax-and-restrictive-rules>.

by requiring the phone manufacturers to use a package of apps, which neither the manufacturer nor the purchaser of the phone can remove from the phone.[51] In the EU, Apple has been accused by Spotify and other app or content providers of discriminating against their apps vis-à-vis competing services or apps that Apple produces on its own. Moreover, the app store agreements may contain clauses that restrict the possibility of making apps dependent on other apps. It seems that Apple store does not want apps to be developed for platforms for other apps, because all apps (at least in theory) should be stand-alone. This prevents app producers from creating their own ecosystems of apps, connected to a platform app, which is the hub of the new ecosystem. Moreover, Spotify was not granted access to consumers on services such as Siri, Homepod, and Apple Watch. Several other companies claim to have been subjected to the same treatment by Apple, such as Epic Games, which produces the Fortnite game.

The German Facebook case deals with Facebook's use of personal data.[52] According to Facebook's terms of use, Facebook in Germany can also collect user data outside of Facebook's website. Facebook thus collects data from services owned by Facebook such as WhatsApp and Instagram, but also from other websites that use Facebook's technology or services, and this data can be combined and assigned to the Facebook user account. Third-party websites refer to websites that contain interfaces where the Facebook 'like' or 'share' buttons can be used. Where such visible interfaces are embedded in websites and applications, the data flow to Facebook will start when these pages are addressed or installed. For example, it is not necessary to scroll or click a like button for Facebook to receive data. If one opens a website with an embedded like button, the data flow starts immediately. Millions of such interfaces are available on German websites and apps, according to the German competition authority, which also claims that even if no Facebook symbol is visible to users of a website, user data will be transferred from those websites to Facebook. This happens, for example, if the website operator uses the Facebook Analytics service in the background to perform user analyses. According to the German competition authority, this constituted an abuse of a dominant position, as the collection constituted a breach of the Data Protection Regulation. Facebook's behavior represented so-called exploitative abuse. Dominant companies must not be allowed to use exploitative methods to the detriment of consumers.[53]

The decision has been appealed and Facebook won a partial victory when the German court inhibited the competition authority's decision until it took a final position in the case. The Court provisionally did not accept the Competition Authority's conclusion that collecting too much personal data in breach of the

51 Commission decision of 18 July 2018 in *Google Android* (Case AT.40099).

52 See German Competition Authority, 'Preliminary Assessment in Facebook Proceeding: Facebook's Collection and Use of Data from Third-Party Sources Is Abusive' (19 December 2017) <www.bundeskartellamt.de/SharedDocs/Meldung/EN/Pressemitteilungen/2017/19_12_2017_Facebook.html >.

53 Sten Nyberg, Richard Friberg, Björn Lundqvist, and Robin Teigland, *Konjunkturrådets rapport 2021: Digitalisering och konkurrens* (SNS Förlag 2021) 168.

Data Protection Regulation would automatically be to the detriment of competition. The competition authority appealed and won in the higher instance, the German Federal Court. The German Federal Court did take into consideration competition-law objects, such as protection of choice, implying that there were elements of exclusionary abuse, while the decisions from lower courts show that the competition authority's decision was controversial from both a practical perspective and a principled point of view. The case was thereafter remanded to the appeal court. The Higher Regional Court (the appeal court) has asked for a preliminary ruling from the ECJ.

According to Advocate General Rantos, in the Meta opinion, confirmed that a competition authority may, in exercising its powers, may take account of the compatibility of a commercial practice with the GDPR. However, the Advocate General points out that a competition authority can only assess compliance with the GDPR as an incidental question, without prejudice to the powers of the competent supervisory authority under that regulation. Therefore, the competition authority must take account of any decision or investigation by the competent supervisory authority, inform the latter of any relevant details and, where appropriate, consult it. The Advocate General was moreover of the opinion that the mere fact that the undertaking operating a social network enjoys a dominant position on the national market for online social networks for private users does not call into question the validity of the consent of the user of that network to the processing of his personal data. Such a circumstance does, however, play a role in the assessment of the freedom of consent, which it is up to the data controller to demonstrate.[54]

The discrimination or leveraging abuse following the steps above, cf. especially the *Google Shopping* case, implies that certain features need to be present or, for that matter, identified. The dominant service provided, for example, the cloud or platform service, does not need to be indispensable, and dominance on the secondary market or elimination of competition on that market does not need to be proven. Nevertheless, exclusionary effect must at least be likely to occur, while it is difficult to prove that innovation is an objective justification or shows a lack of anticompetitive effect.

An example of a more cautious approach vis-à-vis discrimination in access on equal terms is demonstrated in the Brazilian Google cases. The Brazilian authorities have looked into the conduct of Google. Regarding tying, CADE investigated whether Google would be unduly favoring its own specific services, such as *Google Shopping*, to the detriment of price comparison sites, such as Buscapé, positioning itself in a more privileged area of the webpage (among the sponsored links). The analysis did not lead to a finding of violation. Indeed, after an extensive analysis, CADE did not identify a causal relationship between Google's conduct and any harm to competition. CADE also identified that *Google Shopping*'s evolution throughout time showed some genuine features of innovation directed to fulfilling consumers' and retailers' needs. In this context, CADE's GS dismissed the case.[55]

[54] C-252/21 - Meta Platforms and Others ECLI:EU:C:2022:704

[55] Lundqvist et al. (n 23)

Indeed, despite having investigated Google and other tech firms, CADE in Brazil has adopted a cautious approach in digital markets. Practice and case law have shown that in very dynamic markets, CADE is more concerned about intervening in a market when it should not have intervened (false positive error – over enforcement) than about not intervening in a market when it should have done so (false negative error – under enforcement). Interestingly, the EU and the Brazilian Google shopping cases show many similarities, but the respective competition authorities reached different conclusions. The European Commission found that Google, when upgrading the algorithm, demoted rival comparison shopping services. According to the European Commission, Google upgraded an algorithm (known as *Panda*) to push its rival services to at least page four of the results, while Google's own comparison service was not subject to demoting and had a privileged position in the search result. Inter alia, the demotion of competing services, coupled with the promotion of Google Shopping, led to foreclosure of rivals, and the European Commission found evidence of traffic diversion and alleged causal nexus with Google's conduct.[56]

In comparison, CADE in Brazil was unable to prove that the decrease in traffic of competing service providers was caused by Google's conduct. There was a lack of causal nexus. Moreover, the use of algorithms to demote rivals was considered scarce in Brazil.[57]

However, on a deeper level, when creating a framework or methodology for the self-preferencing abuse, further questions may be approached. It seems that CADE and the European Commission applied different standards for an effects-based analysis. CADE required more evidence of (1) competitive harm and (2) causal relation with the conduct (closer to an actual effect standard), while the European Commission applied a standard of 'potential effects' (but still going through some important analysis of actual effects). Finally, more weight is given by CADE to (1) innovation and (2) potential efficiencies/justifications in the analysis. The European Commission seems more skeptical of these effects and tried to weigh them against potential anticompetitive effects.[58]

The above investigations show that even though it takes time, doctrines can be developed under competition law dealing with new forms of abuses and anticompetitive conducts. Given time, new legal equilibriums will be developed under competition law.[59] However, while obstruction of interoperability, data collection, and subsequent data use by gatekeepers to enter their customers' markets could be

[56] Ibid.

[57] Ibid.

[58] Ibid.

[59] Crémer, de Montjoye and Schweitzer (n 10); Federal Ministry for Economic Affairs and Energy (n 10); Furman Report: HM Treasury (n 10). Various authors, 'Digital Era Competition BRICS Report' <http://bricscompetition.org/upload/iblock/6a1/brics%20book%20full.pdf>; ACCC (n 10); BRICS Competition Law and Policy Centre (n 10); Committee for the Study of Digital Platforms (n 10).

addressed as leveraging, self-preferencing, or even obstruction under Article 102 TFEU, it should be stressed that access to data *erga omnes* is not the natural remedy in these cases. For access to data as a remedy, the exceptional circumstance doctrine is exclusively available (see Article 7 of Regulation 1/2003), and as discussed above, is not an effective path to creating markets for liberal economies. Indeed, for access to data, sector-specific rules need to be implemented.

However, could access be addressed under Article 101 TFEU? This matter has not been fully addressed in academia or elsewhere. The issue is how to view the platform provider and the ecosystems: What are these complex arrangements under competition law?

3.3 ANTICOMPETITIVE AGREEMENTS

Business users are clearly facing a looming paradigm shift, when data will be included in the value chain and the development of new products or services. The large amount of data collected by platforms – which function as the consumer interface – will affect how products, entertainment, and content are designed and developed. Easy access to data implies that 'things' can be designed to be adapted to the individual: personal products, personal medicines, and personal entertainment. The development of platforms and data-driven business models on the Internet has shown that data is fundamentally changing how websites, computer programs, search engines, products, and services are developed. Well-known industrial processes for developing new products and services will no longer work. Increasingly in data-driven industries, products are no longer being developed starting with Research and Development (R&D), and then moving to design, testing, and then marketing. Instead, gathering information to develop new products and services – normally part of R&D – takes place in normal sales processes, as each external and internal activity generates the necessary data. Companies with data-driven business models do conduct research and development in their daily business, for example, in their customer relationships; activities are carried out continuously as companies experiment to generate data. In other words, daily sales are an ongoing R&D project, including the possibilities to conduct real-life experiments. The data-driven company must continuously adapt the product and service to the relevant data, that is, to the individual buyer. However, the company must also adapt the buyer to the product through specific marketing and nudging.[60]

[60] See Iain M. Cockburn, Rebecca Henderson, and Scott Stern, 'The Impact of Artificial Intelligence on Innovation: An Exploratory Analysis' in Joshua Gans, Ajay Agrawal and Avi Goldfarb (eds), *The Economics of Artificial Intelligence: An Agenda* (University of Chicago Press 2019); but also generally Susan Athey, 'The Impact of Machine Learning on Economics' in A. Agrawal, J. Gans and A. Goldfarb (eds) *The Economics of Artificial Intelligence: An Agenda* (University of Chicago Press 2018); Susan Athey, 'Beyond Prediction: Using Big Data for Policy Problems. The Econometrics of Randomized Experiments' in S. Athey and G. W. Imbens (eds) 2017 *Handbook of Economic Field Experiments* (Elsevier 2017) 1, 73–140; S. Athey,

It seems that the larger existing platforms, such as Google, Facebook, and Amazon, carry out continuous research through experiments on their users. Users are categorized according to different parameters and are confronted with different commercial situations and choices within the framework established by the system leaders. Various products, content, and services are tested. In other words, a trial-and-error process takes place within platforms and ecosystems. This is a competitive process that the consumer does not control – where the consumer is instead the object of continuous commercial research. Avi Goldfarb states that Amazon, based on continuous research of the customer base on Amazon's platform, can determine to an accuracy of 1 in 20 as to which product a user will buy *before* the user has logged on to Amazon's website. This is an impressive figure in light of the company's astonishing product range. However, the goal is to be able to anticipate user desires and anticipate purchases so that users do not even need to go online (as early as 2014, Amazon applied for patent protection for an 'anticipatory shipping' solution).[61]

As hinted above, platforms – when focusing on the collection and use of data – can be viewed as in-depth and long-term collaborations to develop the platform and the products and services provided on the site. These are R&D collaborations that develop into joint production and marketing between the platform provider and business users. A big part of the collaboration is the collection of relevant data when selling the product or service on the platform. The collection of data – and this also holds true in an IoT setting – is mainly for the benefit of developing the product, service, or platform; personalizing the product or service line; or developing the business model. Therefore, it could be wise to seek some guidance regarding the antitrust regulation of data generated by collaborations between firms.

For long-term collaborations, and under EU competition law, the start of the collaboration determines the rules and guidelines for establishing whether there a breach has occurred.[62] This would imply that several of the ecosystems now being developed could be analyzed as R&D collaborations.[63] Interestingly, the R&D block

E. Calvano, and J. S. Gans, 'The Impact of Consumer Multi-homing on Advertising Markets and Media Competition' (2016) 64 Management Science, Science 1574–1590.

[61] See in general Ajay Agrawal, Joshua S. Gans, and Avi Goldfarb, 'Artificial Intelligence: The Ambiguous Labour Market Impact of Automating Prediction' (2019) 33(2) Journal of Economic Perspectives 31–50; A. Goldfarb and C. Tucker, 'Digital Economics' (2019) 57(1) Journal of Economic Literature 3–43; J. Shaw, F. Rudzicz, T. Jamieson, and A. Goldfarb, 'Artificial Intelligence and the Implementation Challenge' (2019) 21(7) Journal of Medical Internet Research; A. Goldfarb, J. Gans, and A. Agrawal, *The Economics of Artificial Intelligence: An Agenda* (University of Chicago Press 2019).

[62] Horizontal Guidelines, paras 13–14.

[63] The definition of R&D has been restricted in the latest R&D block exemption but remains broad: "research and development' means the acquisition of knowhow relating to products, technologies or processes and the carrying out of theoretical analysis, systematic study or experimentation, including experimental production, technical testing of products or processes, the establishment of the necessary facilities and the obtaining of intellectual property rights for the results'; cf. Commission regulation No 1217/2010 14 December 2010 on the

exemption in Article 3(2) stipulates that should one party to an R&D collaboration not be granted rights to the result of the R&D collaboration,[64] that is, the know-how (the data) for further exploitation, this provision would not apply. The created data must come to the benefit of all parties in the collaboration, because otherwise, the firms that do not receive access to the data may be excluded from relevant future markets. Indeed, such covenants could be regarded as hardcore, putting whole collaborations beyond the scope of the block exemption. However, it is not certain that Article 101(1) TFEU has been violated merely because the collaboration falls outside the block exemption. It is still necessary to present contra-factual evidence, for example, to show potential anticompetitive effects. Nonetheless, not granting data access to a collaborator in a joint R&D collaboration would presumably be considered outside 'competition on the merits' under Article 102 TFEU.

This begs the following questions: Are the principles envisioned in the R&D block exemption more generally applicable? Could data originating from ecosystem – data that is hoarded or collected by the system leaders – be considered accessible by all firms in the ecosystem, *erga omnes*? This issue caters more to Article 102 TFEU and whether the data collection in an ecosystem could be considered an indispensable standard for the firm addressed by the gatekeeper, and whether the dataset is essential for firms' activities in the markets connected to the ecosystem. Indeed, it is conceivable that only global platforms providing something akin to infrastructure for the digital society, and where the markets for these services have tipped in favor of one platform, could be required to share data *erga omnes* under competition law, but such a doctrine needs to be developed under a new EU platform regulation.[65]

Indeed, what seems to be on the table in Brussels with respect to the Digital Markets Act is a function where certain powerful platforms can be obligated, during a period of time, to provide information about performance of customers by informing other undertakings of the scope, quality, or success of the performance they provide or commission on the platform, or making it possible for the business users to assess the value of their performance. Perhaps more intervenient rules can be imagined in bilateral relationships. In cases of dependency on an intermediary to access customers, the new rules would establish a new type of 'relative market power' when undertakings are 'dependent on access to data controlled by another undertaking for its own activities'. 'Denying access to such data may constitute an unfair impediment even if no commerce has yet begun for such data'.

application of Art 101(3) of the Treaty on the Functioning of the European Union to certain categories of research and development agreements OJ L335, 18 December 2010, 36 et seq. (defined as the R&D block exemption or 2010 R&D block exemption).

[64] Commission regulation No 1217/2010 14 December 2010 on the application of Art 101(3) of the Treaty on the Functioning of the European Union to certain categories of research and development agreements OJ L335, 18 December 2010, 36 et seq. (defined as the R&D block exemption or 2010 R&D block exemption).

[65] For a general rule requiring access or licensing, see *Huawei Technologies v ZTE* (Case C-170/13) ECLI:EU:C:2015:477. For the EU Platform initiative, see Chapter 3.

It is difficult to see where the new rules are heading, but it seems clear that competition law uses prohibition and does not create positive rights – and it does not create rights to access and port data, that is, the right to data as a property *erga omnes*.

3.3.1 *Data Pools*

EU Commissioner Margrethe Vestager has addressed data pooling previously, stating that sometimes 'bigger is better' and combining companies' data into a single, large pool might provide insights that could not be obtained independently and in any other fashion. As an example, she mentioned businesses of connected cars and bookstores.[66] She seems, therefore, to consider data pooling as a pro-competitive behavior or, at least as not raising a presumption of antitrust harm. Indeed, it can alleviate the competitive problem with large platforms and even increase competition. The commissioner is promoting an all-industry sharing of data for the development of technology, innovation, or R&D. However, she also stresses the need to use the Horizontal Guidelines[67] for reference when pooling data, as sharing information may also be considered anticompetitive.[68] The issue for analysis is whether making the rules for data pools more lenient would also promote competition in reference to the concentrative effect of platforms.

According to Vestager, one way to circumvent Article 101 TFEU is by sharing information anonymously. Companies could send their data to a platform and receive aggregated data in return, with no indication of the source company. This would still provide companies with information to facilitate more efficient production, while 'it just would not undermine competition'.[69] The commissioner continues: '[o]r companies might limit the type of information they share. So, car companies might decide not to share information that would tell rivals too much about their technology. Online shops might share data without saying when products were bought, or for how much. And companies also need to be sure that pooling data doesn't become a way to shut rivals out of the market. It's one thing to decide who you want to cooperate with. But that decision shouldn't deny the others a chance to compete.'[70]

The Horizontal Guidelines explicitly recognize that cooperation between competitors can lead to substantial economic benefits, especially if competitors share risks, reduce costs, increase investments, *pool know-how* (author's emphasis), enhance product quality and variety, and launch innovation more rapidly. When using the Horizontal Guidelines generally, and looking specifically at technical information

66 Margrethe Vestager, 'Big Data and Competition' <https://ec.europa.eu/commission/commissioners/2014-2019/vestager/announcements/big-data-and-competition_en>.
67 Horizontal Guidelines 27.
68 Margrethe Vestager, 'Big Data and Competition' <https://ec.europa.eu/commission/commissioners/2014–2019/vestager/announcements/big-data-and-competition_en>.
69 Ibid.
70 Ibid.

exchange, R&D collaboration, and standard-setting, exchange of data may fall under several categories or chapters therein. The general rules regarding information sharing are only of interest when analyzing whether the collaboration is a disguised cartel or at least facilitates collusion or engages in other forms of pricing abuses such as price discrimination.[71]

If the data pool concerns only information for the incremental benefit of product development or innovation and is not a disguise for price-exchange mechanism, then making use of the principles and doctrines underlying the antitrust analysis for R&D collaboration and standard-setting could make sense. Indeed, these forms of collaboration might even be more similar to data pooling than pooling intellectual property rights. The infrastructure to set up a data pool is similar to a patent pool, and significant experience and knowledge can be derived from the soft law regulation in the Technology Transfer Guidelines (TT Guidelines).[72] Technology pools often include only patents and are devices to collect royalties, where the technology has already been defined in the standard-setting agreements.[73] Technical data pools, on the contrary, are instead information-gathering mechanisms for future benefits and could thus be filled with nonpersonal industrial data. Data is perceived here as nonexclusive and nonrivalrous.[74] Indeed, data pooling for the development of new services or to enhance products is more akin to agreements on information sharing regarding future use and development of the technology, aimed at creating new forms of products or services, without actually agreeing on the future technology as such.[75] In these cases, the doctrine for assessing R&D collaborations or standard-setting might be more appropriate and similar to the patent-pool rules.[76]

If the principles of R&D collaborations and standard-setting were to be used for data pools, these data pools would thus be treated leniently under EU competition law, under both Articles 101 and 102 TFEU; nevertheless, the risk of anticompetitive exclusionary effect could still materialize. It is thus important that large data pools for a given industry or market are open access, so they do not fall under Articles 101 and 102 TFEU. It is possible that such data pools could be connected to relevant technical standards, as is sometimes the case with patent pools. Data pools may very well be combined with a technical standard and a patent pool. Should the data pool

71 Horizontal Guidelines paras 65 et seq.

72 TT Guidelines paras 244 ff.

73 Even the Commission now recognizes this: '[t]here is no inherent link between technology pools and standards, but the technologies in the pool often support, in whole or in part, a de facto or de jure industry standard'. See TT Guidelines para 245.

74 See further on the concept of ownership of data Eric Tjong Tijn Tai, 'Data Ownership and Consumer Protection' (2018) 7(4) Journal of European Consumer and Market Law 136.

75 See generally regarding standard-setting and patent pools Björn Lundqvist, 'Standardization under EU Competition Rules & US Antitrust Laws: The Rise and Limits of Self-Regulation' (Edward Elgar monograph May 2014 496) 149 et seq.

76 Regarding R&D collaborations, see generally Björn Lundqvist, *Joint Research and Development under US Antitrust and EU Competition Law* (2015).

be closed for newcomers, then it should be scrutinized under Article 101(3) TFEU, if it has market power or industry presence.

Firms that agree to pool data need to define the market or industry to monitor and perhaps the technology to use for collecting and storing data, and, presumably, how they will not use the data in the future. Possibly, examples of unilateral conduct in violation of Article 102 TFEU should be listed in covenants of the pool agreement, providing pool members with a stipulation they can invoke as proof that they do not condone or have not agreed to such unilateral conduct of an individual pool member. At a minimum, the pool agreement should include a reminder that Articles 101 and 102 TFEU (or the equivalent) may be applicable.

The Horizontal Guidelines assume that standard-setting agreements or R&D collaborations are pro-competitive. Only in specific circumstances may these agreements give rise to restrictive effects on competition. This can occur through three main channels, namely: reduction in price competition, hindering of the emergence of innovative technologies, and exclusion of, or discrimination against, certain companies by preventing their effective access to the technology, which in this case would be data.[77] The R&D block exemption reflects this and expresses an R&D collaborators' risk that should any collaboration member be excluded from the R&D result, that is, the data created by the collaboration, the entire collaboration will not be subject to the exemption.[78]

Thereafter, the Horizontal Guidelines define safe harbors. When dealing with standards, where participation in standard-setting is unrestricted (i.e., open access is used) and the procedure for adopting the standard in question is transparent, standardization agreements, which contain no obligation to comply with the standard and provide access to the standard on fair, reasonable, and nondiscriminatory (FRAND) terms, will normally not restrict competition within the meaning of Article 101(1) TFEU.[79] Interestingly, this safe harbor is applicable regardless of the market share of the parties to the standard-setting agreement or the level of the standard's penetration. It is logical that it may also influence the application of Article 102 TFEU.

Data pooling may very well be assessed in a similar fashion, that is, according to a similar structure, but one must keep in mind the specificity of certain issues, for example, that firms should not agree on what to do with the data. The data from the pool must be free to use when competing downstream. Indeed, the pool agreement should not contain restrictions on how a party may use the data obtained through the pool, although an individual firm may still be restricted due to the application of Article 102 TFEU.

[77] Horizontal Guidelines paras 262 et seq.

[78] Regulation No 1217/2010 14 December 2010 on the application of Article 101(3) of the Treaty on the Functioning of the European Union to certain categories of research and development agreements (18 December 2010), OJ L335/36 Article 3(2) et seq. (defined as the R&D block exemption or 2010 R&D block exemption).

[79] Horizontal Guidelines para 280. See also the certification case *SCK and FNK v Commission* (Joined Cases T-213/95 and T-18/96) ECLI:EU:T:1997:157.

However, an important issue to discuss is whether the competition authorities should interfere with the issue of what market, technology, or industry to monitor. How far can the parties go in the effort to collect and share data? This is a difficult problem to solve. Commissioner Vestager seems to imply that a decision about what data is to be pooled could be subject to competition-law scrutiny. However, in standard-setting, competition authorities have refrained from examining exactly what technology is being standardized. Perhaps, by analogy, competition authorities should refrain from determining what technical data is being collected and shared, as long as it does not violate rules for basic antitrust harms.

Finally, it should be stressed that interoperability lies at the heart of the digital market and data pooling. In general, firms try to achieve interoperability or compatibility by increasingly connecting their products to IoT technology and data.[80] This inevitably puts limits on competition policy. To create a virtual infrastructure or interoperability, the pool procedure needs to be an open-access venture, where firms negotiate and collaborate on technology as they compete and conduct unilateral and sometimes collaborative R&D.[81]

In light of the above, by including multiple firms in data pooling, monopolies can perhaps be prevented on the data level and on the downstream product market, yet, to a high price. The risk of collusion is great. Data pools can also become the tool for platforms to start collaborating, thus making the platforms even stronger. Moreover, access to data under Article 101 TFEU does not seem even remotely possible.

3.4 PROCEDURAL CHALLENGES UNDER COMPETITION LAW

It seems clear that it is difficult to extract an access and porting right under substantive competition law, but major institutional or procedural difficulties exist with a competition-law solution to the problem of accessing and porting data. The tests, for example, the exceptional circumstance doctrine, are difficult to apply, and obtaining relevant judgments can take considerable time. *Microsoft*, *Google Shopping*, and even the *Apple* case now being investigated by the EU Commission are examples of where the business case for obtaining a judgment is lost long before the judgment is finally rendered.[82] When the judgment is finally received, the

[80] Claudia Tapia, 'Industrial Property Rights, Technical Standards and Licenssing Practices (FRAND) in the Telecommunications Industry' and references in 20 Geistiges Eigentum und Wettbewerb (C Heymanns 2010).

[81] Josef Drexl, 'Anti-competitive Stumbling Stones on the Way to a Cleaner World: Protecting Competition in Innovation without a Market' (2012) 8 Journal of Competition Law & Economics 534.

[82] It took the EU Commission seven years to render a decision in the *Google Shopping* case, and the case is still lingering in the courts. The *Microsoft* case saga was also long. Few, if any, believe that in the end, Google (or Microsoft, for that matter) will lose their market power as a result of the EU Commission's decision.

relevant market or industry has often fallen into the hands of the dominant firm that committed the abuse.

The established doctrines, such as the exceptional circumstances doctrine or the essential facility doctrine, took decades to develop, and de facto similar cases in the business community are few and far between – even after the implementation of these doctrines on an EU level. Dominant firms use litigation to slow and hamper access to facilities (or to intellectual property rights or technology, for that matter). To imagine that business users, under the doctrines mentioned here, would be able to get access and port data on a real-time basis could be naïve.

The fact that competition law cannot address the issue of data access and portability is not very surprising. Competition law in Europe (and in the United States), as it has developed during recent decades, is not capable of addressing paradigm shifts in society or the economy. It is a legal system that can be used to make a few adjustments to the competitive environment of highly efficient firms and economies. However, on its own, competition law cannot be the basis for an economic regulation of the data-driven economy as such. New systems must be developed to regulate a new economy and new legal systems, including property rights.

Nevertheless, competition law may have several benefits and uses in the data-driven economy. It is a flexible legal system that encompasses the demand and possibility to use both pro- and anticompetitive potential effects in consideration. Several cases are now being investigated and brought by the European Commission as well as national competition authorities. Indeed, the share magnitude will cause new guiding principles and doctrines. We see 'instant' EU Competition Law for the digital markets being created. The anticompetitive issues raised in reference to platforms should be judged under competition law, such as self-favoring – when platforms treat the offers of competitors differently from their own offers when providing access to supply and sales markets, leveraging market power – directly or indirectly impeding competitors on a market in which the respective undertaking can rapidly expand its position even without being dominant, provided that the impediment is likely to significantly obstruct the competitive process and hindering interoperability and data portability – making the interoperability of products or services, or data portability, more difficult and thereby impeding competition. When such breaches have been identified, data access and portability may be a suitable remedy on a case-by-case basis. However, competition law has its limitations, and cannot be used to create general rights schemes (*erga omnes*). Doing so requires the implementation of something akin to a property system.

3.5 NOT ADDRESSING THE ISSUE OF ACCESSING AND TRANSFERRING DATA?

The currently available competition-law test is not sufficient for addressing the fundamental issues troubling data-driven economies. These days, competition law is a sophisticated tool, designed to address certain inefficiencies in highly core service-driven, old-economy firms. It is not truly suited to addressing major changes in the economy; it involves too many steps to identify. Proving market dominance in data-related markets is a difficult undertaking and highly case specific. Similarly, the very stringent requirements for establishing abuse were developed for the old economy and may need to be adapted to those related to the data-driven economy. It is also very difficult to establish open data streams as a remedy under competition law. Finally, the enforcement system of competition law does not seem sufficiently effective to guarantee competitive markets for the mass phenomenon of data lock-ins caused by connected devices. Hence, a better approach could consist of sector-specific, competition-oriented property regulation.

Indeed, forcing collaboration based on competition law is difficult and rare. For such a remedy to work, an authority or independent entity needs to be put in charge, but mandating firms to collaborate is still difficult when they have no desire to collaborate. The only real case where firms were mandated to collaborate, apart from the EU and US *Microsoft* cases, is the US *Aspen Skiing* case, which required ski resorts to collaborate to provide joint ski passes. The EU *Microsoft* case did include a requirement for Microsoft to share source code, etc. but not to collaborate; at any rate, it was a very difficult remedy to uphold.[83] Even to go beyond that, legislation may also be needed to implement some measures that go beyond what a competition authority could order, for example, if there is a desire to assign ownership rights over a defined set of their data.[84]

All in all, while obstruction of interoperability, data collection, and the subsequent gatekeepers' use of data to enter their customers' markets could be addressed as leveraging, self-preferencing, or obstruction under Article 102 TFEU, access to data *erga omnes* is moreover a difficult and far-reaching remedy to create for a Competition Authority or Court in an abuse of dominance case.

[83] *Aspen Skiing Co. v Aspen Highlands Skiing Corp.* 472 U.S. 585 (1985) and *Microsoft Corp v Commission* (Case T-201/04) ECLI:EU:T:2007:289 (2007).

[84] See discussion infra. Moreover, L. Zingales and G. Rolnik. A Way to Own Your Social-Media Data (2017) <www.nytimes.com/2017/06/30/opinion/social-data-google-facebook-europe.html>.

4

General and Sector-Specific Regulations

4.1 NET NEUTRALITY

Sector-specific regulations apply in several network industries. The telecom sector and infrastructures such as utilities have been regulated based on the notion that they are natural monopolies and need to be regulated to prevent facilitation of monopolies. However, in the beginning of the internet era, large tech escaped regulation.[1]

According to Andrej Savin, the fact that the internet content layer was not subject to heavy regulation should invite curiosity.[2] Even though there is an emerging consensus today that big tech firms must be tamed, that has not always been the case. The policy choice in both the United States and the EU throughout the twentieth century was to treat the Internet not as a telecoms network or a regulatory service, subject to sector-specific regulation, but as an information society service.[3] As such, the Internet was subject to significantly less regulation than either telecommunications networks and services or broadcasting media with editorial control.[4] The enormity of this policy choice should not escape us because according to Savin, it created a curious pattern: While cables and radio waves used to convey the Internet were regulated, the content largely remained free.[5]

[1] Jonathan E. Nuechterlein and Philip J. Weiser, *Digital Crossroads*, MIT Press (2005) 1 et seq.; Brett Ryder, 'What If Large Tech Firms Were Regulated Like Swage Companies? – Being Treated as Utilities is Big Tech's Biggest Long-term Threat' *The Economist* (23 September 2017) 54.

[2] Andrej Savin, 'New Directions in EU Policymaking on the Content Layer: Disruption and Law' (29 April 2020) Copenhagen Business School CBS LAW Research Paper No 20-05 <https://ssrn.com/abstract=3588387>.

[3] Ibid.

[4] Nuechterlein and Weiser (n 1).

[5] According to Savin, in 1997, the then-US President Bill Clinton's senior policy advisor Ira Magaziner played a decisive role in outlining the scope of regulatory reach toward information society services, thus defining the shape of the modern Internet. His main contribution was a

The US noninterventistic approach was copied in Europe.[6] This hands-off attitude with the aim to promote a 'free', market-driven, and unregulated Internet at least partially mirrors the original internet dream for a borderless and radically democratic space. While some regulation was implemented – for example, the Internet was not lawless in terms of privacy, copyright, consumer protection, civil law, and jurisdiction – internet content in this early period escaped special (sector-specific) regulation requiring authorization or determining the conditions for providing the services, their extent, their content, or their reach. Moreover, the free internet implied that as a rule, intermediaries were not required to have editorial control; this implied that intermediaries were not generally liable for the illegality of the content they conveyed unless they produced that content themselves or did not take action when alerted to its illegality.[7] Generally, the EU's early internet policy was based on four principles:[8] (i) no regulation for regulation's sake, (ii) all regulation based on single market freedoms, (iii) all regulation to take account of business realities, and (iv) all interests to be reached effectively and objectively.[9]

The burning issue of net neutrality as a principle can be added to this sprawling, yet ideology-driven,[10] approach to the regulation of the digital economy. Net neutrality implies that content providers and applications should be granted access by internet service providers to broadband transmission platforms, generally, to the Internet in a nondiscriminatory and free fashion.[11] The EU net neutrality principle can be identified in the 2009 telecom package and the 2015 Open Internet

'hands-off' approach to regulating the content layer of the Internet. The policy principles that Magaziner introduced were deceptively simple. The Internet is a medium with enormous potential for 'promoting individual freedom and individual empowerment'. To preserve this, where possible, the rules that govern it 'should be set by private, non-profit, stakeholder-based groups'. Governments should refrain from intervening unless absolutely necessary. This approach resulted in a firm policy based on a simple idea: The private sector should lead and, where regulation is needed, it should be kept to a minimum and should foster a 'predictable, consistent, and simple legal environment'. This created a completely different regulatory pattern on the content layer compared to the one found in many other networked industries. cf Savin (n 2). See also Ira C. Magaziner, 'Creating a Framework for Global Electronic Commerce' Future Insight Release 6.1 n (July 1999) <www.pff.org/issues-pubs/futureinsights/fi6.1globaleconomiccommerce.html> and Nuechterlein and Weiser (n 1).

6 See John M. Broder, 'Ira Magaziner Argues for Minimal Internet Regulation' *The New York Times* (30 June 1997) <www.nytimes.com/1997/06/30/business/ira-magaziner-argues-for-minimal-internet-regulation.html>.

7 Savin (n 2).

8 Communication on a 'European Initiative on Electronic Commerce' COM (97) 157 final, 16 April 1997.

9 Savin (n 2).

10 It should be noted that the ideology was not laissez-faire economics, but was instead based on the notion of open-access, free end-to-end Internet, Open Internet Order. See Nuechterlein and Weiser (n 1) 196 et seq. See also in reference to net neutrality, Tim Wu, 'Network Neutrality, Broadband Discrimination,' 2 (2003) Journal on Telecommunications and High Technology Law 141, 149.

11 Nuechterlein and Weiser (n 1) 196 et seq. See also in reference to net neutrality, Wu (n 10).

Regulation. Article 22 of the Universal Service Directive allows Member States to introduce minimum quality-of-service requirements for undertakings that provide public communication networks. The Open Internet Regulation further grants end users the directly applicable right to access and distribute the lawful content and services of their choice via their internet access service. According to the Commission, the regulation enshrines the principle of net neutrality: Internet traffic shall be treated without discrimination, blocking, throttling, or prioritization.[12] The EU Net neutrality principle is a mild protection yet implies that in principle, internet service providers cannot discriminate regarding access to the Internet. They may not charge certain platforms higher fees by giving certain platforms higher quality service.

Interestingly, it is possible that the generally noninterventionist approach to information service providers, such as platform service providers like Google, compared to the regulatory approach vis-à-vis the providers of the underlying layers of technology and internet infrastructure services, benefited the internet service platforms and the providers of infrastructure hardware such as telecom technologies. The platforms provide their services on the basis of infrastructure and service, provided in turn by undertakings that are more or less prevented from charging market prices or discriminating in price for the content services provided. The platforms can compete, without regulatory 'strings', based on infrastructure that charges end users and not content providers. This can also be reflected in real numbers. The online services segment is considerably larger than the other segments in the value chain and is also growing more rapidly. In addition, firms active in the other telecom technology segments have a smaller EBIT margin.[13] Indeed, the value in the value chain(s) making up the Internet seems to flow to the platforms, while other layers of the value chain receive less supracompetitive profits.[14]

Interestingly, the EU Commission is hinting to a future fee or tax for online platforms' use of telecoms infrastructure. All market actors benefiting from the digital transformation should assume their social responsibilities and 'make a fair and proportionate contribution to the costs of public goods, services and infrastructures'.[15] Whether that implies that the system leaders should pay a market price for

[12] Commission, 'Commission Report on Open Internet' <https://ec.europa.eu/digital-single-market/en/news/commission-report-open-internet>.

[13] GSMA, 'The Internet Value Chain: A Study on the Economics of the Internet' (May 2016) <www.gsma.com/publicpolicy/wp-content/uploads/2016/05/GSMA_The-internet-Value-Chain_WEB.pdf>.

[14] In reference to the doctrine of one-monopoly profit, see Joseph Farrell and Phil Weiser, 'Modularity, Vertical Integration, and Open Access Policies: Towards a Convergence of Antitrust and Regulation in the Internet Age' (2003) 17 Harvard Journal of Law and Technology 1 <https://ssrn.com/abstract=452220> or <http://dx.doi.org/10.2139/ssrn.452220>.

[15] <www.politico.eu/article/eu-tech-firm-pay-telecom-infrastructure/>.

the technology provided or be taxed for the use of telecoms infrastructure is still uncertain.

The policy skew in the regulation of internet hardware technology and telecom providers and the stark contrast of nonregulated internet information services have decreased since 2015, and the goal of a level playing field now seems more of a priority for the legislator.[16] The EU Commission is working hard to provide policy recommendations and regulations for the data-driven economy. The ECJ has also struck down the very pro-internal market goal for e-commerce in *Coty*, implying that holder of well-known trademarks can now prevent their goods from being sold by distributors on third-party platforms, for example, Amazon.[17] The Commission's strategy here is rather coherent, yet the legislation that the EU has delivered is less so. Indeed, several of the sector-specific regulations seem to be at odds with each other. Primarily viewed as a bundle of regulations, they tend to fortify the dominance of certain platforms, rather than creating a level playing field. Indeed, they reflect a policy at war with itself.

4.2 REGULATING PLATFORMS AND DATA HOLDERS

To grant access to data, the EU Commission seems keen on using sector-specific regulations in reference to e-platforms[18] and the free flow of data.[19] Indeed, it seems that rules regarding certain conduct by platform providers concerning use and access of data (ex ante regulations) are currently seeping in as sector- or industry-specific regulations, implying an obligation to either share data or grant open and somewhat nondiscriminatory access to platforms and devices that collect the data.[20]

First, the EU Commission did introduce a platform-to-business (P2B) regulation in 2019, which targets the platform-business interface.[21]

[16] Savin (n 2).

[17] *Coty Germany* (Case C-230/16) ECLI:EU:C:2017:941.

[18] The proposed P2B regulation: COM (2018) 238 final 2018/0112 (COD), 26 April 2018 Proposal for a regulation on promoting fairness and transparency for business users of online intermediation services.

[19] There are French national initiatives to open e-platforms for third-party competitors. See e.g. French Senate Report (20 March 2013) <www.senat.fr/rap/r12-443/r12-443.html>.

[20] Alex Chisholm and Nelson Jung, 'Platform Regulation – Ex-Ante versus Ex-Post Intervention: Evolving Our Antitrust Tools and Practices to Meet the Challenges of a Digital Economy' (2015) 11(1) Competition Policy International 7–21.

[21] The Commission's roadmap for the P2B stated that the overall policy objective was to ensure a fair and innovation-friendly platform economy. More specifically, the aims for a P2B, according to the Commission, should be (a) to optimize the innovation and growth potential of online platform ecosystems, by securing a predictable business environment for firms depending on platforms and thus enhancing the general level of trust of all (potential) users; (b) to limit direct negative effects of problems arising in platform-to-business relationships; (c) to prevent, ex ante, abuse of dependencies in the platform economy; (d) to reduce burdensome compliance costs derived from legal fragmentation, which could jeopardize the functioning of the Digital Single Market; and (e) to facilitate the emergence of new online platform firms, including by

4.2.1 *Platform-to-Business and Data Free Flow*

The P2B regulation from 2019 focuses mostly on rules regarding transparency, and it seems clear that this regulation will not directly address access issues. The Commission was somewhat reluctant to regulate P2B activities in detail.[22]

The P2B regulation covers online platform intermediaries and general online search engines that provide their services to businesses established in the EU and that offer goods or services to consumers located in the EU. The definition of platforms covers app stores (e.g., Google Play, Apple App Store, Microsoft Store), as well as websites that locate a nearby restaurant or shop. Online platform intermediaries also include third-party e-commerce marketplaces (e.g., Amazon Marketplace), social media for business (e.g., Facebook pages, Instagram used by makers/artists, etc.), and price comparison tools (e.g., Skyscanner, Google Shopping).[23]

The regulation excludes online advertising, payment services, search engine optimization, services that connect hardware, and applications that do not mediate direct transactions between businesses and consumers; nor does it cover intermediaries that operate only between businesses (e.g., Google and Facebook online advertising exchanges as discussed above). It also excludes online retailers such as grocery stores (supermarkets) and retailers of brands (e.g., Nike.com), to the extent that such online retailers directly sell only their own products, without relying on third-party sellers or facilitating direct transactions between those third-party sellers and consumers.

reducing barriers to entry and by ensuring a level playing field. Commission, 'Fairness in Platform-to-Business Relations' Ref. Ares (2017) 5222469–25/10/2017 <https://ec.europa.eu/info/law/better-regulation/initiatives/ares-2017-5222469_en> accessed 28 May 2018.

22 The Commission begins its proposal in a rather bold manner, stating '[t]hese online intermediation activities usually benefit from important data-driven direct and indirect network effects which tend to result in only a limited number of successful platforms per intermediated segment of the economy. This growing intermediation of transactions through online platforms, combined with strong indirect network effects that can be fuelled by data-driven advantages by the online platforms, lead to an increased dependency of businesses on online platforms as quasi-'gatekeepers' to markets and consumers. The asymmetry between the relative market strength of a small number of leading online platforms – not necessarily dominant in the sense of competition law – is exacerbated by the inherently fragmented supply-side consisting of thousands of small merchants.' However, in the end the obligation to give business users access to term and conditions does not seem to be quite so intrusive. cf the proposed P2B regulation COM (2018) 238 final 2018/0112 (COD), 26 April 2018. Proposal for a regulation on promoting fairness and transparency for business users of online intermediation services.

23 Regulation (EU) 2019/1150 of the European Parliament and of the Council of 20 June 2019 on promoting fairness and transparency for business users of online intermediation services (Text with EEA relevance). PE/56/2019/REV/1 OJ L186, 11 July 2019, 57–79.

The regulation's definition of platforms is wide; however, as discussed below, the definition of platforms in the Digital Markets Act is even broader, including operating systems, cloud services, and advertising exchanges.

The EU has taken a coregulatory approach, requiring online platform intermediaries and online search engines to comply with legal obligations and encouraging them to take voluntary complementary steps. The p2B regulation stipulates the possibility of creating guidelines that further specify and clarify the rules. Guidelines have been provided for rankings.[24] Accordingly, platforms and search engines will have to inform businesses about how they treat and rank goods or services offered by the platforms and search engines or by businesses that they control, compared to their treatment and ranking of goods and services from third-party businesses. Businesses must also be informed about how online platforms can influence their ranking position, for example, through the payment of additional commissions. Online search engines will also need to inform consumers if the ranking result has been influenced by agreements with the website user.

Generally, the regulation shall ensure that businesses using online intermediation services, for example, marketplaces and general online search engines, will have greater legal certainty and clarity regarding the rules governing their relationships with these platforms and how to resolve potential disputes. Platforms should not prevent the business user from making its identity visible, and a platform intermediary that restricts, suspends, or terminates a firm's account (including the delisting of individual goods or services or effectively removing them from search results) is required to give the company in question a statement of reasons for the action. The P2B regulation also provides hard rules regarding access to court and stipulates that business users of platforms shall have easy access to resolve disputes with online platform intermediaries.

Moreover, the standard terms and conditions must be presented in a transparent manner and be readily available, and platforms must announce changes in the standard terms and conditions well in advance. The terms and conditions must state the reasons for suspending or terminating a firm's account and include a description of:

- the supplementary goods and services that online platform intermediaries propose to consumers alongside a business user's offer and the supplementary goods and services that a business user can offer,
- additional distribution channels through which an online platform intermediary will offer a business user's goods or services, and

[24] Commission Notice Guidelines on ranking transparency pursuant to Regulation (EU) 2019/1150 of the European Parliament and of the Council 2020/C 424/01 C/2020/8579 OJ C424, 8 December 2020, 1–26.

- reasons why the online intermediation platform may restrict business users from offering goods and services under different conditions through other intermediation platforms (so-called most-favored-nation clauses).

In the P2B Regulation, the Commission did grasp to some degree the problem with internet intermediates having access to more data than their customers. The regulation obligates providers of online intermediation services to furnish business users with a clear description of the scope, nature, and conditions of business users' access to and use of certain categories of data.

According to the regulation, the description should be proportionate and can refer to general access conditions, rather than supplying an exhaustive list of actual data, or categories of data, so that business users can determine whether or not they are allowed to use the data they have created with the provider of the online intermediation service. Indeed, the online intermediation service provider is not obligated to give the customer (the business user) access to the data that users create through their activities on the platform. The data belongs to the internet intermediate. Moreover, according to the draft P2B regulation and as derived from the General Data Protection Regulation (GDPR), business users must also be informed as to whether they have access to personal data, other data, or both, including in aggregated form, provided by or generated through the provision of the online intermediation services from all of the business users and consumers thereof, and if so, the data categories and conditions for this access.

Moreover, the P2B regulation states that providers need to be transparent if they intend to discriminate by giving better access to affiliated firms than to business users. Online search engines and platforms must be transparent about any preferential treatment they give to their own products and services offered through their sites. The P2B regulation thus addresses the issue of data and who has access, while only providing rules regarding transparency.

Second, in the Data Free Flow Regulation, the European Commission has specifically addressed the issue that firms should be given the right to port non-personal data – especially vis-à-vis cloud providers. The regulation states that, through self-regulation, the industry should develop a procedure and standard technology so that data can be ported. The regulation contains a call for self-regulation of the right to port data.[25] It should be acknowledged that a standards organization has now produced a code of conduct for porting data from cloud to cloud. The code is very detailed and applicable for members of the organization; it

[25] Commission, 'Commission Staff Working Document Impact Assessment Accompanying the Document Proposal for a Regulation of the European Parliament and of the Council on a Framework for the Free Flow of Non-personal Data in the European Union' SWD/2017/0304 final – 2017/0228 (COD) 13 September 2017 (Impact Assessment); Commission, 'Staff Working Document on the Free Flow of Data and Emerging Issues of the European Data Economy' COM (2017) 9 final, 10 January 2017.

can be difficult for firms to penetrate.[26] Whether the code will actually create a right (*erga omnes*) to port data between clouds seems unclear, to say the least.

The result of the Data Free Flow initiative is somewhat surprising, given the enthusiasm the Commission showed in early policy papers toward implementing a mandatory right to port data for business users vis-à-vis cloud providers,[27] and begs the question of whether the right to port should be included in some other legislative effort by the Commission, such as the modernization of the database directive.[28]

However, these regulations do not stipulate any hard rules that would enable a more equal playing field. Access and portability are not rights, but rather topics for discussion. Indeed, the transaction and contracts will presumably still be skewed to the benefit of platform providers.

4.2.2 *The Data Act*

The Commission published a proposal for a substantial and general, that is, non-sector specific, Data Act in February 2022. It applies to all sectors and works as lex generalis, leaving room for sector-specific solutions for separate markets and industries. Such *lex specialis* may thus go beyond the Data Act and implement a different equilibrium between the power of the platforms, or as they are called in the Data Act data holders, and the users. The main objective in reference to data and Internet of Things (IoT) of the proposal is to generally 'facilitate access to and the use of data by

26 See the SWIPO Code of Conduct <https://valtioneuvosto.fi/en/project?tunnus=LVM019:00/2019>. As stated on the EU Commission website, apart from two dedicated Codes of Conduct, addressing Infrastructure-as-a-Service (IaaS) cloud services and on Software-as-a-Service (SaaS) cloud services, respectively, the SWIPO working group also delivered an extensive proposal for a governance structure. This governance structure should make the Codes of Conduct enforceable in practice, for example, through a complaint mechanism for users. The deadline for the implementation of the Codes of Conduct was May 2020, as foreseen by the Regulation on the free flow of nonpersonal data (FFD). As determined in the FFD Regulation, the European Commission will evaluate the impact of those Codes of Conduct before November 2022. This evaluation will notably focus on the effects that the SWIPO Codes of Conduct will have on the fluidity and competitiveness of the cloud market <https://ec.europa.eu/digital-single-market/en/news/presentation-codes-conduct-cloud-switching-and-data-portability>.

27 Commission, 'Communication from the Commission to the European Parliament, the Council, the European Economic and Social Committee and the Committee of the Regions' SWD (2017) 2 final, COM (2017) 9 final, 13; Commission (n 25) 33, making reference to the works of Zech, who claimed that the right way forward is the creation of a property right to nonpersonal goods. Cf Herbert Zech, 'Information as a Tradable Commodity' in Alberto de Franceschi Ferrara (ed), *European Contract Law and the Digital Single Market* (Intersentia 2016) 51–79.

28 It should be mentioned that there is a right for persons to port data, under certain circumstances, according to Article 20 GDPR. cf Björn Lundqvist, 'Regulating Competition and Property in the Digital Economy – The Interface Between Data, Privacy, Intellectual Property, Fairness and Competition Law' (17 January 2018) Faculty of Law, Stockholm University Research Paper No 55.

consumers and businesses, while preserving incentives to invest in ways of generating value through data'.[29]

That objective can be divided into four subsidiary objectives:[30]

> (i) empowerment of consumers and businesses to have more control over the use of their IoT data, and to benefit from more, better, and cheaper products and services on secondary markets. The benefit will, in the proposal, be derived from more intense competition. According to the Explanatory memorandum, a high level of consumer protection is reinforced with the new right to access user-generated data in IoT situations. Ownership, or as the Commission puts it, the 'right to use and dispose of lawfully acquired possessions' is reinforced with a right to access data generated from the use of an Internet of Things object. 'This way, the owner may benefit from a better user experience and a wider range of, for example, repair and maintenance services.' A second (ii) subobjective, dissemination of data: More data shall be available to businesses, especially for more innovation (unlocking the wealth of existing data). The second subsidiary objective seems to empower or create a leveled playing field both horizontally and vertically between undertakings. This is in line with the third subobjective (iii), fairness in the allocation of data and the value from data among actors in the data economy, while still preserving incentives of manufacturers of IoT products, data holders, and others to invest in ways of generating value from data which should still be considered a subobjective (iv).

Even though the Impact assessment report drafts the application of the Data Act more narrowly, limiting the effect within the digital ecosystems and enhancing competition on aftermarkets only, the objectives of Explanatory memorandum and the legal text of the proposal give the Data Act a broader application.[31] The application is meant to generally create a leveled playing field, not only vertically or within ecosystems but also horizontally. However, the proposal fall way short to meet the objectives.

The basic structure of the Data Act for meeting these objectives is the introduction of an obligation in Article 3 that 'products shall be designed and manufactured, and related services shall be provided, in such a manner that data generated by their

[29] Proposal for a Regulation of the European Parliament and of the Council on harmonized rules on fair access to and use of data (Data Act), COM (2022) 68 final, 23 February 2022, 3.

[30] Wolfgang Kerber, 'Governance of IoT Data: Why the EU Data Act Will Not Fulfill Its Objectives' (8 April 2022) <https://ssrn.com/abstract=4080436> or <http://dx.doi.org/10.2139/ssrn.4080436>.

[31] Josef Drexl et al., Position Statement of the Max Planck Institute for Innovation and Competition of 25 May 2022 on the Commission's Proposal of 23 February 2022 for a Regulation on harmonized rules on fair access to and use of data (Data Act), 15 et seq.

use are, by default, easily, securely and, where relevant and appropriate, directly accessible to the user'. The obligation is accompanied with what seems to be a new right of the users to access and share the (raw) data that they have generated through their IoT devices (Articles 4 and 5).[32] It is uncertain, whether Article 4 of the proposal is only applicable when the data is not directly accessible under Article 3 Data Act, or whether Article 4 provides for a right to access data applicable without restrictions and erga omnes, for example, vis-a-vis purchasers of the database originally set up by the manufacturer of the IoT device, including the sensor. Indeed, an important issue – for understanding the system under the Data Act – is whether the right is applicable also when the obligation under Article 3 is violated.

The potential right makes no difference between consumers and businesses. All users of IoT devices (B2C and B2B) should be empowered by the rights and can get access to all data they have created. According to recital 28, the user should be free to use the data for any lawful purpose. According to Article 5, the user also has the right to share the generated data with third parties (firms or other actors), who can use these data for those purposes that are agreed upon with the users, while the third party still needs to negotiate and enter an agreement with the data holder according to Article 8 of the Data Act.

According to recital 14, the scope of data these rights cover is raw data, that is, the data directly and unprocessed generated by the user. Derived data and inferred data are not encompassed by the rights, or the proposal as such. This could be a default setting and that more sector-specific regulations, such as the Digital Markets Act, will go beyond the limitation of only regulating the control of raw data. Indeed, the Cloud regulation in the Data Act itself (cf. chapter IV) has a broader understanding of data to include also inferred data.

Article 3 of the Data Act addresses, in a possibly deliberate way, rudimentary the delicate issue of how the manufacturer or data holder gains control over the data in the first place. Accordingly, before concluding a contract for the purchase, rent, or lease of a product or a related service, certain topics or points of information shall be provided to the user. These points will make the user aware of the collection and use of data conducted by the product or service purchased or used by the user. The topics that need to be raised are as follows:

(a) the nature and volume of the data likely to be generated by the use of the product or related service;
(b) whether the data is likely to be generated continuously and in real time;
(c) how the user may access those data;
(d) whether the manufacturer supplying the product or the service provider providing the related service intends to use the data itself or

[32] Kerber (n 30).

allows a third party to use the data and, if so, the purposes for which those data will be used;

(e) whether the seller, renter, or lessor is the data holder and, if not, the identity of the data holder, such as its trading name and the geographical address at which it is established;

(f) the means of communication that enable the user to contact the data holder quickly and communicate with that data holder efficiently;

(g) how the user may request that the data are shared with a third party;

(h) the user's right to lodge a complaint alleging a violation of the provisions [. . .]

Interestingly, Article 3 does not require the contract to include that the user gives up or sells the right to be monitored, only to be informed. Furthermore, Article 3 indirectly identifies the original data holder (often the manufacturer of the device or part that includes the sensor) and also applies to third-party data holders. The third-party data holder can be purchaser of the product that includes the sensor monitoring the user or, when the user purchases the product directly, the purchaser of the contract where the information mentioned in Article 3 was provided, inter alia the contractual right to monitor the user through the sensor. Although not explicitly discussed, the contract between the user and the data holder, be it the manufacturer or a third party, could be identified as a license agreement.[33] The rights in license agreement can thus be transferred, while still the Data Act does not mention or even dwell on the issue of whether the user entering into this contract has a right that the user can license out. This is unsettling and the legislator needs to identify the subject of the contract.

The Commission has, moreover, in Article 3 of the Data Act circumvented the delicate issue of exhaustion in reference to the product that includes the sensor picking up the data. As will be argued in Section 6.3, the right to the data collected from a sensor would be transferred in an exhaustive sale of a product to the purchaser of the product, and without having such a license agreement as envisioned in Article 3, the data holder would not have access to the sensor and the data originating from the sensor. Indeed, Article 3 of the proposal opens up the possibility to trade the access right to purchasers, renters, or leasees of the product separately, while Articles 4 and 5 give a not as developed right to access and transfer the raw generated data for the benefit of the user.

A major problem with the Data Act is that it accepts or rather resigns the notion that the collector of the data, that is, the firm with the technical de facto possibility to exclude others from mining the sensor is the rightful 'owner' of the data. Thus, even those who find the end result of the Data Act attractive should recognize that the starting point for making the rules should be that the owner of the sensor should be

33 Ibid.

able to collect the data, while others could be given a right to access and transfer the data collected, as stipulated in Articles 4 and 5. The data generated by the users should thus as *default* premises be in the control of the holder of the property right of the sensor and the user, which may be the same person. This should be reflected and emphasized in Articles 3, 4, 5, and 11, which restricts the user to utilize the data and guarantees the data holder to contractually restrict the user and the possibility to make use of technical protection measures (TPMs) under Article 6 InfoSoc to prevent access to the sensor.[34]

The data holder could make a successful claim, for example, that TPMs under Article 6 InfoSoc (or the copyright protections of the API[35]) are available, irrespective of an obligation to grant access and the possibility to port data under Article 5 and create interoperability under Article 28 Data Act. Indeed, among the technical means to enable data access, Article 28 Data Act mentions APIs. Yet, the proposal leaves open how this provision should work, if the APIs are protected by intellectual property law.[36]

Moreover, Articles 5 and 8 of the proposal forward the notion of contractual negotiations with the data holder and third parties that convey the message that system leaders and gatekeepers will be in charge of the data flows and can use their bilateral influence to shape the data structure. Indeed, the third party according to Article 5 should be bound to FRAND commitments, remunerating the data holder. Indeed, the proposed Data Act is very data holder friendly and does not create a levelled playing field.

Article 35 of the proposed Data Act stipulates that the sui generis right 'does not apply to databases containing data obtained from or generated by the use of a product or a related service', 'in order not to hinder the exercise of the right of users to access and use such data … or of the right to share such data with third parties'. The database sui generis protection cannot be invoked by data holders as a defense for not fulfilling their obligations under Articles 4 and 5, without the risk of liability.[37] If they still refuse access, liability under the Data Act can be expected, while the sui generis database right cannot be overridden due to the fact that the Data Act is not a property law. Or, should the right in Article 4 Data Act be viewed as

34 The Data Act emphasizes that these user rights do not diminish in any way the rights of data subjects from EU data-protection law regarding personal data but complement them. This also implies that the DA de facto extends these rights on personal data, for example, with respect to continuous and real-time data access and data sharing (if applicable). See recital 31, discussed in Kerber (n 30).

35 It is highly uncertain that APIs are covered by copyright in the EU.

36 Drexl et al. (n 31) 81 et seq. See also Jörg Hoffmann and Begoña Gonzalez Otero, 'Demystifying the Role of Data Interoperability in the Access and Sharing Debate' (29 September 2020) Max Planck Institute for Innovation & Competition Research Paper No 20-16 <https://ssrn.com/abstract=3705217> or <http://dx.doi.org/10.2139/ssrn.3705217>.

37 Drexl et al. (n 31) 90 et seq.

similar to the data mining and reverse-engineering exemptions under EU Copyright law? Is it a 'countervailing' right hidden in Article 4 Data Act? It is uncertain whether injunctions for accessing data are available under the Data Act for the benefit of the user. The Data Act could be regarded as *lex specialis* vis-à-vis the database directive, yet it seems somewhat unlikely, given it has been presented as a general les generalis legal system for IoT. As regards EU law, before the legislative development reflected in the proposal for the Data Act and Digital Markets Act, only competition law provided a means to limit the availability of intellectual property remedies outside the intellectual property legal system. To be able to grant injunction for accessing data vis-à-vis a holder of a database imply that the Data Act may trump the right based on the database directive.[38]

On the other hand, Article 11(1) confirms that the data holder can make use of TPMs (e.g., Article 6 InfoSoc), which are an additional means to enable and safeguard de facto data control. In reference to technical means to enable data access, the Commission mentions application programming interfaces (APIs). However, the Data Act leaves open how this should work, if the APIs are protected by intellectual property law.

Article 5(2) of the Data Act includes a rule that seeks to exclude platform providers that have been declared gatekeepers according to the Digital Markets Act from benefitting from the application of Article 5(1), that is, gaining access through agreement with user. In reference to the larger picture of Article 5, the provision constitutes a limitation of the right of the user to freely choose the third party to which the data should be made available for the provision of added value services.[39]

The proposal for the Data Act and the Digital Markets Act (discussed below) share similar structural or constitutional point of departure in reference to establishing a legal system of access and transfer of data. The owner of the sensor or platform should be able to collect the data, while others could be given a limited 'right' to access and transfer the data collected. As will be argued, competition and society at large would be better off should the data generated by the users as a *default* be accessible and transferable on equal terms by the owner of the sensor collecting the data and the user. In reference to the Data Act, the proposal should thus be amended so that the data generated by the sensor should be accessible for both parties irrespective of whether it is raw data or inferred or processed data. Moreover, the user should be able to transfer the data the sensor generated without the possibility of the data holder using technical or legal means to disturb such transfer.

[38] Drexl et al. (n 31) 37. A very similar provision can be found in both the Data Governance Act, which in Article 5(7) states that the right of the maker of a database as provided for in Article 7 (1) of Directive 96/9/EC shall not be exercised by public-sector bodies in order to prevent the reuse of data or to restrict reuse beyond the limits set by this Regulation and in Article 1(6) of the 2019 Open Data Directive which contains the same language as the Data Governance Act proposal.

[39] Ibid., 34.

If the sensor collects and processes result that reflects inferred data, such data should also be accessible and transferable on equal terms.

That would imply that the user should have some kind of right that could trump the rights held by the data holder and the person holding the property right to the sensor. There are both competition-law arguments based on the notion of leveraging market power and creating a leveled playing field,[40] and constitutional or incentive arguments that users who invest both intellectually and the work of generating the data should also hold a right to access and transfer such data. Indeed, the right of the user should be on an equal level to that of the data holder.

The Data Act should reflect such an equal access and right to transfer. The proposal falls also short of its goals of integrating the existing legal regimes in a general market law regulation for the data-driven economy. The proposal fails to take into account private rights and interests. Given the above, the Data Act does not suffice as a fundamental constitutional regulation for the data-driven economy. As will be discussed in Chapter 5, constitutional principles would incline that the users should hold equal rights to control the data they generate by using the product they purchase. Nonetheless, the Data Act reflects the notion that the legislator envisioned that a user of an IoT-product should have a right to access and transfer data, while the DMA is unclear in reference to the existence of such right.

4.2.3 *The Digital Markets Act*

The P2B Regulation entered into force in July 2019, but soon thereafter, the EU Commission realized that the P2B Regulation did not go far enough and that a more comprehensive regulation of platforms was needed. The Commission therefore floated proposals during the summer of 2020, seeking to enhance and broaden the regulation's powers and discretions in terms of regulating platforms. First, ex ante rules were proposed, where the EU Commission should be allowed to decide whether certain platforms should benefit from a greater unfair competition-law exposure. Second, an idea was launched to give the Commission a new regulator competition tool. The tool would enable the Commission to impose behavioral and, where appropriate, structural remedies.[41]

[40] *Google Shopping* case, para 180 regarding the discussion of net neutrality.

[41] The Commission could also recommend legislative action to improve the functioning of the market concerned. As under the previous options, there would be no finding of an infringement, no fines, and no damage claims. See Commission, 'Inception Impact Assessments for New Competition Tool' <https://ec.europa.eu/info/law/better-regulation/have-your-say/initiatives/12416-New-competition-tool>.

In December 2020, the EU Commission published a proposal for a Digital Markets Act, which includes ex ante rules and gives the Commission a more lightweight regulatory tool to address certain platforms directly with decisions, including platform-specific rules. It was finally enacted in July 2022. The Digital Markets Act is comprehensive, addressing several of the issues discussed in Chapter 2. It is something just short of a revolution that ex ante rules, that is, a sector-specific regulation, are now proposed in reference to certain gatekeeping platforms. The Digital Markets Act could be compared to the sector-specific regulation for the telecom sector. Sector-specific ex ante rules are a hybrid form of competition law, whereby designated authorities (normally national telecoms authorities) identify actors with significant market power that are in danger of violating competition rules and impose remedies on these actors in advance. By their very nature, such rules are asymmetric (as they do not apply equally to all providers) and sector-specific (as they apply only to telecoms).[42]

The Digital Markets Act, if implemented, will be a valuable tool for the Commission. However, whether it fulfills its goals or creates a leveled playing field is still uncertain. Unlike telecommunications law, which charges national regulatory agencies with enforcement, the Commission will be the regulatory agency for all of the EU – creating centralization and uniformity but decreasing flexibility of the system and potentially raising questions about subsidiarity. This may prevent what sociology researchers call 'capture' and 'agency' dilemmas.[43]

The Digital Markets Act will be applicable only to large platforms that will be identified and designated as 'gatekeepers' according to objective criteria set out in the Regulation. These gatekeepers are companies which, owing to their size and their importance as gateways for business users to reach their customers, play a particularly important role in the internal market.

Gatekeepers control at least one so-called 'core platform service' and have a lasting, large user base in multiple EU countries. These core platform services include (i) online intermediation services (incl. for example marketplaces, app stores, and online intermediation services in other sectors, such as mobility, transport, or energy); (ii) online search engines; (iii) social networking; (iv) video-sharing platform services;

[42] Andrej Savin, 'The EU Digital Markets Act: A Possible Game Changer in Efforts to Regulate Platforms' EU Internet Law & Policy Blog Understanding EU Cyberlaw (20 December 2020) <https://euinternetpolicy.wordpress.com/2020/12/20/the-eu-digital-markets-act-a-possible-game-changer-in-efforts-to-regulate-platforms/>.

[43] For discussion of regulator capture and 'agency' dilemmas from a legal point of view, see, for example, Ernesto Dal Bó, 'Regulatory Capture: A Review' 22(2) Oxford Review of Economic Policy Summer 203–225 https://doi.org/10.1093/oxrep/grj013 and Jean-Jacques Jean Tirole Laffont, 'The Politics of Government Decision-Making: A Theory of Regulatory Capture'(1991) 106(4) The Quarterly Journal of Economics 1089–1127 <https://doi.org/10.2307/2937958>.

(v) number-independent, interpersonal, electronic communication services;[44] (vi) operating systems;[45] (vii) cloud services; and (viii) advertising services, including advertising networks, advertising exchanges, and any other advertising intermediation services, where these advertising services are related to one or more of the other core platform services mentioned above. In addition, during the negotiations with the Parliament and the Council, two more services were added to the list, virtual assistants and web browsers. Some services such as cloud services, operating systems, and advertising services connected to platforms are included in the Digital Markets Act but are not encompassed by the P2B regulation. Moreover, by including cloud computer services, the Digital Markets Act becomes complementary to the Data Free Flow Regulation. Hence, the Digital Markets Act has a wider definition of platforms, and this broad definition is both a blessing and a curse. It implies that several forms of platforms are covered, creating legal certainty and equality before the law, but it also paves the way for more gatekeepers to become business users of other gatekeepers – thus enabling these business users to extract, for example, data from their actions on other platforms. In the Digital Markets Act, the Commission has not been able to address the issue of gatekeepers that are also business users. Indeed, this can become a problem, if gatekeepers utilize the Digital Markets Act as a way to distribute data between each other.

Some services still seem to be excluded from the definition. Internet service providers and other network providers seem to be excluded, even though they collect significant amounts of data. In addition, online retailers or distributors that sell products, such as grocery stores (supermarkets) and retailers of brands (e.g., hm.com or ikea.com) still seem to be excluded from application of the Digital Markets Act.[46]

According to Article 2, point 17, 'business user' means any natural or legal person acting in a commercial or professional capacity, who uses core platform services for the purpose of or while providing goods or services to end users. The definition should be more stringent, and possibly should exclude other platforms with gatekeeper capabilities, at least for the benefit of their respective core platform service. In addition. the interface between services and ancillary services is not entirely clear. Is an ancillary service included in the notion of service? This was probably the

[44] For a definition, see para 7 of Article 2 of Directive (EU) 2018/1972: 'number-independent interpersonal communications service' means an interpersonal communications service which does not connect with publicly assigned numbering resources, namely, a number or numbers in national or international numbering plans, or which does not enable communication with a number or numbers in national or international numbering plans.' (Most OTT services will fall within this category.) For these, at least one natural person must be involved, and the recipients must be taken from a finite number of recipients chosen by the sender. This includes services where the remuneration is data instead of money and excludes broadcast-style services. There is still confusion as to whether services such as Facebook/Twitter fall within this definition.

[45] According to Article 2 para 10, 'Operating system' means a system software which controls the basic functions of the hardware or software and enables software applications to run on it.

[46] There issue is not entirely sorted, see the concern of Zalando: <www.reuters.com/article/eu-digital-enduser-idUSL8N2RN59L>.

intention of the legislator when drafting the Digital Markets Act, but this is not entirely clear.

Specifically, three main cumulative criteria determine whether a company falls within the scope of the Digital Markets Act:

(i) A size that impacts the internal market: This is presumed to be the case if the company achieves an annual turnover in the European Economic Area (EEA) equal to or exceeding € 7.5 billion in the three preceding financial years, or where its average market capitalization or equivalent fair market value amounted to at least € 75 billion in the most recent financial year, and it provides a core platform service in at least three Member States;

(ii) The control of an important gateway for business users toward final consumers: This is presumed to be the case if the company operates a core platform service with more than 45 million monthly active end users established or located in the EU and more than 10,000 yearly active business users established in the EU in the most recent financial year;

(iii) An (expected) entrenched and durable position: This is presumed to be the case if the company fulfilled the other two criteria in each of the past three financial years.

If these quantitative thresholds are met, the specific company is presumed to be a gatekeeper, unless it submits substantiated arguments to demonstrate the contrary. If all these thresholds are not met, the Commission – in the context of a market investigation for designating gatekeepers – may evaluate the specific situation of a given company and decide to identify it as a gatekeeper based on a qualitative assessment. Under the Digital Markets Act, companies identified as gatekeepers will need to implement certain behaviors proactively and will need to refrain from engaging in unfair practices, which are defined in the legislation in the light of market experience to date.[47]

The consequences of being identified as a gatekeeper under the proposed Digital Markets Act are identified mainly under Articles 5 and 6. Article 5 of the Digital Markets Act stipulates stringent rules with which gatekeepers must comply. A gatekeeper shall

2. not (a) process for the purpose of providing advertising services personal data from end users using services of third parties that make use of core platform services of the gatekeeper, (b) combine personal data from the

[47] When a company does not yet enjoy an entrenched and durable position, but it is foreseeable that it will do so in the near future, a proportionate subset of obligations will apply to ensure that the gatekeeper concerned does not achieve by unfair means an entrenched and durable position in its operations.

relevant core platform service with personal data from any further core platform services or other services offered by the gatekeeper or with personal data from third-party services, (c) cross-use personal data from the relevant core platform service in other services offered separately by the gatekeeper, including other core platform services, and vice-versa, and (d) sign in end users to other services of the gatekeeper in order to combine personal data.

Should the end user have been presented with a specific choice and provided a specific consent in the sense of Article 4(11) and Article 7 of GDPR, the obligation in Article 5(2) is not applicable.[48]

Prohibition to combine personal data from the gatekeeper's platform services with personal data from other services mirrors in several aspects the German Competition Authorities Facebook investigation.[49] The prohibition was broadened to capture several interfaces between the core platform service and affiliated services in reference to the use and combination of data. The advantage in data may originate from a right to access and use customers' data, and such a clause may be considered anticompetitive in certain situations, for example, if done in conjunction with violating a data privacy rule (German Facebook case[50]). According to the DMA, combining data can be a violation *per se* against Article 5(2)(b), while still the end user may specifically provide consent, which would allow the gatekeeper to combine personal data in the manner described in Article 5(2)(b).

3. refrain from applying obligations that prevent business users from offering the same products or services to end users through third-party online intermediation services or through their own direct online sales channel at prices or conditions that are different from those offered through the online intermediation services of the gatekeeper;

Article 5(3) seems to be inspired by the Amazon e-book MFN case from 2017, the German Amazon investigation,[51] and also the investigation and decision of national competition authorities in bookingdotcom (price-parity clauses) (Sweden, France, Germany, and Italy) from 2015. Interestingly, it seems to prohibit not only wide price-parity clauses but also so-called narrow price-parity clauses.

48 Whether this is an accurate interpretation is still in doubt and the text may change (see, e.g., preamble 36). Where that consent has been refused or withdrawn by the end user, the gatekeeper shall not repeat its request for consent for the same purpose more than once within a period of one year. This is without prejudice to the possibility of the gatekeeper to rely on Article 6(1) points (c), (d), and (e) of Regulation (EU) 2016/679, where applicable.

49 Cf Section 3.2.

50 See German Competition Authority, 'Preliminary Assessment in Facebook Proceeding: Facebook's Collection and Use of Data from Third-Party Sources Is Abusive' (19 December 2017) <www.bundeskartellamt.de/SharedDocs/Meldung/EN/Pressemitteilungen/2017/19_12_2017_Facebook.html>.

51 Cf Section 3.2.

4. allow business users free of charge to communicate and promote offers, including under different conditions to end users acquired via the core platform service or through other channels, and to conclude contracts with these end users regardless of whether for that purpose they use the core platform services of the gatekeeper.
5. allow end users to access and use, through the core platform services of the gatekeeper, content, subscriptions, features, or other items by using the software application of a business user, including where these items have been acquired by the end users from the relevant business user without using the core platform services of the gatekeeper;
6. refrain from requiring business users or end users to use, and in the case of business users also to offer, or interoperate with, an identification service, web browser engine, payment services, or technical services which support the provision of payment services such as payment systems for in-app purchases, of the gatekeeper in the context of services offered by the business users using the core platform services of that gatekeeper;

Article 5(4) stipulates a prohibition of steering exclusivity clauses as well as requiring some form of interoperability between the platform and the business user's software. At least Article 5(5), in combination with certain prohibitions under Article 6, requires not only portability but interoperability. Article 5(4) read in combination with Article 5(e) moreover seems to draw inspiration from Apple App store investigation in reference to not granting access to certain platforms. The Google AdSense case could also have been used, as well as national cases such as the Swedish decision regarding the Bruce app having exclusive agreements with gym facilities.

7. refrain from directly or indirectly preventing or restricting business users or end users from raising any issue of noncompliance with the relevant Union or national law by the gatekeeper with any relevant public authority, including national courts, relating to any practice of gatekeepers. This is without prejudice to the right of business users and gatekeepers to lay down in their agreements the terms of use of lawful complaint-handling mechanisms;
8. refrain from requiring business users or end users to subscribe to or register with any further core platform services identified pursuant to Article 3(7) or which meet the thresholds in Article 3(2) point (b) as a condition for being able to use, access, sign up for, or registering with any of their core platform services identified pursuant to that Article;

The prohibition against bundling and the rule provided in Article 5(8) seems to be derived from the Google Android case and the German Amazon investigation (discussed in Section 3.2).

9. provide each advertiser to which it supplies digital advertising services, or third parties authorized by advertisers, upon the advertiser's request, with free-of-charge information on a daily basis, concerning each advertisement placed by the advertiser, regarding (i) the price and fees paid by that advertiser, including any deductions and surcharges, for each of the relevant advertising services provided by the gatekeeper, (ii) the remuneration received by the publisher, including any deductions and surcharges, with the publisher's consent; and (iii) the measure on which each of the prices and remunerations is calculated. In case some publishers do not provide their consent to the sharing of information, provide each advertiser with free-of-charge information concerning the daily average remuneration received by those publishers, including any deductions and surcharges, for the relevant advertisements.
10. Provide each publisher to which it supplies digital advertising services, or third parties authorized by publishers, upon the publisher's request, with free-of-charge information on a daily basis, concerning each advertisement displayed on the publisher's inventory, regarding (i) the remuneration received and fees paid by that publisher, including any deductions and surcharges, for each of the relevant advertising services provided by the gatekeeper, (ii) the price paid by the advertiser, including any deductions and surcharges, with the advertiser's consent; and (iii) the measure on which each of the prices and remunerations is calculated. In case some advertisers do not provide their consent to the sharing of information, provide each publisher with free-of-charge information concerning the daily average price paid by those advertisers, including any deductions and surcharges, for the relevant advertisements.

In essence, Articles 5(9.) and 5(10.) stipulate a price and cost transparency requirement regarding online advertising. The articles were extensively rewritten and extended during the negotiations with the Parliament and the Council. The original covenant seems to be derived of the Google AdSense investigation, yet lobbying efforts by European media houses have extended the reach and width of the obligations. Yet, it can also be inspired by the UK CMA Final Report and the Australian Competition Authority (ACCC) report on the same subject.

Article 6 of the Digital Markets Act provides a list of requirements that platforms acting as gatekeepers must comply with, while the Commission should still be able to specify the requirements in individual decisions.

> Article 6(1) states that gatekeepers should refrain from using, in competition with business users, any data not publicly available, which is generated or provided by those business users in the context of their use of the relevant core platform services

> or of the services offered together with or in support of the relevant core platform services, including data generated or provided by the end users of those business users.[52]

Article 6(1) stipulates a prohibition for gatekeepers to use business users' data in competition with said business users on downstream markets. The prohibition seems to be derived from the Amazon marketplace investigation (cf discussion above). Data that is not publicly available shall according to Article 6(2) include any aggregated and nonaggregated data generated by business users that can be inferred from, or collected through, the commercial activities of business users or their customers, including click, search, view, and voice data, on the relevant core platform service or on services offered together with or in support of the relevant core platform service of the gatekeeper. As mentioned above, this is in stark contrast with the Data Act, where the user is only able to gain access to the raw data generated by the same.

> Article 6(3) requires gatekeepers to allow and technically enable end users to easily uninstall any software applications on the operating system of the gatekeeper, without prejudice to the possibility for a gatekeeper to restrict such uninstallation in relation to software applications that are essential for the functioning of the operating system or of the device and which cannot technically be offered on a stand-alone basis by third parties;
>
> The gatekeeper shall allow and technically enable end users to easily change default settings on the operating system, virtual assistant, and web browser of the gatekeeper that direct or steer end users to products or services provided by the gatekeeper, including prompting end users, at the moment of the end users' first use of an online search engine, virtual assistant or web browser of the gatekeeper identified pursuant to Article 3(7), to choose, from a list of the main available service providers, the online search engine, virtual assistant, or web browser to which the operating system of the gatekeeper directs or steers users by default, and the online search engine to which the virtual assistant and the web browser of the gatekeeper directs or steers users by default.

The prohibition in Article 6(3) against technical hindrances to uninstalling software applications was investigated in the Google Android case (discussed above), while it has been broadened to also cover virtual assistants and web browsers more specifically.

[52] Moreover, the preamble (43) states that to prevent gatekeepers from unfairly benefiting from their dual role, it should be ensured that they refrain from using any aggregated or nonaggregated data, which may include anonymized and personal data that is not publicly available to offer similar services to those of their business users. This obligation should apply to the gatekeeper as a whole, including but not limited to its business unit that competes with the business users of a core platform service.

4. allow and technically enable the installation and effective use of third-party software applications or software application stores using, or interoperating with, the operating system of the gatekeeper and allow these software applications or software application stores to be accessed by means other than the relevant core platform services of that gatekeeper. The gatekeeper shall, where applicable, not prevent the downloaded third-party software applications or software application stores from prompting end users to decide whether they want to set that downloaded software application or software application store as their default and technically enable that change to be carried out easily. The gatekeeper shall not be prevented from taking to the extent strictly necessary and proportionate measures to ensure that third-party software applications or software application stores do not endanger the integrity of the hardware or operating system offered by the gatekeeper, provided that such measures are duly justified by the gatekeeper.

   The gatekeeper shall furthermore not be prevented from applying to the extent strictly necessary and proportionate measures and settings other than default settings enabling end users to effectively protect security in relation to third-party software applications or software application stores, provided that such measures are duly justified by the gatekeeper.

Rules regarding side-loading, that is, the ability of end customers to access, install, download, and use apps from business users, Article 6(4) requires open access and interoperability on OS systems, also outside the platform. Here we can also see signs of the Apple App store investigation, as well as *Google AdSense*. Interestingly, the prohibition also seems to target the use of third-party proxies implementing the abuse.

5. refrain from treating more favorably in ranking, and related indexing and crawling, services and products offered by the gatekeeper itself compared to similar services or products of third party and apply transparent, fair, and nondiscriminatory conditions to such ranking;

Prohibition of self-favoring or discrimination in rankings, clearly derived from the *Google Shopping* case and the lengthy Google investigation. The Amazon Buy Box and Marketplace investigation also seem to have inspired the rule.

6. refrain from technically or otherwise restricting the ability of end users to switch between and subscribe to different software applications and services to be accessed using the core platform services of the gatekeeper, including as regards the choice of internet access services for end users;
7. allow providers of services and of hardware, free-of-charge, effective interoperability with, and access for the purposes of interoperability to,

the same hardware and software features accessed or controlled via the operating system or virtual assistant of the gatekeeper identified pursuant to Article 3(7), that are available to services or hardware provided by the gatekeeper. Furthermore, allow business users and alternative providers of services offered together with or in support of core platform services free of charge, effective interoperability with, and access for the purposes of interoperability to, the same operating system and hardware or software features regardless of whether those features are part of the operating system that are available to or used by the gatekeeper when providing such services. The gatekeeper shall not be prevented from taking strictly necessary and proportionate measures to ensure that interoperability does not compromise the integrity of the operating system, virtual assistant, and hardware or software features offered by the gatekeeper provided that such strictly necessary and proportionate measures are duly justified by the gatekeeper.

Obligation to allow third parties to offer support services including software on platforms, that is, it requires interoperability. The rule seems to be derived from Apple Store/Mobile Payment investigation.

8. provide advertisers and publishers, and third parties authorized by advertisers and publishers, upon their request and free of charge, with access to the performance measuring tools of the gatekeeper and the data necessary for advertisers and publishers, to carry out their own independent verification of the ad inventory, including aggregated and nonaggregated data. This data shall be provided in a manner that would allow advertisers and publishers to run their own verification and measurement tools to assess performance of the core services provided by the gatekeepers;

Access to the gatekeeper's performance measurement tools. This issue in reference to the media and advertisement markets is discussed in the UK CMA Final Report as well as in the Australian report regarding competition on the media market.

9. provide end users and third parties authorized by an end user, upon their request and free of charge, with effective portability of data offered by the end user or generated through the activity of the end user in the context of the use of the relevant core platform service including the provision of free-of-charge tools to facilitate the effective exercise of such data portability and the provision of continuous and real-time access;

The obligation to facilitate data portability for end users as well as to give third parties authorized by an end user continuous access to data seems clearly to be derived from the Amazon Marketplace investigation (see above). Interestingly, different from the Commission proposal, the business user as a benefiter of the portability requirement has been erased, and Article 6(9) now only mimics and extends portability right for end users (often individuals) under Article 20 GDPR (see also recital 54). It should also be read in light of the proposed Data Act (see below), which as a de fault proposes that negotiations between data holder and third party should take place, similarly to where a user of an IoT device would like to transfer data to a third party.

10. provide business users and third parties authorized by a business user, upon their request, free of charge, with effective, high-quality, continuous, and real-time access and use of aggregated and nonaggregated data, including personal data, that is provided for or generated in the context of the use of the relevant core platform services or services offered together with or in support of the relevant core platform services by those business users and the end users engaging with the products or services provided by those business users; for personal data, provide access and use only where the data are directly connected with the use effectuated by the end user in respect of the products or services offered by the relevant business user through the relevant core platform service, and when the end user opts in to such sharing by giving their consent;

Similarly, the access for business users to data generated on the platform is also inspired by the Amazon Marketplace investigation. It should however be noted that Article 6(10) does not include a right to port the data for the benefit of the business user.

11. provide to any third-party undertaking offering online search engines, upon their request, with access to fair, reasonable, and nondiscriminatory terms to ranking, query, click, and view data in relation to free and paid search generated by end users on online search engines of the gatekeeper, subject to anonymization for the query, click, and view data that constitutes personal data.

The requirement to share search data is the only requirement directly focusing to boost horizontal competition in the DMA. To require Google to share search data with competitors could be derived from the *Google Shopping* case, while also from the early investigation regarding Google search originating from Microsoft complaint in the 2010s.

12. The gatekeeper shall apply fair, reasonable, and nondiscriminatory general conditions of access for business users to its software application stores, online search engines, and online social networking services listed in the designation decision pursuant to Article 3(9). For that purpose, the gatekeeper shall publish general conditions of access,

including an alternative dispute settlement mechanism. The Commission shall assess whether the published general conditions of access comply with this paragraph.

13. The gatekeeper shall not have general conditions for terminating the provision of a core platform service that are disproportionate. The gatekeeper shall ensure that such conditions of termination can be exercised without undue difficulty.

It seems that Article 6(12) generally requires access to app stores and the like on something similar to FRAND terms. The rule could be inspired by Apple App store investigation but also the US FTC investigation of Google in 2013.

Article 7 addresses gatekeepers providing number independent of interpersonal communications services. Generally, the quite long article requires the gatekeeper to make basic functionalities of its number of independent interpersonal communications services interoperable with another provider by providing the necessary technical interfaces or similar solutions that facilitate interoperability, upon request, and free of charge.

Generally, these requirements are extensive, far-reaching, and detailed in their requirements on interoperability, price-parity restriction, self-preferencing, and access to platforms on equal terms. It represents a Digital Markets regulation for the Internet of today. Indeed, the obligations are in several instances derived from current investigations conducted by the European Commission or national competition authority. In practical terms, the Digital Markets Act means Amazon must stop favoring its own goods over those from business users on its Marketplace. Apple must unlock its App store. Google must no longer collect combine data from Maps and YouTube and use it to target advertising on its search engine without the specific consent from the users. Meta must within four years from the decision by the European Commission allow its WhatsApp messaging service to accept calls from competitors such as Signal and Telegram.

Moreover, it seems possible that gatekeeper platforms also need to open core platform services for third-party (ancillary) service providers. What does this imply? For example, could a competing messaging service (WhatsApp) require access to Facebook on the same terms as Messenger? Can Twitter claim access as an application of Google or on Facebook? Indeed, the requirements stipulated above pave the way for interoperability on a much broader scale than we have experienced thus far. Gatekeepers will bear an extra responsibility to conduct themselves in a manner that ensures an open online environment that is fair for businesses and consumers, and open to innovation by all, by complying with specific obligations laid down in the draft legislation.

It should be noted that the Digital Markets Act empowers the Commission to grant an exemption from Articles 5 and 6 but also to extend the list of requirements under Articles 5 and 6 (cf Article 10), after carrying out a sector inquiry. Inquiries and the regular reports that gatekeepers must provide to the Commission should also include all relevant merger and acquisition activities. In the case of systematic gatekeeper infringements of their obligations, additional remedies may be imposed on the gatekeepers after a market investigation. Such remedies will need to be proportionate to the offense committed. If necessary and as a last-resort option, nonfinancial remedies can be imposed. These can include behavioral and structural remedies, for example, the divestiture of (parts of) a business. The Digital Markets Act opens paths for a new, interoperable Internet, where leveraging (including self-preferencing) is restricted. However, the Digital Markets Act became after the trialogue negotiations very detailed, and there is clearly room for litigations to carve out the fine details of the obligations. This is unfortunate, and it is not certain that the DMA would imply less or less lengthy litigations vis-à-vis general competition law. Moreover, with respect to creating a level playing field in relation to access and use of data, there are possibly some hidden limitations to a genuine interoperable use of services and flow of data. It seems that the Digital Markets Act does not address the interface or limitation set by intellectual property law in reference to accessing intellectual property-protected services, software, interfaces, or data in a comprehensive way.

This book focuses on access to data, but it should be stressed that interfaces (e.g., APIs and websites) and software can be encompassed by copyright protection and possibly other intellectual property rights. Indeed, the question is whether the platforms can use rights to circumvent the implementation obligations set out in Articles 5 and 6. As mentioned above, access to data can be restricted by TPMs, third-party copyright, trade-secret rules, and sui generis database rights; however, the Digital Markets Act does not adequately address the intellectual property-law dimension.[53] In the new recital 70, the DMA stipulates that the gatekeeper should not be allowed to engage in any behavior undermining interoperability as required, such as, for example, by using unjustified technical protection measures or unlawfully claiming copyright on APIs. Whether the breadth of copyright may be restricted by the text in a recital can only be interpreted in light of the property protection reflected in the EU Charter.

Moreover, as concluded in Chapter 3, competition law does not suffice to create a right to data access and portability, neither in practice nor in theory. In practice, it is very difficult to create a workable collaboration for gaining access to the flow of data, and in theory it is difficult to create rights under competition law, available erga omnes.

Interestingly, even though the trialogue led to the increased breadth and depth of several of the obligations stipulated in Articles 5 and 6, the portability obligation in Article 6 (9) was limited during the negotiation. There is no 'right' for business users to port data, implying taking the data they generated on the platform from the platform. Indeed 'business user' as a subject was deleted from Article 6 (9). This is unfortunate. It implies that business users' potential right to data was limited.

[53] Moreover, it should be stressed that the matter of having gatekeepers using each other's services is quite complex, and it is not clear whether an obligation to give access and port data should also be given in these circumstances.

It should still be clear that paragraphs (1.), (9.), and (10.) of Article 6, when read in combination, may – with the help of end users – provide something akin to an access and portability right for business users. However, the DMA does not stipulate a stand-alone portability right for the benefit of business users vis-à-vis gatekeepers.[54] The end user may bring the data from the gatekeeper to the business user and by doing so eliminate the gatekeeper's access to the same data. The use of the notion of portability should imply that the gatekeeper cannot keep a copy of said data. The provisions state that the platform provider is de facto not allowed to use the data generated by the business user on the platform, in competition with the business user (see also Article 5 (1) in the Regulation). Interestingly, the obligation in Article 6 (1), compared to the obligations in (9) and (10), does reflect that business users have some sort of preferential right to the data generated, vis-à-vis the platform provider. Indeed, this is a bilateral, preferential right to each data point, which at first glance seems to override the gatekeeper's general database right. However, on a general level, it is still uncertain whether the Digital Markets Act stipulates rights for for example users or only general obligations for the gatekeepers. The Court may interpret the obligations to reflect corresponding rights for users, should they be sufficiently clear, unconditional and precise, liability rules (right to compensation for users) or only public obligations to be enforced by the Commission. The Digital Markets Act, being a regulation, should be available for private action vis-a-vis designated gatekeepers and given the principles of effectiveness and effective judicial protection, users should have right to action under the DMA. Indeed, this should be more clearly specified in the DMA, giving the users a clear Access and Transfer Right to data.[55]

The gatekeeper still retains the prerogative to make all data available for all users (cf Article 6(1) DMA. Yet, in parallel, business users have been granted a data advantage vis-à-vis the platforms. Indeed, the combination of Article 6 paragraphs (1) and (10) implicitly creates some form of compulsory access obligation that mirrors a limited right to the data generated by the business user on the platform – that is, a right granted to the business users. The combination of the obligations stated in Article 6 of the Digital Markets Act should be interpreted amounting to a right to access for the business user, yet the question is whether it is a right that prevents gatekeepers from using their intellectual property rights to prevent access. Inferred data should also be accessible, but drawing the line between data that originates from the business users and data that originates from the business (model) of the platform can be very difficult. Indeed, the preamble claims that data generated by business users and end users, as well as data inferred from that data, should be encompassed by the obligation, but in the case at hand, it can be difficult to identify the boundaries for that dataset.[56]

[54] This is also reflected in the updated recital 54, which do not contain the notion of portability.

[55] The obligation stipulated in Article 6 (10) of the proposal almost mirrors the right held in Article 7 of the Database Directive. See the discussion in Section 6.2.2.

[56] One possible means of addressing this is to require the use of blockchain, with rights for the business users to access the blocks reflecting the definition in the Article 6 (2), (9), and (10).

The preamble continues by stating:

> [I]n order to ensure that business users have access to the relevant data thus generated, the gatekeeper should, upon their request, provide effective access, free of charge, to such data. Such access should also be given to third parties contracted by the business user, who are acting as processors of this data for the business user. Data provided or generated by the same business users and the same end users of these business users in the context of other services provided by the same gatekeeper may be concerned where this is inextricably linked to the relevant request. To this end, a gatekeeper should not use any contractual or *other restrictions* to prevent business users from accessing relevant data and should enable business users to obtain consent of their end users for such data access and retrieval, where such consent is required under Regulation (EU) 2016/679 and Directive 2002/58/EC. Gatekeepers should also facilitate access to these data in real time by means of appropriate technical measures, such as for example putting in place high quality application programming interfaces or integrated tools for small volume business users.[57]

The text above indicates that the model for data access imagined by the Commission is that the gatekeeper makes a data-access API available to business users. The gatekeeper is not allowed to use contractual or other restrictions to prevent such access. Is this an overriding right to any and all intellectual property rights held by the gatekeeper? The major issue is whether this gateway to access and portability of data is in fact such a revolutionary tool for creating interoperability, or whether, in the end, lack of a global technical API standard, intellectual property legal systems, or the GDPR will de facto prevent data access and portability.

As stated above, the new recital 70 stipulates that the gatekeeper should not be allowed to use 'unjustified technical protection measures' or 'unlawfully claiming' copyright on APIs. Whether the breadth of copyright may be restricted by the text in a recital can only be interpreted in light of the property protection reflected in the EU Charter. Notwithstanding the text in the new recital 70, gatekeepers may try to prevent access to their platforms and most importantly their data by claiming that it is walled in by intellectual property rights. As discussed above, copyright owners regularly resort to TPMs, cf Article 6 InfoSoc, to prevent access to copyright-protected content. 'Hacking', or breaching technical measures to gain access to data, can be a violation of Article 6 InfoSoc. Thus, Article 6 InfoSoc also protects the platforms from being 'hacked' to gain access to unprotected data. APIs *can* be copyright protected.[58] Platforms can also claim that the datasets they collect are trade secrets as defined under the new EU directive,[59] or in the case of personal data, might be off-limits under the GDPR. For the data generated on the platforms, the

[57] The proposal for Digital Markets Act preamble 56.

[58] Discussed in Chapter 6.

[59] Cf Article 3 of the Trade Secret Directive and preamble 16, stating that 'Reverse engineering of a lawfully acquired product should be considered as a lawful means of acquiring information,

gatekeepers would most likely acquire some intellectual property rights when storing the data in databases or in public centralized blockchains, such as sui generis database protection, which may also limit or even prevent the porting of whole datasets.[60] On the other hand, do the obligations stipulated in Article 6(9) and (10) override these rights in order to uphold interoperability? It seems that Article 6(9) and (10) restrict the property rights held by the platforms.

Yet another major problem is that the DMA is unclear as to which data is in fact encompassed by the access and transfer right granted under the regulation; the DMA contains only an obligation for gatekeepers to give access. This could be a matter of litigation and indeed data can originate from both the business users' activities and the platform providers' activities, especially in the case of inferred data.

As discussed in reference to the Data Act above, the Data Act and the Digital Markets Act should be derived from the notion that equal access to the data should be given to the user and data holder/gatekeeper. That would imply that the business user under the Digital Markets Act should hold some kind of right, so to enable data-mining activities or similar without running the risk of violating the gatekeeper's intellectual property right, or risk violating trade-secret protection rules, or for that matter the GDPR. Indeed, the users should be empowered by a access and transfer right that can be used in Court to obtain access and transfer of data.

4.2.4 A *Competition Tool*

As discussed above, the DMA only caters to gatekeepers, which only includes the very largest digital/tech firms. Indeed, few companies will today fall under the definition.[61] Moreover, competition law may possibly not be able to address some of the situations where the ex ante rules presented in the DMA will be applicable, while it can be used for addressing others. Indeed, some recent investigations conducted by the Commission and NCAs under competition law are addressing business conduct, which is now encompassed by ex ante rules under the DMA. This may strike as odd and can complicate the application of competition law and DMA alike.

As a reminder, the European Commission's proposal of creating a 'Competition Tool',[62] which would be a legal system giving power to the relevant authorities to

except when otherwise contractually agreed. The freedom to enter into such contractual arrangements can, however, be limited by law.'

60 Discussed in Chapter 6.

61 However, when Internet of Things has been implemented, several Swedish companies may fall under the definition.

62 It should be mentioned that the proposal had been inspired by the UK Market Investigation powers. In the Online Platforms and Digital Advertising market study, the UK Competition and Markets Authority made recommendations regarding interoperability. The study was being conducted in the context of recent reforms establishing a Digital Markets Unit (DMU) within the Authority, which will have powers to enforce a code of conduct for large digital platforms. The study recommended that the DMU be granted powers to mandate interoperability for

produce sector-specific regulations or platforms-specific regulations should be mentioned. The tool creates a hybrid form of guidance in-between legislation and guidelines. The Commission was playing with the idea of addressing structural competitive problems with a special legal 'tool'.

According to the Commission, the tool should have addressed 'structural competition problems concern structural market characteristics that have adverse consequences on competition and may ultimately result in inefficient market outcomes in terms of higher prices, lower quality, less choice, and innovation. While structural competition problems can arise in a broad range of different scenarios, they can be generally grouped into two categories depending on whether harm is about to affect or has already affected the market:

- Structural risks for competition refer to scenarios where certain market characteristics (e.g., network and scale effects, lack of multihoming and lock-in effects) and the conduct of the companies operating in the markets concerned create a threat for competition. This applies notably to tipping markets. The ensuing risks for competition can arise through the creation of powerful market players with an entrenched market and/or gatekeeper position, the emergence of which could be prevented by early intervention. Other scenarios falling under this category include unilateral strategies by nondominant companies to monopolize a market through anticompetitive means.
- Structural lack of competition refers to a scenario where a market is not working well and not delivering competitive outcomes due to its structure (i.e., a structural market failure). These include (i) markets displaying systemic failures going beyond the conduct of a particular company with market power due to certain structural features, such as high concentration and entry barriers, consumer lock-in, lack of access to data or data accumulation, and (ii) oligopolistic market structures with an increased risk for tacit collusion, including markets featuring increased transparency due to algorithm-based technological solutions (which are becoming increasingly prevalent across sectors).'[63]

The remedies to address such situations were to be included in a legislative tool that inter alia allows the relevant authority to identify and remedy structural competition problems that cannot be addressed (at all or as effectively) under the EU competition rules. Thus, it would not be limited only to companies that are already dominant. The tool would be based on a test allowing the relevant authority to

digital platforms, noting that 'the case for interoperability is greater in respect of functionality which is: directly helpful in overcoming identified network effects; not highly innovative; and in respect of which privacy concerns can be managed effectively.'

63 Commission, 'Impact assessment' (2020) <file:///Users/bjornlundqvist/Downloads/090166e5cff96aa6%20(1).pdf>.

intervene when a structural risk for competition or a structural lack of competition prevents the internal market from functioning properly. The tool would enable the authority to impose behavioral and, where appropriate, structural remedies. The authority could also recommend legislative action to improve the functioning of the market concerned. As under the previous options, there would be no finding of an infringement, no fines, and no damage claims. Similar to the existing EU competition rules, the tool would be generally applicable across all sectors of the economy. These could include certain digital or digitally enabled markets and/or other sectors identified as being especially prone to such concerns due to entrenched dominance, high entry barriers, etc.[64]

[64] Ibid. This is a hybrid of the different proposals in the Impact assessment. It should be mentioned that a package of reforms in Germany have provided the German Bundeskartellamt with the ability to declare a firm to be 'of paramount significance for competition across markets' (Bundeskartellamt, 2020, p. 12[73]). These reforms supplement abuse of dominance tools by giving the Bundeskartellamt the ability to address potential competition problems in markets not yet dominated by a firm. Once the *Bundeskartellamt* has identified a platform with 'paramount cross-market relevance' for five years, the authority can issue an order prohibiting this undertaking from any of the following (exhaustive) practices:

1. favoring its own offers over the offers of its competitors when mediating access to supply and sales markets, in particular
   a) presenting its own offers in a more favorable manner;
   b) exclusively preinstalling its own offers on devices or integrating them in any other way in offers provided by the undertaking;
2. taking measures that impede other undertakings in carrying out their business activities on supply or sales markets where the undertaking's activities are of relevance for accessing such markets, in particular
   a) taking measures that result in the exclusive preinstallation or integration of offers provided by the undertaking;
   b) preventing other undertakings from advertising their own offers or reaching their purchasers through other channels in addition to those provided or mediated by the undertaking, or making it more difficult for other undertakings to do so;
3. directly or indirectly impeding competitors on a market on which the undertaking can rapidly expand its position even without being dominant, in particular
   a) linking the use of an offer provided by the undertaking to the automatic use of another offer provided by the undertaking which is not necessary for the use of the former offer, without giving the user of the offer sufficient choice as to whether and how the other offer is to be used;
   b) making the use of an offer provided by the undertaking conditional on the use of another offer provided by the undertaking;
4. creating or appreciably raising barriers to market entry or otherwise impeding other undertakings by processing data relevant for competition that have been collected by the undertaking, or demanding terms and conditions that permit such processing, in particular
   a) making the use of services conditional on the user agreeing to the processing of data from other services of the undertaking or a third-party provider without giving the user sufficient choice as to whether, how, and for what purpose such data are processed;
   b) processing data relevant for competition received from other undertakings for purposes other than those necessary for the provision of its own services to these undertakings without giving these undertakings sufficient choice as to whether, how, and for what purpose such data are processed;

The DMA does indeed open avenues for a new, interoperable internet, where leveraging (including self-preferencing) and other forms of abuse are restricted. However, the DMA became very complicated after the trialogue. It is an intricate legal tool for the Commission and the complexity of the ex ante rules may lead to lengthy litigation, something which the DMA was supposed to fix in the first place. Moreover, in reference to creating a level playing field in relation to access and use of data, there are possibly some hidden limitations to genuine interoperable use of services and flow of data from the gatekeepers providing so-called core platform services to their business users.[65] Given the fact that DMA equivalent ex ante rules were being developed under competition-law doctrine through the ongoing investigations by the European Commission and national competition authorities, the full set of rules in the DMA may not be needed from a competition-law perspective. However, a competition tool could still be useful. It can provide a basis for creating sector or individual obligations and conditions that can be used vis-a-vis special industries or markets such as the media market, or to employ a specific remedy, such as data access and portability, more broadly.[66] Indeed, in hindsight, the Competition tool was perhaps to be preferred.

5. refusing the interoperability of products or services or data portability, or making it more difficult, and in this way impeding competition;
6. providing other undertakings with insufficient information about the scope, quality, or success of the service rendered or commissioned, or otherwise making it more difficult for such undertakings to assess the value of this service;
7. demanding benefits for handling the offers of another undertaking which are disproportionate to the reasons for the demand, in particular
   a) demanding the transfer of data or rights that are not absolutely necessary for the purpose of presenting these offers,
   b) making the quality in which these offers are presented conditional on the transfer of data or rights which are not reasonably required for this purpose.

According to item 5 above, some data information could be made available up front for these firms. The German bill also includes a broadening of the possibility to access data under the rules addressing firms with relative market power vis-à-vis dependent companies. In addition, firms with little bargaining power may be exposed to unfair impediment if they have not been granted access to data. However, as with general competition law, it will be difficult to enforce these rules, and much litigation will be needed to ensure that firms are obligated to give access to data. Moreover, the firms should be remunerated for the data they transfer. See Thomas Höppner, 'Digital Upgrade of German Antitrust Law – Blueprint for Regulating Systemic Platforms in Europe and Beyond?' <www.hausfeld.com/news-press/digital-upgrade-of-german-antitrust-law-blueprint-for-regulating-systemic-platforms-in-europe-and-beyond>.

65 For definitions of a core platform service and a gatekeeper, and how obligations on gatekeepers are triggered, see the proposal for the Digital Markets Act <https://eur-lex.europa.eu/legal-content/EN/TXT/PDF/?uri=CELEX:52020PC0842&from=en>.

66 The Nordic Competition Authorities made a joint statement in 2020 that seem to be preferring a competition tool, rather than an ex ante regulation. Cf Digital platforms and the potential changes to competition law at the European level – The view of the Nordic competition authorities, 2020 [cit. Nordiska konkurrensmyndigheternas memorandum], available via: <https://konkurransetilsynet.no/wp-content/uploads/2020/09/Nordic-report-2020-memoran dum-on-digital-platforms.pdf>.

Generally, the Commission needs to clarify whether the competition rules being drafted in the Digital Markets Act are behavioral liability rules, or the Digital Markets Act should be viewed as creating rights for business users to actually use and access intellectual property law or trade-secret-protected subject matter (held by the platform or a third party). Or is the Digital Markets Act a sui generis reverse-engineering – data-mining – tool, to be applied by business users and end users? Is it a development of the reverse-engineering tool inherent in copyright law, cf the EU Software Directive, mirroring the data-mining exemption under the new copyright directive? This will be discussed in Chapter 6, but first, the following sub-chapters explore the Open Data Directive and Data Governance Act, which deals with access and portability of public (government) data and also addresses the issue of whether intellectual property-law-protected data can be accessed by business users of governmental data. These legal systems create rights to access data, while still acknowledging the rights of the platform or maker of the database. Second, Chapters 6 and 7 discuss the proposed Data Act and present the legal system for an access and transfer right (ATR).

4.3 SECTOR-SPECIFIC REGULATIONS TARGETING ACCESS TO DATA

Access to data is a disputed issue not only under 'general' competition law but also in the case of sector-specific regulations such as the Public Sector Information Directive,[67] the *eCall* Regulation,[68] in the field of transport[69] and financial services,[70] and in other legislative initiatives.[71]

67 Directive (EU) 2019/1024 of the European Parliament and of the Council of 20 June 2019, on open data and the reuse of public-sector information, OJ L172, 26 June 2019, 56–83 (The old PSI directive: Directive 2003/98/EC, known as the 'PSI Directive') entered into force on 31 December 2003. It was revised by Directive 2013/37/EU, which entered into force on 17 July 2013.

68 Regulation (EU) 2015/758 of the European Parliament and of the Council of 29 April 2015 concerning type-approval requirements for the deployment of the eCall in-vehicle system based on the 112 service and amending Directive 2007/46/EC.

69 OJ L207, 6 August 2010, 1–13.

70 To accelerate retail banking innovation and simplify payments, the European Commission is mandating standardized API access across the EU. The initiative is part of the European Commission's update of the Directive on Payment Services (PSD). The revision to the Directive on Payment Services (PSD2) requires banks to provide access to third parties. See Directive (EU) 2015/2366 of the European Parliament and of the Council of 25 November 2015 on payment services in the internal market, amending Directives 2002/65/EC, 2009/110/EC and 2013/36/EU and Regulation (EU) No 1093/2010, and repealing Directive 2007/64/EC (Text with EEA relevance). cf Commission, 'A Digital Single Market Strategy for Europe' COM (2015) 192 final. See also OJ L337, 23 December 2015, 35–127.

71 Several regulatory initiatives are discussed in this book. A legislative proposal for the European health data space has been introduced. https://health.ec.europa.eu/publications/proposal-regulation-european-health-data-space_en. However, for access data regimes, see also the REACH Regulation, Article 25 Regulation (EC) No 1907/2006 of the European Parliament and of the Council of 18 December 2006 concerning the Registration, Evaluation, Authorisation and

4.3.1 *Open Data Directive*

There seems to be a need for rules regarding fair access to data. As already mentioned, the Open Data Directive[72] stipulates routes for accessing government data.[73] The focus of the Open Data Directive is very specific: to create a level playing field when making public-sector information (PSI) available as an input to a commercial activity, that is, when the PSI is used as components in new products and services. Unfortunately, it is not encompassed under the Data Act and acts in its own universe. This should release the full economic potential of a new emerging area of the ICT sector.[74] If public-sector bodies (PSBs) offer information products or services exclusively, chances are that they will not be able to provide these services as innovatively and efficiently as a structure governed by competition.[75] This could have a negative effect on competition in the European market. Therefore, the Open Data Directive aims to overcome these barriers, which limit the reuse of PSI in EU Member States. The Open Data Directive thereby stipulates that public-sector data collectors must grant access to data (cf Article 3 of the Open Data Directive). The Open Data Directive tries to eliminate barriers, which could include attempts by PSBs to charge supracompetitive prices, unfair competition between the public and the private sectors, practical issues hindering reuse (such as the lack of information

Restriction of Chemicals (REACH), establishing a European Chemicals Agency, amending Directive 1999/45/EC and repealing Council Regulation (EEC) No 793/93 and Commission Regulation (EC) No 1488/94 as well as Council Directive 76/769/EEC and Commission Directives 91/155/EEC, 93/67/EEC, 93/105/EC and 2000/21/EC; OJ L41, 14 February 2003, 26–32; OJ L108, 25 April 2007, 1–14. See furthermore Article 16 of the new Digital Content and Digital Services Directive, making reference to GDPR, discussed in Z Efroni, 'Gaps and Opportunities: The Rudimentary Protection to 'Data-Paying Consumers' under New EU Consumer Protection Law' (2020 Weizenbaum Series 4). Weizenbaum Institute for the Networked Society – The German Internet Institute <https://doi.org/10.34669/wi.ws/4>. See also the new Electricity Directive of June 2019, which imposes the sharing of consumer data, including metering and consumption data as well as data required for customer switching, demand response, and other services. To stimulate competition and innovation among electricity suppliers, Article 23 (2) of the Directive provides that porting of data should be required. Finally, see the Clinical Trials Regulation 536/2014 on clinical trials on medicinal products for human use, and repealing Directive 2001/20/EC.

72 Directive (EU) 2019/1024 of the European Parliament and of the Council of 20 June 2019 on open data and the reuse of public-sector information, OJ L172, 26 June 2019, 56–83.

73 See also the INSPIRE directive regarding spatial data, Articles 5 and 8. For the various legal tools making up the INSPIRE initiative see <https://inspire.ec.europa.eu/inspire-directive/2>.

74 Commission, 'Public Sector Information: A Key Resource for Europe' Green Paper on Public Sector Information in the Information Society COM (1998) 585 final, 5.

75 Björn Lundqvist, 'Turning Government Data into Gold': The Interface between EU Competition Law and the Public Sector Information Directive – With Some Comments on the *Compass* Case in I I C' (2013) 44(1) International Review of Intellectual Property and Competition Law 79–95.

on available PSI), and the attitude of PSBs that are slow to realize the economic potential of PSI.[76]

Interestingly, the Open Data Directive seems to include nondiscriminatory exclusion rules, similar to the ideas put forward in the French *GDF*[77] and *EDF* competition-law cases.[78] Indeed, the Open Data Directive stipulates a prohibition preventing Governments and government authorities from abusing the power inherent in the data collected, by not giving access, without the need to identify dominance in reference to the authority or the database.

In several aspects, the Open Data Directive stipulates something akin to the compulsory licensing scheme for PSB-controlled databases holding reusable public data. From a Nordic law perspective, at least, the public authorities have historically been able to claim database rights (most likely sui generis protected database rights), and while admitting that the Open Data Directive creates an obligation to grant access to data, the database right is the platform for establishing license arrangements with reusers.[79] The fact that the PSBs are funded by tax money does not prevent public authorities from being subject to database protection.[80] It should be noted that the new Open Data Directive from 2019 has somewhat reversed this situation, stating that PSBs shall not exercise their potential database rights to prevent the reuse of documents or to restrict reuse beyond the limits set by the new Open Data Directive.

Indeed, the Open Data Directive could be considered to stipulate a compulsory license scheme, or, more accurately, a general real-time access and portability right for business users to public 'spin-off' data.[81] Such data is not the core activity of the

[76] Katleen Janssen and Jos Dumortier, 'Towards a European Framework for the Re-use of Public Sector Information: A Long and Winding Road' [2011] (2) International Journal of Law and Information Technology 195.

[77] French Competition Authority Decision 14-MC-02 of 9 September 2014. The case is discussed in the German and French Competition Authorities, 'Competition Law and Data' (joint paper 10 May 2016) 20 <www.autoritedelaconcurrence.fr/doc/reportcompetitionlawanddatafinal.pdf>.

[78] French Competition Authority Decision n°13-D-20 of 17.12.2013, confirmed on that point by the court of appeal on 21 May 2015.

[79] The previous PSI Directive stipulated in preamble 24 that '[t]his Directive is without prejudice to Directive 2001/29/EC of the European Parliament and of the Council of 22 May 2001 on the harmonisation of certain aspects of copyright and related rights in the information society (10) and Directive 96/9/EC of the European Parliament and of the Council of 11 March 1996 on the legal protection of databases (11).' It spells out the conditions under which public-sector bodies can exercise their intellectual property rights in the internal information market when allowing reuse of documents.

[80] Estelle Derclaye, *The Legal Protection of Databases: A Comparative Analysis* (Edward Elgar 2008) 72. Compare with Thomas Dreier and Bernt Hugenholtz (eds), *Database Directive in Concise European Copyright Law* (2nd ed, Kluwer Law International 2016) 405.

[81] The 'spin-off' exemption under sui generis data protection has been discussed at length. It seems that the doctrine has been rejected by the ECJ. See *BHB v Hill* (Case C-203/02) ECLI:EU:C:2004:695 paras 31–42; *Fixtures Marketing* (Case C-444/02) ECLI:EU:C:2004:697 paras 40–53; *Fixtures Marketing v Oy Veikkaus AB* (Case C-46/02) ECLI:EU:C:2004:694 paras

public authority but rather a by-product of their core activity. As noted elsewhere in this chapter, such access and portability rights could empower business users vis-à-vis system leaders and platforms because for many of these platforms, their investment is focused on their core activity, and not on creation of databases. Platform concentrate inter alia on acquisition, verification, or presentation of the databases.[82]

It should be pointed out that the Open Data Directive is applicable only for public data that is not restricted by intellectual property rights held by the third party or the public authority or business confidentiality limitations, and under the GDPR, personal data is off-limits. Indeed, the right to access public-sector information concerns only public-good data.[83] This has been viewed as a clear limitation of the Open Data Directive, however, and the Commission has therefore proposed a new Data Governance Act that encompasses public-sector data to make such data available for reuse in situations where such data is subject to rights of others.

4.3.2 *The Data Governance Act*

(i) Access to Data

The new Data Governance Act aims to foster the availability of public data for reuse by increasing trust in data intermediaries and strengthening data-sharing mechanisms across the EU.

Article 5 in the Data Governance Act stipulates that public-sector bodies that are judged competent under national law to grant or refuse access for the reuse of data that is covered by commercial confidentiality, statistical confidentiality, protection of intellectual property rights of third parties, or protection of personal data shall make the conditions for allowing reuse of such data publicly available.[84]

34–49; *Fixtures Marketing v Svenska Spel AB* (Case C-338/02) ECLI:EU:C:2004:696 paras 24–37.

82 Ibid.

83 The preamble 54 of the Open Data Directive states '[t]he intellectual property rights of third parties are not affected by this Directive. For the avoidance of doubt, the term 'intellectual property rights' refers to copyright and related rights only, including sui generis forms of protection. This Directive does not apply to documents covered by industrial property rights, such as patents and registered designs and trademarks. The Directive neither affects the existence or ownership of intellectual property rights of public sector bodies, nor does it limit the exercise of these rights in any way beyond the boundaries set by this Directive. The obligations imposed in accordance with this Directive should apply only insofar as they are compatible with international agreements on the protection of intellectual property rights, in particular the Berne Convention for the Protection of Literary and Artistic Works (Berne Convention), the Agreement on Trade-Related Aspects of Intellectual Property Rights (TRIPS Agreement) and the WIPO Copyright Treaty (WCT). Public sector bodies should, however, exercise their copyright in a way that facilitates re-use.'

84 The DGA does not create any obligation on public-sector bodies to allow reuse of data; nor would the Act release public-sector bodies from their confidentiality obligations. This chapter is without prejudice to Union and national law or international agreements to which the Union

The conditions for reuse shall be nondiscriminatory, proportionate, and objectively justified with regard to categories of data, purposes of reuse, and the nature of the data for which reuse is allowed. These conditions, set out by the authority, shall not be used to restrict competition.

Interestingly, Article 5 further states that public-sector bodies can impose an obligation on the reuser to anonymize or pseudonymize personal data or delete commercially confidential information, including trade secrets, before the data may be reused. Moreover, the public-sector body shall be able to verify any results of the reuser's processing of data and reserve the right to prohibit the use of results that contain information that jeopardizes the rights and interests of third parties. When requested data is considered confidential, in accordance with Union or national law on commercial confidentiality, the public-sector bodies shall ensure that the confidential information is not disclosed as a result of the reuse.

Generally, under the Data Governance Act, the reuse of data is allowed only in compliance with intellectual property rights and the GDPR; if efforts by the public-sector body to comply – for example through anonymization of personal data – are in vain, the reuse of data cannot be granted. However, the public-sector body shall support reusers in seeking consent from the data subjects and/or permission from the legal entities whose rights and interests may be affected by such reuse, where it is feasible and does not incur disproportionate cost for the public sector. However, there is one exemption: The right of a database maker as provided for in Article 7(1) of the Database Directive (96/9/EC) shall not be exercised by public-sector bodies to prevent the reuse of data or to restrict reuse beyond the limits set by the regulation.

(ii) Data-Sharing Service

It should further be noted that the Data Governance Act also proposes rules for a new form of intermediates and platforms, in which infrastructure is created for combining, pooling, providing notification for, and using users' data. According to the Data Governance Act, business users of platforms that would like to combine their data would be able to pool their data, in situations where they can access and port the data held by gatekeepers.

The new Data Governance Act aims to foster the availability of public data for reuse by increasing trust in data intermediaries and by strengthening data-sharing mechanisms across the EU. The Data Governance Act therefore sets out to provide rules and a structure to set up data-sharing services, or data pools, including means for notifying relevant authorities about such a sharing service. The provider

or Member States are parties on the protection of categories of data provided in paragraph 1. This chapter is without prejudice to Union and national law on access to documents and to obligations of public-sector bodies under Union and national law to allow the reuse of data.

of a data-sharing service shall report service to relevant national authorities when the set-up corresponds to the following (cf Article 9):

(a) intermediation services between data holders, which are legal persons and potential data users, including making available the technical or other means to enable such services; those services may include bilateral or multilateral exchanges of data or the creation of platforms or databases, enabling the exchange or joint exploitation of data, as well as the establishment of a specific infrastructure for the interconnection of data holders and data users;
(b) intermediation services between data subjects that seek to make their personal data available and potential data users, including making available the technical or other means to enable such services, in the exercise of the rights provided in Regulation (EU) 2016/679;

vis-à-vis services of data cooperatives, that is to say, services supporting data subjects or one-person companies or micro-, small-, and medium-sized enterprises, who are members of the cooperative or who confer the power to the cooperative to negotiate terms and conditions for data processing before they consent, in making informed choices before consenting to data processing, and allowing for mechanisms to exchange views on data-processing purposes and conditions that would best represent the interests of data subjects or legal persons.

The Data Governance Act also sets out rules for collaboration. These rules originate from unfair competition legislations and practical IT law sources. Data-sharing services shall be subject to the following conditions:

(1) the provider may not use the data for which it provides services for other purposes than to put them at the disposal of data users and data-sharing services shall be placed in a separate legal entity;
(2) the metadata collected from the provision of the data-sharing service may be used only for the development of that service;
(3) the provider shall ensure that the procedure for access to its service is fair, transparent, and nondiscriminatory for both data holders and data users, including as regards prices;
(4) the provider shall facilitate the exchange of the data in the format in which it receives it from the data holder and shall convert the data into specific formats only to enhance interoperability within and across sectors or if requested by the data user or where mandated by Union law or to ensure harmonization with international or European data standards;
(5) the provider shall have procedures in place to prevent fraudulent or abusive practices in relation to access to data from parties seeking access through their services;

(6) the provider shall ensure a reasonable continuity of provision of its services and, in the case of services that ensure storage of data, shall have sufficient guarantees in place that allow data holders and data users to obtain access to their data in case of insolvency;
(7) the provider shall put in place adequate technical, legal, and organizational measures in order to prevent transfer or access to nonpersonal data that is unlawful under Union law;
(8) the provider shall take measures to ensure a high level of security for the storage and transmission of nonpersonal data;
(9) the provider shall have procedures in place to ensure compliance with the Union and national rules on competition.

According to the Data Governance Act, each Member State shall designate in its territory one or more authorities competent to carry out the tasks related to the notification framework. The designated competent authorities, data-protection authorities, national competition authorities, authorities in charge of cybersecurity, and other relevant sectorial authorities shall exchange the information necessary for the exercise of their tasks in relation to data-sharing providers. The competent authority shall monitor and supervise compliance with rules, including having the authority to render decisions. In this regard, the competent authorities shall be able, where appropriate:

(a) to impose dissuasive financial penalties which may include periodic penalties with retroactive effect;
(b) to require cessation or postponement of the provision of the data-sharing service.

In addition to these rules, the Data Governance Act also states that a special organ should be set up to provide best-practice guidelines – a formal expert group (the 'European Data Innovation Board') that will 'facilitate the emergence of best practices by Member States'.

Business users that collect data may thus create a data-sharing facility and use a data-sharing service. They can thereby create their own platform, even to the level of being a gatekeeper, under the Digital Markets Act. Interestingly, the rules above somewhat mirror the rules for patent pools, or what academia has put forward as 'data pools'. These forms of collaboration are normally addressed under competition law and, interestingly, the rules set out above cater to regulation of the relationship between firms, including competitors. Indeed, the regulation carves out a safe harbor for establishing intermediates for providing data-sharing services. Still, the rules are somewhat fuzzy. It is not certain that all comers are welcome and that the platform created to share data can deny access. What if the platform becomes a gatekeeper that provides a core platform service according to the Digital Markets Act, and access then needs to be granted to business users? Is the service of data sharing not a core platform service under the Regulation? Indeed, it seems that an intermediate that establishes a data-sharing service through which business users can store their business user's data must take several access regimes into consideration, including competition law.

Interestingly, under competition law, one could envision safe harbor – provisions for data pools that require dominant data pools to be open to all comers.

(iii) Conclusion

The Data Governance Act attempts to address the difficult issue of enabling access to data to create a vibrant data industry, by making public-sector data available for reuse, in situations where such data is subject to rights under an intellectual property legal system, rules, and covenants in reference to confidentiality or under the GDPR. The Act still does not provide any overriding rules under which access rights to data should trump rights held by others. Nonetheless, it puts in place a methodology, obligations, and pressure on the public-sector bodies to resolve rights issues before granting access to data for reuse. Reluctance on the part of PSBs reflects the constitutional challenges that are present for the EU in its attempt to create an overriding access and transfer right to intellectual property right-protected data. Interestingly, in the Digital Markets Act, the Commission could have elaborated on these issues and indicated a way to address data covered by rights of others.

The Data Governance Act also provides the outlines to create new forms of intermediates – the providers of data-sharing facilities. These entities could grow in importance and de facto become powerful gatekeepers. The question is whether firms defined and identified as gatekeepers under the Digital Markets Act should also be able to pool and access data under such an intermediate. Indeed, these facilities may cater more to large platforms with gatekeeping status that use each other's services than to small business users.

4.3.3 *The Digital Service Act and Directive on Payment Services II*

A similar principle for accessing data can be found in the EU Regulation on providing multimodal travel information services.[85] This regulation requires both private and public transport service providers to grant access to travel data at any time, in a machine-readable format, through a National Access Point

[85] Commission Delegated Regulation (EU) 2017/1926 of 31 May 2017, supplementing Directive 2010/40/EU of the European Parliament and of the Council with regard to the provision of EU-wide multimodal travel information services C/2017/3574 OJ L272, 21 October 2017, 1–13. See also Directive 2010/40/EU of the European Parliament and of the Council of 7 July 2010, on the framework for the deployment of Intelligent Transport Systems in the field of road transport and for interfaces with other modes of transport, OJ L207, 6 August 2010, 1–13.

(NAP);[86] these NAPs will gather travel and traffic data from all types of transport from both private and public entities within and, eventually, beyond the borders of EU Member States. The type of static travel data to be made available through NAPs is detailed in Annex I of the regulation. The regulation stipulates that firms have a right to access transport data at any time.[87]

In reference to cars and vehicles, a number of legislative efforts and private initiatives for access to data have been established. Independent repair shops active in Europe have a right to access repair and maintenance information (RMI) under a FRAND-like mechanism.[88] Repair and maintenance information covers all information required for diagnosis, servicing, inspection, periodic monitoring, repair, reprogramming, or reinitializing of the vehicle, and which manufacturers provide to their authorized dealers and repairers, including all subsequent amendments and supplements to such information. This includes all information required for installing parts or equipment in vehicles.

There is a problem, however, in accessing in-vehicle data in cars, because car manufacturers want to create in-vehicle data architectures that allow them to control access to in-vehicle data.[89] Modern vehicles generate around 25 gigabytes of data every hour and autonomous cars will generate terabytes of data that can be used for innovative, mobility-related services, and repair and maintenance services.[90]

[86] See Parliament and Council Regulation (EU) 2017/1926 of 31 May 2017, supplementing Directive 2010/40/EU with regard to the provision of EU-wide multimodal travel information services [2017] OJ L272/1.

[87] However, access to payment data services (i.e., APIs), as granted by the Finnish and French Mobility Acts, is not granted under this EU regulation. Therefore, a new EU regulation/directive is required to render open/accessible these data to MaaS platform providers. From a user's perspective, the benefits of that would be easy access to various means of transport around EU and the chance to have roaming in mobility (similar to the telecommunication sector), thus cutting mobility costs. For instance, once a user has an MaaS app or acquires an MaaS mobility package in Helsinki and then goes on holiday in Vienna, the Whim app, owned by MaaS Global in Finland, offers the possibility not only to have access and buy Vienna's mobility access but also to use the same mobility package acquired in Helsinki. For discussion regarding MaaS, see Björn Lundqvist and Erion Murati, 'Collaborative Platforms and Data Pools for Smart Urban Societies and Mobility as a Service (MaaS) from a Competition Law Perspective' (2020) Faculty of Law, Stockholm University Research Paper No 75 <https://ssrn.com/abstract=3564135> or <http://dx.doi.org/10.2139/ssrn.3564135>.

[88] See Regulation (EU) 2018/858 of the European Parliament and of the Council of 30 May 2018, on the approval and market surveillance of motor vehicles and their trailers, and of systems, components and separate technical units intended for such vehicles, amending Regulations (EC) No 715/2007 and (EC) No 595/2009 and repealing Directive 2007/46/EC, Official Journal of the European Union, L151/1, 14 June 2018. Discussed in Wolfgang Kerber and Dabile Gill, 'Access to Data in Connected Cars and the Recent Reform of the Motor Vehicle Type Approval Regulation' (2019) 10(2) JIPITEC 244.

[89] Wolfgang Kerber, 'Data Governance in Connected Cars: The Problem of Access to In-Vehicle Data' (14 November 2018) JIPITEC Journal of Intellectual Property, Information Technology and Electronic Commerce Law Forthcoming <https://ssrn.com/abstract=3285240>.

[90] A European strategy for data COM (2020) 66 final.

Innovation in this area requires that car data is shared, in a secure and well-framed way and in line with competition rules, among many different economic players. The access to in-vehicle data has been regulated since 2007 in the EU vehicle approval legislation[91] to ensure that independent repairers have fair access to certain car data. This legislation is now being updated to consider the increasing use of connectivity (3G-4G, so-called remote diagnostics) to ensure that the rights and interests of the car owners generating the data are respected and enforce compliance with data-protection rules.[92] The *eCall* Regulation[93] should be mentioned here as well. According to Recital 16,

> [I]n order to ensure open choice for customers and fair competition, as well as encourage innovation and boost the competitiveness of the Union's information technology industry on the global market, the eCall in-vehicle systems should be based on an interoperable, standardized, secure and open-access platform for possible future in-vehicle applications or services. As this requires technical and legal back-up, the Commission should assess without delay, on the basis of consultations with all stakeholders involved, including vehicle manufacturers and independent operators, all options for promoting and ensuring such an open-access platform and, if appropriate, put forward a legislative initiative to that effect. Furthermore, the 112-based eCall in-vehicle system should be accessible for a reasonable fee not exceeding a nominal amount and without discrimination to all independent operators for repair and maintenance purposes in accordance with ... [author's emphasis].[94]

The *eCall* Directive seems to lay the groundwork for a future regulation where competitors can access data originating from cars used by individuals, in that the device should be (connected to) a standardized, secure, and open-access platform. Interestingly, the idea seems to be that by creating a standard, competitors will not (only) be able to produce *eCall* devices under FRAND licenses but can actually access *eCall* devices in cars with their own applications to collect data. In this way, automobile manufacturers would not have exclusive rights to the personal data created in the car (the device), and this could open the platform in the car, for

91 Regulation (EC) 715/2007.

92 A European strategy for data COM (2020) 66 final.

93 Regulation (EU) 2015/758 of the European Parliament and of the Council of 29 April 2015 concerning type-approval requirements for the deployment of the eCall in-vehicle system based on the 112 service and amending Directive 2007/46/EC.

94 Ibid. See also Arts 6 and 7 Regulation (EC) No 715/2007 of the European Parliament and of the Council of 20 June 2007 on type approval of motor vehicles with respect to emissions from light passenger and commercial vehicles (Euro 5 and 6) and on access to vehicle repair and maintenance information, [2007] OJ L171/1, as well as Article 13 Regulation (EC) No 692/2008 of the European Parliament and of the Council of 18 July 2008 implementing and amending Regulation No 715/2007, [2008] OJ L199/1.

example, to leasing firms, insurance companies, and independent service providers to access the device for collecting data.[95]

On the other hand of the spectrum, the Digital Service Act provides rules for data access by the government of data collected by very large platforms. Indeed, accessing data from platforms may be necessary for government and research. According to Paddy Leerssen, the issue of research access is becoming ever more urgent. Over the past years, dominant platforms such as Facebook have repeatedly interfered with independent research projects, prompting calls for reform. The matter went mainstream in October 2020, when – only weeks before the US elections – Facebook tried to shut down an independent audit by NYU of their political advertising. Facebook also suspended the researchers' Facebook accounts and stripped them of access to the Ad Library API and Crowdtangle research tools. Closer to home, Facebook also retaliated against data collection by the Berlin-based nongovernmental organization AlgorithmWatch, sending those involved 'thinly veiled threats' of legal action on the grounds that independent data collection violated the platform's terms of service. Platforms are becoming gatekeepers not only of online content and commerce but also of research into these phenomena.[96]

The Digital Service Act states in preamble 63 that very large online platforms should ensure public access to repositories of advertisements displayed on their online interfaces, to facilitate supervision and research into emerging risks brought about by the distribution of advertising online, for example, in relation to illegal advertisements or manipulative techniques and disinformation with a real and foreseeable negative impact on public health, public security, civil discourse, political participation, or equality. Repositories should include the contents of advertisements and related data on the advertiser and delivery of the advertisement, in particular where targeted advertising is concerned.

Moreover, in order to appropriately supervise the compliance of very large online platforms with the obligations in Article 26 regarding systemic risk laid down by Member States or the Commission, these entities may require access to or reporting of specific data. Such requirements may include, for example, the data necessary to assess the risks and possible harms brought about by a platform's systems; data on the accuracy, functioning, and testing of algorithmic systems for content moderation, recommender systems, or advertising systems, or data on processes and outputs of

[95] An example of this development could be the announcement on 27 September 2016 by AUDI AG, BMW Group, Daimler AG, Ericsson, Huawei, Intel, Nokia, and Qualcomm Incorporated of the formation of the '5G Automotive Association'. The association will develop, test and promote communications solutions, support standardization, and accelerate commercial availability and global market penetration. The goal is to address society's connected mobility and road safety needs with applications such as connected automated driving, ubiquitous access to services, and integration into smart cities and intelligent transportation <www.ericsson.com/news/160927-telecommunications-and-automotive-players_244039854_c>.

[96] Paddy Leerssen, 'Platform Research Access in Article 31 of the Digital Services Act Sword without a Shield?' 7 September 2021 <https://verfassungsblog.de/power-dsa-dma-14/>.

content moderation or of internal complaint-handling systems within the meaning of the Digital Services Act (DSA) (cf Article 26). According to the DSA, investigations by researchers on the evolution and severity of online systemic risks are particularly important for bridging information asymmetries and establishing resilient risk mitigation systems.

Thus, the DSA provides a framework for providing government and vetted researchers access to data from very large online platforms. All the requirements for access to data under that framework should be proportionate and appropriately protect the rights and legitimate interests, including trade secrets and other confidential information, of the platform and any other parties concerned, including service recipients.

The obligation that advertisement repositories are made available through application programming interfaces (APIs) is stipulated in Article 30. Under the Article 31 framework, regulators can order access for their own monitoring and enforcement purposes (paragraph 1) or for use by third-party researchers (Paragraph 2).

In the Commission proposal, data access was limited to academic ('vetted') researchers, subject to various conditions such as university affiliation, independence from commercial interests, and compliance with confidentiality and security requirements (Paragraph 4). It should be underlined that the Council now wants to go further and create an independent right of access for researchers. Also, the European Parliament wants to broaden the group that may access data to also include independent researchers working for or affiliated with nonprofit organizations. It seems that the European Parliament proposal was successful in the political agreement entered on 23 April 2022. An important limitation, which seems to have been left untouched by the Council and the Parliament, is that researchers may only use the data for the purpose of research into 'systemic risks' as defined in Article 26 DSA.[97]

Platforms may object to data access requests in cases where they do not have the data or where access would create 'significant vulnerabilities' to security or prevent 'protection of confidential information, in particular trade secrets'. Possibly, the same limitations apply to the obligation stipulated in Article 30 DSA. Indeed, as discussed below in the section on the DMA, platforms can claim that the datasets they have collected are trade secrets as defined under the EU Directive, or might be off-limits under the GDPR, in the case of personal data. Moreover, for data generated on their platforms, the gatekeepers would most likely acquire some intellectual property rights when storing the data in databases or in public centralized blockchains, such as *sui generis* database protection – which may also limit or even prevent access and porting of whole datasets. At the very least, this may serve as a ground for refusing access to repositories under Article 30 DSA.

[97] Ibid.

Finally, the updated Directive on Payment Services stipulates a right for third parties to access, under certain circumstances, the banking data of consumers. Consumers should be able to agree that third parties provide services, while accessing consumer bank accounts and internet bank sites. Under PSD2, banks must allow only third-party providers (TPPs) access to customers' payment account data, provided that the TPPs have the 'explicit consent' of the customer (Articles 67 and 94, PSD2). The PSD2 may, as a way to promote competition, require banks to provide standardized API access to third parties under the auspices of the European Banking Authority (EBA).[98] This may enable third parties to tailor their banking service toward customers, while using data collected by a competitor. Thus, the PSD2 implements data portability requirements (but not full interoperability) for consumer data between certain financial institutions. However, in a recent report, the Portuguese Competition Authority highlighted poor performance of APIs as one factor limiting the effectiveness of portability under PSD2 in promoting competition.[99] As discussed in Section 2.6 above, general technical standards for granting access to data need to be developed, and holding up such a development may constitute a competition-law violation.

These four legal systems giving access to data are examples of rules that are, or are close to, requiring public entities and firms to give access to data or devices/platforms to enable data harvesting. It is possibly an indication of an interesting underlying current: that legislators are attempting to boost competition and markets by granting access to data, while circumventing general competition law. The idea is to enhance competition without using any test of antitrust harm, by opening up devices for everyone and everything to collect data. The legal systems do not differentiate between sharing with firms that already possess large amounts of data or are hoarding data on several markets, and sharing with firms that do not possess or hoard much data. Whether such a policy is pro-competitive may be disputed. Not only will new entrants be able to obtain data; incumbent platforms and system leaders will also be granted access to these devices or, in reference to government data, the PSI. Indeed, the greatest beneficiary of these sector-specific access rules is probably Google, which would gain access to huge data streams for free.[100]

98 See Directive (EU) 2015/2366 of the European Parliament and of the Council of 25 November 2015 on payment services in the internal market, amending Directives 2002/65/EC, 2009/110/EC and 2013/36/EU and Regulation (EU) No 1093/2010, and repealing Directive 2007/64/EC (Text with EEA relevance). cf Commission (2015). See also Commission Delegated Regulation (EU) 2018/389 of 27 November 2017 supplementing Directive (EU) 2015/2366 of the European Parliament and of the Council with regard to regulatory technical standards for strong customer authentication and common and secure open standards of communication (Text with EEA relevance.)

99 OECD, 'Data Portability, Interoperability and Digital Platform Competition' (2021) OECD Competition Committee Discussion Paper, 11 et seq. <http://oe.cd/dpic>.

100 For a similar argument in reference to the banking industry, see Jorge Padilla and Miguel de la Mano, Big Tech Banking (4 December 2018). <https://ssrn.com/abstract=3294723> or <http://dx.doi.org/10.2139/ssrn.3294723>.

Moreover, this also begs the question, to be put to the legislator: Why are there no similar access rules for platforms? Why are platform providers as such not subject to the rules when large industries such as the car industry and the financial sector are required to grant access? Indeed, these sector-specific regulations have allowed large platforms to become dominant and show that the EU policy in reference to the data-driven industry is at war with itself.

4.4 DATA PROTECTION: GDPR

The GDPR[101] protects the individual's right to personal autonomy and privacy of natural persons. It is not a property rights regime, yet there are parts of the GDPR that reflect economic rights or that can at least have economic implications.[102] Furthermore, the GDPR has significant economic consequences. It molds the way firms that are active in Europe can conduct their businesses.

The GDPR could be viewed in several aspects as a sector-specific regulation. It acts as a regulation for the business use of personal data in Europe, stipulating the boundaries for what should be considered competition or business within accepted terms and conditions for data protection and privacy. Indeed, the regulation defines 'competition on the merits' when specifically weighing business and entrepreneurial freedom vis-à-vis privacy and data protection.[103] An important aspect of this is the right to data portability, under Article 20 of the GDPR. Article 20 allows individuals to move privacy-related data in a structured, commonly used, and machine-readable format to another service provider/data controller (e.g., personal data from a social media account).

The GDPR stipulates a system based on an individualistic approach; in theory, each data-processing event must be carried out for a specific, legitimate purpose.[104]

[101] Regulation (EU) 2016/679 of the European Parliament and of the Council of 27 April 2016, on the protection of natural persons with regard to the processing of personal data and on the free movement of such data, and repealing Directive 95/46/EC (General Data Protection Regulation) OJ L119, 4 May 2016, 1–88.

[102] Drexl discusses very convincingly that GDPR is not a property regime. See Josef Drexl in 'Data Access and Control in the Era of Connected Devices', in *Study on behalf of the European Consumer Association BEUC, Brussels* (2018) 62 et seq.

[103] The German Competition Authority (*Bundeskartellamt*) investigated Facebook for violating German Competition Law by violating German data-protection provisions. According to the Bundeskartellamt's preliminary assessment, Facebook's terms of service are at minimum inappropriate and violate data-protection provisions to the disadvantage of its users when Facebook can unrestrictedly collect every kind of user data from third sources, attribute it to the user's Facebook account, and use this data for numerous data-processing activities. In addition, in view of the company's dominant position, it cannot be assumed that users effectively consent to this form of data collection and processing. Therefore, the Bundeskartellamt preliminary conclusion is that Facebook's collection and use of data from third-party sources is abusive. <www.bundeskartellamt.de/SharedDocs/Meldung/EN/Pressemitteilungen/2017/19_12_2017_Facebook.html> accessed 30 May 2018.

[104] See Articles 4 and 6 GDPR.

The modus operandi of the GDPR is very case-by-case or process-by-process focused. The regulation mentions several legitimate purposes for processing data (cf Article 6), with the main relevant and legitimate purpose for platforms being consent gained from the individual(s) involved – in other words, a data controller has received consent to perform the process(es) in question.[105] This system could be very tedious and burdensome; holders of large volumes of data would need to be in constant contact with their users to obtain consent for each and every process or procedure, and hence manage large, even enormous consent systems.[106] Indeed, the sensitivity of the data and the database, or the scale of the data being processed or monitored, can trigger the requirement to have a large compliance system that includes a data-protection officer.[107]

Given the above, it could be presumed that the burden of GDPR increases in proportion to the size of the business and data managed. However, it seems that, de

[105] According to Article 6(1) processing shall be lawful only if and to the extent that at least one of the following applies:

a) the data subject has given consent to the processing of his or her personal data for one or more specific purposes;
b) processing is necessary for the performance of a contract to which the data subject is party or in order to take steps at the request of the data subject prior to entering into a contract;
c) processing is necessary for compliance with a legal obligation to which the controller is subject;
d) processing is necessary in order to protect the vital interests of the data subject or of another natural person;
e) processing is necessary for the performance of a task carried out in the public interest or in the exercise of official authority vested in the controller;
f) processing is necessary for the purposes of the legitimate interests pursued by the controller or by a third party, except where such interests are overridden by the interests or fundamental rights and freedoms of the data subject which require protection of personal data, in particular where the data subject is a child.

[106] Samson Yoseph Esayas states '[f]irst, it can be argued that, in most cases, the purpose limitation principle will not allow data aggregation across different processing activities based on distinct purposes. It goes without saying that aggregation constitutes processing under the EU rules and requires an independent legitimate basis when conducted on processing operations based on distinct purposes. This means that, if an entity aggregates data across different processing activities based on separate purposes, without having a legitimate basis, it will constitute a breach of the rules. However, this is complicated by the reliance of many entities on consent as a basis for processing data, including the aggregation practices. Once the user consents to such aggregation practices, the line between the different individual processing activities and data in each box starts to disappear, complicating the application of the data privacy rules to a specific box.' Samson Yoseph Esayas, 'Data Privacy and Competition Law in the Age of Big Data' (PhD thesis, October 2019) 82 et seq.

[107] See Article 37 GDPR. It should be stated, however, that the GDPR has more requirements for large tech firms processing large volumes of data, though these lack something akin to the competition-law doctrine of special responsibilities for dominant data holders. Cf Esayas (n 106).

facto, the system works the other way around. Large players using broad consent covenants and data-driven business models over a multitude of services and markets, such as Google with Google search, Google Maps, and the other Google services within the Google ecosystem, are better equipped to manage GDPR requirements than smaller players.[108] Large, well-known platforms easily obtain broad and detailed consent from individuals. They gain consent to use the data over various services, yet often use the data outside the consent given. Faced with platforms and the share of the business that these platforms control, data-protection authorities may find it difficult to identify incidents in which data is processed without the necessary consent.

The size of platform databases also makes it possible to analytically extract highly personal information, while broad consents mean that the individual data points utilized for the analytical process and the analytical process itself do not violate the GDPR.[109] Indeed, the whole reveals more – sometimes a great deal more – than the sum of its parts.[110] For smaller players, the data obtained may not be very beneficial; the small size of the datasets makes the conclusions less profitable. The GDPR, therefore, becomes much more burdensome when compared to the benefits that might be obtained. The data processing can also be traced more easily and connected to individual consents, and breaches can be more easily detected. Moreover, for small players to scale their data volumes, they might need to share data in data pools or purchase data, which may very well be considered outside the scope of consent given by individuals.[111] The oddity of analyzing the GDPR seems to be that the regulation de facto places a heavier burden on smaller players but shelters large platform providers.[112] Finally, smaller firms do not seem to benefit from the portability right included in Article 20 GDPR. Indeed, few individuals exercise this right,

[108] Ibid., 77 et seq. See also Michal Gal and Oshrit Aviv, 'The Competitive Effects of the GDPR' (2020) Journal of Competition Law and Economics 22 et seq., 30 et seq. Also, to some extent, Michal Gal and Daniel L. Rubinfeld, 'Data Standardization' (2019) 94 NYU Law Review; NYU Law and Economics Research Paper No 19-17 forthcoming <https://ssrn.com/abstract=3326377> or <http://dx.doi.org/10.2139/ssrn.3326377>.

[109] It should be noted that Article 7(4) GDPR stipulates rules for when consent is considered freely given, and the conduct of large platforms may violate these rules and principles. Nevertheless, few if any cases vis-à-vis the larger players have been initiated by the EU data-protection authorities, so no clear answer is available as to whether or not such business conduct with regard to personal data fulfils the rules or the underlying principles.

[110] *US v Maynard* Court of Appeals, Dist. of Columbia Circuit 615 (2010) 558.

[111] The GDPR thus creates the incentive for firms to merge or organically grow horizontally and vertically so that they can include more data streams in-house. See Gal and Aviv (n 108) 21.

[112] This is in stark contrast to legal developments in the United States, where following the 2012 decision of the US Supreme Court in *United States v Jones*, concepts such as the *mosaic theory* and *quantitative privacy* began attracting considerable attention; these theories advocate regulation and prohibition of the whole, rather than individual data points. The US system seems better than its EU equivalent when it comes to protecting individuals' privacy against large data collectors.

and the information transferred may also be difficult to use. The data is not raw and cannot be the basis for more sophisticated analysis.[113]

Large players may also use the GDPR to refuse access to data under competition law and any sector-specific regulation that mandates data access. Owing to the great uncertainty about what is actually restricted by the GDPR and the de facto difference between data-protection authorities' GDPR application and the regulation's theoretical reach, large technology firms use GDPR offensively and limit their data-sharing activities far beyond the apparent obligations of the GDPR.[114] In fact, empirical evidence demonstrates that when the GDPR was introduced, data-driven markets suffered from increased concentration.[115] The data-protection rules, and the matter of whether they should be used as a benchmark for determining competition-law violations[116] and whether they should be considered akin to intellectual property rights that could shield dominance and anticompetitive behavior, and the notion that competition law can trump other regulations are issues to be resolved by twenty-first-century researchers and practitioners.[117]

When reusers or data brokers are interviewed and asked whether they encounter obstacles when trying to access data from large platforms, the brokers cite data-protection rules as the grand 'showstopper'. The issue for these firms is thus to investigate whether competition law can be used to override data-protection rules. Can competition law trump data-protection rules? When one considers EU

[113] See, for early works arguing that the GDPR creates anticompetitive effects, Damien Geradin and Dimitrios Katsifis, 'An EU Competition Law Analysis of Online Display Advertising in the Programmatic Age' (2019) 15 European Competition Journal 55 <www.tandfonline.com/doi/full/10.1080/17441056.2019.1574440>; Damien Geradin and Dimitrios Katsifis, 'Trust Me, I'm Fair: Analysing Google's Latest Practices in Ad Tech from the Perspective of EU Competition Law' European Competition Journal forthcoming <https://doi.org/10.1080/17441056.2019.1706413>.

[114] See Damien Geradin, Dimitrios Katsifis, and Theano Karanikioti, 'GDPR Myopia: How a Well-Intended Regulation Ended up Favouring Google in Ad Tech' (2020) TILEC Discussion Paper No 2020-012 <https://ssrn.com/abstract=3598130> or <http://dx.doi.org/10.2139/ssrn.3598130>. See furthermore their research on third-party cookies in Damien Geradin and Dimitrios Katsifis, 'Online Platforms and Digital Advertising Market Study: Observations on CMA's Interim Report' (13 February 2020) <https://ssrn.com/abstract=3537864> or <http://dx.doi.org/10.2139/ssrn.3537864>. See also Gal and Aviv (n 108) 22 et seq.

[115] Christian Peukert, Stefan Bechtold, Michail Batikas, and Tobias Kretschmer, 'European Privacy Law and Global Markets for Data' (6 March 2020) <https://ssrn.com/abstract=3560392>.

[116] Bundeskartellamt, 'Bundeskartellamt initiates proceeding against Facebook on suspicion of having abused its market power by infringing data protection rules' (Press release 2 March 2016) <www.bundeskartellamt.de/SharedDocs/Meldung/EN/Pressemitteilungen/2016/02_03_2016_Facebook.html>.

[117] Björn Lundqvist, 'Big Data, Open Data, Privacy Regulations, Intellectual Property and Competition Law in an Internet-of-Things World: The Issue of Accessing Data' in Mor Bakhoum, Beatriz Conde Gallego, Mark-Oliver Mackenrodt, and Gintare Surblytė-Namavičienė (eds), 'Personal Data in Competition, Consumer Protection and Intellectual Property Law' (MPI Studies on Intellectual Property and Competition Law, vol 28, Springer 2018) 30 https://ssrn.com/abstract=2891484.

Commission case law, it seems this would be difficult. In *Asnef-Equifax* the CJEU stated '…any possible issues relating to the sensitivity of personal data are not, as such, a matter for competition law, they may be resolved on the basis of the relevant provisions governing data protection.'[118] Moreover, in the *Facebook/Whatsapp*[119] merger case, the Commission states, '[a]ny privacy related concerns flowing from the increased concentration of data within the control of Facebook as a result of the Transaction do not fall within the scope of the EU competition law rules but within the scope of the EU data protection rules.' It is not yet clear whether the relevant competition authorities are thereby implying that Article 6(1) c) GDPR is also not applicable. Finally, the argument put forward against using competition law to trump data-protection rules is that reduction in privacy equals reduction in quality – and that is not the same thing as using competition law to trump an intellectual property right. 'Quality' may be an objective of competition law itself, while upholding property rights is less so.

In 2014, the European Data Protection Supervisor indicated a shift in policy and a 'more holistic approach to enforcement', in which a more systematic dialogue is maintained between competition-, consumer- and data-protection authorities. Therefore, the interface between data-protection rules and competition law may become more intense. Cases are coming out of the EU Commission and Member States' legal systems in which privacy is considered a competition parameter. Moreover, access to data has been obtained, and individuals have been granted the possibility to refuse transfer of data to a competitor, for example, in the French *GDF Suez* case.

4.5 NOT ADDRESSING THE ISSUE OF ACCESSING AND TRANSFERRING DATA

In light of the above, it seems clear that the Commission was aiming to implement several sector-specific regulations for the digital economy paradigm and some more general regulations, with a view to creating a level playing field. The underlying idea was to facilitate matters for the business users and users of platforms, help small- and medium-sized enterprises (SMEs) benefit from the digital economy, and create competition. However, beginning with the lenient legal system enacted in the P2B and Data Free Flow regulations, the question is whether the Commission can truly fulfill its aim with the Data Act, Digital Markets Act, and other sector-specific regulations. The regulations stipulate a number of game changers and should be viewed as a comprehensive legal system for the platform or even the data-driven industry of today. Depending on one's interpretation of platform

[118] C-238/05 Asnef-Equifax ECLI:EU:C:2006:734 para 63.

[119] *Facebook/Whatsapp* (Case COMP/M.7217) dated 03 October 2014, para 164.

services' operating systems[120] and cloud services, the Digital Markets Act is focused on the digital economy as it is today, thus excluding the future IoT paradigm, while the Data Act is possibly premature since it is too cautious in reference how to regulate and structure the equilibrium of power between platforms and data holders on the one hand and users on the other hand in an IoT setting.

The Digital Markets Act does indeed open avenues for a new, interoperable Internet, where leveraging (including self-preferencing) and other forms of abuse are restricted. However, the DMA became after the trialogue very complicated. In its indeed, now an intricate legal tool for the Commission and the complexity of the ex ante rules may lead to lengthy litigation, something which the DMA was supposed to be the antidote to in the first place. Moreover, in reference to creating a level playing field in relation to access and use of data, there are possibly some hidden limitations to genuine interoperable use of services and flow of data from the gatekeepers providing so-called core platform services to their business users.[121]

As discussed above, it should be clear that when Article 6 paragraphs (2), (9), and (10) in the regulation are read in combination, they stipulate an obligation for gatekeepers to give access and transfer data to their business users – to a level that could be regarded as an access and portability right for business users vis-à-vis gatekeepers (an ATR) and possibly overriding rights held by the gatekeepers. This is a right for which business users could presumably make a claim in court to override the rights held by the gatekeeper; it stipulates that gatekeepers are not allowed to use the data generated on the platforms by the business users or their end users, in competition with the business users, while the obligation in Article 6 (10) reflects that the business users have some sort of right to gain access and reuse the data generated by their action on the platforms. Indeed, this is a right to receive a steady stream of data (also inferred data) from the platforms – a stream that can also be transferred to third parties.

This could be a game changer. The combination of Article 6 paragraphs (2), (9), and (10) creates a compulsory access regime, stopping just short of a property right, to the data generated on the platform by the business user and its end users. In comparison to Articles 3, 4, and 5 of the proposed Data Act, the scope of the data is much more generous, since the access right for the users under the Data Act only reflects the raw data generated by the same. Data that is not publicly available shall according to Article 6(2) include any aggregated and nonaggregated data generated by business users that can be inferred from, or collected through, the commercial activities of business users or their customers, including click, search, view, and

[120] According to Article 2 para 10, 'Operating system' refers to system software that controls the basic functions of the hardware or software and enables software applications to run in this system.

[121] For definitions of a core platform service and a gatekeeper, and how obligations on gatekeepers are triggered, see the proposal for the Digital Markets Act <https://eur-lex.europa.eu/legal-content/EN/TXT/PDF/?uri=CELEX:52020PC0842&from=en>.

voice data, on the relevant core platform service or on services offered together with or in support of the relevant core platform service of the gatekeeper.

However, the issue is how and whether the gatekeepers can and will retaliate. Can they legally close the gateways for business users to access and port data? Can they use the intellectual property legal system or the GDPR so that in the end, they can de facto prevent data access, reuse, and portability? It seems obvious that the gatekeepers will try to claim that the obligation to give access and the right for the business users to reuse the data generated on their platforms should not be enforced, because the data is walled in by intellectual property rights or reflects personal data.

Generally, the Court should grant the business users the right of access in reference to both the Digital Markets Act and the other sector-specific legal systems, such as the Open Data Directive. Alternatively, the Commission should clearly state that these legal systems are behavioral liability rules and should not be viewed as also creating rights for users to actually use and access intellectual property law-protected subject matters (held by the platform or a third party).

The Open Data Directive, the transport regulation,[122] the Directive on Direct Payment Services II, and the other sector-specific data access regulations discussed above grant access to certain unique data, which may create competition and innovation and increase business in specific sectors. However, these sector-specific rules still lack overriding rules that could penetrate intellectual property-protected gateways for accessing the data. The Data Governance Act also addresses the interface between the access right to public data in the Open Data Directive and third-party intellectual property rights, and both the Open Data Directive and the Data Governance Act address the issue of database rights held by government authorities.[123] Accordingly, government authorities should not be able to claim that right vis-à-vis a business user. However, the Open Data Directive as well as the Digital Markets Act are also in need of overriding rules to allow for data mining should the holder of the data refuse to grant access to the data by claiming third-party copyrights or other forms of IPRs.

Moreover, the objective of the Open Data sector-specific directive as well as other sector-specific regulations was to encourage entrepreneurs and SMEs to create a data-driven economy, but in hindsight, the regulations seem de facto to benefit one kind of monopoly – the data-driven platforms – by opening up traditional oligopoly markets, e.g., local transport and banking and financial markets. It could be that the Digital Markets Act will primarily benefit other platforms and that through the

[122] EU Regulation on providing multimodal travel information services. The Regulation requires both private and public transport service providers to grant access to travel data at any time, in a machine-readable format, through the National Access Point (NAP). Parliament and Council Regulation (EU) 2017/1926 of 31 May 2017 supplementing Directive 2010/40/EU with regard to the provision of EU-wide multimodal travel information services [2017] OJ L272/1.

[123] Clarification of this interface in the Digital Markets Act could possibly be drawn from the Data Governance Act.

Digital Markets Act, the EU will de facto create an infrastructure for huge data commons between the large platforms.[124]

With more sophisticated, data-driven business models and access to much more personal and nonpersonal data, it is possible that tech platforms will be able to compete successfully in the oligopoly markets targeted by sector-specific access regulations. Indeed, they may use their data advantage and cross-market presence to gain substantial market access in the fintech or banking business.[125] They gain significance through these legal instruments by having a legal, granted access right to data that is business sensitive and, in addition, by enjoying a data advantage through being present and in their capacity as the leading data collector across several other digital markets. Often these access regulations also grant access to data for free, or where the remuneration should be calculated to represent the marginal cost of the data host.[126] Even the GDPR seems to benefit large platforms instead of new entrants or entrepreneurial ingenuity.[127]

Generally, the data-driven economy's most prominent problem with the sector-specific regulations – except for the Digital Markets Act – is that they do not take into consideration the dominance and market power of the firms that demand data access. Perhaps firms that pursue data-driven business strategies, that is, to hold, seek access to, and use data, and are economically powerful (such as certain tech platforms), should not be subsidized by having access to data almost for free. Whether we will see an increased concentration in these markets is still difficult to predict, but the general trend is toward much higher concentration levels. Moreover, if the goal of the digital agenda was to benefit start-ups, entrepreneurial competition, and innovation, the sector-specific regulations granting access to data seem instead to benefit large enterprises: They benefit large platforms.

According to the EU Commission's latest communication from February 2020, the Commission seems to want to pursue even further the strategy of enacting data-access regimes on a sector-specific level. It indicates that the EU will support so-called common data spaces, through investments and possibly sector-specific regulations. Both public and private entities should be encouraged and obligated to provide their data-to-data pools or data commons.[128] According to the Commission, the following areas should hold common data spaces:

[124] Indeed, gatekeepers should be excluded from the definition of a business user in the Digital Markets Act (cf Article 2 (16)).

[125] See Jorge Padilla and Miguel de la Mano, 'Big Tech Banking' (4 December 2018) <https://ssrn.com/abstract=3294723> or <http://dx.doi.org/10.2139/ssrn.3294723>. The Facebook initiative of creating its own currency should possibly be viewed in this light.

[126] See the discussion above in reference to the Open Data Directive.

[127] Gal and Aviv (n 108).

[128] Commission, 'A European strategy for data' COM (2020) 66 final, 19 February 2020, 21 et seq. See also the Appendix 'Common European data spaces in strategic sectors and domains of public interest.'

- A Common European industrial (manufacturing) data space, to support the competitiveness and performance of the EU's industry, allowing to capture the potential value of use of nonpersonal data in manufacturing (estimated at € 1.5 trillion by 2027).
- A Common European Green Deal data space, to use the major potential of data in support of the Green Deal priority actions on climate change, circular economy, zero-pollution, biodiversity, deforestation, and compliance assurance. The 'GreenData4All' and 'Destination Earth' (digital twin of the Earth) initiatives will cover concrete actions.
- A Common European mobility data space, to position Europe at the forefront of the development of an intelligent transport system, including connected cars as well as other modes of transport. Such data space will facilitate access, pooling, and sharing of data from existing and future transport and mobility databases.
- A Common European health data space, which is essential for advances in preventing, detecting, and curing diseases, as well as for informed, evidence-based decisions to improve the accessibility, effectiveness, and sustainability of the healthcare systems.
- A Common European financial data space, to stimulate, through enhanced data sharing, innovation, market transparency, sustainable finance, as well as access to finance for European businesses and a more integrated market.
- A Common European energy data space, to promote a stronger availability and cross-sector sharing of data, in a customer-centric, secure, and trustworthy manner, as this would facilitate innovative solutions and support the decarbonization of the energy system.
- A Common European agriculture data space, to enhance the sustainability performance and competitiveness of the agricultural sector through the processing and analysis of production and other data, allowing for precise and tailored application of production approaches at the farm level.
- Common European data spaces for public administration, to improve transparency and accountability of public spending and spending quality, fighting corruption, at both EU and national levels, and to address law enforcement needs and support the effective application of EU law and enable innovative 'gov tech', 'reg tech', and 'legal tech' applications supporting practitioners as well as other services of public interest.
- A Common European skills data space, to reduce the skills mismatches between the education and training system on the one hand and the labor market needs on the other.

A legislative proposal for health data spaces has now been introduced by the Commission. Neither this common data space concept[129] nor the strategy as a whole seems to take into consideration the size or the market presence of the entities that should be allowed access to these data spaces. Indeed, they may become access tools and further fortify the dominance of already powerful platforms. Indeed, it is possible that sector-specific regulations granting access to data from public and private entities should not be available to large platforms. However, the issue is whether from a constitutional perspective, large platforms can be excluded from gaining access to public data, for example, or whether restricting access to SMEs would be considered discriminatory.

The sector-specific legal systems have a further major drawback. As with competition law, these systems still stipulate liability rules in terms of access and portability of data. This is asking for trouble and shows that a sector-specific regulation granting access rights to platform-held data is not a good idea. Access and claims for having the possibility to port data might not be refused by the large platforms, but the relevant data may be slow to access and difficult to obtain, and the set-up may become unsatisfactory owing to significant litigation regarding both access and remuneration. Indeed, dominant platforms will give preferred access to their own affiliated companies and ecosystems. Litigation regarding access will be long and cumbersome and thus act as a tool to force firms several rungs down the ladder in the ecosystem run by a single platform or system leader.

The proposal for the Data Act, the Digital Markets Act, and the Directive on Payment Services share similar structural or constitutional points of departure in reference to establishing a legal system of access and transfer of data, while the Open Data Directive and the Data Governance Act and the Digital Service Act use a different constitutional structural. Each sector or industry has its rule for accessing data.

In reference to G2P (government to platform), all government data should in principle be available for any comer for free or at marginal cost under the Open Data paradigm, while for P2G (platform to government), data transfer is to be required certain requirements in reference to systemic risk need to be fulfilled. However, there are also users for several of the service provided by the government platforms. The large data holders within the public system are often organized with platforms in the center of digital ecosystems. Indeed, real estate data, corporate information, weather data, and so on are organized with users and business users providing and generating data for the platforms. That could imply that they could be regulated in a similar fashion as the Data Act, the DMA, and the PSD2 and legally obliged to share access to their data with their users. Indeed, in principle, the regulation of access to data G2P could be built around the principle of empowering the users to have a right to access and transfer of the data they generate.

[129] Also including the Gaia-x initiative, see <www.data-infrastructure.eu/GAIAX/Navigation/EN/Home/home.html>.

The guiding principle for the data-driven economy should reflect an equal access and transfer right to data for users and data holders. The right should also address the general intrinsic limitation and restriction reflected by the intellectual property rights held by data holders while also addressing the restriction of competition created by the claiming use of GDPR. Indeed, users should have equal access also under GDPR when providing the same level of protection. This will solve the general problems faced by all the sector-specific access and transfer of data legal systems now being implemented.

It can be argued that the proposal for Data Act, the Digital Markets Act, the DPS2 and the Open Data/DGA, or the regulation of the data-driven economy could be amended with a right for accessing and transferring the data that is collected and stored on the data holders' server interface, that is, most likely a database. Such an access right taking inspiration from data-mining or reverse-engineering principles would allow users to circumvent or trump the data holders' right to protection under TPMs, database rights, and trade-secret legislation to gain access to the data generated by themselves. Such a limited ATR could be included in a stand-alone Data Act as a lex generalis applicable within the whole field of the data-driven economy or perhaps in an updated version of the database directive.

Moreover, the right to access and transfer for users should also be aligned with the GDPR, giving a user the right to also access personal data when the user can provide equal protection under the GDPR as the original data holder. Indeed, the GDPR must also be included in the general legal system for data-driven economy and should be judged and analyzed in reference to the rights held by the party wanting access to the data under the notion of providing equity and fairness for the system as a whole. Indeed, the rights of privacy and data protection must therefore be weighed against such a backdrop.

The right could be supplemented in an updated version of the database directive, for the benefit of users generating data. The database directive could moreover go further and grant a more elaborated right when users have invested time and/or effort to create useful data to the level that it would become a database right in its own right, that is, with a limited exclusive right to prevent certain large data dumps. This would normally apply to business users of platforms.

5

The Objectives of Regulating the Data-Driven Economy

5.1 INTRODUCTION

Data-related technology advancements have brought about a paradigm shift and have created a data-driven economy that requires a legal framework to regulate the economic behavior of its participants – both companies and consumers. However, legislators' hands-off attitude, intended to promote a 'free' and unregulated Internet, has not realized the original internet dream of a borderless and radically democratic space. Some observers have even suggested that the Internet is beyond the sovereignty of governments, or even a fifth dimension, not subject to the same regulation as other domains of human activities.[1] This laissez-faire approach to the digital economy has created a lawless arena where the strong prevail. These powerful participants also dominate in terms of data – the Internet's most valuable asset – and through their actions, system leaders and silo providers are in fact hindering the free flow of information by 'hoarding' data (or, as the Commission formulated it, 'data lock-in').[2] These barriers seem destined to increase in the future.

To be precise, the internet movement did not imply a totally lawless Internet. Gradually, rules regarding privacy, copyright, consumer protection, civil actions, and jurisdiction were either implemented in the virtual environment or developed with time and experience. However, the Internet escaped the sector-specific regulation normally applied to network services, with laws on authorization, conditions for providing the services, and services' extent, content, or scope of their reach. Moreover, the free Internet did imply that as a rule, intermediaries should not be

[1] See discussion in Pål Wrange, 'Sovereignty, Belligerency and the New Normal in Cyberspace' in Linda Bishai (ed), *Law, Security and the State of Perpetual Emergency* (Palgrave 2020) 67–105.

[2] The EU Commission's aim in reference to the suggested data producer rights is to prevent data lock-ins and promote competition on open markets, to achieve a multitude of choices for consumers. See Commission, 'Communication from the Commission of January 10, 2017 – Building a European Data Economy' COM (2017) 2 final, 13.

liable for the illegality of the content they convey unless the intermediaries (i.e., platforms) produced that content themselves or did not take action when alerted to the content's illegality.[3] Indeed, though it should be acknowledged that sector-specific rules for an industry often lead to rigid legal instruments and seldom are successful, the hands-off policy of a free Internet implied that even basic legal systems for establishing a functional liberal economy should be frowned upon or even rejected. The public became uncertain as to whether some users (often young persons) should be made liable for illegal downloads, while the political internet movement was critical of the notion of property as such. Against this backdrop, the introduction of functional property systems for the Internet seems generally to have stalled or even to have been rejected.[4] Indeed, the grassroots internet movement reflected the policy of a 'free' and liberal Internet, while legislators argued over who should be held liable for infringement when illegal content was uploaded on the Internet. The consequences of these parallel worlds are clear: Basic rules for implementing a liberal economy have been lacking, or application of rules for the internet-based, data-driven economy has been sluggish at best.

Historically, as the free economy was envisioned and developed starting with the first industrial revolution, certain freedoms were considered essential to the proper function of such an economy. The main objective of these freedoms is to uphold and protect the liberal economic system as such.[5] However, from a realistic perspective, these freedoms implied the objective of guaranteeing functioning and competitive markets.[6]

The number of freedoms and scope can be disputed, but certain freedoms were considered necessary to the establishment of something akin to a liberal economy with functioning and competitive markets. The first is the freedom to conduct and establish businesses, that is, to establish, develop, and terminate business operations, without requirements on certain certified competences or licenses (in contrast to the guild-based or regulated economy that preceded the first industrial revolution). The second is the freedom to compete, that is, to access markets and to enter into business conduct that could negatively affect other firms' success, while such behavior would still be considered competition on the merits. The third is the

3 Andrej Savin, 'New Directions in EU Policymaking on the Content Layer: Disruption and Law' (2020) Copenhagen Business School CBS LAW Research Paper No 20-05 <https://ssrn.com/abstract=3588387>.

4 In the Nordics, the original idea of a free internet was most clearly perceived in the long Pirate Bay saga, where basic rules for a liberal economy were surprisingly difficult to implement. For the story of Pirate Bay, which illustrates the force of the free internet movement, see <https://en.wikipedia.org/wiki/The_Pirate_Bay_trial>.

5 Ulf Bernitz, 'Market Law as a Legal Discipline' (1979) 23 *Scandinavian Studies in Law* 53–76, 56 et seq.; Ulf Bernitz, *Svensk och Europeisk Marknadsrätt* (2015) 33 et seq., making reference to Johan Myhrman, Stig Strömholm and Gustaf Petrén (eds), Marknadsekonomins rättsliga grundvalar (Timbro 1987).

6 Josef Drexl in 'Data Access and Control in the Era of Connected Devices', in Study on behalf of the European Consumer Association BEUC, Brussels 2018 49 et seq.

freedom to enter into contracts and trade with any party, with the content of the contracts being determined solely by the involved parties. The fourth, 'consumer' freedom, means that purchasers should master the market and freely select products and services. These days, however, few if any would dispute that in a liberal tradition one foundation for these freedoms is the right to property.[7] Today, these freedoms, in conjunction with the four freedoms of the EU, form a 'European economic constitution'.[8]

These freedoms are protected to a certain extent by human-rights conventions and charters but are often inherent in the general legal system. For example, Article 16 of the EU Charter protects the freedom to conduct a business and the freedom to enter into contracts and to select business partners.[9] Freedom to compete is protected by Article 16 but is also spelled out in Article 120 TFEU. However, the full picture of these freedoms is rather intrinsic, and these freedoms must be exercised with the application of other social freedoms and principles. For example, the protection of property must be applied proportionally with freedom of information (Article 10 ECHR).[10]

The notion of a European Economic Constitution is controversial, as is the perceived limitation of the European Economic Constitution as societies and governments acknowledge the importance of the social dimension and the need for balancing economic rights and freedoms against other fundamental rights. It should be noticed, however, that the notion and effect of the European Economic

7 Bernitz (1979) (n 5) 53 et seq. In reference to ordoliberal theory of economy and property, see the contribution in Alan Peacock and Hans Willgerodt (eds), *Germany's Social Market Economy: Origins and Evolution* (Springer 1989), for example Walter Eucken, 'What Kind of Economic and Social System?' See also Werner Bonefeld, 'Freedom and the Strong State: On German Ordoliberalism' (2012) 17(5) New Political Economy 633–656, doi: 10.1080/13563467.2012.656082. Even economist Milton Friedman saw property rights as 'the most basic of human rights and an essential foundation for other human rights'. Rose D. Friedman and Milton Friedman, *Two Lucky People: Memoirs* (University of Chicago Press 1998) 605. See also Ludwig von Mises, *Economic Policy: Thoughts for Today and Tomorrow* (Ludwig von Mises Institute 2006) 18. For the reasons for using 'property' as a concept in relation to IP, see Ole-Andreas Rognstad, *Property Aspects of Intellectual Property* (Cambridge University Press 2018).

8 Bernitz (2015) (n 5). Generally regarding the European Economic Constitution, Nils Wahl, 'The Freedom to Conduct a Business: A Right of Fundamental Importance for the Future of the European Union' in Fabian Amtenbrink, Gareth Davies, Dimitry Kochenov and Justin Lindeboom (eds), *The Internal Market and the Future of European Integration: Essays in Honour of Laurence W. Gormley* (Cambridge University Press 2019) 273–287; Hermann-Josef Blanke, 'The Economic Constitution of the European Union' in Hermann-Josef Blanke and Stelio Mangiameli (eds), *The European Union after Lisbon – Constitutional Basis, Economic Order and External Action* (Springer 2012). See also Michele Everson and Rui Correia Gonçalves, 'Article 16 – Freedom to Conduct a Business' in Tamara K. Hervey et al., (eds), *The EU Charter of Fundamental Rights. A Commentary* (Hart 2014) 446.

9 See Case C-283/11 *Sky Österreich* ECLI:EU:C:2013:28 paras 42 and 43. See also C-426/11 *Alemo-Herron* ECLI:EU:C:2013:521 para 32.

10 C-283/11 *Sky Österreich* ECLI:EU:C:2013:28. See also C-469/17 *Funke Medien* ECLI:EU:C:2019:623.

Constitution have greatly increased in importance with the latest ECJ case-law developments regarding intellectual property regimes and the charter.[11]

In the Nordic legal tradition, 'market law' (*marknadsrätt*, *marknadsret*) was developed in the late 1960s and during the 1970s as a specific discipline for creating a framework for the free-market economy.[12] When introduced, the legal discipline included competition law, intellectual property law, and unfair competition law, including rules for the marketing of goods and services to consumers. A large number of European directives now deal with the protection of consumers from various marketing methods (misleading advertising, comparative advertising, distance contracts, e-commerce, etc.). The influence of EU law is perhaps even stronger in competition law, which is developed in reference to EU competition law.[13]

Market law in the Nordic discipline was distinguished from the core European notion of general economic law (*Wirstshaftrecht* or *droit économique*), as being more precise and a more functional approach to creating a framework for free markets, intended to protect inter alia the freedom to compete and the right to establish and conduct a business (*näringsfrihet*), including freedom of contract. The various legal systems worked together toward a vision of the discipline's main function: to keep competition free and fair, with a firm basis in private rights, as a property system, and to complement this system with rules regarding unfair competition, for example, prohibitions against unfair trading terms, protection for trade secrets and know-how, and so on.

The identification of the legal discipline of market law has not been promoted after the introduction of EU law, which is based on the broader concept of economic law, and certain important objectives such as efficiency are now decisive for market law regulation in Nordic EU member states. Nevertheless, as with market law, the use of legal disciplines – with a smaller set of main goals or objectives – has several advantages. It makes the legal systems more transparent and more prone to legal certainty and can also provide more effective guidance when the legislator regulates new forms of industries.

[11] Increasingly, national courts have begun to consider the impact of the Charter of Fundamental Rights on EU copyright law. In *Funke Medien, Pelham GmbH*, and *Spiegel Online v Volker Beck*, the ECJ discussed a series of important questions about the relationship between the Charter, copyright law, and national constitutional norms. Generally, it should be acknowledged that the CJEU has ruled that freedom of information and of the press cannot justify a derogation from the rights of copyright holders beyond allowed exceptions and limitations. C-469/17 *Funke Medien* ECLI:EU:C:2019:623; C-476/17 *Pelham GmbH* ECLI:EU:C:2019:624; and C-516/17 *Spiegel Online v Volker Beck* ECLI:EU:C:2019:625.

[12] Ulf Bernitz, *Marknadsrätt* (1969) 63 et seq. See also Bernitz (1979) (n 5) 55 et seq.

[13] See also Antonina B. Engelbrekt, 'The Scandinavian Model of Unfair Competition Law' in Reto Hilty and Frauke Henning-Bodewig (eds), *Law Against Unfair Competition* (1 MPI Studies on Intellectual Property, Competition and Tax Law, Springer 2007).

We need a legal discipline of digital market law to regulate and develop the digital or the narrower data-driven economy, and it is very interesting that the Commission is now proposing a digital market law regulation. The energy and speed with which EU institutions are developing diverse (and sometimes dysfunctional) sector-specific regulations for the digital economy certainly call for a more holistic approach. A general approach to the legal system is now being developed in a piecemeal fashion to protect a number of freedoms and objectives for the digital economy, ensuring that a sturdy legal platform for the new paradigm is put in place without over-regulating the data-driven economy.

Several authors in academia discuss the objectives for establishing a regulatory theory for the data economy, which seems to reflect the constitutional framework of fundamental rights in its entirety.[14] The four objectives are to (i) establish functioning and competitive markets, (ii) promote innovation, (iii) protect consumer interests with a particular focus on protecting the privacy of natural persons, and (iv) promote additional public interests. Under the objective of establishing functioning and competitive markets, it is possible to include freedom of contract, the right to compete, and freedom to conduct a business, while including a multitude of different public interests and objectives as part of objectives for protecting consumer interests and promoting public interests. The objectives also form an integrated test for regulating the digital economy, including what appears to be a test to establish something akin to a property right for data.[15] However, from a Nordic market law perspective, the need for a right system should be established primarily in the light of the first and second objectives – establishing a functioning and competitive market and promoting innovation – because generally, the economic freedoms in a liberal economy can be included under these objectives. This perspective notwithstanding, the economic freedoms as well as a new property regime and its application must be applied proportionately with other social freedoms and principles.

Indeed, the four objectives stated above reflect the core European notion of a general economic discipline (*Wirstshaftrecht* or *droit économique*), but in this case for the digital economy. The aim is inter alia to include the constitutional framework of human rights in its entirety. From the viewpoint of a Nordic legal tradition, a narrower approach could be developed when regulating the digital or data-driven economy, where objectives still need to be weighed against each other. However, for establishing a legal discipline, not every part of the legal discipline needs to fulfill each objective; only the sum of the parts must meet the objectives, that is, a legal discipline as such must cater to all rights in reference to the liberties and freedoms that are at stake. Moreover, there might be freedoms and objectives that are only remotely connected to business conduct in data-driven markets and thus can be protected by other parts of the general economic legal system. Indeed, an economic

[14] See, for example, Drexl (n 6).

[15] Ibid 58.

regulation for the governing of a digital economy should be enacted when the need arises in reference to the economic freedoms indicated above – to conduct and establish businesses and compete (i.e., to access markets) and ensure consumer freedom, which allows consumers to master the market and freely select the products and services to their liking and according to their needs. Nevertheless, rights such as privacy cannot form an objective for creating a digital competitive economy as such; they can only be a counterweight to limiting economic freedoms.

Both the proposed Data Act and the Digital Markets Act are comprehensive regulations for data holders and gatekeepers that are connected to the Internet and that apply a data-driven business model, and they generally fulfill the four objectives for a general economic legal system.[16] They aim to establish functioning and competitive markets when the contractual and technical restrictions imposed by data holders and gatekeepers on users are eliminated. The core connected markets might be contestable by the users under the proposed Regulations, or, at least, they will level the playing field in the core markets of (business) users. The (business) users *might* be able to compete with the data holders and gatekeepers on their own markets. Access to data will also limit the data holders and gatekeepers from having a competitive advantage due to asymmetric information. However, neither the Data Act nor the Digital Market Act goes far enough in providing equal terms for competition when addressing the issue of access to and transfer of data. The scope of the data accessible by the relevant parties under the regulations should be similar, while intellectual property rights or other legal systems that de facto favor the data holder or the gatekeeper and restrict access for users and property holders of sensors should be neutralized through a right of the user and owner. Innovation is promoted when data is accessible for many, and consumer and public interests are also promoted. Yet, if the Data Act and the Digital Markets Act do not stipulate an 'overriding' or 'countervailing' right to data, one may conclude that they will not go far enough, and the objectives listed above will not be met. At least innovation would be restricted, while competition would be limited as well. Or, as will be developed below, the access and transfer regime stipulated in the Data Act and Digital Markets Act should, in light of Articles 16 and 17 of the EU Charter, be considered a hard right giving a user a countervailing and non-waivable right to access and transfer data.

The need to consider the multitude of objectives posed by general economic law also increases the number of rationales regarding the three basic requirements for establishing a property regime. As indicated above, there are generally three fundamental rationales for intellectual property protection: the incentive function, the disclosure function to promote the objective of innovation, and the general need for creation of proper markets. (These rationales are discussed in more detail below.) While these rationales should be used, and objectives such as freedom of information, privacy, and other liberties can be weighed against them, they cannot constitute a rationale or objective in themselves for the establishment of a new property regime.

[16] The other sector-specific legal systems discussed in Chapter 4 are not as comprehensive.

The issue addressed in this book is whether there should be an access and transfer right to a *user's data* – something akin to a limited property right to a limited set of data, but that does not necessarily need to include all the rights that are normally included in the general notion of property. Foremost, the right held by users should not be an exclusive right. Data holders, platforms, and gatekeepers should have access to the data, and the users' right entails an access and transfer regime only. Whether that is a property right, or not, depends on the legal system it will be enacted.

Several arguments have been put forward as to why a right in data should be created. For example, many assert that data is very valuable, that data is the magic material for predicting and controlling the future, and that a property right in data would promote innovation. All these arguments are discussed below, but a fundamental theoretical argument and major underlying thrust of arguments to support the introduction of a right is the emergence of technology that has resulted in the separation of data and information from individuals' personalities and skills. The new paradigm implies that data can be controlled, collected, and stored, that is, it has left the room of thoughts and ideas to become tangible items, at least in the virtual world. This was something that the proponents of the original internet dream – a free space filled only with public goods – did not realize.[17] Data is the new raw material, information in data format is de facto no longer a public good, and data can be used for creating innovations and markets.[18] However, the relevant information as a good for developing products and services for suppliers of platforms is in the control of the platforms, and to prevent the market failure inherent in this state of affairs, this asymmetry in information must be corrected.

Data has thus become a separate means for production,[19] similar to other means of production such as old-economy raw material, tools, or machinery. As a means of

[17] Moreover, a property-based solution may bring other benefits. As discussed above, the regulatory policy for the Internet was based on the idea of a 'free' or lawless Internet. The low level of regulation of the Internet means that (a) no special approval is needed for conducting a business, (b) information society services should not be subject to sector-specific regulation (i.e., regulation that applies to them only because they are such services), (c) no special regulatory oversight is put on those services, and (d) liability rules should be kept to a minimum. This regulatory policy, enacted in the 1990s, reflects the goals and ideas of liberal market regulation that were developed in the beginning of the twentieth century; however, the policy lacked the fundamental structure of a property system, so it could not be truly successful for a liberal, data-driven economy. The fundamental flaw is the lack of a property regime for data, as data is the raw material of such an economy. Without a property regime, the policy is instead a recipe for a winner-take-all approach, especially in a network-driven environment where network effects are present. See Savin (n 3).

[18] OECD, 'Data-Driven Innovation: Big Data for Growth and Well-Being' 7 (2015).

[19] In economics and sociology, the means of production (also called capital goods) are physical and nonfinancial inputs used in the production of economic value. These include raw materials, facilities, machinery, and tools used in the production of goods and services owned or controlled by the company, while labor was controlled by the workers. In the terminology of

production, its inherent property is that parties to a market would seek to control data, limit its availability, and de facto own it. There are other items that may be considered means of production but that are not owned in a classical sense; however, because technological developments have made data a fundamental means of production in the data-driven economy, the property aspect of data comes to the fore; this aspect is analyzed below.[20]

5.2 CONSTITUTIONAL ASPECTS OF THE ENACTMENT OF AN ACCESS AND TRANSFER RIGHT

Ownership is not defined at the EU-law level, and the Member States legal systems define ownership differently.[21] There is a dichotomy between the civil law and the common law in an understanding of ownership. While civil law recognizes a limited number of property rights and a limited number of legal objects that can be subjected to these property rights, the common law is more flexible and allows private parties more freedom in the types of ownership interests which they can create.[22] In civil law jurisdiction, property is based on law or legal acts. Ownership is thus an absolute dominion encompassing all the listed rights over the relevant object.[23] On the contrary, in the common law tradition, the notion of ownership includes a variety of different rights over the same property. Ownership can be a sliding scale. As Janeček identifies, under common law, you can have more or less ownership depending on how large the bundle of your property rights in the object is.[24] Moreover, civil law jurisdictions consider property or ownership to be absolute, erga omnes, while common law recognizes personal property (in personam) and real property rights – in rem.[25] In light of this, the proposal for the Data Act may

classical economics, the means of production are the 'factors of production' minus financial and human capital. See Wikipedia and John Eatwell, Murray Milgate, and Peter Newman, *Marxian Economics: The New Palgrave* (W W Norton 1990) 76. According to the conception of capital within orthodox economics, the term 'capital' generally refers to the means of production. James M. Henslin, *Essentials of Sociology* (Taylor & Francis US 2002) 159.

20 The above theoretical framework for establishing a market regulation for the data-driven economy reflects what can be considered 'just' in a liberal economy, while the historical function of a liberal economic ideology also meant a break with the regulated economic ideas, to allow more participants to enter the economy and to break down the old silo structures of the guilds.

21 Václav Janeček, 'Ownership of Personal Data in the Internet of Things' (2018) 34(5) Computer Law & Security Review 1039–1052, 1041 <https://doi.org/10.1016/j.clsr.2018.04.007>. See also Sjef van Erp, 'Ownership of Data: The Numerus Clausus of Legal Objects' (2017) 6 Brigham-Kanner Property Rights Conference Journal 235, 242 et seq.

22 Janeček (n 21) 1041 et seq.

23 van Erp (n 21).

24 Janeček (n 21).

25 Ibid.

from a common law tradition be viewed as including something akin to a property system in Articles 3 to 5.

A fundamental thrust of arguments that support introduction of a right to data is how technological advancements have brought us to a point where data and information are separated from individuals' personalities and skills. The new paradigm implies that data can be controlled, collected, and stored, that is, that it has left the room of thoughts and ideas to become tangible items,[26] at least in the virtual world. Data is the new raw material for many diverse services.[27] Data is also the cornerstone of developing models to predict future events.

Indeed, one fact cannot be avoided in this context: A property legal system is an allocation-of-power regime that distributes and disseminates power. Such allocation of power can be based on various factors: as a reward for labor or investment, as an expression of personality, as a basis for economic freedom, or in terms of economic utility (efficiency based).[28] In several aspects, various justice-related arguments are presented to alter the paradigm of dominance of the strong and powerful over the weak in an unregulated scenario, or when the legal system promotes the wrong group over other groups in society.[29] With this viewpoint, the economic rights inherent in property are not an end in themselves but a means to protect something else – often the investment in capital or time to create tangible goods or intangible information – which on a grander scale implies that property protects the distribution of opportunities and the function of the liberal market economy as such.[30] In essence, a property right is the foundation of a legal system and a major function in the protection of the liberal economy. Clearly defined rights enable transactions and efficient allocation of resources. Indeed, a regime reflecting an access and transfer right for users is necessary, because it often reflects a reward for labor and/or is an expression of personality, or a reward for an investment, while it often directs the data to the entities that need it for trade and innovation, that is, business user's data to business users collected by platforms. The new right system also diffuses the inherent power of information resting in the hands of a few and disseminates data among several stakeholders, to the benefit of innovation, progress, and the creation of markets for trading data. An access and transfer right will increase trade in data; the access and transfer right will function as a tool to increase the volume of data in

26 Daria Kim, 'No One's Ownership as the Status Quo and a Possible Way Forward: A Note on the Public Consultation on Building a European Data Economy' (2017) Gewerblicher Rechtsschutz und Urheberrecht Internationaler Teil 697.

27 OECD (n 18).

28 For a similar list, see Heiko Richter, The Power Paradigm in Private Law' in Mor Bakhoum, Beatriz Conde Gallego, Mark-Oliver Mackenrodt, and Gintare Surblytė-Namavičienė (eds), *Personal Data in Competition, Consumer Protection and Intellectual Property Law* (MPI Studies on Intellectual Property and Competition Law, vol 28, Springer 2018) 552 et seq.

29 Guido Calabresi and A. Douglas Melamed, 'Property Rules, Liability Rules, and Inalienability: One View of the Cathedral' (1972) 85 Harvard Law Review 1089, 1093.

30 Bernitz (1969) (n 12) 54 f. See also Bernitz (1979) (n 5).

the market. Moreover, the market for licensing of an access and transfer right will introduce a new market, created by enacting an access and transfer right and which could become an additional layer for competition and prosperity.

Moreover, the scope of the data accessible by the relevant parties should be similar, while intellectual property rights or other legal systems that de facto favor the data holder or the gatekeeper and restrict access for users should be neutralized through an access and transfer right for the users. Leveling the playing field by giving equal access.

The previous attempt in academia to promote a producer data right has argued that producers should have a right to individual data points, and indeed, any information they produce.[31] Moreover, the proponents for such a property regime have been unclear as to whether the protected subject matter is information or merely syntactical elements of data. These two aspects may indeed create a risk that the producer data right develops into a stranglehold on the right to information, with the potential to greatly increase transaction costs. It could increase the bureaucracy of data-driven markets, and it is unclear whether such a right would truly benefit innovation and the creation of data markets and data-driven markets.[32]

The concept proposed above for an access and transfer right would not entail such risks; in addition, it provides a clear distinction: Information is protected but not the syntactical elements of data (i.e., 1s and 0s). The access and transfer rights are not vested in individual data points. Business users and subcontractors would obtain access to datasets consisting of the data generated by or at least reflecting their intellectual or quantitative investments in the dataset or database provided on the platform.

Such a right will boost and increase innovation because it will teach business users how to create better products; the data from the marketing segment will become available to these providers. Indeed, this right will transform the marketing and distribution process into an R&D effort, where information regarding customer satisfaction is obtained in real time, by the entities with the greatest need of such information. These entities will innovate based on the information received because market forces will incentivize them to act immediately in reference to the data obtained. Interestingly, this will boost innovation, perhaps even beyond traditional levels. Their data-driven products and business models need to be developed continuously. Access to data generated by business users will no longer be the prerogative of platforms.

The access and transfer right (ATR) also creates something more: It increases potential access to information in the commons. Implementing strong ATRs will

[31] Stressing that data includes any and all information, see Bernt Hugenholtz, 'Data Property in the System of Intellectual Property Law' in Sebastian Lohsse, Reiner Schulze, and Dirk Staudenmayer (eds), *Trading Data in the Digital Economy: Legal Concepts and Tools* (Nomos 2017) 75.

[32] Several authors discuss this' see, for example, ibid., and Drexl (n 6).

transfer data from the gatekeepers to users that can transfer or sell data, or even make the data available to the commons. Indeed, data will be more available than before, giving journalists, activists, and civil society the possibility to access data, because data will be traded and marketed to a larger extent than when platforms hoard data. The vision or dream of having a free and democratic Internet, where data and services were freely available for all, is more likely to be fulfilled with an ATR than without.

As discussed above, the legislator's hands-off attitude, intended to foster a 'free' and unregulated Internet, created a lawless arena for the digital economy; this approach will not promote freedom. For a liberal economy to develop properly, certain freedoms must be present and protected: the freedom to conduct and establish businesses; the freedom to compete; the freedom to enter into contracts and trade with any party, along with freedom of the involved parties to determine contract content; and purchaser freedom, allowing purchasers to master the market and freely select products and services according to their liking and needs. These freedoms must be in place, in conjunction with the four freedoms of the controversial notion of a European economic constitution.[33]

However, for these freedoms to materialize in a liberal economy, private property regimes must be put in place.[34]

These freedoms for regulating the digital economy are protected to a certain extent by human-rights conventions and charters but are often inherent in the legal system. The right to property is stipulated in Article 17 of the EU Charter; everyone has the right to own, use, dispose of, and bequeath his or her lawfully acquired possessions. Intellectual property shall be protected. Article 16 of the EU Charter protects the freedom to conduct a business, to enter into contracts, and to select business partners.[35] Article 11 of the Charter provides the right to freedom of expression and information, subject to certain restrictions that are in accordance with law and necessary in a democratic society. This right includes the freedom to hold opinions and to receive and impart information and ideas. Freedom to compete is spelled out in Article 120 TFEU. Article 8 of the EU Charter stipulates that every person has the right to the protection of personal data concerning him or her. Such data must be processed fairly for specified purposes and on the basis of consent from the person concerned or some other legitimate basis laid down by law. Everyone has the right of access to data that has been collected concerning him or her, and the right to have the data rectified.

It should be noted that the idea and (direct) effect of the European Economic Constitution in EU national legal systems has greatly increased in importance owing

[33] Bernitz (2015) (n 5). Generally regarding European Economic Constitution, Wahl (n 8) 273–287; Blanke (n 8). See also Everson and Gonçalves (n 8) 446.

[34] Bernitz (1979) (n 5); Friedman and Friedman (n 7). See also von Mises (n 7).

[35] See C-283/11 *Sky Österreich* paras 42 and 43 and C-427/11 *Alemo-Herron* para 32.

to the latest ECJ case-law development in reference to the charter for human rights.[36] It seems that the ECJ is developing the notion of economic freedoms and the European Economic Constitution under the indulgence of the Charter. Weak, passive rights are starting to develop into strong, active rights.[37]

In reference to the legal systems discussed in this book, numerous rights are being triggered. They therefore need to be applied in conjunction with other rights and in a proportionate manner. For example, as Drexl argues, control over the use of data depends on the constitutional right to data protection acting as a specific justification that, from a fundamental-rights perspective, can explain the exception to the principle of freedom of information. As for protection of trade secrets, the justification relates to the procompetitive effect of such protection, which according to Drexl is weaker. Drexl continues, arguing that a data ownership right, which would result in exclusive control by the data owner without any additional substantive requirement for protection and without the requirement of secrecy, would risk violating the principle of freedom of information.

It should be noted that the ATR proposed in this book does not entail an exclusive right; it is an access and portability right that increases the number of holders of data. Interestingly, when letting go of the exclusivity requirement as a right in the bundle of rights we collectively call ownership, a right to data based only on the rights to access and transfer data becomes much more acceptable. Indeed, much of the controversy in reference to creating a property right to nonpersonal data can then be circumvented.[38] The risk of introducing such an ATR is far less.[39]

36 Increasingly, national courts have begun to consider the impact of the Charter of Fundamental Rights on EU copyright law. In C-469/17 *Funke Medien*, C-476/17 *Pelham GmbH*, and C-516/17 *Spiegel Online v Volker Beck*, the ECJ discussed a series of important questions about the relationship between the Charter, copyright law, and national constitutional norms. Generally, it should be acknowledged that the CJEU rules on freedom of information and of the press cannot justify a derogation from the rights of copyright holders beyond allowed exceptions and limitations under EU, for example, those stipulated in the InfoSoc.

37 Eduardo Gill-Pedro, 'A Company's Fundamental Right to Conduct Business: Reverse Engineering a Free Market as an Objective of EU Law' (Draft Paper) Faculty of Law Lund University [in archive with the author].

38 See for example Osborne Clarke LLP, 'Legal Study on Ownership and Access to Data' (European Commission 2016) <https://bookshop.europa.eu/en/legal-study-on-ownership-and-access-to-data-pbKK0416811/> or <https://perma.cc/82D8–9787>; Nestor Duch-Brown, Bertin Martens, and Frank Mueller-Langer, 'The Economics of Ownership, Access and Trade in Digital Data' (JRC Digital Economy Working Paper 2017-01, European Commission 2017); Anette Gärtner and Kate Brimsted, 'Let's Talk about Data Ownership' (2017) 39 EIPR 461; van Erp (n 21); Herbert Zech, 'Information as a Tradable Commodity' in De Franceschi, *European Contract Law and the Digital Single Market* (2016) 51–79; Josef Drexl and Reto Hilty et al., 'On the Current Debate on Exclusive Rights and Access Rights to Data at the European Level' in *Max Planck Institute for Innovation and Competition Position Statement* (16 August 2016) 12; Wolfgang Kerber, 'A New (Intellectual) Property Right for Non-Personal Data? An Economic Analysis' (2016) GRUR International 989.

39 The EU Commission also envisioned something similar. Instead of creating the data producer right as a right in rem, the Commission purport that it could be conceived of as a set of purely

Moreover, ATRs will boost markets and create markets. This would imply that the Charter Article 16 right to conduct a business and Article 17 right to property act as constitutional justifications for enacting an ATR legal system or even identifying such a legal system within the Data Act and the Digital Markets Act, while also creating a constitutional balance against other rights that might be triggered by the enactment of an ATR legal system – such as the right to freedom of expression and information, and the right to the protection of personal data. However, as stated earlier, it is difficult to see how the freedom of expression and information would be seriously violated by ATRs that would increase information in the public arena, rather than decrease the amount of freely available information in the current situation. A different matter, however, is the right to privacy. As the right has been defined by the General Data Protection Regulation (GDPR), privacy is enhanced by limited personal data in the public sphere, and the natural person should be granted some right to personal data; the introduction of an ATR legal system could restrict these rights. The issue therefore is whether this is constitutionally sound. In several jurisdictions, the right to privacy is a fundamental right of great importance, while the right to property and conducting a business are weak rights. However, this is not the case in the EU. The Charter explains that the right to privacy can be restricted by law, and under EU law, by giving consent for firms to collect their personal data, individuals are clearly in control of their right to privacy.

The right to conduct a business has seen an interesting rise in the hierarchy of human rights stipulated in the Charter. From its original state as a weak and passive right, it has ascended to become much greater prominence in the European Economic Constitution now being enhanced by the ECJ.[40] Previously, the right to conduct a business was weak and unclear because it could not be used to strike down national legislation. However, it should be noted that then-Advocate General

defensive rights. This option would follow the choice made in the design of the protection given to know-how by the Trade Secrets Protection Directive. Its objective would be to enhance the sharing of data by giving at least the defensive elements of an in rem right, that is, the capacity for the de facto data holder to sue third parties in case of illicit misappropriation of data. This approach thus equates to a protection of a de facto 'possession' rather than to the concept of 'ownership'. According to the Commission, a number of civil law remedies could be introduced such as:

(i) the right to seek injunctions preventing further use of data by third parties who have no right to use the data,
(ii) the right to have products built on the basis of misappropriated data excluded from market commercialization, and
(iii) the possibility to claim damages for unauthorized use of data.

Cf. Commission, 'Staff Working Document on the Free Flow of Data and Emerging Issues of the European Data Economy' COM (2017) 9 final, 10 January 2017, 33 et seq. See also Kerber (n 38).

40 Gill-Pedro is among the first to see the signs that this understanding of Article 16 may be gaining traction in the CJEU. See Gill-Pedro (n 37).

(now Judge) Nils Wahl, in the opening to his Opinion in *AGET Iraklis*,[41] stated that: '[t]he European Union is based on a free-market economy, which implies that undertakings must have the freedom to conduct their business as they see fit.'[42] It should also be also acknowledged that Judge Wahl developed this further in an essay, stating that 'the freedom to conduct a business forms part of the EU's economic constitution according to which Member States have undertaken to commit to a specific form of political economy and market within the European Union.'[43] However, Judge Wahl is not the only person who seems eager to increase the ambit and importance of Charter Article 16. In *Alemo Herron*,[44] which concerned an employee dispute, the ECJ seems to have used the right to conduct a business as a method to set aside national legislation that prevents an undertaking from using this right to exploit the market.

In light of the above, it should be clearly considered that the ECJ could be positive to an ATR, although it might restrict the right to privacy in a limited way. A balance must be struck between the right to property and the right to conduct a business on the one hand, and the freedom of information and expression, on the other, enshrined in Article 11 of the Charter and Article 10(1) of the European Convention for the Protection of Human Rights and Fundamental Freedoms, as well as the right to privacy and data protection set out by the Charter. The welfare gains of enacting an ATR and the positive effects that some believe would be realized by increasing the amount of data available in society seem to outweigh the decreased protection of privacy and data protection, as articulated in Articles 7 and 8 of the Charter and in the GDPR; the GDPR also seems to facilitate exemption mechanisms that could in turn facilitate introduction of an ATR legal system.[45]

However, to begin generally with the three fundamental rationales for intellectual property protection – the incentive function, the disclosure function, and the need for creation of proper markets – they should be considered fulfilled. Internet and the data-driven economy would greatly benefit from having a sui generis property regime, as the principles of a regulatory system for a free liberal economy would be complete. Indeed, ATRs could be the protection against the EU's current

[41] Opinion of AG Wahl, C-201/15 *Anonymi Geniki Etairia Tsimenton Iraklis (AGET Iraklis) v Ypourgos Ergasias, Koinonikis Asfalisis kai Koinonikis Allilengyis* EU:C:2016:429 para 1.

[42] Ibid.

[43] Wahl (n 8) 276. See also K. Lenaerts, 'Federalism: Essential Concepts in Evolution – The Case of European Union' (1997) 21(3) Fordham International Law Journal 746.

[44] C-426/11 *Mark Alemo-Herron and others v Parkwood Leisure Ltd* ECLI:EU:C:2013:521.

[45] According to Article 6(1)(f) of the GDPR, access and sharing of personal data can be lawful without user's consent when: 'processing is necessary for the purposes of the legitimate interests pursued by the controller or by a third party, except where such interests are overridden by the interests of fundamental rights and freedoms of data subject [user] which require protection of personal data'. Moreover, it should be recognized that Articles 5(1), 6(4), and 89 could enable firms to conduct R&D based on personal data, under certain circumstances and without the need for consent. It should also be noted that both Article 15(4) GDPR and Article 20(4) GDPR provide that these two rights 'shall not affect the rights and freedoms of others'.

interventionistic, sector-specific regulation approach, which seems to lack a holistic idea or aim and instead reflects a development toward a regulated economy. At the very least, an ATR legal system would complement the sector-specific regulation movement and make certain aspects of this movement superfluous. Innovation would be promoted, and indeed incentives to promote data creation and public availability of data would be enhanced by making use of aspects or rights from the general bundle of rights included in a property system. The greatest benefit of an ATR system is in regard to the establishment of markets, where the consumers will evaluate the product, the data, or the ATRs, and the transfer of such data will be based on the market value of the data or right. Furthermore, the establishment of property-based markets also clarifies the application of competition law, where relevant markets can be identified and analyzed. Access and transfer right would place data as an item in the value chain or as a commodity firmly within the established boundaries of the liberal market economy and legal system.

At this point, the four objectives reflecting the test for a general economic regulation, used in this case for regulating the digital economy, also seem to be fulfilled – or at least noneffected by enacting an access and transfer right. It seems clear that giving the users the right to communicate or distribute the dataset to the public would establish functioning and competitive markets for data, while also increasing innovation in the product or service markets, that is, the core markets of the users. Consumers benefit from more competition and better products, while their inherent rights for protecting the privacy of natural persons are not infringed. Moreover, freedom of information is upheld and even promoted by having more data in the public domain and by not protecting or having individual data points as business secrets held outside the public domain.

5.3 EU OR THE MEMBER STATES

In federal systems as well as in the EU, it is sometimes difficult to determine the level of government that should regulate a matter of interest.[46] The special position of intellectual property rights under the EU treaties can be detected in both Article 345 TFEU and Article 36 TFEU, which state that property is the prerogative of the Member States and that the protection of industrial and commercial property constitutes a derogation from the right to freely move goods within the EU. The CJEU has tried to reconcile this potential conflict by creating a very complicated compromise between the rights to property, trade, and competition.

However, since the entry into force of the Treaty on the Functioning of the European Union (TFEU) in 2009, the EU has had explicit competence for intellectual property rights (Article 118). Although governed by different national laws, intellectual property rights (IPR) are also subject to EU legislation. Article 118 of

[46] Lenaerts (n 43).

the TFEU provides that in the context of the establishment and functioning of the internal market, Parliament and the Council, acting in accordance with the ordinary legislative procedure, shall establish measures for the creation of EU intellectual property law – in order to provide uniform protection of IPR throughout the EU – and for the setting up of centralized, EU-wide authorization, coordination, and supervision arrangements. The legislative activity of the European Union consists chiefly of harmonizing certain specific aspects of IPR through the creation of a single European system, as is the case for the EU trademark and design, and as will be the case for patents. The European Union Intellectual Property Office (EUIPO) is responsible for managing the EU trademark and design.

Regulating intellectual property in the internal market remains shared competence between the EU and Member States.[47] The EU has exclusive competence in the field of commercial aspects of intellectual property regarding common commercial policy.[48]

In addition, in reference to the interface between competition law and unfair competition law, there are areas of exclusive and of shared competence. In reference to unfair competition rules, such as several of the rules included in the Digital Markets Act, Member States still have competence. Moreover, according to Regulation 1/2003, Article 3(3), provisions of national law that predominantly pursue an objective different from that pursued by Articles 101 and 102 of the Treaty are not violating the regulation or the treaties. The preamble to the 1/2003 regulation states that EU-exclusive competence does not

> preclude Member States from implementing on their territory national legislation, which protects other legitimate interests provided that such legislation is compatible with general principles and other provisions of Community law. In so far as such national legislation pursues predominantly an objective different from that of protecting competition on the market, the competition authorities and courts of the Member States may apply such legislation on their territory. Accordingly, Member States may under this Regulation implement on their territory national legislation that prohibits or imposes sanctions on acts of unfair trading practice, be they unilateral or contractual. Such legislation pursues a specific objective, irrespective of the actual or presumed effects of such acts on competition on the market. This is particularly the case of legislation which prohibits undertakings from imposing on their trading partners, obtaining or attempting to obtain from them terms and conditions that are unjustified, disproportionate or without consideration.

Member States should be able to regulate platforms that do not fall within the ambit of the Digital Markets Act, and EU law cannot prevent a Member State from enacting a right that mirrors an access and transfer right.

[47] *Spain and Italy v Council* (Case C-274/11) ECLI:EU:C:2013:240 para 25.

[48] In accordance with Article 207(1) TFEU, the common commercial policy, which under Article 3(1)(e) TFEU falls within the exclusive competence of the European Union, relates inter alia to 'the commercial aspects of intellectual property'.

6

The Intellectual Property Law System and Data

6.1 INTRODUCTION

Generally, the political consensus at the beginning of the internet era was that platforms should have only limited liability under intellectual property law for content that users uploaded on these platforms.[1] Now, however, the platforms are the center of gravity for the Internet, drawing in (for technical reasons and owing to network effects) all data streams in the respective ecosystems, for the benefit of the system leader controlling the platform. Furthermore, the contracts that system leaders conclude with business users, and which control their business relationship, not only normally grant the exclusive right to data generated on the platform to the platform provider but also generally neutralize any intellectual property rights held by the business user. Indeed, the system leaders are regulators of their respective ecosystems and use their system of contracts to control the ecosystems and exclude the use and importance of intellectual property rights. The platform or cloud provider contractually secures the right from the platform or cloud user, not only to store the data but also to analyze it and make use of it for the provider's own benefit, and for the benefit of others in the ecosystem, on all connected markets. The platform providers thus become the masters of their respective data ecosystems; they do indeed hoard the data and generally do not trade or share the data.

Moreover, system leaders' use of far-reaching contracts to regulate the ecosystems has additional consequences. Generally, the ecosystem agreements provided by the platforms seem to include restrictions for the users of platforms or clouds, such as exclusivity, nontampering, and a ban on reverse engineering. Some platform- and cloud-service providers include, as stated above, broad nonassert provisions that prevent customers from asserting their intellectual property rights against the system leaders, or any other cloud-service customer or partner in the ecosystems, also in

[1] See discussion in Chapter 5.

reference to behavior and business conduct outside the ecosystem.[2] Indeed, the ecosystems are regulated and controlled by platform providers.

Future system leaders will likely use their similar market position and contractual systems in the upcoming Internet of Things (IoT) era. As this age gains momentum, all things (devices) will include embedded sensors in both mechanical parts and the human interface. Cars, for example, will become platforms where data is collected from several sensors embedded in different parts of the vehicle. A wide range of service providers, OEMs, and aftersales service providers as well as leasing companies and vehicle loan providers are keen to access the data generated in the car by the parts or services that these suppliers have provided. Manufacturers of parts will most likely be contractually bound to transfer or port data from the sensors inserted in the parts to the brand-holder, the car manufacturer. Car manufacturers can design the car data architecture to ensure their exclusive access to in-vehicle data. Doing so gives them exclusive data access for in-vehicle data from their brand, while also often granting far-reaching immunity vis-à-vis subcontractors' intellectual property rights through nonassertion clauses in the subcontracting agreements.[3]

In reference to the data architecture, vehicle manufacturers seem to mirror the platform model originally pioneered by Amazon, Facebook, and Google: Collect data and control it to fortify one's already achieved platform position in the ecosystem, while remaining reluctant to trade or give access to data that would migrate from the platform.[4] Indeed, they will become gatekeepers in their ecosystems.[5]

We may see similar developments in reference to kitchen appliances and in other industries or systems that will soon enter the Internet of Things realm. For example, the producers of parts, such as refrigerators for kitchens, can transfer data to a system leader while having their own patent portfolios; the system leader controlling the relevant platform could require access to these patent portfolios in exchange for access to the platform, with the platform being a kitchen provider or a food platform.[6] Years or decades of investment in R&D could be lost because in the future, the device producers need to be able to access the relevant platform to provide interoperability to their customers, and hence connect to the ecosystems.

[2] Björn Lundqvist, 'Cloud Service as the Ultimate Gate(keeper)' (2019) 7(2) The Journal of Antitrust Enforcement 220–248. What is problematic with these agreements from a competition law perspective is that they are vertical and a no-go for many competition authorities and economists. Indeed, in accordance with vertical or licensing guidelines, it would be difficult not to have such covenants accepted under competition law.

[3] Bertin Martens and Frank Mueller-Langer, 'Access to Digital Car Data and Competition in Aftersales Services' (September 2018) EUR – Scientific and Technical Research Reports <https://ec.europa.eu/jrc/sites/jrcsh/files/jrc112634.pdf>. See also Wolfgang Kerber, 'Governance of IoT Data: Why the EU Data Act Will Not Fulfill Its Objectives' (8 April 2022) <https://ssrn.com/abstract=4080436> or <http://dx.doi.org/10.2139/ssrn.4080436>.

[4] Wolfgang Kerber, 'Data Governance in Connected Cars: The Problem of Access to In-Vehicle Data' (2019) 9 JIPITEC 310 para 1.

[5] Kerber (n 3).

[6] Stigler Report (2019) 110.

Thus, parts and device producers will likely need to transfer their property rights to the parts and devices to the system leader or platform provider. Nonassertion clauses, if they are broad in scope, eliminate the incentive to conduct R&D when the firm knows that it cannot prevent a platform provider from entering the market. Using these clauses and their data advantage, platform providers may become very potent potential competitors for any part, device, or thing producer.[7]

A business or manufacturing right to access and port data becomes important, given the often far-reaching de facto control system leaders obtain in the ecosystems. Platform or system providers seem to be immune to the patent portfolios held by business users and subcontractors. The platform provider within its IoT ecosystem will not be stopped from entering the business users, subcontractors, or brick-and–mortar firms markets inside and possibly outside the ecosystem.[8] Moreover, platform providers seem to have superior bargaining power when negotiating the contracts that make up the ecosystems. Therefore, a right to access and port data for business users of these ecosystems should be considered. Such a right needs to be mandatory and nonnegotiable, and also focused on the digital economy, where services and users are interoperable.

By hoarding data, platforms that provide infrastructure data-driven services or that succeed in tipping markets can create several different problems for the upcoming IoT era. These platforms become central administrative units in ecosystems that control large parts of the industry. They become the dominant forces – and even acquire quasi-monopoly status – by holding market power both inside their respective ecosystem and generally in the relevant industry. Systems in which a few platforms hold all or significant amounts of data, where these platforms may act as gatekeepers or bottlenecks in the flow of this data between suppliers and customers, users and end users, imply loss of creativity. The Digital Markets Act provides an interesting definition of gatekeepers controlling core platform services, identifying these undertakings through the combination of the services provided and the size of the platforms. The newly proposed Data Act also provides definitions of data holders and users, providing something akin to a sui generis access and user right to data.

The gatekeeping platforms under the Digital Markets Act (DMA) and the data holders under the Data Act generally collect and hold knowledge that could benefit users when they develop new devices and products. However, by hoarding the data, these firms may allow only certain expressions of creativity to reach consumers. Indeed, the firms creating data by providing content to platforms, or by using the products that generate data under the Data Act scenario, may not be able to access the data they created and use that data for research and development, while the data

7 Ibid.

8 Lundqvist (n 2).

holders control and keep confidential all technical, customer, or user data. Increasing access to data would boost not only innovation and creativity but also the commercialization and trade of data; it would also increase multihoming and dampen the trend of hoarding on the part of large data holders. The issue is whether giving business users a right to access and use the data generated on platforms would solve the problem of platforms' exclusive data hoarding. This right would need to be effective and give the business users an edge, while still honoring the business model of the platforms. Indeed, it needs to be a right, or at least something akin to a functioning, reverse-engineering, data-mining tool.

It should be stressed that currently available tools are narrow in their effect. Despite the conferral of an unwaivable right, through the Software Directive or a data-mining right under the new copyright directive, to reverse engineer through either decompilation or black-box testing, the carve out from legal protection that the directives offer to platform providers is far from an effective method for guaranteeing access and portability of data or interoperability. It is not certain that business users will gain access to the data through these directives because the platform system leader may refuse access by claiming protection under intellectual property or trade-secret law. Technical protection measures (TPMs), cf Article 6 InfoSoc, can be used to de facto keep data confidential, because business users cannot mine the data without risk of violating the prohibition in Article 6 InfoSoc. Furthermore, the new trade-secret directive restricts data access because the information can be defined as business secrets. Providers could also claim that the dataset represents personal data, and it is thus off-limits. Other legal systems can protect gatekeepers as well. For the data generated, data holders *may* hold some intellectual property rights, such as sui generis database protection. These issues will be explored below, as well as the issue of exhaustion of rights in reference to the IoT paradigm.

Several options, implemented unilaterally or in combination, could create something akin to a data access system for natural or legal persons acting in a commercial or professional capacity and who use IoT devices and core platform services for providing goods or services to end users. These persons are often referred to as (business) users of platforms; however, a more accurate term would be data or business users or content providers to the platforms or the IoT systems, because these persons or undertakings create the content provided on the platforms or information for the development of the goods and services for IoT system leaders.

First, one could imagine an Open Data solution, where data holders have an obligation to give access and allow anyone to access and port all data. This resembles the set-up in which public sector data-holder bodies are obliged to provide access and the possibility to reuse data held by them. In reference to G2P (government to platform), all government data should in principle be available for anyone for free or at marginal cost under the Open Data paradigm. The large data holders within the public system are often organized with platforms in center of digital ecosystems.

Indeed, real estate data, corporate information, weather data, etc., are organized with users and business users providing and generating data for the platforms.[9]

Second, one could imagine a right, including a developed reverse-engineering or data-mining right, for accessing and transferring the data that is stored on the data holder's server interface, that is, most likely a database. Such a right would allow users to circumvent the data holders' right to protection under TPMs, database rights, and trade-secret legislation to gain access to the data generated by themselves. A limited access and transfer right (ATR) could be included in a stand-alone Data Act. The right could be supplemented in an updated version of the database directive, for the benefit of users. The database directive could go further and grant a more elaborated right when users have invested time and/or effort to create useful data to the level that it would become a database right in its own right.

The Digital Markets Act and Data Act mirror something in between these alternatives. Digital Markets Act stipulates an obligation for the gatekeepers to grant access to the data that business users provided or generated in the context of using the relevant core platform services. This obligation could presumably be enforced in court by a business user. However, it does not fully address whether intellectual property regimes may restrict the obligation. The Data Act grants a more limited right to access and copy the data generated by a user. The right under the proposed Data Act is narrower in reference to what data can be accessed compared to the right in the Digital Markets Act, while the Data Act addresses the intellectual property rights issues to some extent better than the Digital Markets Act. Moreover, the portability possibility under Article 6 in the DMA may be interpreted to imply that the gatekeeper needs to erase the data ported from its database, while the Data Act only implies that the data holder needs to give access and a copy of the data.[10] It can thus hold on to the data transferred to a user or third party. Nonetheless, both proposed regulations are not going far enough and should instead be replaced by a more thorough regulation for creating a ATR for users in general.

The ATR option is explored in Chapter 7 while starting to examine the current intellectual property right's landscape in reference to access and use of data collected by platforms with gatekeeping capabilities or by manufacturers in IoT settings in Section 6.2. Hence, first, under Section 6.2, the rights and exemptions currently benefiting either the platforms provider or the business user in the new copyright directive from 2019, the database directive from 1996 and the newly enacted trade-secret directive from 2016 will be identified. In Section 6.3, the effect of exhaustion in reference to products with sensors sold and transferred under the IoT setting will

[9] That could imply that they could be regulated in a similar fashion as data holders or gatekeepers according to the Data Act, the DMA, and the PSD2 and be legally obliged to share access to their data with their users. Indeed, in principle, the regulation of access to data G2P could be built around the principle of empowering the users to have a right to access and transfer of the data they generate.

[10] Continuous access should be give under the Data Act.

be explored. Second, in Chapter 7, the solution to enable access and reuse of data, an ATR to data, will be explored and presented.

6.2 RIGHTS AND EXEMPTIONS IN THE DIGITAL ECONOMY

6.2.1 *The New Copyright Directive: New Rights and Exemptions*

Ten to fifteen years ago, a growing body of literature suggested that we would be far better off with fewer property rights, and less patent and copyright protection, both in duration and in scope. Perhaps the intellectual property system we have now is worse than not having any protection at all. Something close to a general consensus had been reached regarding the notion that intellectual property rights need to be restricted and limited. According to Hovenkamp, this poor fit would call into question any presumption that competition policy should yield to intellectual property policy:

> We know pretty well what competition is and that it should be protected. However, we hardly know what intellectual property is and if it should be protected.[11]

As discussed above, the general sense that the Internet should be free from regulation and property accurately reflected the movement that accused property legal systems of being too developed and creating bottlenecks.[12] However, with the current change of policy vis-à-vis intermediates or internet content service providers, new rights are being created for the benefit of content producers. The new copyright directive (DSM Directive) includes an expansion of intellectual property protection for news writing.[13] A similar right is included for press publishers. Article 15 in the new copyright directive expands the 2001 Copyright Directive to cover publishers' direct copyright over 'online use of their press publications by information society service providers' for a period of twenty years. This right is derived from the ancillary copyright for press publishers that was introduced in Germany in 2013. Press

[11] Herbert Hovenkamp, 'Signposts of Anti-competitive Exclusion: Restraints on Innovation and Economies of Scale' in Barry E. Hawk (ed), *International Antitrust Law & Policy 2006* (Juris Publishing, Fordham Competition Law Institute 2007) 413 et seq.

[12] The recent opinion by Advocate General Øe in *YouTube* (C-682/18) reflects this. Advocate General Øe confirms that platforms are not directly liable because they are not primary posters and do not engage in acts of communication to the public. Any act of automatic classification or other similar identifying act is not an act of communication as long as there is no selection or determination of content. See C-682/18 *YouTube* ECLI:EU:C:2020:586. See also Andrej Savin, 'AG Opinion on YouTube: No New Developments, Only a Summary of Current EU Law on Intermediaries' (16 July 2020) EU Internet Law & Policy Blog Understanding EU Cyberlaw <https://euinternetpolicy.wordpress.com/2020/07/16/ag-opinion-on-youtube-no-new-developments-only-a-summary-of-current-eu-law-on-intermediaries>.

[13] Directive (EU) 2019/790 of the European Parliament and of the Council of 17 April 2019 on copyright and related rights in the Digital Single Market and amending Directives 96/9/EC and 2001/29/EC.

publishing, 'whose purpose is to inform the general public and which are periodically or regularly updated', is distinguished from academic and scientific publishing (Recital 33).

Moreover, the new copyright directive reinforces the position of right holders to negotiate and to be remunerated for the online exploitation of their content on platforms. Online content-sharing services that provide access to a large amount of copyright-protected content that is uploaded by their users should pay royalties. Article 17 removes the 'safe harbor' exemption from copyright infringement that is extended to online content-sharing service providers, according to the definition stated in the Electronic Commerce Directive of 2000, thus making these providers liable for infringement.[14]

These rights enforce the notion that content is also protected by an intellectual property right, primarily copyright, in the digital environment. They are aimed to encompass Google, YouTube, Facebook, and similar social sites and encourage these platforms to pay royalties to the content providers. Thus, the covered sites are social in nature, communicating to the public, while content on these sites is produced by others. However, the new right does not give the right holders any control over the data generated by the content uploaded on the platforms. This requires access and portability rights.

Furthermore, an issue is whether these sites will start paying royalties or whether they will instead try to exclude content covered by Articles 15 and 17. Publishers such as newspapers, who rely on Google and Facebook for about 40 percent of their traffic, have expressed concerns about unexplained dramatic changes in the number of people visiting their websites due to changes in Google's search and Facebook's news algorithms.[15]

Moreover, it seems that these sites have reached a level of penetration in the market, that is, market power, so that platform providers may threaten to exclude content producers that try to enforce the new rights and push platforms to allow sites to provide the content for free.[16] The market position of Google and Facebook potentially may be undermining the ability of newspapers and other publishers to

[14] Article 17 was held-up by the CJEU recently in case C-401/19 – *Poland v Parliament and Council* ECLI:EU:C:2022:297.

[15] CMA, 'CMA Lifts the Lid on Digital Giants' (Press release 18 December 2019) <www.gov.uk/government/news/cma-lifts-the-lid-on-digital-giants>.

[16] 'Critics also note that national versions of this law don't tend to work. In Spain, for example, in 2014, a law was passed that forced publishers to charge news aggregators for sharing snippets. Google reacted by shutting down Google News; local aggregators couldn't afford the fees and collapsed; and overall traffic to sites fell by as much as 15 percent. A similar opt-in law was passed in Germany in 2013. Google reacted by dropping sites who wouldn't let their content be shared for free and again, traffic fell and publishers bent the knee.' cf James Vincent and Russell Brandom, 'Everything You Need to Know about Europe's New Copyright Directive, The Fight over the European Internet Is Just Getting Started' (13 September 2018) <www.theverge.com/2018/9/13/17854158/eu-copyright-directive-article-13-11-internet-censorship-google>.

produce valuable content, as their share of revenues is squeezed by large platforms.[17] Indeed, at the moment, there is a European stand-off between the collecting societies and the large platforms regarding whether the platforms will or will not pay royalties.

In light of the above, it is not certain that system leaders – the gatekeepers in the data-driven economy – will honor intellectual property rights which, ten years ago, were perceived as all-encompassing, or even the new intellectual property rights developed to specifically target the platforms. It seems that the system leaders, in the ecosystems, through network effects, market tipping, and contracts (and indeed the use of economic monopolistic power), can use content without being required to honor the intellectual property rights held by content providers. They control the platforms, which gives them the power to use contracts that diminish the threat of intellectual property rights infringements through inter alia nonassertion clauses and other terms and conditions. From the above, it should be acknowledged that business users may need a mandatory right for accessing and porting data in relation to platforms. Otherwise, this right may be contractually derogated, given the clear indication that platform providers have superior bargaining power.

Users and business users, respectively, have an indirect or even direct right to access and port data under the proposed Data Act and Digital Markets Act; however, were the platform provider to claim that the data (or the technology in which the data is embedded) would benefit from intellectual property law protection, it is highly uncertain whether (business) users could use of the method for access and porting data. Nevertheless, it is possible that a (business) user could claim the right to demand access, based on the obligation for the gatekeepers. The proposal for the Data Act and the Digital Markets Act can be interpreted as tools to access data – tools that are analogous to other forms of tools for accessing intellectual-property-protected subject matter as a means to access nonprotected data, such as the reverse-engineering tool in the software directive[18] or the data-mining tool referred to in

[17] CMA (n 15).

[18] For reverse engineering, cf Article 5 of the Software Directive, which provides for the exceptions for reverse engineering in general. Such rights are not subject to the authorization of the author when these acts are necessary to enable the legitimate purchaser to use the computer program in a manner consistent with its intended purpose, including correcting errors. There are a few conditions that must be satisfied here. First, the reverse engineer must have acquired the program lawfully, that is, through a licensing agreement and purchase. Second, the reverse-engineering needs to occur while performing any activities that one is entitled to perform, such as loading, displaying, running, transmitting, or storing the program. This phrase ensures appropriate limitation of the permitted acts. These appropriate limitations are not fully specified, but one limitation is decompilation as provided for in Article 6. Another possible limitation could derive from the wording of the licensing agreement itself. In response to general cases of reverse engineering, the Court of Justice has already ruled in a case referred by the UK (*SAS Institute Inc v World Programming Ltd*) that copyright of a program cannot be infringed where the lawful acquirer of the licence merely studied, observed, and/or tested the program in order to reproduce its functionality in a second program. Indeed, would an 'idea' be

Article 4 of the new copyright directive (previously defined as the DSM Directive). Indeed, perhaps the proposal contains an overriding right, or rather an overriding obligation, that forces gatekeepers to give access to data, even when holding rights protected the gateways to the data.

Article 2 (2) of the DSM Directive defines 'text and data mining' as 'any automated analytical technique aimed at analyzing text and data in digital form in order to generate information which includes but is not limited to patterns, trends and correlations'. Text and data mining (TDM) generally refers to the computer-based analysis of large bodies of data in order to gain knowledge.[19] Article 4 of the DSM Directive requires EU Member States to allow the reproduction of copyrighted works and extraction of information using TDM technologies, as long as the miner has lawful access to the contents being mined. However, Article 4 suffers from several limitations.

An important aspect is that rights holders can override the TDM exception in Article 4 of the DSM Directive through contract restrictions. Moreover, rights holders can use technology to ensure the security and integrity of their networks and databases; this opens the possibility of technology overrides, but with the limitations stated in Article 7 of the DSM Directive.[20] The DSM Directive assumes that profit-making firms can and should get a license to engage in TDM research from the owners of the affected IP rights. On the other hand, Article 4 (3) at least applies only on the condition that rights holders have not expressly reserved their rights 'in an appropriate manner, such as machine-readable means in the case of content made publicly available online'. According to Recital 18, 'This exception or limitation should only apply where the work or other subject matter is accessed lawfully by the beneficiary, including when it has been made available to the public online, and insofar as the rightsholders have not reserved in an appropriate manner the rights to make reproductions and extractions for text and data mining.' In other words, under Article 4, rights holders may effectively prohibit text and data mining

protected through the 'expression of the idea', that is, in the functionality of the source code. But only the source code is protected, not the idea itself. Indeed, as was stated in *SAS Institute Inc v World Programming Ltd*: '. . .to accept that the functionality of a computer program can be protected by copyright would amount to making it possible to monopolize ideas, to the detriment of technological progress and industrial development. . .'; see Komal Shemar (Legal Consultant @ Gerrish Legal), 'Reverse Engineering: When Can Users Lawfully Decompile Software?' (February 2020) <www.gerrishlegal.com/legal-blog/2020/4/7/reverse-engineering-when-can-users-lawfully-decompile-software>.

[19] Pamela Samuelson, 'The EU's Controversial Digital Single Market Directive – Part II: Why the Proposed Mandatory Text- and Data-Mining Exception Is Too Restrictive' (Berkeley Law School 12 July 2018) <http://copyrightblog.kluweriplaw.com/2018/07/12/eus-controversial-digital-single-market-directive-part-ii-proposed-mandatory-text-data-mining-exception-restrictive>.

[20] Ibid. This limitation is also available under Article 3 of the DSM Directive.

for commercial uses.[21] Yet, indeed, the data-mining rules may be used as inspiration for the legislator to widen and deepen the ATRs in the proposal for the Data Act and Digital Markets Act to become rights benefitting business users and users by countervailing the rights of the data holders.[22]

For the two legal systems to be in tandem, and to create an attractive solution for users, the obligations in the Digital Markets Act and the proposed Data Act could be construed as limiting a right holder to contractual and technical restriction of data mining under Article 4 of the DSM Directive, and that the obligations under Article 6 (10) of the Digital Markets Act or Article 4 of the proposed Data Act cannot be refused by a platform provider or data holder, thus providing the argument that the data is protected by intellectual property law, falls under the trade-secret directive or is covered by the General Data Protection Regulation (GDPR).

Without these amendments, it is highly uncertain whether this systematic interpretation of the legal system would prevail. The platform provider could make a successful claim, for example, that TPMs under Article 6 InfoSoc (or the copyright protections of the API[23]) are available, irrespective of an obligation to grant access and the possibility to port data. Indeed, before we analyze the interface between the legal systems in detail, the matter of whether the platforms have copyright or even trade-secret protection in the first place needs to be addressed. Identifying the relevant right holder *de lege lata* is complicated in the systems that are currently being developed. Initially, the following explores the issue of copyright protection for the system leaders. Moreover, the application of the data-mining exception will be discussed. Thereafter, the application of the trade-secret directive and the reverse-engineering tool will be discoursed, and, finally, the interface between access and portability of data and the GDPR is analyzed.

6.2.2 *Copyright Protection*

6.2.2.1 Technical Protection Measures and APIs

Technical protection measures (TPMs) or Digital Rights Management tools (DRM), cf Article 6 InfoSoc, do not deal with copyright per se, but with technical measures introduced by the right holder, to prevent circumventions of certain conduct that might be in violation of a copyright. Thus, InfoSoc requires the Member States to harmonize rules for copyright but also to regulate the conduct

[21] Bernt Hugenholtz, 'The New Copyright Directive: Text and Data Mining (Articles 3 and 4)' (Institute For Information Law (Ivir)) 24 July 2019) <http://copyrightblog.kluweriplaw.com/2019/07/24/the-new-copyright-directive-text-and-data-mining-articles-3-and-4>.

[22] Cf Josef Drexl et al., Position Statement of the Max Planck Institute for Innovation and Competition of 25 May 2022 on the Commission's Proposal of 23 February 2022 for a Regulation on harmonized rules on fair access to and use of data (Data Act), 99 et seq.

[23] It is highly uncertain that APIs are covered by copyright in the EU.

of trying to circumvent the technical tools that prevent, for example, accessing and copying of works. This part of InfoSoc is not unique, and similar regulations exist in other jurisdictions, including in the United States.[24] Nonetheless, this part of InfoSoc has been heavily criticized because it allows and (often) validates large firms' strategies to restrict reverse engineering and to create different copyright regions (jurisdictions), in which prices and output may differ considerably.[25] Moreover, TPMs constitute a powerful tool for enforcement of copyright; they can be used to prevent extraction of data and therefore hinder interoperability – even when users in principle have a legal right to interoperability.[26]

The protection is twofold: (i) One part is the circumvention prohibition, and the (ii) second part is the antitrafficking provision. Article 6 InfoSoc stipulates that Member States shall provide adequate legal protection against the circumvention of any effective technological measures, which the person in question carries out either in the knowledge or with reasonable grounds to know that he or she is pursuing that objective. Moreover, Member States shall provide adequate legal protection against the manufacture, import, distribution, sale, rental (i.e., any trafficking) of devices, products, or components used for the purpose of circumvention of any effective technological measures.[27]

There are several issues regarding the interpretation of Article 6 InfoSoc, such as the definition of 'purpose', 'use' and 'in knowledge' and what constitutes an effective technology measure. 'In knowledge' does not refer to the intent to infringe on copyright; it refers only to the general knowledge that the conduct engaged in would lead to circumvention. The expression 'technological measures', according to Article 6 (3) InfoSoc, means any technology, device, or component which, in the normal course of its operation, is designed to prevent or restrict acts, in respect of works or other subject matter, that are not authorized by the right holder. Technological measures shall be deemed 'effective' where the use of a protected

[24] Worldwide, many laws have been created that criminalize the circumvention of TPMs or DRM, communication about such circumvention, and the creation and distribution of tools used for such circumvention. Such laws are part of the United States' Digital Millennium Copyright Act.

[25] Article 5 of the Software Directive specifies that reverse engineering is allowed in reference to computer programs, see (n 18). According to Zingales, despite the conferral of an unwaivable right to reverse engineer (cf preamble 16 of the Software Directive), either through decompilation or black-box testing, the carve out from legal protection offered by the directive is far from constituting an effective method for the attainment of interoperability. See Nicolo Zingales, 'Of Coffee Pods, Videogames, and Missed Interoperability: Reflections for EU Governance of the Internet of Things' (1 December 12015) TILEC Discussion Paper No 2015-026, 11 <https://ssrn.com/abstract=2707570> or <http://dx.doi.org/10.2139/ssrn.2707570>; Jan Trzaskowski, Andrej Savin, Patrik Lindskoug, and Björn Lundqvist, *Introduction to EU Internet Law* (2nd ed, Ex Tuto 2018) chapter 4.

[26] See G. Ghidini, *Innovation, Competition and Consumer Welfare in Intellectual Property Law* (Edward Elgar 2010) 114.

[27] Trzaskowski et al. (n 25).

work or other subject matter is controlled by the right holders through the application of an access control or protection process, such as encryption, scrambling, or other transformation of the work, other subject-matter or a copy-control mechanism, which achieves the protection objective. Thus, effectiveness does not refer to the technical aspect of whether the copyright-protected work is effectively protected but to whether the right holder controlled the technology measure and thereby access to the copyright-protected work.[28]

In *Nintendo and Others v PC Box*, the European Court of Justice addressed the issue of whether modchips in gaming consoles should be considered circumvention devices forbidden by Article 6 (2) of the Copyright Directive.[29] The decision established that the legal protection offered by Member States must comply with the principle of proportionality and could not prohibit devices or activities that have a commercially significant purpose or use other than circumventing a TPM for unlawful purposes. Thus, there are limitations to the protection of TPMs.

According to Article 6 (4) InfoSoc, some of the exemptions in Article 5 InfoSoc are also available under Article 6 InfoSoc. At first glance, it may seem a bit strange that the list given in Article 6 (4) has not been added to Article 5 (1) InfoSoc, as Member States are obligated to implement the latter article. The idea behind Article 6 (4) InfoSoc is that the exemptions stated in Article 6 (4), read in conjunction with Article 5 InfoSoc, would allow the beneficiaries of these exemptions also to cite the exemptions when faced with technical countermeasures introduced by rights holders. If the rights holders do not comply voluntarily, the Member States should step in and allow the circumvention.[30]

The protection of antiaccess technology under Article 6 of the InfoSoc Directive, which restricts the freedom to access and use works, data, and information that is not necessarily covered by copyright, has been criticized. According to Ghidini, 'the problem is not simply that all such provisions are too broad and leave excessive scope for arbitrary conduct. The fact is they lack teeth. The Directive does not provide any effective means to prevent and chastise, with appropriate sanctions and procedures, the application of TPM to non-copyrightable data and information'.[31]

Interestingly, the first, third, and fifth subparagraphs of Article 6 (4) of InfoSoc shall also apply to Articles 3 to 6 of the DSM Directive, according to Article 7

[28] Andrej Savin, *EU Internet Law, United Kingdom* (Edward Elgar 2013) 138. In some respects, Article 6 InfoSoc is out of date. It originated in the time of regional DVD and Blu-Ray players and discs, and thus does not apply well to the problems of today, for example, contractually and technically based geo-blocking of streamed movies on the Internet. Trzaskowski et al. (n 25).

[29] *Nintendo Co Ltd and Others v PC Box Srl, 9Net Srl* (Case C-355/12) [2012] OJ C 295.

[30] Trzaskowski et al. (n 25).

[31] See Ghidini (n 26). See also Jacopo Ciani, 'A Competition-Law-Oriented Look at the Application of Data Protection and IP Law to the Internet of Things: Towards a Wider "Holistic Approach"' in Mor Bakhoum, Beatriz Conde Gallego, Mark-Oliver Mackenrodt, and Gintare Surblytė-Namavičienė (eds), *Personal Data in Competition, Consumer Protection and Intellectual Property Law: Towards a Holistic Approach?* (Springer 2018).

DSM. Thus, it seems that under certain limited circumstances, data mining is exempted from violating Article 6 InfoSoc, while these exemptions are not readily available for the platform-and-business-users scenario discussed here. Thus, in the DSM Directive, the problem identified by *Ghidini* remains unaddressed by the legislator.[32]

As stated above, for business users of platforms, application programming interfaces (APIs) are a major gateway to the platforms. Application programming interfaces are software entities that allow a program to access and interact with other programs, sharing data and functionality. Application programming interfaces provide a standardized way to access and port data. Platforms therefore use thousands of APIs to enable third-party developers and service providers to use and interact with the platforms. In the EU, APIs could be possibly considered copyright protected, while the US Supreme Court recently in *Oracle v Google* found that APIs fell under the fair use exception.[33] This could promote calls for the EU to protect APIs under some form of copyright protection.

In Europe, the Software Directive (2009/24/EC) clarifies that ideas and principles underlying any element of a computer program, including – presumably – those underlying its interfaces, for example, APIs, are not protected by copyright.[34] The

32 However, the proposed Digital Markets Act can be seen as the kind of teeth that would provide the appropriate sanctions and procedure for not granting access to noncopyright-protected content.

33 Ciani (n 31) explaining that the CAFC reversed Judge William Alsup's (Northern District of California) ruling that APIs are not subject to copyright. The CAFC treated patents and copyrights as providing overlapping protection for computer program innovations. The US Supreme Court decision not to review the CAFC ruling left this finding intact. However, the case returned to Judge Alsup's district court for a jury trial focused on Google's fair-use defence. In May 2016, the jury unanimously agreed that Google's use of the Java APIs 'constitutes a fair use under the Copyright Act'. cf Google, *Inc. v Oracle America*, Inc., 135 S.Ct. 2887 (2015). Oracle appealed the retrial. On 27 March 2018, the US Court of Appeals for the Federal Circuit reversed the retrial's decision, concluding that Google's use of the Java API packages was not fair and violated Oracle's copyrights. Google's commercial use of the API packages weighed against a finding of fair use. Google merely copied the material and moved it from one platform to another without alteration this is not a transformative use. The court remanded the case for a trial on damages, but Google may still appeal to the Supreme Court. See *Oracle America, Inc v Google, Inc* No 17-1118 (Fed Cir 2018). See an interesting paper discussing APIs by Jörg Hoffmann and Begoña Gonzalez Otero, 'Demystifying the Role of Data Interoperability in the Access and Sharing Debate' (2020) Max Planck Institute for Innovation & Competition Research Paper No 20-16 <https://ssrn.com/abstract=3705217> or <http://dx.doi.org/10.2139/ssrn.3705217>.

34 According to Band, 'The Software Directive does not directly address the protectability of interface specifications. Rather, Article 1 (2) provides that "[i]deas and principles which underlie any element of a computer program, including those which underlie its interfaces, are not protected by copyright . . .." Commentators interpreted this provision to mean interface information necessary to achieve interoperability must fall on the idea side of the idea/expression dichotomy; otherwise, the detailed decompilation provision in Article 6 would have little utility.' Jonathan Band, 'The Global API Copyright Conflict' (2018) 31 Harvard Journal of Law & Technology 615. See also Kemp IT Law, 'APIs and Copyright: Who Owns the Glue that

Court of Justice has already ruled in a case referred by the UK (*SAS Institute Inc. v World Programming Ltd*) that copyright of a program cannot be infringed where the lawful acquirer of the license merely studied, observed, and/or tested the program in order to reproduce its functionality in a second program. Although the Court did not specifically address the question of whether copyright attaches to APIs, it did state that 'neither the functionality of a computer program nor the programming language and the format of data files used in a computer program in order to exploit certain of its functions constitute a form of expression of that program'. Although the judgment does not specifically address the matter of APIs and copyright protection, it has been recognized as stating that the accepted EU position appears to be that APIs are not protected by copyright because they are functional in nature.[35]

However, this situation could change if APIs come under copyright protection in the United States. A protection of APIs would likely have significant implications for accessing data and platforms for business users and would clearly imply that business users would need an overriding right to access data, going beyond the stipulations in the Digital Markets Act.

6.2.2.2 Copyright-Protected Databases

According to Article 2 of the Database Directive, accessible collections of data need to be systematically and methodically arranged to enjoy protection. The individual elements of data need to be accessible for a user.

The database directive stipulates copyright for databases that constitute the author's own intellectual creation and a sui generis right in cases where a qualitatively and/or quantitatively substantial investment has been made to set up the database. These rights are separately regulated in the directive, yet they can exist together and in parallel to the same database, since we are dealing with separate rights and, possibly, separate rights holders.[36]

Sticks the Digital World Together?' <www.lexology.com/library/detail.aspx?g=a124eb8e-d92c-4729-a2a2-8fbef75806c0>; Shemar (n 18).

35 On APIs and potential issues of IPRs, see Jörg Hoffmann and Begoña González Otero, 'Demystifying the Role of Data Interoperability in the Access and Sharing Debate' (2020) 11 JIPITEC 252, para 49. In Europe, the CJEU has clarified that data languages and data file formats are not protected under copyright law.
See Case C-406/10 SAS Institute ECLI:EU:C:2012:259, paras 29–46.

36 See generally for the Database Directive, F. Willem Grosheide, 'SUI Generis Protection for Databases the European Way: An Analysis' in Hugh C. Hansen (ed), *International Intellectual Property Law & Policy* (Juris Publishing; Sweet & Maxwell 2000) 68-1–68-16; Estelle Derclaye, *The Legal Protection of Databases: A Comparative Analysis* (Edward Elgar 2008); generally, Lucie M. C. R. Guibault and Andreas Wiebe (eds), *Safe to Be Open Study on the Protection of Research Data and Recommendations for Access and Usage* (Universitätsverlag Göttingen 2013) <http://webdoc.sub.gwdg.de/univerlag/2013/legalstudy.pdf>. See also Johan Axhamn, *Databasskydd* (PhD thesis, Stockholm University 2016).

For the copyright to be triggered, the selection or arrangement of the database should be original, and the 'author's own intellectual creation'; that is, if it expresses creative ability in an original manner by reflecting the author's free and creative choices.[37] Copyright protection extends only to the structure of the database, not to its content (Article 3 (2) of the Directive). This does not preclude independent protection of database content by other means, for example, by copyright on works or trade-secret information. Indeed, websites can be protected by copyright, as long as they are original – meaning that they reflect the creativity of expression of their authors. Copyright law also (in theory) protects only the creative expression of ideas but not the idea as such.[38] Copyright protection arises automatically upon the creation of the website. However, according to Article 6 of the database directive, lawful users of a database have a mandatory right to access content or of a copy thereof.[39]

Identifying the database author can be a complex matter, especially when several persons have taken part in setting up and developing the database. The difficulty stems in part from the fact that few harmonized principles and rules have developed on a European level in relation to author identification for a copyright-protected work. Two different approaches remain to solve the problem. The Anglo-Saxon perspective allows initial rights ownership to be conferred on the investor. The second system, on the other hand, represented by the continental countries, is rooted in natural rights and confers these rights exclusively upon the natural person.[40] EU has solved this problem by delegating the matter of author identification in the database directive to the Member States. In accordance with the respective Member States' legal tradition, the identification of individual database authors is the prerogative of the national legislator.[41] However, this is only one part of

[37] Michal Koščík and Matěj Myška, 'Database Authorship and Ownership of Sui Generis Database Rights in Data-driven Research' (2017) 31(1) International Review of Law, Computers & Technology 43–67. See *Infopaq International* (C-5/08) ECLI:EU:C:2009:465, para 45; *Bezpečnostní softwarová asociace* (C-393/09) ECLI:EU:C:2010:816, para 50, and *Painer* (C-145/10) ECLI:EU:C:2013:138, para 89.

[38] There is a clear difference between technical copyright and classical copyright. Technical copyright may de facto protect ideas, with limitation due to reverse engineering, while classical copyright serves the public interest by enhancing the free flow of information to the benefit of newspapers, media and the democratic exchange of ideas and knowledge.

[39] As discussed infra, if a business user has been active and has added collected data on a platform to the degree that database copyright protection has been triggered, the platform provider would still have a mandatory right to access the database.

[40] Koščík and Myška (n 37). See also Lucie M. C. R. Guibault and Bernt Hugenholtz, 'Study on the Conditions Applicable to Contracts Relating to Intellectual Property in the European Union' Study contract No ETD/2000 /B5–3001/E/69 (Institute for Information Law 2002) <http://dare.uva.nl/record/1/202080> accessed 12 December 2016.

[41] According to Article 4, the author of a database shall be the natural person or group of natural persons who created the base or, where the legislation of the Member States so permits, the legal person designated by that legislation as the rights holder.

the problem. The issue is how to identify the acts that are necessary to establish authorship of a copyright-protected database.

For example, a discussion is currently taking place in academia regarding whether individual websites could be included in the copyright-protection realm of the database directive. A website, such as one on Wikipedia or Amazon Marketplace, is a collection of independent elements containing information. This can be images, texts, and copyright-protected elements. Some authors claim that such a website could enter the level of protection under the database directive if the website could be considered to contain a collection of data.[42] Similarly, a profile site on a social platform could include similar, independently arranged images, texts, and other expressions. The issue is whether these elements or data could be considered systematically and methodically arranged and accessible by individuals, to the extent that the database protection is triggered in reference to the structure of the dataset.[43]

However, what about the copyright? Whether regulator copyright or database copyright, should these rights be allocated to the Wikipedia foundation and social platform provider, respectively, or to the 'authors' who create and arrange these sites or collections of data? This matter is the prerogative of the Member States, and thus it is not beyond the reach of copyright logic to allocate the right to the platform provider, for example, Amazon Marketplace or the Wikipedia foundation and/or individual(s) who created and developed the websites, such as a wiki page or even a social-platform site. This means that profile sites on social platforms could be covered not only by the GDPR but also by copyright, and protected to the benefit of the individuals creating these sites. However, the copyright can be transferred to undertakings such as platform providers; lawful users of databases have a mandatory access right, and individuals, at least, can give consent under the GDPR to social sites and other platforms to use the information contained in these platforms, when applying their business model, based for example on selling personalized ads.[44]

[42] Axhamn (n 36) 114. See also Simon Stokes, *Digital Copyright: Law and Practice* (5th ed, Hart 2020).

[43] In the EU, websites are usually protected by copyright, as long as they are original, meaning that they reflect the creativity of expression of their author. Copyright protection arises automatically upon the creation of the work, and therefore requires no registration in order to be effective.

[44] The issue of whether APIs are copyright protected is up for scrutiny in the US Supreme Court, see *Google LLC v Oracle America, Inc* 886 F.3d 1179 (Fed Cir 2018), cert. granted (US 24 January 2019) (No 18–956), petition hosted by SCOTUSBlog. On 15 November 2019, the Supreme Court of the United States granted certiorari to *Google LLC v Oracle America, Inc* 886 F.3d 1179 (Fed Cir 2018). The issues to be decided are whether copyright protection extends to software interfaces and whether Google's use of Oracle's application programming interfaces (APIs) constituted fair use. cf Justin Cho – Edited by Jeewon Lee, Harvard Law, 'Google v. Oracle: SCOTUS to Determine How Copyright Laws Apply to APIs' (1 December 2019) <https://jolt.law.harvard.edu/digest/google-v-oracle-scotus-to-determine-how-copyright-laws-apply-to-apis>.

According to Article 5 of the Database Directive, the author of a database has inter alia the following exclusive rights in a bundle of copyright: (i) temporary or permanent reproduction by any means and in any form, in whole or in part; (ii) translation, adaptation, arrangement, and any other alteration; (iii) any form of distribution to the public of the database or of copies thereof. The directive explains however that the first sale in the community of a copy of the database by the rightsholder or with his consent shall exhaust the right to control resale of that copy within the community; (iv) any communication, display, or performance to the public in reference to certain databases, for example, web-based database;[45] and (v) any reproduction, distribution, communication, display, or performance to the public of the results of the acts referred to in (ii).

However, the data generated on the platform website or by the sale of the goods or service by the business user are not normally controlled by the same; instead, such data collection are, generally, exclusively controlled by the platform provider, who also keep such data confidential. Indeed, that data are firmly embedded in the platform provider's business model. Nonetheless, it should be acknowledged that such data are generated as a result of the business users' work on the platforms, while the data reflect, and are collections of data representing, a reaction on the content the business users utilized on the platform website.[46] It is also very valuable information for the business user, and to understand and view in real time the reaction by customers to the products marketed can indeed spur innovation. To give the business users a right to access and use these datasets, which include information on the customers reaction on the products or services provided by the business users, could thus enhance the business users' ability to innovate in reference to the products or services provided. Such information would likely not go unnoticed. Indeed, before the Internet, it was difficult to obtain such reactions, and constant receipt of feedback in real time may revolutionize the way products and services are developed.[47] It would enable product development in real time but also create and develop data markets where business users may trade and share their data.[48] Moreover, the platforms' provider retains the overall picture, the aggregated data from not only the sales of the individual business users but also in reference to other sales conducted by other business users of the platforms and the data generated by their own conduct. Unilateral access under an ATR to the business data generated by the creative works of an individual business user would thus not inflict on the

45 Axhamn (n 36).

46 Regarding the issue and discussion about 'spin-off' data, see Section 6.3.4.

47 See of Iain M. Cockburn, Rebecca Henderson, and Scott Stern, 'The Impact of Artificial Intelligence on Innovation: An Exploratory Analysis' in Joshua Gans, Ajay Agrawal, and Avi Goldfarb (eds), *The Economics of Artificial Intelligence: An Agenda* (University of Chicago Press 2019).

48 Cf Maximilian Becker, 'Rights in Data – Industry 4.0 and the IP Rights of the Future' (2017) 9 Zeitschrift für Geistiges Eigentum 253.

business models of platforms, these business models being centered around aggregated data and data analytics.[49]

It is unlikely that databases for business user's data would be covered by copyright database protection; it does not reach the level of originality. Copyright protection also extends only to the structure of the database, not to its content, Article 3 (2) of the Directive. So, should the requirements for copyright protection be met, it would likely be to the benefit of the platform provider. It should however be noted that the data-mining exemption under Article 4 DSM Directive, possibly in conjunction with the Digital Markets Act, in theory is applicable in reference to copyright-protected databases.

However, what about the database that does not fulfill the rules of being copyright protected? Moreover, the datasets created under B2B and in an Internet of Things setting and provided by users to platforms and IoT systems will most likely not be copyright protected. Here, instead, the sui generis right to databases can be applicable and act as an inspiration for upcoming ATR legal system.

6.2.2.3 Sui Generis Database Protection

It should be acknowledged from the outset that several of the conception and rules in reference to the sui generis database protection lack clarity, or at least sparked a debate regarding the scope of the protection of the sui generis right. To one extent it could be attributed to the lack of case law from the ECJ, not enabling the Court to carve out fruitful doctrines. It can also be connected to a general feeling in academia that the sui generis database protection is not a 'proper' intellectual property right, should never have been enacted and a need to limit is attribution. However, what is clear is that the database directive was developed before the paradigm shift and that the database directive is in dire need to be updated from viewpoint to take the data-driven economy into consideration.[50]

A foremost discussed issue in reference to data generated on platforms, be it web-based platforms or more complex systems in reference to IoT systems for vehicles, marine vessels, airplanes, homes, or kitchens,[51] is whether the sui generis database protection could be available for the platform provider. In reference to the sui

[49] Cristina Alaimo and Jannis Kallinikos, 'Computing the Everyday: Social Media as Data Platforms' (2017) 33(4) The Information Society 175–191; Ashley P. Jones, Richard D. Riley, Paula R. Williamson, and Anne Whitehead, 'Meta-Analysis of Individual Patient Data versus Aggregate Data from Longitudinal Clinical Trials' (2009) 6 Clinical Trials 116–127 (published correction appears in (2009) 6(3) Clinical Trials 288).

[50] As discussed in this book, there is a process for updating the database directive; see Section 6.6.

[51] José van Dijck, Martijn de Waal, and Thomas Poell, *The Platform Society: Public Values in a Connective World* (Oxford University Press 2018); Murray Goulden, '"Delete the Family": Platform Families and the Colonisation of the Smart Home' (2019) 24(4) Information, Communication & Society 1–18; and generally Rob Kitchin, Tracey P. Lauriault, and Gavin McArdle (eds), *Data and the City* (Routledge 2018).

generis protection, the maker of a database obtains the protection if he shows that there has been a substantial qualitatively and/or quantitatively investment in either the acquisition, verification, or presentation of the contents of that database.[52]

As with copyright-protected databases, a sui generis database right needs to correspond to the basic requirements of a database. Article 1 (2) of the Database Directive defines a database as a 'collection of independent works, data or other materials'. it has been argued that this definition 'squarely rules out protection – whether by copyright or by database right – of (collections of) raw machine-generated data'.[53] According to Drexl, the strongest argument in this regard seems to be that the data needs to be arranged in a systematic or methodical way, which will typically not be the case where large amounts of data are collected by a connected device.[54]

Others claim that the threshold for 'systematic or methodical' has been set. Leistner states that most authors agree that this is a very wide definition, which accordingly will be fulfilled by the overwhelming majority of big data collections of any kind.[55] In the German *Autobahnmaut* case,[56] the German Federal Supreme Court (Bundesgerichtshof) seem to favor the interpretation according to which machine-generated data would be included in the sui generis right according to

[52] The court has decided on the notion of the database itself (*OPAP* (Case 444/02) ECLI:EU:C:2004:697, *Ryanair* C-30/14) and on the issues as to the activity to which the substantial investment must be related (*BHB* (C-203/02) paras 31–32; *Fixtures Marketing* (C-444/02) ECLI:EU:C:2004:697, para 41; *Fixtures Marketing v Oy Veikkaus AB* (Case C-46/02) ECLI:EU:C:2004:694, paras 34–49; *Fixtures Marketing v Svenska Spel AB* (Case C-338/02) ECLI:EU:C:2004:696, paras 24–37.

[53] P Bernt Hugenholtz, 'Data Property in the System of Intellectual Property Law' in Sebastian Lohsse, Reiner Schulze, and Dirk Staudenmayer (eds), *Trading Data in the Digital Economy: Legal Concepts and Tools* (Nomos 2017) 75, 88.

[54] Josef Drexl, 'Data Access and Control in the Era of Connected Devices', Study on behalf of the European Consumer Association BEUC, Brussels 2018, et seq.

[55] See Matthias Leistner, 'Big Data and the EU Database Directive 96/9/EC: Current Law and Potential for Reform' (7 September 2018) <https://ssrn.com/abstract=3245937> or <http://dx.doi.org/10.2139/ssrn.3245937>, stating further that as the originally wide definition of database (cf Matthias Leistner, 'The Protection of Databases' in Estelle Derclaye (ed), *Research Handbook on the Future of EU Copyright* (Research Handbooks in Intellectual Property, Edward Elgar 2009) 427, 429) has been even further extended (in respect of the crucial condition of independency of the elements) by recent ECJ case law, such as in Case C-490/14 *Freistaat Bayern v Verlag Esterbauer* [2015] ECLI:EU:C:2015:735. Leistner also makes reference to Timo Ehmann, 'Big Data auf unsicherer Grundlage – was ist "wesentlich" beim Investitionsschutz für Datenbanken?' [2014] K&R 394, 396; Herbert Zech, '"Industrie 4.0" – Rechtsrahmen für eine Datenwirtschaft im digitalen Binnenmarkt' [2015] 117(12) Gewerblicher Rechtsschutz und Urheberrecht 1151, 1157; Andreas Wiebe, 'Schutz von Maschinendaten durch das sui-generis-Schutzrecht für Datenbanken' [2017] Gewerblicher Rechtsschutz und Urheberrecht 338, 339 et seq.

[56] Bundesgerichtshof, Case I ZR 47/08, Autobahnmaut (25 March 2010).

the Commission.[57] That is the reason to include a limitation of the sui generis database right under Article 35 of the proposed Data Act.[58]

It should be noted that the above discussion is important not only from an academic standpoint. The Digital Markets Act stipulates an obligation for gatekeepers providing core platform services to give 'effective, high-quality, continuous and real-time access and use of aggregated or non-aggregated data' to their business users. It could be argued that such an obligation could be enforced as a right for the business users, while the gatekeeper does not hold a sui generis database protection. Giving access in accordance with Article 6 (1) in the Digital Markets Act excludes the possibility of having a 'collection of independent works, data or other materials arranged in a systematic or methodical way and individually accessible by electronic or other means' according to Article 1 (2) of the Database directive. Indeed, the obligation to share data is triggered before a database is created.

Whether an argument loosely sketched as the above would hold in court is uncertain, yet it should be noted that the Open Data Directive also provides a route to obtain real-time data through APIs (so-called dynamic data) and acknowledge that a maker could still utilize that database right in when making data available for reuse.[59]

The further issue of discussion in reference to the platform business model has been whether the crucial condition of a substantial investment in 'obtaining' data is fulfilled.[60] The assumption that it might not be fulfilled is based on the ECJ's judgments in *BHB v Hill* and the *Fixtures Marketing* cases, where the ECJ held that only investments into obtaining the contents of a database (i.e., the 'seeking out' of existing independent material) will be relevant for the substantiality threshold, whereas investments into the 'creation' of information and data are irrelevant in that regard. According to Mathias Lesner, from this ruling, many authors have derived that in typical big data scenarios, the investments of 'producers' of sensor or machine-generated data of all kinds will be excluded from the sui generis right because in most practical cases, such investments would have to be regarded as investments in the 'creation' of data, and not in obtaining data.[61] However, the ECJ rulings should not be found so restricted, according to Leistner, and there are cases, where the ECJ has held in different factual settings that investments into the establishment of a measuring, obtainment, or documentation infrastructure in order

[57] Impact Assessment Report, 136.

[58] Ibid.

[59] As discussed above, the Open Data Directive states that the 'right for the maker of a database provided for in Article 7 (1) of Directive 96/9/EC shall not be exercised by public sector bodies in order to prevent the re-use of documents or to restrict reuse beyond the limits set by this Directive.'

[60] EU Commission DG Connect, 2018, Study in support of the evaluation of Directive 96/9/EC on the legal protection of databases <https://ec.europa.eu/digital-single-market/en/news/study-support-evaluation-database-directive>.

[61] Leistner (n 55).

to obtain certain preexisting use, sales, or geographical data will be relevant for assessing substantiality under Article 7 (1).[62] This seems to be supported by German case law, cf The *Autbahnmaut* case discussed by Drexl.[63]

Moreover, the legal status of the spin-off doctrine, that datasets which is only a by-product of the investment in the core activity cannot benefit from database protection, is unclear on an EU level. It seems that the doctrine is not available on an EU level, or at least that it is too early to state whether the doctrine has any relevance in reference to the legal doctrine of the scope of 'substantial investment' developed by the ECJ.[64]

In reference to the issue discussed in this book, there has been a substantial investment in obtaining data and the database by the platform provider or the business users for the data. The database could be regarded as a collection of *spin-off* data of the core business of either the platform provider or the business user[65] – possibly, the spin-off data of the intellectual work created by the business user or, for that matter, as a spin-off on the platform provider's investment in the creation of the platform as such. However, the business user's data is valuable both for the business user and for the platform provider. On an aggregated level, indeed, the data are the raw material needed for the platform business model as such. In light of this, it seems clear that the database directive and the case law of the ECJ should be reevaluated. The recent *CV-Online Latvia* judgment limits the availability of the sui generis database right, recognizing that the right should only be considered as infringed, where the unauthorized use would result in 'depriving [the right holder] of revenue which should have enabled him or her to redeem the cost of [the] investment' for making the database. Whether the case actually endorses the spin-off doctrine or whether the sui generis database right now generally is not applicable to machine-generated data is still unclear. It seems that investment in sensors collecting data could be included in 'substantial investment'. However, if the current case

62 Case C-490/14 *Freistaat Bayern v Verlag Esterbauer* ECLI:EU:C:2015:735.

63 Drexl (n 54) 72 et seq.

64 Leistner (n 55) in footnote 10, '[i]n particular, this concerns cases where a machine "produces", stores and transmits *real-time operational data* which is vital to the very functioning of the machine. In such cases, indeed, it would not be far-fetched to argue that such data are "created" by the very operation of the machine if and to the extent that the operation cannot be separated from the measuring, storing and transmitting of the data and if such data are not available by any other means than the very operation of the machine. Such situations, indeed, are situated on the thin red line between the *BHB v Hill* doctrine and the spin-off doctrine (which latter the ECJ essentially rejected). Hence, in such cases legal uncertainty prevails, until the ECJ further clarifies the scope of the sui generis right in a future judgment.'

65 The spin-off doctrine has its origin in the Netherlands, see Annemariue Cristiane Beunen, *Protection for Databases, the European Database Directive and Its Effects in the Netherlands, France and the United Kingdom* (Wolf Legal Publishers 2007). For its implication of the PSI directive, seeEstelle Derclaye, 'Does the Directive on the Re-Use of Public Sector Information Affect the State's Database Sui Generis Right?' in Jens Gaster, Erich Schweighofer, and Peter Sint (eds), *Knowledge Rights – Legal, Societal and Related Technological Aspects* (Austrian Computer Society 2008) <https://ssrn.com/abstract=1316115>.

law is unclear whether in data-driven business model scenarios the spin-off doctrine[66] would exclude the core business activities of the participants, it should be clarified. It should therefore be clear that the doctrine is somewhat inadequate and obsolete as a tool for identifying when the sui generis right is not applicable, because collecting machine-readable data from sensors is the focal point of the investment and business, as such. In an updated database directive, the dichotomy between creating and obtaining data should possibly be scrapped. At least, should investments in sensors collecting data in an IoT setting be included in what is considered under substantial investment in obtaining data?

The database sui generis protection under the 1996 Database Directive[67] is applicable to makers of collection of data. Public and private entities that collect personal or nonpersonal data in databases might, thus, also fulfill the requirements for obtaining database sui generis protection, if the maker of the database has made a substantial investment in the creation of the database.[68]

According to the Commission, subject to exceptions, use by others (e.g., extraction of the content, reproduction of reuse of the database) can be prevented by the database author or maker but only to the extent that either its database in its entirety or substantial parts thereof are concerned, cf Article 7 (1), or when others seek to use insubstantial parts of the database in a 'repeated and systematic' manner, cf Article 7 (5). As for the exceptions, the maker of a sui generis database may inter alia not prevent a lawful user of the public database from normal use of the database or extracting and reusing insubstantial parts of its contents for any purposes whatsoever. As with the normal use exception under copyright-protected databases, the exemption under sui generis databases is mandatory.[69] The business users' right to access and port data under the Digital Markets Act could thus work in conjunction with the exemption, where the business user could be considered lawful user under the directive, in case the platform provider would claim sui generis or even copyright-protected database right. Possibly, the database directive, when being updated, could refer to the Digital Markets Act in this respect.

In reference to the Internet of Things, the Commission however concludes that the protection offered under the sui generis database protection, thus, does not apply

66 As discussed below, ECJ has not endorsed the spin-off doctrine, as applicable in reference to the database directive.

67 Directive No. 96/9/EC of the European Parliament and of the Council, of 11 March 1996 on the legal protection of databases. There is a two-tier protection scheme: copyright protection for creative databases. In the scientific and technical field, copyright protection relating to the individual structure of a database is not highly relevant. However, the sui generis right protecting the investment of setting up and maintaining databases is more applicable for big data databases. See Article 3 of the Database Directive.

68 C-203/02 British Horseracing Board, ECLI:EU:C:2004:128, paras 30 et seq. See also Josef Drexl, Designing Competitive Markets for Industrial Data – Between Propertisation and Access (31 October 2016) Max Planck Institute for Innovation & Competition Research Paper, No 16-13 21 <https://ssrn.com/abstract=2862975> or <http://dx.doi.org/10.2139/ssrn.2862975>.

69 See Articles 6, 8 and 9 of the Database Directive.

to machine-generated data, while a certain amount of data needs to have been used for an infringement to be at hand.[70] Others disagree and argue that machine-generated data can be encompassed by the sui generis right and that infringements might be at hand.[71] Thus, it seems rather unclear whether the Database Directive is effectively applicable for the IoT, or not. Moreover, 'extraction' should not be read literally and can be triggered when the database is simply consulted, assessed, and used, without physical transfer of data from the database.[72] In other words, the sui generis database protection may have limits, and, like the trade-secret directive, was not drafted for the IoT or platform paradigm.[73]

The database directive does not elaborate in detail on the notion of the maker of the database. Article 7 of the directive states only that the maker of the database who has made a qualitatively and/or quantitatively substantial investment should be granted sui generis database right. Recital 41 of the directive provides, however, a working definition of the maker of the database as the person who takes the initiative and the risk of investing and specifically excludes subcontractors as possible makers of a database (and consequently as initial rights owners).[74] The quality requirement makes it possible to also include intellectual investments in the creation of sui generis databases.[75] Here, possibly, the investments put by business users could be taken into consideration. Could it be so that the business users may have a claim on being the maker or at least joint maker with the platform provider of sui generis databases including data from the sale and marketing of their products or services on the platform? It is likely that the platform provider holds sui generis database protection to data from the use and utilization of the platform and that the business user has no rightful claim for database protection over said collection of data. A business user could possibly have a joint claim to the sui generis database protection as being the investor of the qualitative aspects of the database. However, there is no current case law that stretches the database directive in such a direction.

Notwithstanding the above, as discussed below, a business user may still try to make use of the data-mining exemption under Article 4 DSM Directive applicable possibly in conjunction with the Digital Markets Act to gain at least short-term access to a sui generis database consisting of data the business user has generated on the platform.

[70] Commission Staff Working Document on the free flow of data and emerging issues of the European data economy, COM (2017) 9 final, 10 January 2017, 20.

[71] Leistner (n 55).

[72] C-304/07 *Directmedia Publishing* ECLI:EU:C:2008:552, paras 46–54.

[73] Indeed, the database directive is in need of modernization, see the EU Commission website for the second public consultation: <https://ec.europa.eu/info/consultations/public-consultation-database-directive-application-and-impact-o_en>.

[74] Koščík and Myška (n 37).

[75] Axhamn (n 36) 222 et seq.

It should finally be noted here that a difference could be made between platforms that act only as agents to the business users[76] on the one hand, and on the other, where the business users act as a subcontractor to the platform. Where the platform acts as an agent the sui generis right may be available for the business user (cf preamble 41 of the Database Directive), while also under the directive for self-employed commercial agents, the agent is obliged to give access to commercial relevant data.[77] As will be discussed further below, there is a clear dichotomy between platforms obtaining data by being agents and system leaders providing complex products with multitude of data-collecting sensors and platforms with subcontractors in connection to a data-creating system (such as smart homes,[78] kitchens, aircraft, or vehicles under IoT settings). These different ecosystems should be judged differently.

6.2.3 *Trade-Secret Protection and GDPR*

Until recently, whether or not data may be covered by rules regarding trade secrets has been regulated in various ways in different Member States.[79] However, the regulatory landscape for trade secrets is dramatically changing with the introduction of harmonized rules based on Directive 2016/943/EU of 8 June 2016 on the protection of trade secrets. Unfortunately, neither modern transfer of data nor the IoT seems to have been on the minds of the authors of the directive, and its implication for the digital economy is uncertain.[80] It is probable that data, as information,[81] may be protected under the rules in the directive. Individual pieces of data might not constitute trade secrets, but datasets, that is, the combination of data or information

[76] Pinar Akman, 'Online Platforms, Agency, and Competition Law: Mind the Gap' (12 July 2019) 43(2) Fordham International Law Journal 209 <https://ssrn.com/abstract=3419067>.

[77] Articles 3 and 17 Council Directive 86/653/EEC of 18 December 1986 on the coordination of the laws of the Member States relating to self-employed commercial agents OJ L382, 31 December 1986, 17–21.

[78] Goulden (n 51).

[79] Sweden was one of few EU Member States that had enacted a specific act on the protection trade secrets, while trade secrets in the UK and in Denmark, for example, have been protected under case law and the marketing law (unfair competition law), respectively. In Sweden, collections of customer data, for example, addresses, have been protected under the Trade Secret Act.

[80] Andreas Wiebe, 'Protection of Industrial Data – A New Property Right for the Digital Economy?' (2016) Gewerblicher Rechtsschutz und Urheberrecht Internationaler Teil 877, 880; Josef Drexl, 'Designing Competitive Markets for Industrial Data – Between Propertisation and Access' (31 October 2016) Max Planck Institute for Innovation & Competition Research Paper No 16-13, 22 et seq. <https://ssrn.com/abstract=2862975> or <http://dx.doi.org/10.2139/ssrn.2862975>.

[81] See Article 2 of the Trade Secret Directive.

(that as such is not publicly available), might well be covered.[82] The same argument also applies with regard to the requirement of commercial value under the directive.[83] Even if the available data, as such, might not have commercial value, their combination can acquire a certain value, conferring a competitive advantage on the data holder.[84] It all hinges on data analytics. However, what about trade secrets in reference to databases?

Presumably, the aggregated data contained in a database controlled by the platform provider would be protected under the trade-secret directive, if the data has not been made available or collected from public third-party sources. It should be noted that the contractual relationship between the business user and the platform provider often explicitly or implicitly provides that the data generated by the business users is accessible for the platform provider and that the data should be considered a trade secret for the benefit of the platform provider and that the data provided by the business user should be considered confidential information. The trade-secret directive would most likely not be applicable because the issue of trade secrets would be bilaterally regulated in the agreements.[85]

If data is not stored in databases, but instead is available in a nonsystematized manner in the cloud, the datasets would not fall under the database sui generis protection in the first place, and neither would databases in which no substantial investments have been made.[86] Here, the trade-secret directive could still have effect.

It should be stressed that neither the DSM Directive in general nor Article 4 regarding data mining refers to the trade-secret directive. The Digital Markets Act also fails to mention the trade-secret directive. However, it is conceivable that the business user of a platform could a possibility to access and port datasets that the platform provider claims include trade secrets. According to the preamble of the

[82] See Josef Drexl et al., 'Data Ownership and Access to Data, Position Statement of the Max Planck Institute for Innovation and Competition' (2016) Max Planck Institute for Innovation and Competition Research Paper No 16-10, 6 et seq.

[83] Ibid.

[84] Ibid.

[85] Article 3 of the trade-secret directive states: The acquisition of a trade secret shall be considered lawful when the trade secret is obtained by any of the following means:

(a) independent discovery or creation;
(b) observation, study, disassembly or testing of a product or object that has been made available to the public or that is lawfully in the possession of the acquirer of the information who is free from any legally valid duty to limit the acquisition of the trade secret;
(c) exercise of the right of workers or workers' representatives to information and consultation in accordance with Union law and national laws and practices;
(d) any other practice which, under the circumstances, is in conformity with honest commercial practices.

[86] Stanley Greenstein, 'Our Humanity Exposed' (Doctoral thesis, Stockholm University 2017) 112 et seq.

trade-secret directive (para. 39), the directive should not affect the application of any other relevant law in other areas, including intellectual property rights and the law of contract. Furthermore, preamble 16 states '[i]n the interest of innovation and to foster competition, the provisions of this Directive should not create any exclusive right to know-how or information protected as trade secrets. Thus, the independent discovery of the same know-how or information should remain possible. Reverse engineering of a lawfully acquired product should be considered as a lawful means of acquiring information, except when otherwise contractually agreed. The freedom to enter into such contractual arrangements can, however, be limited by law.' Hence, reverse engineering is accepted, yet in comparison to the Software Directive, the practice can be contractually restricted within the limits of the law.[87]

From the above, one could try to construe a line of argument proposing that a user should have access to data generated by the activities of the user, which in certain instances is covered by the trade-secret directive because there is a right to access it through the principle of reverse engineering, and the obligation to give access and allow transfer of data under the Data Act and Digital Markets Act that cannot be contractually limited.[88] However, this argument contains several weaknesses. Access to and porting of data do not constitute reverse engineering as we have previously come to understand this principle.[89] Access and porting obligations or rights to data in other sector-specific regulations are available only for data that is not covered by trade-secret rules.[90]

Moreover, the Commission rigorously claims that the GDPR and the *lex specialis* ePrivacy Directive fully regulate the processing of personal data. There is a fundamental right to protection of personal data in the EU, under Article 8 of the Charter of Fundamental Rights. The GDPR sets out the rules for processing personal data, including, inter alia, the collection, use of, access to and portability of personal data, as well as the possibilities to transmit or transfer personal data. According to the Commission, the right to data portability under Article 20 of GDPR will allow individuals to obtain copies of personal data they have provided to a service provider/data controller and to move that data to another service provider/data controller (e.g., personal data on a social media platform). This may minimize potential lock-in

[87] Cf Preamble 16. Trade Secret Directive. For discussion of the reverse-engineering exemption in the trade-secret directive, see e.g., Zingales (n 25) 11 et seq.

[88] See preamble 55 in the proposal; a gatekeeper should not use any contractual or other restrictions to prevent business users from accessing relevant data and should enable business users to obtain consent from their end users for such data access and retrieval, where such consent is required under Regulation (EU) 2016/679 and Directive 2002/58/EC. Gatekeepers should also facilitate access to this data in real time by means of appropriate technical measures, for example by establishing high-quality application programming interfaces.

[89] See, for example, the Software Directive. See also Noam Shemtov *Beyond the Code Protection of Non-Textual Features of Software* (Oxford University Press 2017); Pamela Samuelsson and Susanne Scotchmer, 'The Law and Economics of Reverse Engineering' (2002) 111 The Yale Law Journal 1575–1663.

[90] See the discussion regarding the Open Data Directive for example Chapter 4.

effects. However, device producers do not have a similar right.[91] Furthermore, both producers and individuals may hold rights to the same data. The individual's right to port data is not a commercial right, while a right to port datasets would benefit the collector.

Moreover, the relationship between the rules on trade secrets and the right to data portability under the GDPR has not been fully elaborated.[92] While the old data protection directive could give data subjects an overriding right to transfer personal data, the data porting right under the new regulation is less clear on this point.[93] For example, customer data could be covered by the trade-secret directive, while also falling under the GDPR. The reason for this shift could be that the GDPR aims to establish a high threshold for data protection and for the free movement of data, that is, the fifth freedom of the internal market.[94] The commercial reasons for this may have been the overriding goal of data protection, so that data defined as trade secrets is not covered by the porting right in the GDPR.

In reference to access and porting of data, the end user must provide consent. The Digital Markets Act states in preamble 55 that a gatekeeper 'should ... enable business users to obtain consent of their end users for such data access and retrieval, where such consent is required under the GDPR'. However, according to Article 6 (1) (f) of the GDPR, access and sharing of personal data can be lawful without user's consent when 'processing is necessary for the purposes of the legitimate interests pursued by the controller or by a third party, except where such interests are overridden by the interests of fundamental rights and freedoms of data subject [user] which require protection of personal data.'[95] Thus, consent is not required in a limited number of cases, when the risks of data access and sharing are small and potential usefulness of data sharing is high. With consent or without, the GDPR provides an avenue that facilitates data sharing – if it increases welfare when privacy risks are low.[96] For the benefit of access and portability and what that may entail in terms of increased innovation and the creation of markets, the business users and holders of ATRs should be allowed to use Article 6 (1) (f) exemption of the GDPR.[97]

91 Commission Staff Working Document on the free flow of data and emerging issues of the European data economy, COM (2017) 9 final, 10 January 2017, 20.

92 Gintare Surblytė, 'Data Mobility at the Intersection of Data, Trade Secret Protection and the Mobility of Employees in the Digital Economy' (2016) Max Planck Institute for Innovation & Competition Research Paper No 16-03, 14 et seq. <http://ssrn.com/abstract=2752989> or <http://dx.doi.org/10.2139/ssrn.2752989>. cf Article 20 (4) and recital 63, General Data Protection Regulation.

93 Ibid.

94 The Swedish Trade Council (2016) 1 et seq.

95 Geoffrey Parker, 'Georgios Petropoulos and Marshall W. Van Alstyne, Digital Platforms and Antitrust' (22 May 2020) <https://ssrn.com/abstract=>.

96 Ibid.

97 Moreover, it should be recognized that under certain circumstances, Articles 5 (1), 6 (4), and 89 could enable firms to conduct R&D based on personal data, without the need of consent.

Because of the great uncertainty around what is actually restricted by the GDPR, the de facto application of the GDPR seems to differ from its theoretical scope. As discussed above, large technology firms use the GDPR offensively and limited their data-sharing activities far beyond what was needed when the GDPR was introduced.[98] In fact, there is empirical evidence that data-driven markets suffered from increased concentration after the GDPR was introduced.[99] It is indeed clear that, as with other rules in the GDPR, Article 6 must be interpreted in light of creating competition and a level playing field. It should therefore be a clear presumption that a holder of an ATR should retain access and portability rights to ex post personal data, even without the consent of the concerned individual(s).[100] However, this needs to be analyzed on a case-by-case basis, and individuals may occasionally have the right to have their data erased, for example.

6.2.4 *The Interface*

The proposed Data Act and Digital Markets Act indeed offer opportunities for a new, interoperable Internet, where leveraging – including self-preferencing and other forms of abuse – are restricted. However, in terms of creating a level playing field in relation to access and use of data, there may be some hidden limitations to a genuine, interoperable use of services and flow of data from the gatekeepers that provide so-called core platform services to their business users.[101]

Articles 3, 4, 5, and 35 of the Data Act and Article 6 paragraphs (2), (9), and (10) in the Digital Markets Act, read together, stipulate an obligation for data holders and gatekeepers to give access and transfer data to users, to a level that could be regarded as a countervailing ATR that overrides the sui generis right to databases under Article 7 of the Database Directive.

As discussed above, the right is more straightforward in the Data Act. Presumably, business users under the Digital Markets Act could go to court to make a claim vis-à-vis gatekeepers. The article stipulates that gatekeepers are de facto not allowed to use the data generated by business users, and their end users, on the platforms, are in competition with the business users, while the obligation in Article 6 (9) and (10)

98 See also Michal Gal and Oshrit Aviv, 'The Competitive Effects of the GDPR' (2020) Journal of Competition Law and Economics 22 et seq.

99 Christian Peukert, Stefan Bechtold, Michail Batikas, and Tobias Kretschmer, 'European Privacy Law and Global Markets for Data' (2020) <https://ssrn.com/abstract=3560392>.

100 See discussion infra regarding the interplay between rights and freedom from a constitutional perspective.

101 For definition of a core platform service and a gatekeeper, and how the obligations for the gatekeepers are triggered, see the proposal for the Digital Markets Act <https://eur-lex.europa.eu/legal-content/EN/TXT/PDF/?uri=CELEX:52020PC0842&from=en>.

reflects that business users may apply a compulsory access regime to gain access to, port, and reuse the data generated by their action on the platforms. Indeed, this entails a right to receive a steady stream of data from the platforms – a stream that can also be transferred to third parties.

This could be a paradigm shift in the relation between core platform service providers and business users of the same. The combination of Article 6 paragraphs (1), (9), and (10) creates a compulsory access regime, stopping just short of a property right, to the data generated by the business user and its end users on the platform. It might be considered legally binding for the gatekeepers, even though the gatekeepers still hold intellectual property rights that might prevent access and reuse. Still, this is uncertain. The issue, as discussed above, is whether the gateway for business users to access and port data is in fact such a revolutionary tool for creating interoperability, or whether, in the end, the intellectual property legal system or the GDPR will de facto prevent data access, reuse, and portability. It seems obvious that the gatekeepers will try to claim that the obligation to give access and for the business users to reuse the data generated on their platforms should not be enforced because the data is walled in by intellectual property rights or reflects personal data.

Data as such is not covered by any property right. However, data can still be walled in and legally protected. Technical protection measures, cf Article 6 InfoSoc, can prevent access to copyright-protected content and, unfortunately, unprotected data as well. 'Hacking', or breaching technical measures and other DRMs to gain access to unprotected data can be a violation of Article 6 InfoSoc. Moreover, the gates to platforms – the APIs – may be copyright protected, also restricting access.[102] However, perhaps the biggest hurdle to gaining access to the data is that the gatekeepers, when storing the data in databases or in private, centralized blockchains, could most likely hold sui generis database protection as stipulated under the 1996 directive.[103]

It is possible that application of these rules in reference to the obligation in the proposed Data Act and Digital Markets Act can be rejected with the argument that in the end, there is no infringement inherent in the access and reuse of the data by business users. Nevertheless, the rights described above, together with the right to trade secrets and the rule making personal data off-limits, seem to create sufficient uncertainty that could allow gatekeepers and data holders to deny applicability of the obligation to grant access to data, because such access and reuse could allegedly infringe the rights and obligations of the gatekeepers and data holders. This is indeed a pity.

[102] See discussion above regarding US *Google LLC v Oracle America, Inc*, which may have EU policy implications.

[103] They can, moreover, claim that the datasets they collect are trade secrets under the new EU Trade-secret Directive, or in the case of personal data, might be off-limits under the GDPR.

It is true that under the intellectual property law system, business users also have tools for accessing data. The new data-mining regulation in the (new) software directive, used in conjunction with the proposed Data Act and Digital Markets Act, could perhaps pry open the gates to allow access to keepers' data. It is possible that the reverse-engineering doctrine in the Software Directive could also be used, together with the Digital Markets Act, in the analogy of breaching the keepers' gates. However, the application of these exemptions is uncertain at best.

Generally, the Commission or the European legislator needs to clarify whether the unfair competition rules being drafted in the Digital Markets Act and the Data Act are capable of creating access and portability of data unilaterally or in combination with the exemption of data mining and reverse engineering in the area of copyright. Should the rules be viewed as creating an obligation for the gatekeepers to actually grant access also to intellectual property law or trade-secret-protected subject matters (held by the platform or third party)? Are the regulations developed reverse-engineering and data-mining tools that business users and end users can apply? Could they develop under the scrutiny of the ECJ to become reverse-engineering rights, paralleling the data-mining exemption under the new Copyright Directive?

What is necessary, therefore, is the establishment of an access and portability right for business users of platforms, accompanied by the appropriate legal and technical tools for gaining access to data; this right must be able to penetrate subject matter protected by intellectual property law, to ensure that business users can exercise their rights. Indeed, the regulations could be given a property angel, or include an incontrovertible data-mining right (an extended reverse-engineering right) designed to cover the situations addressed by the regulations. These ideas will be developed below under Chapter 7.

6.3 EXHAUSTION

6.3.1 *Exhaustion and the Internet*

Applying the doctrine of exhaustion of rights is a difficult matter when it comes to the Internet, especially because some of the 'transfers' occurring on the Internet involve the use of services rather than the transfer of products, and may thus fall outside the doctrine; generally, on the Internet, the use of a service constitutes communication to the public under Article 3 InfoSoc, not distribution of a tangible item, and Article 3 is exempted from the exhaustion doctrine. However, we need to remember that the Internet transforms several activities that were previously viewed IRL as services into tangible items. Services were commoditized to be included, for example, in software for distribution on the Internet. Perhaps the problems and uncertainty involved in transfer and exhaustion with respect to services and tangible digital items on the Internet will be transferred to real life through the use and increased importance of the Internet of Things.

A case that involves several of these aspects is *Premier League*,[104] where the ECJ indirectly addressed the issue of exhaustion. The case dealt with the transmission, communication, and broadcast of English football matches. In the United Kingdom, certain restaurants and bars had begun using foreign decoding devices (originating mainly in Greece) to access Premier League matches, instead of purchasing/licensing the more expensive UK decoding devices. The cards and decoder boxes that restaurant and pub owners bought from dealers allowed them to receive a satellite channel broadcast in another Member State. The decoder cards had been manufactured and marketed with the authorization of the service provider but were subsequently used in an unauthorized manner – the broadcasters made the sale of these cards subject to the condition that customers did not use them outside the national territory concerned. The 'hot topic' of the case was whether this parallel import of decoders from another EU Member State constituted a violation of UK (IP) law and whether the contract had been violated.

The ECJ reached an interesting conclusion. It stated that 'on a proper construction of Article 56 TFEU, that article precludes legislation of a Member State which makes it unlawful to import into and sell and use in that State foreign decoding devices which give access to an encrypted satellite broadcasting service from another Member State that includes subject-matter protected by the legislation of that first State.' Article 56 TFEU concerns the free movement of service provisions, yet it seems that the rights covering the decoding devices were exhausted. However, could the Court's ruling imply that the service/right of broadcasting the game may also be exhausted? This could have far-reaching consequences with respect to the Information Society Directive (see below) and the dichotomy between Article 3 (Communication) and Article 4 (Distribution). Can communication under Article 3 InfoSoc be exhausted under Article 56 TFEU? Moreover, these questions could have implications for the right to collect data sent by sensors in system parts under the IoT paradigm discussed in this book.

Several other cases regarding use of the doctrine of exhaustion and the meaning of 'communication to the public' under Article 3 InfoSoc have been brought (see below).[105]

[104] Joined Cases C-403/08 and C-428/08 *Football Association Premier League and Murphy* ECLI: EU:C:2011:631.

[105] See, for example, *ITV Broadcasting Ltd and Others v TVCatchUp Ltd* Case C-607/11 [2013] ECLI:EU:C:2013:147; Case C-466/12 *Nils Svensson and Others v Retriever Sverige AB* [2014] ECLI:EU:C:2014:76; Case C 277/10 *Luksan* [2012] ECLI:EU:C:2012:65; Case C-160/15 *GS Media BV v Sanoma Media Netherlands BV and Others* [2016] ECLI:EU:C:2016:221 Opinion AG Wathelet; Case C-301/15 *Marc Soulier and Sara Doke v Premier ministre and Ministre de la Culture et de la Communication* [2016] ECLI:EU:C:2016:878; Case C-138/16 *Staatlich genehmigte Gesellschaft der Autoren, Komponisten und Musikverleger registrierte Genossenschaft mbH (AKM) v Zürs.net Betriebs GmbH* [2017] ECLI:EU:C:2017:218; Case C-610/15 *Stichting Brein v Ziggo BV and XS4All Internet BV* [2017] ECLI:EU:C:2017:456 and C-265/16 *VCAST Limited v RTI SpA* ECLI:EU:C:2017:913.

It seems clear that services that are communicated to the public in accordance with Article 3 InfoSoc are not exhausted; nevertheless, there are several means of distributing games, software, films, TV, etc., on the Internet, and the doctrine of exhaustion needs to be taken onto consideration depending on the means of distribution.

Article 3 InfoSoc deals with the right of public communication, now adapted for the Internet, with regard to copyrights. The article stipulates that Member States shall provide authors with the exclusive right to authorize or prohibit any communication to the public of their works, by wired or wireless means, including making available to the public their works in such a way that members of the public may access them from a place and at a time chosen by the individual. The Member States are obligated to introduce this latter feature in respect to performers, phonogram producers, and broadcasting organizations. Moreover, the term 'communication to the public' under the EU harmonizing measures can be found in the variety of legislative measures that encompass several subject-matter-specific areas, such as works, beneficiaries, and pecuniary rights.[106] This concept can be found for databases (as works) under the Database Directive,[107] satellite broadcasting (as a work) under the SatCab Directive,[108] related rights (encompassing works, beneficiaries as well as remunerative and exclusive pecuniary rights) under the Rental and Lending Rights Directive,[109] and copyright (works, beneficiaries, and exclusive

[106] Marusic Branka, *Communication to the Public* (PhD thesis, forthcoming; text on file with the author). More specifically, as explained by Branka, the autonomous legal concept can be found in four different directives. Under Article 5 (d) of the Database Directive, a right is granted for communication, display, or performance for the public of a database (work). The SatCab Directive in Article 2 provides for an exclusive right of communication to the public by satellite broadcast. The Rental and Lending Rights Directive covers three different subject-matter situations (relating to works, beneficiaries, and pecuniary rights). Under Article 8 (1), performers are granted an exclusive pecuniary right to the communication to the public of their performances (works). Under Article 8 (2), phonogram producers are granted a remunerative pecuniary right to the communication to the public of their phonograms (works). Lastly, under Article 8 (3), broadcasting organizations are granted an exclusive pecuniary right to the communication to the public of their broadcasts if such communication is made in places accessible to the public in return for payment of an entrance fee. The InfoSoc Directive's Article 3 (1) provides for an exclusive pecuniary right of communication to the public, including the provision of copyright works, and Article 3 (2) extends the subject matter of the making available right to related rights. However, as previously noted, the substance of the autonomous legal concept itself remains undefined in these harmonizing measures. See also Justin Koo, *The Right of Communication to the Public in EU Copyright Law* (Hart 2019) 45.

[107] Directive 96/9/EC of the European Parliament and of the Council of 11 March 1996 on the legal protection of databases OJ L77, 27 March 1996, 20–28 (hereafter the 'Database Directive').

[108] Council Directive 93/83/EEC of 27 September 1993 on the coordination of certain rules concerning copyright and rights related to copyright applicable to satellite broadcasting and cable retransmission OJ L248, 6 October 1993, 15–21 (hereafter 'the SatCab Directive').

[109] Directive 2006/115/EC of the European Parliament and of the Council of 12 December 2006 on rental right and lending right and on certain rights related to copyright in the field of intellectual property (codified version) OJ L376, 27 December 2006, 28–35 (hereafter: the 'Rental and Lending Rights Directive').

pecuniary rights) under the InfoSoc Directive.[110] Generally, the right to communication referred to in Article 3 InfoSoc, as well as under other directives, shall not be exhausted by any communication to the public or by making the works available to the public. Because the right to communicate cannot be exhausted, the creator will retain the copyright if the creator communicates the work (for example through public performance, broadcast, or streaming).[111]

> The *Retriever* case is an example of the use of Article 3 and the principle of exhaustion.[112] In February 2014, the ECJ delivered its decision in the case. The applicants – all journalists – wrote press articles that were published in the Swedish newspaper *Göteborgs-Posten* and on the newspaper's website. *Retriever Sverige* operated a website that provided its clients with lists of clickable Internet links to articles published by other websites, according to the needs of its clients. It was agreed between the parties that those articles would be freely accessible on Göteborgs-Posten's website. According to the applicants in the main proceedings, if a client clicks on one of the links, it is not apparent to that client that he or she has been redirected to another site where the client can access the work in which he or she is interested. According to Retriever Sverige, however, it should be clear to the client that clicking on one of the links will redirect to another site. The issue of the case was thus whether 'linking' could constitute 'communication to the public' according to Article 3 InfoSoc. ECJ dwelt on the issue, but in the end concluded that Article 3 InfoSoc must be interpreted as meaning that a website's provision of clickable links to works freely available on another website does not constitute an 'act of communication to the public', as referred to in that provision. Moreover, the ECJ stated that Article 3 must be interpreted as precluding a Member State from giving wider protection to copyright holders by establishing that the concept of communication to the public includes a wider range of activities than those referred to in that provision.

The new Copyright Directive includes an expansion of the intellectual property protection for news writing, which may have implications in reference to the doctrine developed in *Retriever*. Article 15 in the new Copyright Directive expands InfoSoc to cover publishers' direct copyright over 'online use of their press publications by information society service providers' for a period of twenty years. Press publishers, 'whose purpose is to inform the general public and which are periodically or regularly updated', is distinguished from academic and scientific publishing (Recital 33).[113]

[110] Directive 2001/29/EC of the European Parliament and of the Council of 22 May 2001 on the harmonisation of certain aspects of copyright and related rights in the information society OJ L167, 10 (hereinafter: the 'InfoSoc Directive').

[111] See also recital 25 of InfoSoc. See, however, the *Premier League* case referred to above.

[112] Case *Svensson (Retriver)* C-466/12 ECLI:EU:C:2014:76.

[113] Moreover, the new Copyright Directive reinforced the position of rights holders to negotiate and be remunerated for the online exploitation of their content on platforms. Online content-sharing services that provide access to a large amount of copyright-protected content uploaded

Article 4 of InfoSoc covers the distribution right, which can be exhausted in accordance with the case law discussed above. It stipulates the obligation on the Member States to provide authors, in respect of the original of their works or of copies thereof, with the exclusive right to authorize or prohibit any form of distribution to the public by sale or otherwise. Thus, the distribution right shall not be exhausted within the Union with regard to the original or copies of the work, except where the right holder makes the first sale or other transfer of ownership in the Union (or consents to such sale or transfer) of that work. According to recital 28, Article 4 deals only with the distribution of works that have been incorporated into a tangible item, for example, on a DVD disc. On the Internet, intellectual property revolves around digital copies, and while the Software Directive or even the TFEU may sometimes be applicable,[114] it is difficult to see when Article 4InfoSoc can be used with reference to the Internet. In addition, according to its wording, Article 4 is applicable only to authors.

Articles 3 and 4 InfoSoc were created so that the EU could regulate the complex nature of communication and distribution of rights on the Internet. Generally, these provisions demonstrate that the doctrine of exhaustion of rights applies only to the right to control distribution (resale, export, or import). It does not generally apply to the right to rent, perform, or broadcast, including streaming, a (copyright-protected) work in public for which the specific subject matter of the right allows the owner to control each and every use (for it is through charging for each use that the essential function of the right is achieved).[115] This complexity is also visible in other situations where other directives are applicable, for instance in the *Premier League* case that was discussed above. The famous *UsedSoft* case[116] deals with both licensing and exhaustion of distribution rights in reference to the Software Directive and could illustrate the difficult dichotomy between communication to the public and distribution:

> In *UsedSoft*, the case was about the plaintiff Oracle, which distributes software on the Internet. Customers of Oracle downloaded a copy of the software directly to their computer from Oracle's website and paid a fee, and the software was known as 'client-server-software'. In the case, the user right for such a program, which was granted by a license agreement, included the right to store a copy of the program permanently on a server and to allow a certain number of users (i.e. 25 users per license) to access it by downloading it from their server to the main memory of their

by their users should pay royalties. Article 17 removes the 'safe harbour' exemption from copyright infringement, given to online content-sharing service providers, according to the definition stated in the Electronic Commerce Directive of 2000, making these providers liable for infringement. Proposal for a directive on copyright in the Digital Single Market (PDF) (25 May 2018) 30, para 37.

114 See the interesting case *UsedSoft* (C-128/11) [2012] ECLI:EU:C:2012:407.

115 There is also the dichotomy between intangible and tangible goods. See also WIPO Copyright Treaty Article 6 with thereto connected Agreed Statements.

116 *UsedSoft* (C-128/11) [2012] ECLI:EU:C:2012:407.

> workstation computers. Oracle's license agreements for the software at issue contained the following term, under the heading 'Grant of rights': 'With the payment for services you receive, exclusively for your internal business purposes, for an unlimited period a non-exclusive non-transferable user right free of charge for everything that Oracle develops and makes available to you on the basis of this agreement.' UsedSoft (the defendant) marketed used software licenses, including user licenses for the Oracle computer programs. For that purpose, UsedSoft acquired such user licenses, or parts of them, from the Oracle customers; the original licenses related to a greater number of users than required by the first acquirer. Customers of UsedSoft who were not yet in possession of the Oracle software in question downloaded a copy of the program directly from Oracle's website, after acquiring a used license from UsedSoft. Customers who already had the software and then purchased more licenses for additional users were induced by UsedSoft to copy the program to the workstations of those users.
>
> The first issue for the courts was whether there had been an exhaustive distribution of the software from Oracle to the customers; in other words, had the customers obtained ownership (property) of the program, the license from Oracle or the license from a copy of the program? According to the ECJ, the right of distribution of a software license is exhausted if the copyright holder who has authorized the download of a copy of the program from the Internet onto a data carrier has also conferred, in return for payment of a fee intended to enable the holder to obtain a remuneration corresponding to the economic value of the copy of the work, a right to use that copy for an unlimited period. Should the user license be resold, entailing the resale of a copy of a computer program downloaded from the copyright holder's website, and the license was originally granted by that right holder to the first acquirer for an unlimited period in return for payment of a fee intended to enable the right holder to obtain a remuneration corresponding to the economic value of that copy of the work, the second acquirer of the license, as well as any subsequent acquirer of it, will be able to rely on the exhaustion of the distribution right, and hence be regarded as lawful acquirers of the copy of the computer program.[117]

The *UsedSoft* case illustrates the difference between purchasing and licensing, as well as the difference between distribution and communication to the public. Oracle was found to have sold and distributed a license and a copy of the program, but the company had not licensed and communicated the software. An interesting feature here is that the digital copy of the program could be considered a dataset and, in *UsedSoft*, the ECJ indirectly acknowledged that datasets can be transferred and exhaustively purchased.[118]

[117] *UsedSoft* (Case C-128/11) [2012] ECLI:EU:C:2012:407para 88.

[118] Drexl (n 54) 61. See also 61 et seq., discussing why personal data and the rights under the GDPR are not exhausted because the GDPR does not create a property right. Ownership in data is not related to personal data as the object of a property right, while personal data in the current framework is only an intermediary tool for protecting personality rights. See also Václav

It should be acknowledged that the *UsedSoft* case concerned the Software Directive and not InfoSoc.[119] In *UsedSoft*, the CJEU regarded the provisions of the Software Directive as *lex specialis* and thus left unresolved the matter of how a similar case should be adjudicated for other categories of works under the InfoSoc.[120] Indeed, the integration of the internal market logic and the exclusion of the exhaustion principle for the communication right can be found in the legislative narrative of Article 3 (3) of the InfoSoc Directive, and the inclusion of the exhaustion principle in the distribution right in Article 4 (2) of the InfoSoc Directive.[121] Similar logic should also be applied for nonharmonized communication rights, such as direct communication for copyright-protected works (including databases), because the nature of the act of communication predisposes an instantiation's consumption of the work by users.[122] This creates a situation where a new, direct communication must be established every time a user wishes to enjoy a work being directly communicated, for example, in the form of performance or display.[123]

Janeček, 'Ownership of Personal Data in the Internet of Things' (2018) 34(5) Computer Law & Security Review 1039–1052 <https://papers.ssrn.com/sol3/papers.cfm?abstract_id=3111047>. Moreover, it should be noted that *UsedSoft* could also have a bearing with respect to a cloud server set-up, where the resale of software licences is generally permitted under the following conditions:

1. The computer program was put on the market within the EEA with the rights holder's consent.
2. The original rights holder granted a perpetual licence, meaning without time limitations.
3. The rights holder received reasonable remuneration.
4. The initial acquirer (who later resells the licence) deletes all remaining program copies.

[119] As stated by the CJEU in the recent *Tom Kabinet* case para 55: '. . . as the Court expressly stated in paragraphs 51 and 56 of the judgment of 3 July 2012, UsedSoft (C-128/11, EU:C:2012:407), Directive 2009/24, which concerns specifically the protection of computer programs, constitutes a *lex specialis* in relation to Directive 2001/29. The relevant provisions of Directive 2009/24 make abundantly clear the intention of the EU legislature to assimilate, for the purposes of the protection laid down by that directive, tangible and intangible copies of computer programs, so that the exhaustion of the distribution right under Article 4 (2) of Directive 2009/24 concerns all such copies (see, to that effect, judgment of 3 July 2012, UsedSoft, C-128/11, EU:C:2012:407, paras 58 and 59).'

[120] See *UsedSoft* para 51.

[121] Branka (n 106).

[122] Ibid. See generally *Nederlands Uitgeversverbond and Groep Algemene Uitgevers* (*Tom Kabinet*) (C-263/18) ECLI:EU:C:2019:1111. For criticism of the judgement see Péter Mezei, 'The Doctrine of Exhaustion in Limbo – Critical Remarks on the CJEU's *Tom Kabinet* Ruling' (2020) Zeszty Naukowe Uniwersytetu Jagiellonskiego – Prace z Prawa Wlasnosci Intelektualnej (2/2020 Jagiellonian University Intellectual Property Law Review 130–153 <https://ssrn.com/abstract=3560138> or <http://dx.doi.org/10.2139/ssrn.3560138>.

[123] See Marušić Branka, 'Author's Right to Choose: Right of Divulgation in the Online Digital Single Market of the EU' in Tatiana-Eleni Synodinou, Philippe Jougleux, Christiana Markou, and Thalia Prastitou (eds) *EU Internet Law in the Digital Era: Regulation and Enforcement* (Springer 2020) 137–160.

Databases can be protected under both copyright and sui generis protection, according to the Database Directive, and these databases can be web-based or held on nonaccessible servers. Moreover, this book also deals with databases that are confidential and not accessible for the general public. Hence, server-based or web-based databases, including the communication to the public rule, should be exposed to the exhaustion principles.

However, sensors included in parts that are transferred are not necessarily required to fulfill the principles and rules for exhaustion in reference to databases. In analogy with the *UsedSoft* case, the sale of parts containing a sensor or software that collects data could be considered to include the explicit or implicit possibility for the transferee or owner of the device to conduct reverse engineering and to mine the data from the sensor. This also seems to reflect the outcome of the *Premier League* case, where the sale of decoding devices did indeed trigger the exhaustion principle. Therefore, the sensor, including a right to obtain data and embedded in the part sold to the system leader or the manufacturer, should be transferred or assigned to the subsequent purchaser.

Indeed, the sensor as such should be encompassed by the principle of exhaustion and should be transferred when the part or device is being purchased and legal ownership is transferred. The purchaser should have the possibility to access the sensor and the data that it generates, as well as the authority to grant sensor access to others.[124] The legal set-up of exhaustion of the right to the sensor and the data it collects for the benefit of the owner is thus somewhat neutralized by an ATR to the data associated with the provided part.

6.3.2 *Exhaustion and the Internet of Things*

In reference to the Internet of Things, the principle of exhaustion plays an important role. In the general situation of the emerging IoT industry, a manufacturer of large machines (e.g., a road vehicle, aircraft, or ship) purchases parts from subcontractors and then assembles the machine, and the parts producer will most likely include sensors in their supplied parts to obtain information (data). According to the EU Commission, an airplane engine, for example, will have several sensors monitoring the engine in real time; the sensors are active during the machine's operation.[125] Likewise, the drive line of a large ship will have multiple sensors allowing the producers of the drive line and its parts to follow all distributed drive lines in the world, in real time, from their IoT headquarters.

[124] It could be argued that the purchaser of a device should also have the right to 'turn down' the amount of data generated by the device. Here, a balance must be achieved between the inherent right to access data under an ATR and the purchaser's right to control the device and the sensor.

[125] Commission, 'Wireless sensors make aircraft maintenance more efficient' <https://cordis.europa.eu/article/id/116391-wireless-sensors-make-aircraft-maintenance-more-efficient>.

According to the Data Act presented above, parts producers should retain a right to obtain necessary data from the device owner, or the manufacturer or system provider of the platform, be it a web-based platform such as Amazon or an IoT-based platform such as a vehicle, airplane, marine vessel, factory, or even a smart city.[126] Thus, these producers should have access to the data generated by the sensor embedded in their parts, while the legal basis for such an access and porting right is based on Article 3 of the Data Act, that is not exhausted with the sale of the device, that is, the container of the sensor. However, as discussed below, the sensor as such should be encompassed by the principle of exhaustion and should be transferred when the part or device is being purchased and legal ownership is transferred. Indeed, the purchaser should have the possibility to access the sensor and the data that it generates, as well as the authority to grant sensor access to others.[127] The legal set-up of exhaustion of the right to the sensor and the data it collects for the benefit of the owner is thus somewhat neutralized by the set-up in Articles 3 to 5 of the proposed Data Act.

When the ownership of the car is transferred, the ultimate purchaser of the car (a lessor or private individual) should obtain the right to collect the data from the car or vehicle. Included in the transfer of ownership should be control also of the sensor. It follows from the system for exhaustion, the purchaser – including individuals – should indeed have the right to data generated by the vehicle, while the producers of parts and the manufacturer of the complex system, for example, the car, should retain something akin to an access and portability right under Article 3 of the Data Act, in reference to the data generated by the car. The manufacturer and the subcontractors should also have the contractual possibility to access their respective generated data in reference to the vehicle owner.[128] Individuals have access under the GDPR. In this light, Articles 4 and 5 of the Data Act actually restrict the notion of exhaustion and limit the property right held by the user. This is unsettling.

The above system would not disrupt the vehicle manufacturer's business model in terms of in-vehicle data and dynamic technical data. Manufacturers retain the exclusive possibility to combine the data from all vehicles, especially from the manufacturer's own sensors or other sensors to which the manufacturer has access. The valuable information is not obtained by access to individual sensors in single vehicles but the real-time access to the sensors embedded by the manufacturer and the manufacturers' data architecture, collecting large datasets of vehicle data. This data is aggregated from all or most of the vehicles under a brand and produced or

[126] van Dijck et al. (n 51); Goulden (n 51); and generally Kitchin et al. (n 51).

[127] It could be argued that the purchaser of a device should also have the right to 'turn down' the amount of data generated by the device. Here, a balance must be achieved between the inherent right to access data under an ATR and the purchaser's right to control the device and the sensor.

[128] In the Nordic legal tradition, an exclusive right such as an ATR would not be encompassed by the notion of *köp bryter legostämma*.

assembled by a manufacturer. It should also be acknowledged that the ultimate purchaser could be the lessor – who is often identical to the car manufacturer, being an affiliated firm within the company group of the manufacturer. Furthermore, the future development where vehicles will rather be devices for transport service, where even autonomous driving will be controlled by the manufacturer, the ownership of the sensors will be retained by the manufacturer, giving the manufacturer direct access to the data generated by all sensors in the device/system because the devices will not be exhaustively sold. Here, Articles 4 and 5 of the Data Act have an independent meaning.

As to software that is either included in the system at car purchase or downloaded by the driver or purchaser, the question is this: Which entity should be in control of the data collected by devices or software such as a GPS and map system or even an independent driving system? In these situations, the principle of exhaustion must also be taken into consideration, as presented in this chapter. The question is whether the copy of the software is licensed or purchased of the producer of the car, or more accurately, whether a transfer of property is de facto at hand.[129] If a transaction of property has taken place, the possibility to collect data and monitor the car should be transferred to the purchaser; an ATR could be available for the software provider for the data created by the software. The claim for data access should be addressed to the car's provider in the purchase, that is, normally the producer of the car – and the party in control of the software-generated data. Indeed, this could enable the purchaser of the car to acquire the necessary control over which data is collected by the vehicle, while the software provider still retains a right to access and port its generated data.

[129] See discussion later in this book in reference to the *UsedSoft* case, C-128/11 [2012] ECLI:EU:C:2012:407.

7

An Access and Transfer Right to Data

7.1 INTRODUCTION

Providing access and transfer rights (ATRs) to data for the benefit of business users (i.e., content providers and other firms) in their relationship with platforms is not an easy fix. However, such rights can be identified as intellectual property rights and, in Germany (the jurisdiction where this has been discussed most), the idea of covering data with property rights has been strongly rejected by both intellectual-property and competition-law academics.[1]

[1] For an interesting discussion, reflecting this, see Hanns Ullrich, 'Technology Protection and Competition Policy for the Information Economy. From Property Rights for Competition to Competition without Proper Rights?' (12 August 2019) Max Planck Institute for Innovation & Competition Research Paper No 19-12 <https://ssrn.com/abstract=3437177> or <http://dx.doi.org/10.2139/ssrn.3437177>. See also, for example, Josef Drexl et al., 'Data Ownership and Access to Data – Position Statement of the Max Planck Institute for Innovation and Competition of 16 August 2016 on the Current European Debate' (16 August 2016) Max Planck Institute for Innovation & Competition Research Paper No 16-10 <https://ssrn.com/abstract=2833165>. Josef Drexl et al., 'Position Statement of the Max Planck Institute for Innovation and Competition of 26 April 2017 on the European Commission's 'Public Consultation on Building the European Data Economy', Max Planck Institute for Innovation and Competition Research Paper No 17-08 <ssrn.com/abstract=295992>; Josef Drexl, 'Designing Competitive Markets for Industrial Data – Between Propertisation and Access' (2017) 8 JIPITEC 257 para 1; Bernt Hugenholtz, 'Against "Data Property"' in Hanns Ullrich, Peter Drahos, and Gustavo Ghidini (eds), *Kritika Essays on Intellectual Property* (Edward Elgar 2018), 48 et seq.; Jacques Crémer, Yves-Alexandre de Montjoye, and Heike Schweitzer, 'Competition Policy for the Digital Era' (Final Report 2019); Wolfgang Kerber, 'A New Property Right for Non-Personal Data? An Economic Analysis' (2016) Gewerblicher Rechtsschutz und Urheberrecht, Internationaler Teil 989; Wolfgang Kerber, 'Rights on Data: The EU Communication "Building a European Data Economy" from an Economic Perspective', in Sebastian Lohsse, Reiner Schulze, and Dirk Staudenmayer (eds), *Trading Data in the Digital Economy: Legal Concepts and Tools* (Nomos 1 September 2017) <https://ssrn.com/abstract=3033002>; Daniel Zimmer, 'Property Rights Regulating Data?' in ibid., 101.

The strong rejection by some German scholars was a reaction to the proposal for creating a property right to individual, nonpersonal data elements or points. The original idea and the relevant discussion of creating a European property right for nonpersonal data points originated in Germany.[2] According to some scholars,[3] the champion of this cause was the former Commissioner of the European Commission's Directorate-General for Communications Networks, Content and Technology (DG Connect), Germany's Günther Oettinger. He and several others perceived data as the gold of the future and felt that the uncertainty around ownership of data must be resolved.[4]

The discussion regarding creating a property right to nonpersonal data has shuttled back and forth,[5] while the European Commission has also put forward the idea in several policy papers of creating a property right to nonpersonal data, for the benefit of the business users.[6] The EU Commission's proposals seem to mirror the proposal presented by Professor Herbert Zech.[7]

In this chapter, it will be argued that the regulation of the data-driven economy could be amended with a right for accessing and transferring the data that is collected and stored on the data holders' server interface, that is, most likely a database. Such an access right taking inspiration from or including data-mining or

2 Thomas Hoeren, 'Big Data and the Ownership in Data: Recent Developments in Europe' (2014) 7 European Intellectual Property Review 751–754; A. de Franceschi and M. Lehmann, 'Data as Tradable Commodity and New Measures for Their Protection' (2015) 1 Italian Law Journal 51–72; Herbert Zech, 'A Legal Framework for a Data Economy in the European Digital Single Market: Rights to Use Data' (2016) 11 Journal of Intellectual Property Law & Practice 460–470; Karl-Heinz Fezer, 'Data Property of the People – An Intrinsic Intellectual Property Law Sui Generis Regarding People's Behavior-generated Informational Data' (2017) Zeitschrift für Geistiges Eigentum 356, 356–357.

3 See, for example, Hugenholtz (n 1) 48 et seq.

4 It should be acknowledged that in 2017 in Japan, there also was a discussion regarding a property right to data. The discussion ended with a METI producing guidelines for data contracts. See, for example, Contract Guidelines on Utilization of AI and Data Version 1.1 Formulated <www.meti.go.jp/english/press/2019/1209_005.html>.

5 See, for example, the summary of the stakeholders, where most seem to purport that a general one-size-fits-all policy does not suffice when it comes to ownership of data. Commission, 'Synopsis Report – Consultation on the "Building a European Data Economy" Initiative' (2017) 4 et seq.

6 Commission, 'Towards a Common European Data Space' COM (2018) 232 final of 25 April 2018. European Commission, 'Communication from the Commission to the European Parliament, the Council, the European Economic and Social Committee and the Committee of the Regions' SWD (2017) 2 final, COM (2017) 9 final, 13; 'Communication from the Commission of 10 January 2017 – Building a European Data Economy' COM (2017) 2 final; European Commission, 'Commission Staff Working Document on the Free Flow of Data and Emerging Issues of the European Data Economy' COM (2017) 9 final, 10 January 2017, 33, making reference to the works of Herbert Zech, who claimed that the right way forward is the creation of a property right to nonpersonal data.

7 Zech (n 2). See also Herbert Zech, 'Building a European Data Economy – The European Commission's Proposal for a Data Producer's Right' (2017) 9 Zeitschrift für Geistiges Eigentum 317.

reverse-engineering rights would allow users to circumvent the data holders' right to protection under technical protection measures (TPMs), database rights, and trade-secret legislation to gain access to the data generated by themselves. Such a limited access and transfer right could be included in a stand-alone Data Act.

Moreover, the right to access and transfer for users should also be aligned with the General Data Protection Regulation (GDPR), giving a user the right to also access personal data when the user can provide equal protection under the GDPR as the original data holder.

The right could be supplemented in an updated version of the database directive for the benefit of users. The database directive could moreover go further and grant a more elaborated right when users have invested time and/or effort to create useful data to the level that it would become a database right in its own right. This would normally apply for business users of platforms.

In reference to the sensor or the system that will collect the data in an Internet of Things (IoT) device, the starting point should be that the holder of the property right to the device or the sensor should also hold the right to extract data from the sensor. Indeed, such a principle would be derived from the doctrine of exhaustion. The property holder should have the right to license access to the sensor for third-party access to data. The user of IoT devices with sensors should have equal right to access and transfer the user-generated data, including such inferred data originating from the sensor. Indeed, a right (an ATR) should be granted to the user in reference to the principles drawn up above.

It is argued in this book that creativity, innovation, and the general development of markets for data can be promoted by creating something akin to a users' ATR to data held by platform providers. Under the Digital Markets Act dichotomy, such a right should cover the datasets generated by the business user's commercial activities on the platform and include aspects of property. However, an ATR does not necessarily need to be exclusive or even property based. It could also be viewed as something similar to a data-mining right – or analogous to a compulsory licensing or access scheme.[8] Business users have a mandatory right to access data from platforms under a scheme, while platform providers are obliged to grant access under licenses.[9] The access and portability obligations for platforms in the Digital Markets Act resemble a countervailing data-access right or compulsory grant

8 It should be noted that a discussion arose during the evaluation of the Database Directive, regarding whether to impose a compulsory licence system in the directive: however, the directive's authors refrained from suggesting such a system, while still recommending a close watch on sensor-produced technologies. See Commission, 'Study in Support of the Evaluation of Directive 96/9/EC on the Legal Protection of databases' (Final Report 2018) 40 et seq.

9 Josef Drexl, 'Data Access and Control in the Era of Connected Devices', Study on behalf of the European Consumer Association BEUC, Brussels 2018 <www.beuc.eu/publications/beuc-x-2018-121_data_access_and_control_in_the_area_of_connected_devices.pdf>. Drexl opposes a property regime, while considering competition law to be necessary – but not sufficient – for establishing 'Competitive Markets for Industrial Data', and therefore recommends introducing

scheme, because the right to access and portability according to the regulation is incontrovertible, even though its interface with intellectual property rights and protections – which benefit the platform provider – is not clear cut. The rules in the DMA must also be identified as a right to access and portability, which can be claimed, in court, by business users of platforms. A future revised Digital Markets Act, being a regulation, should have horizontal applications, giving rights that business users can exercise against the gatekeeper, at least for the benefit of obtaining redress. It will be enforced not only by the Commission but also by private parties.[10]

'Access' and 'porting' are still rights that are included in the bundle of rights claimed to be included in ownership. Indeed, it is suggested in this book to pick up the benefits of a property regime for datasets, yet to reject the drawbacks with the same regime. Property, or some aspects included in the bundle of rights that normally is by legal scholars considered applicable to property, may empower the device or content producers vis-à-vis the platforms, and thus enhance competition by reducing network effects and increasing creativity; more firms – and not only the platform providers – will be able to access relevant data to conduct research and develop their business models. It may well be that access to generated data and a porting right to datasets created through firms' activities on a platform comprise the solution. Porting may create competition between platforms, as it enables users – brick-and-mortar firms – to choose among platforms and cloud service providers, thus enhancing competition and reducing network effects, and may promote development of new platforms and e-ecosystems. This in turn could increase both competition and creativity, and thus the number of potential inventors. On the other hand, a system where a few platforms hold all data and act as gatekeepers or bottlenecks between manufacturers. The platforms holding all the data, that is, knowledge, that is necessary to develop new products may allow only certain expressions of creativity to reach the consumers. Indeed, the firms that create data by providing content to platforms may not be able to use the data for R&D, as long as the platforms hoard all customer or user data.

Given the above, it seems that a right to data generated by business activities on platforms, for the benefit of brick-and-mortar firms providing products or content that cannot be contractually eroded or derogated, could be the way to create markets and increase creativity and innovation. This transfer right would

specific general and/or sectoral access regimes. Indeed, he draws inspiration from the Open Data Directive that obligates public-sector bodies to give access to data.

10 The Commission seem to believe that the DMA will be applicable in private enforcement suits. See the website presenting the proposal, stating: 'The Digital Markets Act is a Regulation, containing precise obligations and prohibitions for the gatekeepers in scope, which can be enforced directly in national courts. This will facilitate direct actions for damages by those harmed by the conduct of non-complying gatekeepers.' <https://ec.europa.eu/commission/presscorner/detail/en/QANDA_20_2349>.

resemble the right given to individuals under the GDPR. However, from an economic perspective, the new right should belong to the content providers and include all data, that is, both personal and nonpersonal data.[11]

It is not the incentive to collect data that needs to be 'boosted' by property rights.[12] Rather, it is creativity that should be promoted by enabling device manufacturers to access the customer information they need to conduct R&D and develop their products. Moreover, a right to port such data would create competition, that is, the dataset commercialization and transfer that need to be supported, so that the benefits of a digital economy can be realized. A right for device producers to port datasets between platform providers would certainly enhance trade; business users, on the other hand, are more likely to sell data.

From general theory, we know that property and competition are not incompatible in reference to 'boosting' trade: They are complementary. Property is one of the foundations of trade and thus of competition.[13] Without a legal system protecting the transfer (porting) of property, great inefficiencies will emerge when trade takes place, resulting in high transaction costs; without or with limited trade, there are no real markets or competition. Property, for instance, intellectual property, creates markets by limiting information (knowledge) and commercializing it, thus giving the inventor or collector specific rights to this information.[14] This facilitates trade because it generates rivalry by limiting the free supply of specific knowledge for the purpose of commercial use.[15] By transforming knowledge or information into products, the intellectual property system constitutes the framework for markets.[16] In addition, we need more markets for data and more competition between platforms, and strong porting rights could decrease indirect network effects and tipping.

[11] Fezer argues that a right to data should include both personal and nonpersonal data. See Fezer (n 2).

[12] Josef Drexl, 'Designing Competitive Markets for Industrial Data – Between Propertisation and Access' (31 October 2016) Max Planck Institute for Innovation & Competition Research Paper No 16-13, 33 <https://ssrn.com/abstract=2862975> or <http://dx.doi.org/10.2139/ssrn.2862975>.

[13] Hanns Ullrich, 'Legal Protection of Innovative Technologies: Property or Policy?' in Owe Granstrand (ed), *Economics, Law and Intellectual Property* (Springer Science+Business Media Dordrecht 2003) 447 et seq.

[14] According to some scholars, Kenneth Arrow was the first to conclude that patents and other intellectual property rights concern the market for information. cf Kenneth Arrow, 'Economic Welfare and the Allocation of Resources for Invention' in R. Nelson (ed), *The Rate and Direction of Inventive Activity: Economic and Social Factors* (National Bureau of Economic Research 1962) 609 et seq. The rights included within a patent are, for example, a distribution right (including a rental right), a manufacturing right, and a user right.

[15] Ullrich (n 13) 448 et seq. Participants in the FTC hearing regarding the interaction between competition law and intellectual property law support the proposed concept that granting a patent marks the beginning of commerce. When the US Supreme Court granted a patent in *Diamond v Chakrabarty* 447 US 303 (1980) for a living, human-made microorganism, it laid the groundwork for the genetic engineering industry as such. See FTC, 'To Promote Innovation: The Proper Balance of Competition and Patent Law and Policy' (FTC 2003) 21, with references.

[16] Ullrich (n 13) 450.

If the risk is that platform providers would vertically integrate, the porting right would empower the brick-and-mortar firms to change platforms or retain their data in-house. Thus, a strong porting right to datasets might provide a solution. However, which data should business users have the right to port? What is the subject matter of the right?

7.2 LEGAL DEFINITION OF DATA

Several authors discuss semantics in reference to data, implying that by creating protection of individual data points, data would be protected on the syntactical level, and such protection would severely hamper access to information on the level of semantics and pragmatics. Thus, protection of individual data points, implying that protection of the level of syntactics (i.e., 0s and 1s) could have a strong chilling effect on the access to and use of information for creating artistic works, design, know-how, innovations, etc.

Information and data do not constitute singular objects but instead should be understood as collective terms comprising different categories of data that can be defined in more detail.[17] Data as it is discussed in this book refers first and foremost to digital data and not analog data. It is true that to some extent, the term 'digital data' relates to electronic or magnetic signals that are represented by syntactics – the numeric characters 0 and 1 – ultimately constituting continual series of bits and bytes. This represents *data points*, while *data* implies information. One can also distinguish between locally stored data, for example, data on an in-house server, and online data, which is often placed in a virtual cloud structure. In addition, the notions of 'metadata', that is, data about user data, and 'derived data', that is, new data generated through the analysis of user data or metadata, need to be understood in this context. Finally, personal data is any information that relates to an identified or identifiable living individual. Personal data is subject to the legal framework of data protection, and thus includes all kinds of digital information that relates to an identified or identifiable living individual.[18]

If data were protected as a subject matter, individual words and, more accurately, individual volumes of information could be at least indirectly protected. Compare this to copyright, for example, which does not protect information as such; it protects only the creative elements of a song, novel, or painting. Copyright refers only to certain aspects of information. Using individual data points as the subject matter for a data right would potentially cause a fundamental paradigm shift from the principle

[17] Lennart Chrobak 'Proprietary Rights in Digital Data? Normative Perspectives and Principles of Civil Law' in Mor Bakhoum, Beatriz Conde Gallego, Mark-Oliver Mackenrodt, and Gintare Surblytė-Namavičienė (eds), *Personal Data in Competition, Consumer Protection and Intellectual Property Law* (MPI Studies on Intellectual Property and Competition Law, vol 28, Springer 2008) 254 et seq.

[18] Ibid.

of free use of information to one of protection of information. In addition, 'if we search for the right balance in reference to intellectual property protection, our focus should be on the information/semantics level, and under this perspective the introduction of a broad data right on the syntactic level would have serious consequences.'[19]

Indeed, the exclusive right to or ownership of individual data points – at least in terms of the syntactic level – should be avoided.[20] Otherwise, significant bottlenecks may arise. However, this does not preclude firms or individuals from having a right to datasets or databases; the information contained in the dataset or database is not walled in merely because it is only the database structure that is being protected or the database is protected only against substantial extractions of data.[21] Interestingly, the obligations in Article 6 (2) compared to the obligations in (9) and (10) of the Digital Markets Act reflect that the business users have some sort of preferential right to the data generated by its commercial activities, vis-a-vis the platform provider. Indeed, a preferential right to each data point. Yet, the platform business models have benefited society, and perhaps society should not disqualify the business models as such. The user right in the Data Act is more limited in scope both in reference to the data it encompasses and that it is only right to copy, while transferring the data is more challenging. The Data Act only concerns raw data generated by the user under Article 4, while Article 3 encompasses all data generated for the benefit of the data holder.

There is no comprehensive legal definition of data that satisfies the discussion in academia regarding how data should be defined. The Public Sector Information (PSI) Directive and other data-access regimes focus instead on the subject matter of the access tool. According to Article 5 of the Open Data Directive, for example, data should be made available in a preexisting format or language and, where possible and appropriate, by electronic means, in formats that are open, machine-readable, accessible, findable and reusable, together with their metadata, and preferably through an application programming interface (API),[22] while in the field of transport and financial services[23] and in other legislative

[19] Andreas Wiebe, 'Protection of Industrial Data – A New Property Right for the Digital Economy?' (2017) 12(1) Journal of Intellectual Property Law & Practice 62–71, 67

[20] Drexl (n 12) 17 et seq.

[21] The scope of the sui generis database right is discussed infra Section 6.3.4.

[22] The Directive on the reuse of public-sector information, Directive (EU) 2019/1024 of the European Parliament and of the Council of 20 June 2019 on Open Data and the reuse of public-sector information, OJ L172, 26 June 2019, 56–83 (The old PSI directive: Directive 2003/98/EC, known as the 'PSI Directive') entered into force on 31 December 2003. It was revised by Directive 2013/37/EU, which entered into force on 17 July 2013.

[23] In order to accelerate retail banking innovation and simplify payments, the European Commission is mandating standardized API access across the EU. The initiative is part of the European Commission's update of the Directive on Payment Services (PSD). The revision to the Directive on Payment Services (PSD2) requires banks to provide access to third parties. See Directive (EU) 2015/2366 of the European Parliament and of the Council of 25 November

initiatives,[24] the definition or rather the subject matter of the access rule for data can be focused on semantics.

The Database Directive, however, does contain something akin to a legal definition of data. According to Article 1 (2) of the Database Directive, 'database' shall mean 'a collection of independent works, *data* or other materials …'. The word 'data' was included to bring the definition in line with the TRIPS agreement.[25] Data can imply both information and syntactics, yet it seems that the legislator has implied that data should be understood as information. The term 'information' is used in several places in the preamble as a synonym for data.[26] Syntactic data which is not yet information – because it cannot be perceived as information by humans – should not be understood as 'data' in the meaning of the directive.[27] This is supported by the Advocate General Stix-Hakl in *Oy Veikkaus*: '[t]he question whether the main proceedings concern data or materials need not be considered in greater depth, because in practice they concern either data, in the sense of combinations of signs representing facts, that is to say, elementary statements with potentially informative content, or materials as recognizable entities.'[28]

2015 on payment services in the internal market, amending Directives 2002/65/EC, 2009/110/EC and 2013/36/EU and Regulation (EU) No 1093/2010, and repealing Directive 2007/64/EC (Text with EEA relevance). cf EU Commission, 'A Digital Single Market Strategy for Europe' COM (2015) 192 final.

24 Several regulatory initiatives are discussed below. However, for access data regimes, see also the REACH-Regulation, Article 25 Regulation (EC) No 1907/2006 of the European Parliament and of the Council of 18 December 2006 concerning the Registration, Evaluation, Authorisation and Restriction of Chemicals (REACH), establishing a European Chemicals Agency, amending Directive 1999/45/EC and repealing Council Regulation (EEC) No 793/93 and Commission Regulation (EC) No 1488/94 as well as Council Directive 76/769/EEC and Commission Directives 91/155/EEC, 93/67/EEC, 93/105/EC and 2000/21/EC. See furthermore Article 16 of the new Digital Content and Digital Services Directive, referring to the GDPR, discussed in Z. Efroni, *Gaps and Opportunities: The Rudimentary Protection to 'Data-Paying Consumers' under New EU Consumer Protection Law* (Weizenbaum Series, 4, Weizenbaum Institute for the Networked Society – The German Internet Institute 2020) <https://doi.org/10.34669/wi.ws/4>. See also the new Electricity Directive of June 2019 imposes the sharing of consumer data, including metering and consumption data as well as data required for customer switching, demand response and other services. In order to stimulate competition and innovation among electricity suppliers, Article 23 (2) of the Directives provides that porting of data should be required. Finally, the Clinical Trials Regulation 536/2014 on clinical trials on medicinal products for human use, and repealing Directive 2001/20/EC.

25 Johan Axhamn, *Databasskydd* (PhD thesis, Stockholm University 2016) 96.

26 See, for example, preambles 3, 9, 10 and 12.

27 Axhamn (n 25).

28 Case C-46/02 *oy Veikkaus*, 33. The AG continues and states in p. 36 that the criterion of 'independence' should be understood as meaning that the data or materials must not be linked or must at least be capable of being separated without losing their informative content; this is why audio and images from a film are not covered. One possible approach to interpretation is to focus not only on the mutual independence of the materials from one another, but instead on their independence within a collection.

The issue is also the requirement on *independent* data or material. It seems that for both data and the notion of *material* to be recognized by the directive, they need to have independent meanings, that is, individual data points should contain information that can be understood by an individual (possibly using a machine). They should have independent meanings. In *OPAP*, concerning whether football team schedules could be protected under the directive, the EU Court states that '. . . the date and the time of and the identity of the two teams playing in both home and away matches are covered by the concept of independent materials within the meaning of Article 1 (2) of the directive in that they have autonomous informative value.'[29] The EU Court has even found in another case that an individual point on a map can constitute a relevant element.[30] Moreover, individual pieces of information in combination can constitute independent material.[31]

The definition of data and independent material and the notion that individual pieces of information in combination can constitute 'independent material', within the meaning of Article 1 (2) of Directive, point to the fact that 'data' should be viewed as information rather than syntactic figures or numbers.[32] On the whole, it seems that the Database Directive does focus on datasets that contain comprehensible information, but it should be acknowledged that the scope of these datasets can be limited.[33] Indeed, a map can be considered a database.[34] Independent data is information.

Article 2 of the Digital Markets Act provides a vague definition of data, yet which resembles the definition in the Database Directive: 'data means any digital representation of acts, facts or information and any compilation of such acts, facts or information, including in the form of sound, visual or audio-visual recording'. The notion of data should also be considered to include 'raw data' and metadata, even though the article does not provide a clear definition of either term. Data according to the Data Act is defined in a similar fashion as any digital representation of acts, facts, or information and any compilation of such acts, facts, or information, including in the form of sound, visual, or audio-visual recording.

29 Case 444/02 *OPAP*, ECLI:EU:C:2004:697, 33.

30 Case C-490/14 *Verlag Esterbauer*, ECLI:EU:C:2015:735, 20 et seq.

31 Ibid. See Wiebe (n 19).

32 It should be acknowledged, however, that the definition of data under the Database Directive is uncertain, and developments are taking place that may mean that basic information or 'raw data' could be considered as covered by the Directive; cf Discussion supra regarding case 444/02 OPAP, ECLI:EU:C:2004:697, 33 and case C-490/14 *Verlag Esterbauer*, ECLI:EU:C:2015:735, 20 et seq. The EU Commission's first evaluation of the Database Directive states: '[h]owever, as evidenced by the ECJ's differentiation between the "creation" of data and its obtaining demonstrate, the "sui generis" right comes precariously close to protecting basic information.' See also Drexl (n 9) discussing this at 33.

33 Axhamn (n 25) 98. See C-444/02 *Fixtures Marketing*, ECLI:EU:C:2004:697, para 35, and C-604/10 *Football Dataco and Others*, ECLI:EU:C:2012:115, para 26.

34 Case C-490/14 *Verlag Esterbauer*, ECLI:EU:C:2015:735, 20 et seq.

Moreover, in the Digital Markets Act, the obligation on platform providers to share data covers only the data that is provided for or generated in the context of the business users' interaction with the relevant core platform services and the end users' engagement with the products or services provided by those business users.

In reference to the definition above, however, the issue is how to distinguish the business users' data from the data generated by the business of the platform. As will be discussed below, different APIs or even blockchain technology could be used to find gates and identify which data originates from which entities, that is, pinpoint data 'provided for or generated in the context of the use of the relevant core platform services by those business users and the end users engaging with the products or services provided by those business user...' However, referred data can in fact have several sources.

This book proposes that the subject matter of an ATR should thus be information, the user's data representing 'any digital representation of acts, facts or information and any compilation of such acts, facts or information, including in the form of sound, visual or audio-visual recording'. Indeed, *business user's data* under the Digital Markets Act is the platform data that refers to the data created by activities or contributed by the business user: In an IoT setting, it refers to sensor-collected data collected.[35] The platform provider should provide business user's data just as public entities do when giving public-sector information to reusers according to national laws and under the Open Data Directive, that is, aggregated or nonaggregated data, in a preexisting format or language, in real time by electronic means, in formats that are open, machine-readable, accessible, findable and reusable, together with the corresponding metadata, and preferably through an API.[36] An ATR could also include a reengineering and data-mining right to enter the platform to gain access to the data, or a requirement on the platform to set up a specific gateway such as an API that gives business users access to data.

A further issue is whether each and every data point should fall under an ATR or under the Digital Markets Act, and whether there should be a threshold requirement for more extended protection. One could imagine that a business user should obtain a stand-alone database protection when the data generated has reached a volume – sufficient proof that the business users have interacted to such an extent with the platform that the created data actually reflects a real investment or for that matter personal creativity.

An ATR could be connected to datasets or a database consisting of such *business user's data*. One could imagine an ATR to business user's datasets. Therefore, there

[35] As discussed below, the aggregated data should be controlled by the platform provider.

[36] The Directive on the reuse of public-sector information Directive (EU) 2019/1024 of the European Parliament and of the Council of 20 June 2019 on Open Data and the reuse of public-sector information, OJ L172, 26 June 2019, 56–83 (The old PSI directive: Directive 2003/98/EC, known as the 'PSI Directive') entered into force on 31 December 2003. It was revised by Directive 2013/37/EU, which entered into force on 17 July 2013.

is no counterfactual right to individual data points, only an intellectual property right to the datasets, reflecting the similarly limited right in the Database Directive.[37] Indeed, business users should have a right to access and port dataset(s) or database(s), while technically such rights could reflect a block of data in a blockchain.

Interestingly, the obligation in Article 6 (2) compared to the obligations in Article 6 (9) and (10) may reflect business users' indirect, bilateral, right to the generated business user's dataset, vis-à-vis the platform provider. Indeed, it is possible that this is a preferential right to each data point that overrides the possible sui generis right of the gatekeeper. An interesting consequence of having an ATR that focuses only on *user's data* is that obtained information will not contain (or is very unlikely to contain) works covered by third-party intellectual property rights.[38] Moreover, by focusing only on the data generated by the actions of the business user or provider, the legal system presented in this book still preserves the business model of the system leader. All inferred data from the actions of several users, industries, and markets connected to the platform belongs to the platform, and hence benefits the platform providers' general business model.

However, discussing the definition of the subject matter in more detail first requires an answer to the question: Who should be able to exercise the ATR?

7.3 GDPR FOR INDIVIDUALS AND ATR FOR USERS

The business users of platforms (which in theory could be an individual) or a user under the Data Act would be the persons with the right to access and port user's data, because this will enable markets to develop and will boost competition and creativity. The purchasers of devices or the viewers of content – often individuals – may have their personal user rights, including rights to portability, to personal data according to the GDPR.[39] The Commission rigorously claims that the GDPR and the *lex specialis* ePrivacy Directive (soon regulation) fully regulate the processing of

[37] As discussed infra, under both the copyright database protection and the sui generis database protection, individual data points are not protected and accessing individual data points is not an infringement. The proposed ATR system, therefore, differs significantly from the data producer's right proposed by other scholars and the EU Commission. This right is available only for nonpersonal data, but it covers individual data points. See Communication from the Commission to the European Parliament, the Council, the European Economic and Social Committee and the Committee of the Regions 'Building a European Data Economy' COM (2017) 9 final, 13. In reference to academia, see, for example, Zech (n 7) 317–330 (14); or a property right for individuals to their personal data, see Fezer (n 2) 356–370 (15).

[38] For the problems associated with third-party rights when porting data, see Barbara van der Auwermeulen, 'How to Attribute the Right to Data Portability in Europe: A Comparative Analysis of Legislations' (2017) 33 Computer Law & Security Review 57, 60 et seq.

[39] In complex systems where devices or systems consisting of multiple devices, for example, cars, are purchased by individuals, these buyers may also come into possession of sensors that collect data; as discussed in this book, these individuals should also be granted the property right to these sensors.

personal data in terms of data privacy. Under Article 8 of the Charter of Fundamental Rights, EU citizens have a fundamental right to protection of personal data in the EU; indeed, the autonomous legal system created by the GDPR and the *lex specialis* ePrivacy Directive should be respected. It should be acknowledged that natural persons as users should be the exclusive right-holders according to this legal system, while the Database Directive and ATR can be applicable only when the thresholds are exceeded for triggering and obtaining such rights. One should also acknowledge that in complex systems (discussed later in this book), where the generated data undergoes various steps of refinement and analysis, the question is whether the data that actually reaches the database is the data that is provided predominantly by individuals.

The GDPR sets out the rules for processing personal data, including, inter alia, the collection, use of, access to, and portability of personal data, as well as the possibilities to transmit or transfer personal data, and to revoke consent(s) for processing of the personal data. The access right vis-à-vis the data controller is stipulated in Article 15 of the GDPR, which includes a right to receive a copy of the personal data held by the processor. According to the Commission, the right to data portability under Article 20 of the GDPR will allow individuals to obtain copies of the personal data that they have provided to a service provider/data controller, and to move that data to another service provider/data controller (for example, personal data on a social media platform). This may minimize potential lock-in effects. However, it may not prevent users from having a similar, yet different, economic right.[40] Indeed, both users and individuals may hold rights to the same data. The individual has a right to individual data points, while the users may hold an economic right to the dataset. The individual's right to port data is not a commercial right, while a right to access and port datasets would be for the benefit of the business user, and individuals should still be allowed to port individual data points under the GDPR in reference to the economic right holder.

Consent of the individual is required to access and port personal data. However, according to Article 6 (1) (f) of the GDPR, access and sharing of personal data can be lawful without user's consent in the following cases: 'processing is necessary for the purposes of the legitimate interests pursued by the controller or by a third party, except where such interests are overridden by the interests of fundamental rights and freedoms of data subject [user] which require protection of personal data.'[41] Article 6 (1) (f) stipulates a test, where the interest of the individual and interest of the business user should be weighed against each other. As discussed below, consent should not be required in cases where the risks of unwanted data access and sharing are small and potential benefits of data sharing are high. Therefore, with or without

[40] Commission (n 6) 20.

[41] Geoffrey Parker, 'Georgios Petropoulos and Marshall W Van Alstyne, Digital Platforms and Antitrust' (22 May 2020) <https://ssrn.com/abstract=>.

consent, the GDPR provides an avenue that facilitates data sharing – if it increases welfare when privacy risks are low.[42] For the benefit of ATRs and what a porting and access right for business users might entail in terms of increased innovation, improved competitiveness, and the creation of markets, the business users and holders of ATRs should generally be allowed to use the Article 6 (1) (f) exemption in the GDPR.

Economic rights to data can thus coexist with personal data protection. Even though the data is personal in the sense that individuals hold rights to it under the GDPR, economic rights to the data can be held by other entities.[43] Consider, for example, the personal (or consumer) mandatory porting right (Article 20 GDPR); it is not economic, but it may still serve as a source of competition.[44] In fact, it works as a consumer protection rule. Individuals have the right to port data, and this right cannot be contractually eroded or derogated.[45] If the platform or business user does not satisfy the consumers' needs, the individuals can select a different service provider and port the necessary data to that new provider. Indeed, the personal rights created by the GDPR may be viewed from an intellectual property law perspective as moral rights similar to the noneconomic rights of authors to be named and recognized as the authors of their works. The absence of economic rights in the GDPR implies that it could be possible to create an economic right for the firms that collect data from individuals. For example, this could be a right to portability or communication that still honors the rights in the GDPR (including the right to be forgotten). The individual's rights cannot be infringed.[46]

It is possible that individuals could have an economic right to their data. For example, if an individual uploads a collection of data as a copyright-protected database on their Facebook site, the data would meet the requirements for copyright database protection. Giving individuals additional economic rights to personal and nonpersonal data created by their activities on a platform would not create more competition between platforms or increase investments in R&D. The risk would instead be that the platforms could become even more dominant because individuals

[42] Ibid.

[43] Drexl (n 12) 18.

[44] See also Pamela Samuelson, Privacy as Intellectual Property (2000) 52 Stanford Law Review 1125.

[45] Due to a number of problems (e.g., legal uncertainty about the scope of portable data, lacking technical feasibility, high transaction costs), this data port-ability right has so far not been effective for leading to more competition and innovation. See Wolfgang Kerber, 'Specifying and Assigning "Bundles of Rights" on Data: An Economic Perspective (26 April 2021) <https://ssrn.com/abstract=3847620> or <http://dx.doi.org/10.2139/ssrn.3847620>.

[46] Giving individuals an economic right to data does not meet any objectives of enacted a property right. See Drexl (n 9). However, it is in terms of nonpersonal data, especially in reference to industrial internet, that the discussion about property rules and a porting right has flourished. See also Herbert Zech, 'Information as a Tradable Commodity' in De Franceschi (ed), *European Contract Law and the Digital Single Market* (2016) 51–79; Kerber (n 1) 989; Drexl et al. (n 1).

will likely abandon such rights to popular dominant platforms. Indeed, a porting right to the data, that is, data on customers, viewers, and dynamic data regarding connection between content and consumers, should be given to the business users that generate this data on platforms. Business users have the incentive to promote innovation and competition.[47]

So, if creativity and competition would be enhanced by giving business users access and the right to transfer their data on platforms or in the IoT, how should that right be packaged? Should it be a right or a compulsory licensing scheme, or should such a right be indirectly protected under competition law? Below, the rights route is presented first, including a discussion regarding sui generis database protection, trade secrets, and whether a compulsory licensing scheme may suffice; the competition-law route will be presented thereafter.

7.4 AN ACCESS AND TRANSFER RIGHT TO DATA FOR BUSINESS USERS

Generally, the Court needs to clarify whether the rules in the Digital Markets Act and the future Data Act are behavioral liability rules or whether the Digital Markets Act and Data Act should be viewed as creating rights, a right that users can genuinely use and hence be able to access also intellectual property law protected subject matters (held by the platform or a third party). Indeed, this would be a definition of property that is applicable erga omnes. And, is the Digital Markets Act and Data Act a developed data-mining/reverse-engineering tool intended for application by business users and end users, and if not, should it be amended to create such a tool?

As purported above, there are ample reasons for enacting an ATR that will benefit business users to platforms – a right to datasets for business users, whether sellers of goods on marketplaces such as Amazon Market or subcontractors in more complex data-driven systems, to be used in their relationship with the platform providers. However, how could this right be designed in more detail? Similarly, there are ample reasons for enacting an ATR for users under the Data Act, creating an equal right to access and transfer data.

Can a right to data be negative in the sense that it grants neither exclusivity of data nor a right to refuse to use individual data points, while at the same time this right includes a mandatory right to access and transfer? That would imply that users have an EU-sanctioned right to access data, and a right to transfer data that reflects the business user's intellectual or quantitative data collection activities on the platform to a different provider, without being locked in by the platform. Could this be achieved without legislation? The Court could by making use of the access and transfer obligations in the Digital Markets Act and the Data Act identify an ATR, while

47 Giving individuals an economic right to data does not meet any objectives of an enacted property right. See Drexl (n 9).

otherwise new legislation and even a new right would probably need to be implemented – in the form of a right to transfer sales and user data for users of transaction platforms, and a right to access and port data for users of manufacturer's things or parts in relation to system leaders of more complex Internet of Things systems.

The best solution could be to amend the newly proposed Data Act to clearly visualize a reverse-engineering and decompilation tool combined with a data-mining exemption that benefits users, while clearly stating that a data holder may not prevent a lawful user to access and transfer its data. This could be included in a Data Act, stipulating not only an access and transfer obligation for the data holders but also an ATR for users that offsets the rights held by the gatekeeper, and create equal access to data.

Indeed, the indispensable attribute here is that an access and portability right for business users of platforms must be accompanied by the appropriate legal and technical tools for gaining access to the said data; these tools must be able to penetrate contingent subject matter that is protected by intellectual property law. The Digital Markets Act could also be connected to an unwaivable reverse-engineering and data-mining right, extended to cover the situations addressed by the Digital Markets Act. Another alternative could be to state that the rights of the TPM creator as provided in Article 6 of InfoSoc, the creator of a database as provided in Article 7 (1) of Database Directive, the copyright owner in accordance with applicable copyright legal systems or the trade-secret beneficiary shall not be exercised by the platform provider in order to prevent access, porting, or the reuse of data beyond the limits set by the regulation. This would amount to creating a right for business users of platforms. This exemption should not be applicable for platforms that have not acquired gatekeeper status.

A second solution could be to grant a 'proper' property right to the business users. An ATR could be included in an updated version of the Database Directive, granting a business user an ATR to the dataset that represents its data, when the business user has invested time and effort, qualitatively and/or quantitatively, in the platform, to the degree that the selection or arrangement of the data collection that was provided to the platform is original, and the 'author's own intellectual creation', or when the business user database contribution to the platform is so substantial that a sui generis database right could be obtained.[48]

The ATR to the business user's data should thus be triggered when the business user holds a sui generis database protection to the database it has contributed to the platform. An example of this database could be a collection of information references to the business user's product line that is marketed on the platform, when the business user invests sufficient time and effort to reach the triggering level for database protection. The included data would also have reached a volume that

[48] Indeed, business user's data is platform data – data that is collected by sensor, created through business-provider activities or contributed by the business user. As discussed below, the aggregated data should be controlled by the platform provider.

reflects a value for the business user as well as for a potential market. The platform provider should then be obligated to respect the business user's ATR for dataset generated by the users' database on the platform, inter alia, relevant sales and customer data generated by the actions of customers and users of the database that the business user has furnished for the platform. Technically, the dataset should be accessed through an API. The platform provider normally retains a sui generis database right in the database, in reference to all activities on the platform, but cannot prevent the business user from accessing and porting the dataset associated with the business user's right and data.[49] The business user should have a right to port the dataset in its entirety or substantial parts thereof. The business user's ATR should also cover situations where users wish to access and use insubstantial parts of the database that reflect users' data in a 'repeated and systematic' manner; compare Article 7 (5) of the Database Directive. Indeed, neither Article 7 (1) nor /(5) of the Database Directive should be applicable vis-à-vis a business user in reference to the user's data.

An ATR should still be available, even though the dataset or database held by the platform provider is not available to the public or protected under law, that is held exclusively for the platform provider, and inaccessible and confidential for the business users with the use of TPMs, sui generis database rights, or protected by the trade-secret directive.[50] The access and porting right would be mandatory and no remuneration would need to be transferred between the business user and the platform provider, in either direction, for accessing or porting data.

The different ATRs described above respect the platform provider's or data holder's business model. Indeed, the business model should still be respected, given that the platform provider or data holder still retains a sui generis database right and can access and use the users' data. The platform provider will have access to individual user data points and can build a general database that reflects the aggregated data of all business users; this database will be necessary to provide the platform service and respect the platform provider's business model. The platform provider or data holder will have the possibility to obtain the aggregated data of all users – a dataset not covered by users' ATR rights.[51] Moreover, the platform provider should have the right to provide access to the public for the general database covering the aggregated data.[52] Therefore, platform provider should bear the cost of setting up and storing the database and datasets.

49 An updated version of the Database Directive could clarify that the platform provider should hold the sui generis right to the database and thus considered the main investor and bearer of the risk for setting up that database. The legislator should not pursue a strategy to respect joint ownership (makers) of the sui generis database for aggregated data. cf Drexl (n 9).

50 C-30/14 – *Ryanair* ECLI:EU:C:2015:10.

51 The issue of data pooling is discussed in Chapter 7.

52 It should here be noted that a platform provider, for example, a car manufacturer, can organize and systematize the collection and storage of data as it pleases. However, if this manufacturer stores everything in a general database, this database would include not only

Such an ATR could also be amended with a [sole] right of distribution and communication to the public and granted to the user for the dataset representing the user's data, implying that the platform provider or data holder can use only data accessed from the dataset for internal entrepreneurial and development work. In essence, by stipulating in Article 6 (1) that platforms or data holders cannot use user's data that is not publicly available, the Digital Markets Act and Data Act, respectively, offer a kind of exclusivity for the user. The regulations also permit users to transfer the data-access right to third parties.[53]

If an ATR were included in an updated Database Directive, Article 7 (2) of the directive could be redrafted to mirror this transferal of rights. Indeed, what is suggested here is a form of limited intellectual property right for the benefit of the users; however, it should be emphasized that this right will not increase the scope of protection regarding access to what should be considered publicly available data or information. In this sense, the ATR would not increase the data protection granted by the Database Directive.

Interestingly, the Digital Markets Act and Data Act do not encompass internet service provider (ISPs). However, an ATR system could also be implemented in reference to ISP. As a result of legislative efforts in various areas, ISPs can and are obligated to collect data from users.[54] Globally, ISPs have become a source of data and they do trade data. The general principle of granting users access to data could also be complemented in relation to ISPs that provide connections, websites, or storage space.

parts manufacturers' data but also information from the system leaders' own sensors and data from third parties (e.g., smart roads). This general database will logically be larger and will include data to which parts producers and individual drivers will not have access under an ATR right. Indeed, the car will be connected to several external intermediates and service providers. In reference to cars and how data is collected and processed, see generally Wolfgang Kerber, 'Data Sharing in IoT Ecosystems and Competition Law: The Example of Connected Cars' (2019) 15(4) Journal of Competition Law & Economics 381–426 <https://doi.org/10.1093/joclec/nhz018> and Drexl (n 9) 41.

53 This opens up the possibility for other platforms to collect data from each other.

54 According to Wikipedia: '[I]nternet service providers in many countries are legally required (eg via Communications Assistance for Law Enforcement Act (CALEA) in the U.S.) to allow law enforcement agencies to monitor some or all of the information transmitted by the ISP, or even store the browsing history of users to allow government access if needed (eg via the Investigatory Powers Act 2016 in the United Kingdom). Furthermore, in some countries, ISPs are subject to monitoring by intelligence agencies. In the US, a controversial National Security Agency programme known as PRISM provides for broad monitoring of Internet users' traffic and has raised concerns about potential violation of the privacy protections in the Fourth Amendment to the United States Constitution. Modern ISPs integrate a wide array of surveillance and packet-sniffing equipment into their networks, which then feed the data to law-enforcement/intelligence networks (such as DCSNet in the United States, or SORM in Russia), thus allowing monitoring of Internet traffic in real time.'

7.5 A PROPERTY SYSTEM OR A LIABILITY SYSTEM?

As we proceed in this discussion, we must avoid the trap of jurisprudence of concepts.[55] In a data-driven economy, old economy concepts and notions of what constitutes relevant market, property, and liability regimes should not hamper us as we attempt to adapt and create an economic legal system for data-driven markets. In several aspects, the access and portability right system proposed in this book borrows from both property legal systems and liability systems. The proposal is in essence an attempt to find a middle ground, a sui generis right in between property and liability.

Normally, three forms of incentive systems for creating, or collecting, information and knowledge (innovations) are discussed in academia:[56] first, a system where the creator is rewarded or granted funds (a prize), through either public funds or private investment; second, a liability system where the inventor is given fair compensation for his/her creation but may not prevent the dissemination of the information or knowledge created;[57] third, a property system, similar to the patent system, where the inventor is able (with some exceptions) to claim an exclusive right to the knowledge that is protected.

However, behavioral economics also teaches us that individuals act differently in reference to different forms of incentives. Individuals tend to assign more value to objects that they perceive as belonging to them than to things owned by other persons or by the public in general.[58] This 'endowment effect' applies not only to tangible objects, such as movable and immovable assets, but can be transferred to intangible objects, such as ideas, intellectual property, or data.[59] However, several studies show that individuals or business users do not feel that they own or control 'their' data, and that is why they do not value or protect it – or, for that matter, cultivate it and use it to innovate. Data fatigue has set in: Individuals and firms

[55] *Begreppsjurisprudens* in Swedish, Norwegian and Danish and *Begriffsjurisprudenz* in German.

[56] See, for example, Paul David, 'Intellectual Property Institutions and the Panda's Thumb: Copyrights and Trade Secrets in Economic Theory and History' in National Research Council (ed), *Global Dimensions of Intellectual Property Rights* (1993) 29 et seq. with references.

[57] Cf Pamela Samuelson et al., 'A Manifesto Concerning the Legal Protection of Computer Programs' (1994) 94 Columbia Law Review 2308; Ullrich (n 13) 463; and Robert Merges, 'Institutions for Intellectual Property Transactions: The Case of Patent Pools' in Rochelle Dreyfuss et al. (eds), *Expanding Boundaries of Intellectual Property* (2001) 128 et seq., 131 et seq. with reference to his own article: Robert Merges, 'Contracting into Liability Rules: Intellectual Property Rights and Collective Rights Organizations' (1996) 84 California Law Review 1293.

[58] See Salomon Reed, 'Information in the Cloud: Ownership, Control and Accountability' in Anne Cheung and Rolf H. Weber (eds), *Privacy and Legal Issues in Cloud Computing* (Edward Elgar 2015) 139 et seq.; Greg Lastowka and Dan Hunter, 'The Laws of the Virtual Worlds' (2004) 1(3) California Law Review 36. See also Chrobak (n 17) 258.

[59] See (n 58). For a US economic perspective of the advantages and drawbacks of a property right in personal data: Samuelson (n 44); Lawrence Lessig, *Code: And Other Laws of Cyberspace, Version 2.0* (SoHo books 2006) 200 et seq.; cf Mark Lemley, 'Private Property' (2000) 52(5) Stanford Law Review 1547.

choose to ignore the fact that through their actions, they create the valuable asset of data. This fatigue likely stems from the de facto situation in which neither individuals nor firms own their data.

The property system offers several advantages compared to the other systems. Primarily, a property system leaves the consumers or customers to evaluate the result. Thus, the reward for the created knowledge is given ex post, based on its utility in competition on functioning markets. Innovation that does not facilitate utility will not be rewarded and will thus become a cost for the inventor or investor. This might seem harsh, but it constitutes a preeminent part of the innovation process: In the end, scarce resources are efficiently allocated.

The ATR system, as envisioned above, is borrowing aspects from a general property system, where the end consumer will retain the possibility to select the winner of the innovation race and the competition. The system will allow users to obtain necessary data for innovation and development and further the development of the product or service, while also allowing the sale and transfer, for remuneration, of the user's data to purchasers – industry players, private equity brokers, or data brokers. However, in several aspects, the ATR system borrows the best part of the property legal system while also capturing the benefits of keeping information nonexclusive and thus preventing bottleneck problems.[60]

The access and portability obligation as presented in Article 6 of the Digital Markets Act is more a liability solution, where neither property nor intellectual property rights with effects erga omnes are created. There are legal systems catering to the digital economy that also provide liability solutions for accessing and porting data.

In the realm of Open Data, as discussed above, the PSI Directive opens up for anyone and everyone to extract and purchase data at a marginal cost or market value, often under license agreements, from the public-sector bodies that collected the data.[61] These so-called reusers – often data brokers – prefer this set-up, compared with being granted access to data available on a website and without an agreement.

Indeed, reusers want the public-sector bodies to have some rights on which to base the transaction, even if it involves paying a license fee. They would rather enter contracts in reference to datasets. Otherwise, reusers run the risk that the collected data will be put on a website for anyone to download, and they will not have the possibility to enter into special agreements with clauses (e.g., warranties) regarding quality or just-in-time delivery of real-time data, etc. In this way, commercial transactions can also increase the value for those buying services. The Open Data

[60] The ATR as defined in this book lacks some aspects of the foundational notion of property as 'the right to exclude'. Discussed later in this book.

[61] Björn Lundqvist, 'Turning Government Data into Gold: The Interface between EU Competition Law and the Public Sector Information Directive – With Some Comments on the Compass Case' (2013) 44(1) IIC – International Review of Intellectual Property and Competition Law 79–95.

Directive is in essence a compulsory access and porting scheme, where public-sector bodies are required to give access to public data in return for (a small) remuneration. Public data that is acquired or collected by the public-sector bodies when these authorities carry out their main public-sector task should be made available for private bodies to access, collect, and reuse, if the authority is reusing the same data outside its public task. However, as described above, the PSI obligation to share data is triggered only when the data is not subject to third-party property rights and is 'cleaned' from personal references, that is, the data does not constitute personal data.

The Digital Markets Act is bilateral, regulating the relationship between gatekeeping platforms and business users, while the Open Data Directive creates a right for all comers to access public data. Nonetheless, the preamble of the Digital Markets Act states that the right to access data can be transferred to third parties authorized by a business user. One could thus imagine a legal system for platforms similar to that for public-sector bodies, at least for platforms of infrastructure type, where the platform must give access to data erga omnes, that is, to any comer. The data platforms collect when conducting their main or core business activity should be made available for everyone, at least if the platforms reuse data outside the main or core business activity. This is of course a far-reaching obligation to make data available to anyone, and indeed to create data commons. This obligation should be put into action only with regard to monopolistic platforms that provide infrastructure-type services (services of general interest) and that also obtain large amounts of data in the process of providing that service.[62] This amounts to forcing infrastructure-type platforms to become a data commons.[63] Perhaps a Private Sector Information Directive, catering to infrastructure-type platforms, could be developed and included in something akin to a platform neutrality principle.[64] Indeed, such platforms should be obligated to remain open to all comers. This sounds great in theory, but this system has several drawbacks. How should the powerful platforms be defined and distinguished from regular platforms, for inclusion in the private sector information system? In addition, what should be done with all other platforms? It should be noted that the recent evaluation of the Database Directive included a discussion regarding whether to impose a compulsory license system in the directive; however, the authors refrained from suggesting such a system while still recommending a close watch on sensor-produced technologies.[65] Moreover, the private-

[62] BMWI, 'The German Commission of Experts on Competition Law 4.0 presents final report to Minister Altmaier: A New Competition Framework for the Digital Economy seems to propose similar ideas, in a European Platform Regulation' cf <www.bmwi.de/Redaktion/EN/Pressemitteilungen/2019/20190909-commission-of-experts-on-competition-law-40-presents-final-report-to-minister-altmaier.html>.

[63] Ibid. See also <www.d-kart.de/en/blog/2019/09/09/competition-4-0>.

[64] Discussing guidance for sharing private data, see Commission, 'Staff Working Document of 25 April 2018 – Guidance on Sharing Private Sector Data in the European Data Economy' SWD (2018) 125 final. For a similar discussion, see Drexl (n 12) 33.

[65] See Commission (n 8).

sector information system invites litigation in reference to determining which platforms to include in the system, as well as the remuneration for the platforms (licensors). As with the ex ante rules in the Digital Markets Act, future litigation will likely address the definition of platforms – the gatekeepers – for real-time access and injunctions. Moreover, do we really want to start regulating the economy in this manner? The liberal market-driven economy and light regulatory touch that we have come to appreciate should be protected. It could be that the problems we see in the digital economy stem from our lack of a general property system for data, the main means of production. Perhaps this is the 'easy' legislative fix: releasing the data-driven economy from chaperoning by authorities.

What is suggested in this book is that the user (including content providers and device users) should have an ATR that is applicable erga omnes to 'its' data created on platforms. The platforms need to provide effective and immediate access to the data that business users provided or generated when using the gatekeeper's relevant core platform services, in a structured, commonly used, and machine-readable format. The business user should be allowed to port this data. This would encourage commercialization, quality in data, and the incentive to contractually agree on the means of distribution. However, holding an ATR does not imply holding an exclusive right. The platform provider should also have access to the same data, ensuring that no firm would hold an exclusive right to an individual data point. Moreover, platform and cloud providers should be able to access data in the datasets belonging to the business users.

Notwithstanding the above, a property system normally implies that the owner may refuse access to the property.[66] In comparison, the ability to price and decide what to do with property is circumscribed in a liability system, where the property holder cannot refuse access.[67] In reference to data, however, and especially when dealing with specific generic data points, an exclusive right to refuse access may cause significant bottleneck problems.[68] Indeed, it would not be possible to have exclusive rights to individual data points. However, the ATR should not create exclusivity for the data; it should create a right to access, transfer, and reuse. In analogy, the sui generis database protection is in a sense a property right, giving the

66 Mark A. Lemley and Phil Weiser, 'Should Property or Liability Rules Govern Information?' (2007) 85 Texas Law Review 783 <https://ssrn.com/abstract=977778>. See also Richard A. Epstein, 'Takings, Exclusivity and Speech: The Legacy of *PruneYard v. Robins*' (1997) 64 University of Chicago Law Review 21 22 ('[I]t is difficult to conceive of any property as private if the right to exclude is rejected.'); cf Adam Mossoff, 'What Is Property? Putting the Pieces Back Together' (2003) 45(371) Ariz Law Review 417–418 (arguing that property should include affirmative rights to develop, not just rights to exclude). See also Guido Calabresi and A. Douglas Melamed, 'Property Rules, Liability Rules, and Inalienability: One View of the Cathedral' (1972) 85(1089) Harvard Law Review 1106–1107. The concept of a 'property rule' does not mean that the only or necessarily appropriate property-law remedy is an injunction but merely that injunctions are the quintessential response to trespass claims.

67 Cf Ullrich (n 13) 464.

68 Drexl (n 9); Lemley and Weiser (n 66).

holder a right to access the database but not the individual data points stored in the database. It is instead an exclusive right to a database under certain circumstances.

It should be pointed out that an access and porting right without an exclusive right to the data has been contemplated before. In reference to datasets comprising data, can an access and porting right be imagined? In the run-up to the recently published regulation for the free flow of data, the Commission did envision a dataset porting right for undertakings, regarding nonpersonal data.[69] The Commission's impact assessment addressed the problem of how providers of cloud services or other digital services could distort competition and prevent free movement of data by preventing or obstructing companies from switching providers. It was therefore rather surprising that in the end, the Data Free Flow Regulation contained only a call for self-regulation regarding the right to port data (Article 6).[70] Indeed, when the Data Free Flow Regulation was published, the Commission left it to the industry to self-regulate the issue of porting rights.[71]

According to the Commission, one of the main reasons for not creating a right to port data was insufficient investigation of the interface between such a right and sui generis database protection, trade-secret protection, and other intellectual property rights covering data. The Digital Market Law is proof that the Commission has changed its opinion on this point.

7.6 ACCESS AND TRANSFER OF DATA FOR COMPLEX IOT SYSTEMS

In the digital era of today, we pretty much know that Google, Amazon, Facebook, Netflix, Spotify, HBO, and others are platforms, but what about when they start purchasing platform services and platform space from each other?

[69] Commission, 'Communication from the Commission to the European Parliament, the Council, the European Economic and Social Committee and the Committee of the Regions' SWD (2017) 2 final, COM (2017) 9 final, 13; Commission (n 6) 33, making reference to the works of Herbert Zech, who claimed that the right way forward is the creation of a property right to nonpersonal data. cf Zech (n 46) 51–79.

[70] Moreover, in a regulation that otherwise stipulates hard rules and prohibitions for Member States regarding creation or maintenance of barriers to the free movement of data, it is asymmetric to include only a plea to private actors, asking them to self-regulate to avoid limitation or prevention of competition and free movement of data. This plea prevents coherence between the requirements on free movement and the requirements under competition law. See (n 69).

[71] By not proposing a right to port data, the Commission also paves the way for Member States to introduce their own right to nonpersonal data. The Commission states that there is support in France and Estonia for introducing a right to port data. The Commission does not disclose the discussion in Germany about creating an intellectual property right for device producers in regard to nonpersonal data. The German discussion also includes negative rights and a right to port data. Would Article 6 in the proposed Data Free Flow Regulation preempt Member States in enacting porting rights for data under EU law? There is room to argue that, by calling for self-regulation, the EU has not exercised its competence; this would give room for Member States to act. Zech (n 46) 51–79; Kerber (n 1) 989; and Drexl et al. (n 1).

However, what about IoT ecosystems? Take cars for example; BMW or Volvo could be regarded as platforms that exclusively hoard data from their branded vehicles and their users.[72] Are they platforms? What about Google or Apple, which are creating successful technical platforms for vehicles that cut across brands? Would that make BMW a device producer or business user for that platform, while still being a platform vis-à-vis its subcontractors, possibly including Google and Apple? These are difficult matters to resolve, and according to many, including a property right in this mix could be toxic. However, a limited ATR circumscribed by competition law and policy could still be useful.

When the device or product being sold also contains sensors or software that collects data from the purchaser of the device or product (be it individuals or commercial actors), a more sophisticated legal analysis is required, including an IoT-adapted right to data mining and reverse engineering.

What about the data generated by the sensor in the product, or when the product is included in larger ecosystems? For more complex data-driven systems, for example, in vehicles where sensors can be embedded in components and software that make up the systems, data access and rules are also needed. However, ATRs in this setting could work differently, and the inherent exhaustion principle must be respected. Parties to distribution networks should be free to negotiate access and portability rights, while from the outset, the rule should be that the right to obtain data from sensors should be transferred when the part or the software is exhaustively transferred – in the end to the end user.[73] The system leader, for example, a car manufacturer or platform provider for the in-vehicle data, will probably be the beneficiary of the data generated in the vehicle through its own sensors but also through technical and contractual arrangements (discussed in Chapter 2 regarding the John Deere ecosystem), while also receiving data from various other external sensors and sources. However, what about the suppliers of various parts to the system, for example, suppliers to a vehicle manufacturer? Should they retain an access and portability right to data generated by the sensor that they install in the part, which is in turn used in the general IoT system, for example, the vehicle ecosystem?

To a large extent, data transfer in IoT systems and its associated problems mirror the problem of distribution systems for manufacturing firms in general, where branded firms control a system of parts suppliers, including suppliers of outsourced services or production. However, the difference is that in data-driven economies and markets all data from a market or ecosystem can wind up with one system leader. That can cause the system leader to become more powerful in the ecosystem and

[72] Bertin Martens and Frank Mueller-Langer, 'Access to Digital Car Data and Competition in Aftersales Services' (September 2018) EUR Scientific and Technical Research Reports <https://ec.europa.eu/jrc/sites/jrcsh/files/jrc112634.pdf>.

[73] See Chapter 6, especially the discussion around the Joined Cases C-403/08 and C-428/08 *Football Association Premier League and Murphy* ECLI:EU:C:2011:631.

give it power to leverage its power to supplier markets, after markets, and neighboring markets. This supports the policy of allowing suppliers in IoT systems that embed sensors in parts of a larger system to retain the right to collect data from the sensors. Indeed, these suppliers should hold some form of an ATR vis-à-vis the user – as in Article 3 of the proposed Data Act – but also against system leader of the IoT ecosystem. It is conceivable that suppliers' rights to access and transfer data in these systems should mirror the ATR held by the user. If the supplier needs access to the sensor or to the data-holders database, an ATR benefitting the supplier could either be stand-alone under an amended Article 3 of the Data Act, or, even making the right more forceful, include it as part of the supplier's patent covering the device or product. The ATR is not exhaustively transferred with the device or product. A developed reverse-engineering and data-mining rights could be included in the ATR held by both the supplier and user of the system or product, while still allowing the property older of the device and the platform or hub provider access to the data generated by the system.

Suppose that a smart kitchen is constructed. The individual or firm purchasing the kitchen components (the devices) to be included in the system should have the right to access and transfer data generated by the components' sensors. That right would be derived from the principle of exhaustion. The component providers (e.g., the refrigerator manufacturer) should, under an ATR (included in an amended Article 3 of the Data Act), retain the right to access the refrigerator's sensor-generated data, while the platform provider or system leader, for example, by 'Google kitchen' or the IKEA or Lidl kitchen platforms should obtain data from agreements with user and the components provider (according to Articles 3 and 5 of the Data Act). The system leader will moreover have access through its own sensors, and it is possible that under the GDPR the consumer will grant the system leader the right to access and port data from the sensors.[74] Under the GDPR, the consumer retains some control of the data collected by the components. However, as will be discussed below, in complex systems, the data sensor-generated is not necessarily the only data used to ensure the functioning of the system or individual devices. This fact is accentuated in larger systems, such as houses or kitchens, where the system acquires data from various sensors inside the system, as well as external information, for example, from stores, weather forecasts from other smart houses or smart cities, and other connected devices. The combination of all the data necessarily needs to be controlled by a platform or hub, and by a system leader or gatekeeper.

[74] José van Dijck, Martijn de Waal, and Thomas Poell, *The Platform Society: Public Values in a Connective World* (Oxford University Press 2018); Murray Goulden, '"Delete the Family": Platform Families and the Colonisation of the Smart Home' (2019) Information, Communication & Society 1–18; and generally Rob Kitchin, Tracey P. Lauriault, and Gavin McArdle (eds), *Data and the City* (Routledge 2018).

7.6.1 *Complex Systems in Reference to Vehicles*

As stated above, for more complex data-driven systems, such as vehicles, vessels, aircraft, and even large metallurgical factories, where sensors can be embedded in the different components and software that make up the core of the data-driven production systems, a more subtle and sensitive approach must be taken. Indeed, the issue is whether the Data Act provides such a delicate approach.

Several authors have discussed vehicles, and especially cars.[75] For cars and vehicles, an intricate network of subcontractors makes up the system or platform that eventually becomes a car or a vehicle, while platform providers also try to use vehicles as a means to extract driver-generated data. Moreover, there are several stakeholders for a vehicle. Often, several legal and physical persons could claim some right to the information and data generated by the car: The driver(s), the owner of the car, and other stakeholders, such as lenders or insurance companies, could claim an interest in receiving vehicle information. Moreover, branded and independent repair shops, licensors of GPS or map systems, and even independent self-driving software/systems, ISPs, and Government authorities for traffic control, eCall and toll systems, and law enforcement authorities may claim a right to access and transfer the (in-)vehicle and technical dynamic data generated by the vehicle.[76] In complex systems, sensor-generated data is not necessarily the only data used to ensure the device's function. This is accentuated in larger systems, such as vehicles, where the vehicle acquires data from various sensors inside the vehicle, and also externally, for example, from a smart road, other vehicles (at least from vehicles of the same brand), and other connected devices.

Several of the parties mentioned here cannot claim a right to access and transfer of data under the rules discussed above or, for that matter, under the proposed Data Act. Instead, they may have a claim to access necessary data under other legal systems. Individual drivers and passengers have this right when it comes to personal data according to the GDPR, while they may have a right as users under the proposed Data Act. Independent repair shops may have the possibility to access static and dynamic data under the competition-law block exemption for vehicles. Governments have a right to access data through various legal systems, such as the eCall regulation or the Digital Service Act, for criminal investigation purposes and in the legal system making up the relationship between the ISP and the Member States.[77] Insurance companies and banks that provide lending services may have a

[75] Wiebe (n 19); Wolfgang Kerber and Jonas Frank, 'Data Governance Regimes in the Digital Economy: The Example of Connected Cars' (3 November 2017) <https://ssrn.com/abstract=3064794> or <http://dx.doi.org/10.2139/ssrn.3064794> accessed 2 January 2018.

[76] Ibid.

[77] For an excellent analysis of the public right to access information, see Liane Colonna, 'Legal Implications of Data Mining: Assessing the European Union's Data Protection Principles in Light of the United States Government's National Intelligence Data Mining Practices' (2016)

contractual right to access data about the driver; in the future, such contracts can imply an obligation to include sensors in the vehicle.[78] Researchers and others may have a right to access data under the Digital Service Act. Indeed, given this web of ATRs being enacted, identifying the party having the 'best' right under classical property theory becomes unnecessary. It is a dead end. Again, because the rights to the data are not exclusive, an intricate analysis of best right is not needed.[79]

Vehicles involve delicate issues in terms of identifying the platform providers or system leaders, vis-à-vis the user or subcontractor. Several stakeholders would not be able to claim an ATR to the vehicle-generated data. The difficult issue is to identify the right of subcontractors, vehicle producers, and vehicle purchasers. For subcontractors of parts for the vehicle, the right to access data from the sensors should normally cease upon sale of the part to the car owner, garage, or vehicle manufacturer.

The heart of the matter is whether the producer (the manufacturer of the vehicle) or the ultimate purchaser of the vehicle (be it a lessor or private individual) should obtain the right to collect the data from the car or vehicle once the property is transferred. According to the system envisioned in this book for rights exhaustion and ATRs, the purchaser – including individuals – should indeed have the right to access data generated by the vehicle and, when applicable, under the GDPR, while the subcontractors should retain control of the data generated by their respective sensors under a system of ATRs. The system leader or platform provider will gain access through its own sensors and through contractual arrangements with subcontractors, producer, property holder, and user.

Faculty of Law Stockholm University Research Paper No 5 <https://ssrn.com/abstract=2924541> or <http://dx.doi.org/10.2139/ssrn.2924541>.

78 See EU Data Protection Board, Guidelines 1/2020 on processing personal data in the context of connected vehicles and mobility related applications Version 1.0 Adopted on 28 January 2020 <https://edpb.europa.eu/sites/edpb/files/consultation/edpb_guidelines_202001_connectedvehicles.pdf>.

79 The EU Commission also envisioned something similar. Instead of creating the data producer right as a right in rem, the Commission purport that it could be conceived of as a set of purely defensive rights. This option would follow the choice made in the design of the protection given to know-how by the Trade Secrets Protection.

Directive. Its objective would be to enhance the sharing of data by giving at least the defensive elements of an in rem right, that is, the capacity for the de facto data holder to sue third parties in case of illicit misappropriation of data. This approach thus equates a protection of a de facto 'possession', rather than the concept of 'ownership' According to the Commission, a number of civil law remedies could be introduced such as:

(i) the right to seek injunctions preventing further use of data by third parties who have no right to use the data,
(ii) the right to have products built on the basis of misappropriated data excluded from market commercialization, and
(iii) the possibility to claim damages for unauthorized use of data.

cf Commission (n 6) 33 et seq. See also Kerber (n 1) 989.

Indeed, the ultimate purchaser, as the rights-exhaustive property holder of the sensors, should then have the possibility to purchase or enter into a transport service agreement or platform agreements with third parties that could provide data analytic services for the vehicle via the sensors.[80] However, the vehicle producer would still retain data generated by the sensors, and can thus also provide a platform based on the data generated by the vehicles, while parts providers may have access through an ATR to their data.[81]

It should also be noted here that current vehicle development seems to suggest that connected cars will soon have automated or fitted autonomous driving provided by manufacturers – that generally, cars will become a transport service and not a driving experience, and car sales to individuals or leasing companies will become the exception and not the rule.[82] In these situations, the manufacturer would retain control of and access to the sensors.

Vehicle manufacturers use technological protection measures to exclude others from accessing in-vehicle data and dynamic data and so-called extended vehicle concept.[83] The so-called extended vehicle concept implies that all data generated in the car are directly transmitted to a proprietary server of the manufacturer and that the car is technically designed as a closed system. Hence, the manufacturers have not only exclusive control over the car data but also exclusive control over the technical access to the car, which has caused concern with other providers.[84] However, the system suggested above would not disrupt vehicle producers' business models for these types of data. The end purchaser would have access to the data, but the vehicle manufacturer would retain the possibility to combine the data from all vehicles under its brands.[85] The valuable information would not be obtained through access to sensors in individual vehicles but through real-time access to large sets of aggregated data from all or the great majority of the vehicles connected under a brand and produced or assembled by a single producer. The manufacturer could transfer the data if he or she chooses to do it, while also engaging cloud service providers or other data processing service providers. It should be noted that the Data Act presumably excludes undertakings that have been designated as gatekeepers from accessing the data from the vehicle under the proposed Data Act.[86]

80 Drexl (n 9) 35 notes that start-ups are currently developing data analytics services for the IoT systems, while not providing any hardware.

81 Thus, vehicle manufacturers such as John Deere would still be able to provide and use their data-driven business models. See Christian Williams, 'Farm to Data Table: John Deere and Data in Precision Agriculture' (12 November 2019) <https://digital.hbs.edu/platform-digit/submission/farm-to-data-table-john-deere-and-data-in-precision-agriculture> See also Mark Ryan, 'Agricultural Big Data Analytics and the Ethics of Power' (2020) 33 Journal of Agricultural Environmental Ethics 49–69 <https://doi.org/10.1007/s10806-019-09812-0>.

82 Drexl (n 9) 35. See also the interesting discussion regarding pills and doctors.

83 Kerber (n 52).

84 Ibid. See also Kerber (n 45).

85 Data pools are discussed in Chapter 7.

86 See Article 5 (2) of the Data Act.

For software that is either included in the system when the car is purchased or downloaded by the driver or purchaser, the question is this: Which entity should be in control of the data collected by these devices or software, for example, a GPS and map system or even an independent driver's system? A related issue here is whether the software license to the software or the software itself is purchased from the car producer – or more accurately, whether the transaction represents a de facto transfer of property.[87] If the license or software is indeed purchased and ownership is transferred, the possibility to collect data and monitor the car could be transferred under contracts to the purchaser and the software provider could have recourse to an ATR for the data created, while the claim to access rights for data should be directed toward the direct purchaser of the software, that is (normally) the producer of the car. The producer has control of the data generated by the software. Indeed, this could enable the car's purchaser to acquire the necessary control regarding which data the vehicle collects, while the software provider still retains a right to access and port data.

Interestingly, the vehicle or car should also be considered a device in reference to the platform that may be controlled by the software. For example, Google provides software for cars, and in reference to that platform, the car is a device, and the producer of the car could claim ATR under the system proposed in this book to the data collected by the Google platform. Notwithstanding this, it might be the case that both firms function as business users and platforms in reference to their bilateral business relationship, giving them equal right to access each other's information under the Digital Markets Act. As discussed above, the challenge of gatekeepers becoming business users for each other is a complexity that the Digital Markets Act does not address, and it is possible that the opportunity for gatekeepers to exchange data as business users under a future Digital Markets Act will be restricted.[88]

It should be acknowledged that patent law does protect technical information. Inventions that fulfill certain standards, most importantly for novelty and inventive aspects, merit protection. This triggers rights for the patentee, and an ATR should be included in the patentee's bundle of rights under a patent. The ATR should be

[87] See discussion later in this book in reference to [2012] ECLI:EU:C:2012:407.

[88] The complexity could also vary. It seems that the B2B relationship for data-driven business models enables expert firms to extract highly sensitive data from within production processes of other firms. There are firms that produce certain key components, and including sensors in these components, they can monitor and control whole industries. For example, the producer of a key component in the powertrain for all major oil tankers can track and monitor all these powertrains in reference to efficiency, capacity, speed and wear and tear, and is indeed able to track, in real time, the cost structure of all major shipping companies in the world, without the shipowners having access to the same information. This transforms the producer of a key powertrain component into a system leader that enjoys a beneficial situation. Similar firms exist in the metallurgical industry, and these manufacturers provide a key component to all or the great majority of industry participants and can monitor all industry participants in real time. Here we have a large industrial complex that acts as a platform for several subcontractors and consulting firms, while all necessary data is still controlled by a key-component provider.

included as a follow-on right. As implied above, in complex IoT systems, patent law and copyright regimes for technical copyright could include a limited ATR in their respective bundle of rights granted to the right holder. When a device or parts producer provides a part to a larger IoT system and this part contains a sensor, an ATR to sensor-generated data should be granted when the producer holds a technical property right to the part or device provided to the system. The ATR should be connected to intellectual property rights held by suppliers in Internet or IoT settings. Indeed, when the ATR is included in the copyright or sui generis-protected databases, the ATRs are also generally granted as a supplier right vis-à-vis platforms. Finally, it is conceivable that ATRs should be included in the general copyright regime; when a work (e.g., a website) has reached the level of copyright protection, the website author should have an ATR to obtain data from ISPs or other platforms associated with individuals who visit the author's website. Perhaps such a right should even be included for obtaining data generated by sensors in artistic works so that artists can understand how purchasers and others use the artists' works.

7.7 A GENERAL ACCESS AND TRANSFER RIGHT

The discussion in this book hinges on the theory that data needs to be accessible and transferable so that we can have a functioning data-driven economy. While on one hand, data can be accessible through an obligation for the data holder – as in the proposal for the Data Act and the Digital Markets Act – access to data can also be achieved with a general ATR in the industrial intellectual property rights system. There are several benefits with such a system, foremost will data be disseminated through society eliminating the hold-up problem and even eliviating the anticommons problem in reference to data.

The proposal for the Data Act, the Digital Markets Act, and also, for example, the Directive on Payment Services share similar structural or constitutional points of departure in reference to establishing a legal system of access and transfer of data, while the Open Data Directive and the Data Governance Act and the Digital Service Act use a different constitutional structural. Each sector or industry has its rule for accessing data.

In reference to G2P (government to platform), all government data should in principle be available for any comer for free or at marginal cost under the Open Data paradigm, while for P2G (platform to government), data transfer to be required certain requirements in reference to systemic risk need to be fulfilled. However, there are also users for several of the service provided by the government platforms. The large data holders within the public system are often organized with platforms in center of digital ecosystems. Indeed, real estate data, corporate information, weather data, etc., are organized with users and business users providing and generating data for the platforms. That could imply that they could be regulated in a similar fashion as data holders under the Data Act, the DMA, and the PSD2 and legally be obliged to share access to their data with their users. Indeed, in principle, the regulation of access to data G2P could be built around the principle of empowering the users to have a right to access and transfer of the data they generate, rather than all and everyone having right to access. Indeed, creating a leveled playing field between Government and Platform could require this restriction of the Open Data paradigm.

The guiding principle for the data-driven economy should reflect an equal ATR to data for users. The right should also address the general intrinsic limitation and restriction reflected by the intellectual property rights held by data holders, while also addressing the restriction of competition created by the claiming use of GDPR. Indeed, users should have equal access also under GDPR when providing the same level of protection. This will solve the general problems faced by all the sector-specific access and transfer of data legal systems now being implemented.

It can be argued that the proposal for Data Act, the Digital Markets Act, the DPS2, and the Open Data/DGA, indeed, the law of the data-driven economy, should be amended with a right for accessing and transferring the data that is collected and stored on the data holders' server interface, that is, most likely a database. Such an access right should include rights to data mining or reverse engineering and would allow users to circumvent or trump the data holders' right to protection under TPMs, database rights, and trade-secret legislation to gain access to the data generated by themselves. Such a limited ATR could be included in a stand-alone Data Act as a lex generalis applicable within the whole field of the data-driven economy or perhaps in an updated version of the database directive.

Moreover, the right to access and transfer for users should also be aligned with the GDPR, giving a user the right to also access personal data when the user can provide equal protection under the GDPR as the original data holder. Indeed, the GDPR must also be included in the general legal system for data-driven economy, and should be judged and analyzed in reference to the rights or principles held by the party wanting access to the data.

The right could be supplemented in an updated version of the database directive for the benefit of users generating data. The database directive could moreover go further and grant a more elaborated right when users have invested time and/or effort to create useful data to the level that it would become a database right in its own right, that is, with a limited exclusive right to prevent certain large data dumps. This would normally apply for business users of platforms.

Amendments of the proposed Data Act and Digital Markets Act, or generally to the regulation of the data-driven economy, to include a genuine, overriding right for users to access and transfer data have been discussed throughout this book and, in several senses, this is the preferred solution. It will certainly be a game changer and create a level-playing field for competition; it will also be a vital tool that enables business users and users to challenge established core platform markets. In reference to IoT systems, the principle of exhaustion should be guiding and give to property holders of the IoT device the general right to access and utilize the data, while parts manufacturer, producers, and users should hold ATRs to parts of the data of interest to them. Such ATRs may be included in the Data Act but may also be included as part of intellectual property rights such as patents and copyright. Finally, platform providers for IoT systems may contractually be granted the right to access and utilize the data. All this may fit in the Data Act and in intellectual property law systems.

Nevertheless, the alternative or complementary solution of an updated database concept will be explored below. Some benefits that are not available for a boosted or amended Digital Markets Act or Data Act are available for the database solution. Primarily, the database or dataset solution creates a threshold for the user. As presented above, to obtain an ATR, users must have invested time and effort in the platform to obtain the then-valuable datasets generated by the business users' actions on the platform. Such a threshold rule creates incentives to invest and thus create valuable data in the platform, which in turn creates incentive for both the platform and the business users to obtain the valuable datasets. It also creates a right in databases (or, rather, datasets), erga omnes, rather than individual data points, which is preferable. By giving users the right to access and port individual data points, the Digital Markets Act and Data Act is indeed a step toward ownership of individual data points – a road that few commentators would want to take.[89] Moreover, it is possible the dataset solution can create a level playing field between users and platforms, while protecting the business model of data-driven platforms.

Second, the dataset solution, where business users obtain an intellectual property right, would apply not only to the core platform providers (gatekeepers) but to all platforms, including the platforms that will be established in the Internet of Things, thus, making rights to access and port data available erga omnes.

It should be acknowledged that the Commission is in the process of reforming and updating the Database Directive.[90] The Commission's evaluation seems to conclude that the Database Directive requires a substantial overhaul to function in an Internet of Things setting.[91] It should also be noted that several of the directive's stakeholders were not enthusiastic about the database directive and that the EU Commission seems to be hesitant regarding how to deal with database rights. The European Commission found that most stakeholders did not see the benefit of the Database Directive. However, as Dreyfuss states, there is a cautionary tale here. Were the EU ultimately to decide that database protection is ineffective, it may well find that it is difficult to roll back a property system, because these rights may not be

[89] See discussion in Section 6.1.

[90] Commission, 'Protection of Databases' <https://ec.europa.eu/digital-single-market/en/protection-databases>.

[91] Commission, 'Staff Working Document and Executive Summary on the Evaluation of the Directive 96/9/EC on the Legal Protection of Databases' <https://ec.europa.eu/digital-single-market/en/news/staff-working-document-and-executive-summary-evaluation-directive-969ec-legal-protection>. See more precisely Commission (n 91).

easy to claw back once investments have been made.[92] From a global perspective, it should be noted that the US Supreme Court has refused a rule for database-copyright protection.[93]

An ATR could be included in an updated version of the Database Directive, where a business user is granted an ATR for the dataset that represents its generated data,[94] and when the business user has invested time and effort, qualitatively and/or quantitatively in the platform, to a certain level. There is thus a threshold requirement reflecting that a certain amount of data has been created on the platform due to the actions of the business users and its end users. The business user should have invested time, for example, in the selection or arrangement of the collection of products or services that it provided for the transaction platform. The user thus gains a right to access and port the data generated by the user's investment in the platform. The data should be stored in datasets that users may have access to under an ATR in real time, through an API.

The data holder (platform) should retain the sui generis database right to the collection of aggregated data originating from the platform and the ecosystem as a whole, which will thus include data from the activities of various users on the platform, as well as other data. In these circumstances, both parties have a genuine and legitimate interest in the generated data, and while the cost of setting up the database should be borne by the data holder, neither the platform provider nor the business user should charge one another for accessing the data.

The data holder and users thus have separate rights to the data, while the scope of their respective datasets and databases are different. Indeed, it is to some degree a collective set-up, lacking the notion of right in rem that grants exclusive control over the use of data. Nonetheless, the set-up with an ATR still favors the user – the party most likely to use the data to invest in the production and commercialization based on the subject matter of protection. It should be acknowledged that access rights are normally countervailing rights to property,[95] but ATRs are more than access rights; they also vest the holder with the right to transfer data, and to create markets for data generally, with the business user. ATRs could also be boosted by a reverse-engineering or data-mining alternative, giving business users a right to open up the platform to search for data, through either an API or a right to access the blockchain of data generated by the platform.

The Database Directive needs to be updated in several other aspects, and while not every detail can be mentioned here, the following issues need to be addressed: (i) The dichotomy between copyright-protected and sui generis-protected databases

[92] Rochelle C. Dreyfuss, 'The Challenges Facing IP Systems: Researching for the Future' in Peter Drahos, Gustavo Ghidini, and Hanns Ullrich (eds), *Kritika: Essays on Intellectual Property* (Edward Elgar 2020) 2.

[93] *Feist Publications, Inc v Rural Telephone Service Co* 499 US 340 (1991).

[94] Previously defined as 'business user's data', see Section 2.4.

[95] Drexl (n 9) 134.

as well as the definition of joint ownership compared to joint makers must be resolved and clarified to give platform providers a sui generis right in the main database created by the platform, while giving business users of the platform access to their respective business user's datasets;[96] (ii) the Database Directive needs to be adapted and must clearly include machine-readable data; (iii) the obsolete principle of the spin-off doctrine and the dichotomy between creating and obtaining data should be scrapped, because everything will be about data. Indeed, irrespective of whether the investment creates or obtains data as a by-product of main or core activity, the investment should be included in the assessment, because it will be very difficult to distinguish between main activity and by-product activity with respect to data. The required scope and thresholds for the collection of data and obtaining database protection must (iv) be clarified. It should also be clarified that (v) public authorities can also obtain database protection. The Database Directive also needs to adapt to the technology of storing data, that is, blockchain and similar technologies, and the name should be changed to the Dataset Directive.[97] In addition to this, mandatory access and portability rights should be included for both copyright-protected databases and sui generis databases.

96 See ibid., 77.
97 See generally Commission (n 91).

8

Conclusion

The content of this book is rather controversial. It paints a rather bleak picture, that the current EU legal economic system being developed for the data-driven economy is both outdated and – to some extent – a policy at war with itself. It promotes dominant platforms to detriment of others. Moreover, the fundamentals for creating rules are also missing. A liberal economic system needs to be based on aspects of a rights system, otherwise, we risk losing innovation, the establishment of new markets, and the creation of wealth, while we will see increasing market failures. Without a legal system for rights to data, we will lose out of a just system for the distribution of wealth. Indeed, it is time that the data-driven economy and the internet economy are granted their 'property' rights, reflecting the new paradigm of the data-driven industrial revolution. Moreover, such a regime fits well with the European economic constitution now being established.

It should be acknowledged that platforms, specifically Google and Facebook, do collect a vast amount of data from their own walled gardens. The notion of a 'walled garden'[1] or silo is often used to describe the digital ecosystem – such as Google's and Facebook's respective systems – where the platform leaders exclusively collect the data and where individual-level data remains under the control of these platforms and is generally not shared with other market participants.[2] That data is not disseminated causes market failures and prevents efficient use of the main resource in the

[1] 'Walled gardens' are closed ecosystems in which a platform provides a complete end-to-end technical solution for advertisers and publishers, and advertisers and publishers are restricted in their ability to choose other technical solutions. These ecosystems can be very large – for instance Google's includes Android and Chrome operating systems; YouTube, Gmail, and Google Maps. Facebook's ecosystem includes WhatsApp, Instagram, Messenger, and Marketplace. CMA Final Report 4.24, fn 225

[2] See CMA Final Report 4.24. Platforms share to some extent aggregate-level data with other market participants.

digital economy, the data. It creates an anticommons plagued with hold-up problems. The data and the knowledge derived therefrom is the core asset of the platform's business model(s), and while their business model should be protected, the data they generate should also be accessible by the businesses that create the content that draws the public to voluntarily give up data when they enter the walled gardens. Indeed, business users of platform as well as subcontractors in Internet of Things (IoT) systems should have access to data.

In reference to their own ecosystems, platforms collect data regarding the individual user when a user surfs or logs on to a platform. Everything from web and search history, hardware used, uploaded or written information on the web, clicks, information that the mouse may have hovered over, etc., is collected. Generally, all individual activities in the ecosystems and also background information regarding the users are collected, categorized, and stored as data.

They however not only collect data from their own respective ecosystems or walled gardens. Data is also provided by third parties, the business users of platforms, for example, advertisers and publishers, including news and other content providers. They provide data voluntarily to the platforms, while also indirectly giving access to their websites for Google and Facebook to collect data. As stated in a final report from July 2020, CMA claims that for platforms in reference to digital advertisement there are two broad sources to use for collecting data: (i) data gathered from the platforms' own walled garden (or as CMA defines it: their 'consumer-facing services and products'), and (ii) data collected from third parties, notably those that use the platforms' services and technology on their own websites.[3]

Not only Google and Facebook collect data. According to some estimates, Amazon captures 46 percent of online shopping, selling for example around 90 percent of all e-books in the United States,[4] and more than 70 percent of online shoppers use Amazon to compare products found on a brand's website. Amazon collects data from these activities on its own platform and closed ecosystem, while also receiving information from third-party publisher sites, where a publisher monetizes its ad inventory through Amazon Publisher Service or Amazon ad exchange.[5]

[3] CMA Final Report Appendix F

[4] Lina Khan, 'Amazon's Antitrust Paradox' (2017) 126 Yale Law Journal 712 et seq. <https://ssrn.com/abstract=2911742>; Olivia LaVecchia and Stacy Mitchell, 'Amazon's Stranglehold: How the Company's Tightening Grip Is Stifling Competition, Eroding Jobs, and Threatening Communities' (November 2016) The Institute for Local Self-Reliance 10 <http://ilsr.org/wp-content/uploads/2016/11/ILSR_AmazonReport_final.pdf> or <http://perma.cc/A4ND-2NDJ>.

[5] From a review of their privacy policies, it appears that Amazon probably does not sell personally identifiable Echo data to third parties such as music streaming services, though the policy is not clear in this respect; there do not appear to be any limits on the transfer of aggregated data, and the policies could be changed by Amazon at any time. It is not evident from Amazon's privacy policies that there are limits on the company's ability to purchase data from a third party such as Fitbit, to aggregate that database with Amazon's own data, and then to identify particular kinds of consumers (e.g., long-distance runners) on that basis. See Stigler Final Report 232. For a critical analysis of other firms' collection and mining of data, see W. Christl, *Corporate*

Amazon also collects cookie IDs when customers use a web browser and mobile advertising IDs when using mobile devices.[6] Amazon seems to collect vast amounts of data from purchasers and users of the platforms, but Amazon also has access and the right to use supplier or business users' data. Access and the right to use that data would under certain situations give Amazon much leverage in knowledge.

'Walled garden' platforms are thus able to combine the ability to accurately monitor conversions with the ability to track users across different devices and sessions and so attribute consumers' actions more accurately. In the case of Google, it is able to track users across more than fifty-three consumer-facing services that it controls. However, its access to mobile data from Android also gives it some ability to monitor the actions of consumers offline (IRL), for example, to identify store visits. Google can thereby quite accurately conclude whether a marketing activity on its platform has been successful. Did the individual exposed to the ad, the target purchaser, indeed purchase the marketed goods by physically transferring him or herself to the store in question within a time period after being exposed to the ad? Yet, also more broadly, the effects content provided on the platform has generated can be monitored. Given the enormous penetration of Google and other platforms, the ability to monitor effects globally, yet on an individual level, originating from specific events or conduct is unprecedented in history.[7]

The above presentations of Google, Facebook, and Amazon show that platforms are 'walled gardens' or silos and networks for collecting data, where the center of gravity is the hubs, the platforms. They receive all data from the ecosystems, while they have technical and legal systems that allow them to prevent sharing the data and limit interoperability of data. The business strategy is closely connected to collecting, analyzing, and using services based on data, while not giving access to data. Data is the key to the set-up and where the data generated is caused not by the actions of the platforms. Rather the data is generated by the parties on either side of the platforms – either consumer or business users. The platforms technically control and general benefit of the data, while denying access to the rest. Indeed, the data generated by the platform are generated by other firms active on the platforms, including their end users or potential end users, while the service or cloud contracts used by platforms do not allow access to data. In addition, platforms may claim intellectual property protection vis-à-vis claims or actions for accessing the data.

There are several options for legally allowing users and others to access the data they generate on large platforms.

First, one could imagine a solution depicted in the Open Data Directive, where all have a right to access and port *all* available data. It could be similar to the set-up

Surveillance in Everyday Life. How Companies Collect, Combine, Analyze, Trade, and Use Personal Data on Billions (Cracked Labs 2017) 6.

[6] CMA Final Report Appendix F

[7] Ibid.

of the Open Data/PSI regulation, indicating that any comer has a right to access all data available and generated by the digital service provided. The general scheme of granting access to data was enacted toward the public sector with an aim to enhance the available data in society and for business users to create innovation, increase wealth, while also creating a dichotomy between the public sector providing digital infrastructure are the private sector. Applying this principle to gatekeepers providing platform of infrastructure type would certainly increase the level of data in society, yet it would transform the platform into infrastructure and destroy their business model and decrease their incentive to innovate and develop their business models. Moreover, the transparency in society and of markets in such a set-up could lead to unpredicted consequences. Competition and Innovation could lessen, collusion could increase, and the surveillance of activities could generally be too great.[8]

In the Digital Markets Act, business users should have access to the data that (i) the business users and its end users generate, and (ii) referred data originating from such data. The access rule should be viewed as overriding the gatekeeper's right to said data. Whether the Digital Markets Act actually includes an overriding right, and its general interface with intellectual property legal system, needs to be clarified. Yet, the rules granting access to data to business users and limiting the gatekeepers' control of data in the Digital Markets Act could be interpreted as a bilateral overriding right benefitting the business users vis-à-vis gatekeepers. However, the gatekeeper may still use General Data Protection Regulation (GDPR) as a tool to deny access to data. In the end, end users' personal data can be off-limit for business users. Indeed, the Digital Markets Act should either be declared providing a right for business user erga omnes to data by the Court or be amended with a clear access and transfer right for business users.

In reference to Google, Facebook, Amazon, and other platforms, the business user's data that should be available for respective business user under an access and transfer right should be both the data it generates in the walled gardens and also the data originating from the actions of their end users or potential end users on third-party websites. A business user should have access to data regarding purchaser, potential purchasers. Everything should be provided: from web and search history, hardware used, uploaded or written information on the web, clicks, and information that the mouse has hovered over, to whether the individual or business purchased the marketed goods or services. Generally, all individual activities in the ecosystems and also background information regarding the users that is collected, categorized, and stored as data should be provided by the platforms. Yet, the data generated by the actions of other business users should not be provided, protecting the business model of that business user and of the platform provider.

8 Indeed, as discussed above, possibly the Open Data paradigm should instead be lessened to improve the competitiveness of public sector bodies and to level the playing field vis-à-vis platforms.

The above implies that the collaboration between the business user and the gatekeeper is somewhat on a level playing field, where the data they are able to access reflects their joint effort on the platform.[9]

One could imagine that the obligation as described in the Digital Markets Act is boosted with not only an overriding right vis-à-vis the gatekeepers' rights but also a sui generis database right, and, moreover, that the business users should hold something akin to a reverse-engineering right and data-mining right. Such a bundle of rights would benefit the business users to gain open access to the platform and the data collected and stored in platform server interface. The business users should have their own access application programming interfaces (API) to the relevant datasets giving the right to the business user to technically access data through such a gateway. A reverse-engineering right would break or trump the gatekeeper's potential claim that access to the data could be refused because the gatekeeper holds intellectual property rights to technical protection measures (TPMs), APIs, or databases, or that the data reflects trade secrets.

It should also be the obligation of the gatekeeper to store the data in such a way that third-party rights are not violated by the access and portability of the business user. Such an obligation could be encompassed in the Digital Markets Act.

Moreover, the business users should only be limited by GDPR to the same extent as gatekeepers. The need for a level playing field call for equal access under GDPR for gatekeepers as well as business users using the same platform. The gatekeepers need to either provide similar access to business users through consent provisions or limit their own access under GDPR to personal data, should the individual in question refuse to encompass business users in the consent given to the platform.

Under the IoT, will issues in reference to access, use, and transfer of data be an even greater concern? In reference to the vehicle industry, perhaps, John Deere's data-driven business model 'precision agriculture' may best depict the future for connected vehicles. John Deere produces farm vehicles, holding by some estimates the largest market share, around 30 percent of the global tractor market,[10] yet today these pieces of machinery are part of IoT for precision agriculture, where John Deere, vehicles, farmers, and third parties may access the John Deere platform. Data, including agronomic (crop management) data and machine operation data (e.g., fuel level, location, machine hours, engine RPM), is collected primarily from sensors embedded both in the machines and in the field (soil) but also pulls from external sources (e.g., weather prediction data, commodity pricing). Through telematics, the data is automatically uploaded onto the cloud via cellular network, Wifi, or Bluetooth. Farmers access and manage the data through the cloud software platform. Through the Operation Centre app on this platform, farmers – and John

9 See discussion in Chapter 3 regarding joint R&D efforts.

10 See, for example, statistics from Farmer Insight <www.fginsight.com/news/news/tractor-sales-breakdown-john-deere-still-out-in-front-but-kubota-is-charging-up-the-outside-18529>.

Deere – can monitor activity in real-time, analyze performance, determine how best to utilize equipment, and collaborate with partners for insights and 'prescriptions' using algorithms that help the farmer decide what to plant, where, and when with optimized conditions. John Deere runs an Open Data platform, where farmers are encouraged to share their data with the third party. Software providers access the data through John Deere's APIs. The more data that is collected, the more valuable the platform becomes to all stakeholders; farmers may benefit from analyzing data collected over time and from other farmers' data to inform decisions, and software developers glean more insights paving the way for development of new value-added products and services. Yet, John Deere will be the holder of the platform controlling much of the data and is perhaps not so keen on sharing the same. John Deere can also share the data with input suppliers (seeds, fertilizer, chemicals) and it can be connected to trigger automatic ordering from the same firms.[11] What John Deere is trying to create with the data-driven business model is network effects, where John Deere, its platform, and its tractors will be the hub in the system. Indeed, it can be a strategy to try to become a monopolist, where the platform services, multisided features, and indirect network effects will tip the market to the benefit of John Deere, elevating it to a monopoly.[12]

The basic structure of the proposed Data Act for meeting these challenges of the IoT paradigm is the introduction of an obligation that 'products shall be designed and manufactured, and related services shall be provided, in such a manner that data generated by their use are, by default, easily, securely and, where relevant and appropriate, directly accessible to the user.' The obligation is, as it seems, accompanied with a new non-waivable and possibly countervailing right of the users to access and share the (raw) data that they have generated through their IoT devices (Articles 4 and 5).[13] It is uncertain, whether the right in Article 4 of the proposal is applicable when the data is directly accessible under Article 3 Data Act, and whether the right to access data is without restrictions and erga omnes, for example, vis-à-vis purchasers of the database originally set up by the manufacturer of the IoT device, including the sensor.

The right makes no difference between consumers and businesses. All users of IoT devices (B2C and B2B) should be empowered by the rights and can get access to all data they have created. According to recital 28, the user should be free to use the data for any lawful purpose. According to Article 5, the user also has the right to

[11] See C. Williams, 'Farm to Data Table: John Deere and Data in Precision Agriculture' (12 November 2019) <https://digital.hbs.edu/platform-digit/submission/farm-to-data-table-john-deere-and-data-in-precision-agriculture>. See also M. Ryan, 'Agricultural Big Data Analytics and the Ethics of Power' (2020) 33 Journal of Agricultural and Environmental Ethics 49–69 <https://doi.org/10.1007/s10806–019-09812-0>.

[12] Network effect and tipping is discussed in Section 2.3.

[13] Wolfgang Kerber, 'Governance of IoT Data: Why the EU Data Act Will Not Fulfill its Objectives' (8 April 2022) <https://ssrn.com/abstract=4080436> or <http://dx.doi.org/10.2139/ssrn.4080436>.

share the generated data with third parties (firms or other actors), who can use these data for those purposes that are agreed upon with the users, while the third party still needs to negotiate and enter an agreement with the data holder according to Article 8 of the Data Act.

According to recital 14, the scope of data these rights cover is raw data, that is, the data directly and unprocessed generated by the user. Derived data and inferred data are not encompassed by the rights or the proposal as such. This could be a default setting and more sector-specific regulations, such as the Digital Markets Act, will go beyond the limitation of only regulating the control of raw data.

Similar problems arise with the Data Act, as with the Digital Markets Act, they are not going far enough in reference to not giving a right to data and where the data holder actually controls the data field. The Data Act should therefore be boosted with an access and transfer right (ATR) benefitting subcontractors, producers, and users. Amendment of the Data Act to include a genuine, overriding right for users to access and transfer data has been discussed throughout this book and, in several senses, this is the preferred solution. It will certainly be a game changer and create a level playing field for competition; it will also be a vital tool that enables business users and users to challenge established core platform markets. In reference to IoT systems, the principle of exhaustion should be guiding and give to property holder of the IoT device the general right to access and utilize the data, while part manufacturers, producers, and users should hold ATRs to parts of the data of interest to them. Such ATRs may be included in the Data Act but may also be included as part of intellectual property rights, such as patents and copyright. Finally, platform providers for IoT systems may contractually be granted the right to access and utilize the data. All this may fit in the Data Act and in intellectual property law systems.

Indeed, in reference to the upcoming IoT paradigm, a right to access and transfer data could be included in other intellectual property legal systems. When the supplier of parts or devices has included sensors in their intellectual property protected parts or devices that are included in larger smart ecosystems, for example, smart house, they should have a right to access the data generated by the sensor within the protected part of the device. They should retain an ATR to the data generated by the sensor also after the part or device has been exhaustively sold to the smart system leaders or to end users. In reference to the John Deere smart system for precision agriculture, the parts suppliers of the system, that is, the part producers to the machines, the suppliers of seeds (including sensors), and software providers should thus hold ATRs. If the device or part they provide to the system is encompassed by intellectual property rights, including an ATR, the ATR will not be exhausted. So, for example, the EU patent legal system should include an ATR for patentees that is not exhausted when the patented device is transferred.

The system leader for the technical control and design of the smart system should also have access through its own sensors, while the individuals will access and port data in such a system under the GDPR.[14] Users may give access to, for example, independent service providers under the proposed Data Act. However, in complex systems, the data generated by sensors are not necessarily the only data used for the system or individual devices to function. This is accentuated in larger systems, such as houses or kitchens, where the system gains data from various sensors inside the system, and also from the outside, for example, from stores, weather forecasts from other smart houses or smart cities, and other connected devices. The combination of all the data necessarily needs to be controlled by a platform or hub, be it under the control of a system leader or a gatekeeper. They will necessarily gain access through contracts and cloud access.

Farmers in the example above should have ATRs to the data generated by the sensors. Would they have purchased the machinery, they can make use of direct access, while access and portability rights under the Data Act and GDPR can be achieved.

However, John Deere would most likely be the lessor of the equipment and machinery to the farmers, holding ATRs to its sensors; while should John Deere exhaustively have transferred the equipment and machinery to the farmer, John Deere would most likely have access to data under contracts with the farmer and with the parts supplier.

It has been argued in this book that the regulation of the data-driven economy should be amended with a right, drawing inspiration from reverse-engineering or data-mining doctrines, for accessing and transferring the data that is collected and stored on the data holders' server interface, that is, most likely a database. Such an ATR, would allow users to circumvent the data holders' right to protection under TPMs, database rights, and trade-secret legislation to gain access to the data generated by themselves. Such a limited ATR could be included in the Data Act and the right should require an equal right to data for users compared to data holders.

Moreover, the right to access and transfer for users should also be aligned with the GDPR, giving a user the right to also access personal data when the user can provide equal protection under the GDPR as the original data holder.

The right to equal access and transfer of data could alternatively be supplemented in an updated version of the database directive for the benefit of users. The database directive could moreover go further and grant a more elaborated right when users have invested time and/or effort to create useful data to the level that it would become a database right in its own right, that is, with a limited exclusive right to prevent certain large data dumps. This would normally apply to business users of platforms.

14 José van Dijck, Martijn de Waal, and Thomas Poell, *The Platform Society: Public Values in a Connective World* (Oxford University Press 2018); Murray Goulden, '"Delete the Family": Platform Families and the Colonisation of the Smart Home' (2019) Information, Communication & Society 1–18; and generally Rob Kitchin, Tracey P. Lauriault, and Gavin McArdle (eds), *Data and the City* (Routledge 2018).

It should be clear that a system with ATRs would increase the volume of data available in society for licensing and use. Datasets or the right to obtain data from a platform can be licensed or traded as such under a license agreement, implying either a transfer of data or granting of access to data under the stipulated term of contract. Presumably, data transfer or licensing to reusers of data will mainly be initiated by the business users selling datasets by giving access to data under licenses. Moreover, ATRs can be licensed, and possibly even assigned, under the system described above. Business users may grant access rights to data brokers, for example. This will provide opportunities for new businesses and markets for data. Indeed, the reuse of data will increase, and data markets with data brokers will increase in volume and in number. Moreover, data pools, where business users join datasets, will presumably increase. These data pools might be very useful for business users because, as many authors have argued, it is the aggregated data from industries, platforms, ecosystems, or markets that creates the best result for understanding and developing products, services, and markets. While the platform providers will hold such aggregated data and be in control of the aggregated data from a platform or ecosystem, and business users will control their respective datasets, the business users can combine their datasets to create something similar to the databases held by the platform providers. Establishment of an access and transfer legal system could expose system leaders and platform providers to natural competition under a new system of economic regulations in data-driven markets.

In the end, it should be emphasized that the book provides the argument that a rights system or governance system for the Internet and IoT is indispensable. Competition without such a system as an incentive structure does not seem to work well in reference to creating functioning data-driven markets. On the contrary, they seem to easily tip and become failing markets in the hands of strong monopolies. Neither individuals nor brick-and-mortar firms value their data without a property right. Moreover, competition does not seem to work well to boost creativity or benefit innovation in reference to the markets where the data is harvested (collected). The platforms are on control of the relevant information and to prevent the market failure inherent in this asymmetry in information needs to be corrected.

Apart from the problem of dysfunctional markets, there are several important arguments for enacting a right system in reference to access and portability of data; this right could in fact mitigate the failures of sector-specific regulations that have developed and are in the process of being enacted.

Intellectual property rights are needed to create incentives for producing or developing new knowledge. If that new knowledge were instantly copied and the creator would not be able to benefit from the creation of the new information, the creator would not spend time and resources to come up with the new knowledge. However, competition also works as an incentive. From an economic welfare policy viewpoint, the collection of data, be it personal or nonpersonal, is a sign of developing, competing firms and the creation of more efficient markets, providing goods that consumers are willing to pay for. As several commentators have acknowledged competition works well as an incentive for firms to collect data. All the incumbent internet service providers (ISPs), platforms, and brick-and-mortar firms collect data under the IoT paradigm. A property right is perhaps not needed for firms to monitor and collect data, yet we do not know the counterfactual situation. Both business with data-driven business strategies and regular brick-and-mortar firms collect data under the current settings, while an access and portability system seem to be needed for business users to use the data to develop their business models, invest in R&D, and innovate in reference to their core market and products[15] – indeed, to use the data to innovate. Otherwise, they risk becoming subcontractors to large platforms or IoT system providers.

A reason for creating such a limited rights regime is that the rights granted to users may help to create markets (for goods and innovations).[16] A limited property regime in data will likely boost data markets, something which is badly needed in Europe. A rights system also makes the protected information transparent, so that others (i.e., third parties, not the right-holder) may access the information and pursue further research or effort to collect and create more information. The property right creates transparency that leads to competition in innovation. The ATR system explained in this book provides for this because there is no exclusivity to data, it only provides a mandatory access and portability right to datasets in the control of the business users, while the aggregated data originating from the platform are still the prerogative of the platform providers. The business users to the platforms hold ATRs including the distribution rights to their respective data, that is, the data produced by their effort for the platform and while they can combine data into pools, their respective datasets are centered on their business model, product, or service.

The ATR will only grant access and portability to the relevant set of data. It is not an exclusive right. Indeed, several interested parties may have right to gain access and port the same data (or copies of said data). Transfer data implies a right to copy; not granting exclusive or excluding rights is the key to a functioning property or governance system to data. Such a system can create a better balance between business users and platform providers, and ATRs should be applicable vis-à-vis all platform providers, not only the large platform providers, that is, the gatekeepers.

When having a rights system in place, competition law plays an important role, to form a framework for licensing of datasets and when setting up data pools that can be

[15] See, for example, Andreas Wiebe, 'Protection of Industrial Data – A New Property Right for the Digital Economy?' (2017) 12(1) Journal of Intellectual Property Law & Practice 62–71, 67 <https://doi.org/10.1093/jiplp/jpw175> accessed 2 December 2017. See also Josef Drexl, 'Data Access and Control in the Era of Connected Devices' (2018) Study on behalf of the European Consumer Association BEUC, Brussels (book publication forthcoming 2019).

[16] Hanns Ullrich, 'Intellectual Property: Exclusive Rights for a Purpose' in Ksiega Pamiatkowa Profesora Mariana Kępińskiego, *Problemy Polskiego e Europejskiego Prawa Prywatnego* (LEX Warszawa 2012) 425–459.

used to compete on data-driven markets. Competition law will also govern whether a platform provider may license in ATRs from business users and users using the platform. Generally, competition authorities should be cautious with such licensing set-ups, due to the fact that the platform providers already hold the data from the platform, and a licensing of ATRs could generally only be conducted with the aim to create barriers to entry for its platform market. Indeed, the more likely development would be that business users of platforms combine their ATRs in data pools to mitigate the market power of platforms, something which has been explored in this book.

Finally, with a property right system in place, current market failures will be eliminated, while the remaining market failures can be addressed under competition law. The ATR systems envisioned above will level the playing field fundamentally and indeed create competition and innovation; technical and contractual hinders may then be litigated under competition law, while sector-specific rules in the DMA et al. can be reduced in ambit or even eliminated.

Index

abuse of dominance, 73–86
application programming interfaces and, 75–76
in CJEU cases, 74–75
leverage theory and, 76–77
Magill case, 74
Public Sector Bodies and, 73
ACCC. *See* Australian Competition Authority
access and transfer rights (ATRs), 4. *See also* data access; data transfer
for business users, 215–222
business-to-business relationships and, 233
under Charter of Fundamental Rights, 217
in civil law contexts, 158–159
in common law contexts, 158–159
competition law and, 249
for complex Internet of Things systems, 227–234
conceptual approach to, 206–211
constitutional aspects of, 158–165
under Data Act, 171, 212, 220, 222, 234–236, 245–247
Data Free Flow Regulation, 206–227
under Data Governance Act, 234
data points and, 160, 211
under Database Directive, 208–223, 236–238
in data-driven economy, 56–67
data collection and, 56
distribution through property regimes, 62
entitlements and, 61
intellectual property rights, 62–64
under Digital Markets Act, 209, 212, 214–216, 220, 222, 225–226, 234–236
under Digital Services Act, 230–231
under Directive on Payment Services, 234
as economic right, 159, 218–219
Electricity Directive, 213
under EU Charter, 161
EU Commission and, 162–163, 231
European Convention for the Protection of Human Rights and Fundamental Freedoms and, 164
in European Court of Justice case law, 161–164
European Economic Constitution and, 161–162
freedom of information and, 162
general, 234–238
under General Data Protection Regulation, 4, 164, 216–219, 235
in Germany, 206–207
implementation of, 160–161
incentive systems, 223–227
independent, 214
for individuals, 216–219
in Japan, 207
legal definition of data, 211–216
market creation by, 163
Open Data Directive, 212–213, 224–226, 234
ownership and, 158–159
porting rights, 209–210
property rules, 226
property systems, 224–227
Public Sector Information Directive, 212–213, 224
purpose of, 157
risks of, 162
trade facilitated by, 210–211
Trade Secrets Protection, 231
under Treaty for the Function of the European Union, 161
user's data and, 157
for vehicles, 230–234
advertising. *See* digital advertising
Alsup, William, 7

Amazon
  cloud services, 55
  competition laws and, 78–79
    German Competition Authority investigation of, 81–82
  data collection by, 11–12, 29, 240–241
    EU Commission findings on, 11–33
    privacy policies for, 11
    US House Antitrust Committee oversight of, 12, 33–34
  as monopoly platform service, 36
anticommons
  market failures and, 22–34
    data collection and, 29–30
    definition of, 23
    Internet of Things and, 23–24
    tragedy of, 30–31
anticompetitive agreements, 86–92
  collaborations and, 87–88
  data pools and, 89–92
  research and development projects, 86–88
  Technology Transfer Guidelines in, 90
antivirus software, 6
API. *See* application programming interface
Apple
  competition laws and, 82–83
  as monopoly platform service, 36
application programming interface (API), 7
  abuse of dominance and, 75–76
  copyright protections for, 45, 176–180, 182
  under Data Act, 106–107
  data and, 59–60
  in data-driven economy, 47–48
  under Digital Services Act, 138
  Facebook and, 59–60
  Google v Oracle, 7
  platform services and, 35
  under Software Directive, 47–48
  walled gardens in, 7–8, 21, 239–241
    Facebook and, 8, 17
    Google and, 8, 14, 17
ARC. *See* German Competition Act
Arrow, Kenneth, 65, 210
ATPs. *See* digital agricultural operations
ATRs. *See* access and transfer rights
Australian Competition Authority (ACCC), 9–10

B2B relationships. *See* business-to-business relationships
big data, 31–32
block chain technology
  centralized, 49
  decentralized, 49–50
  public, 50
  technology restrictions on, 48–51
Brazil, competition laws in, 84–86
business models, in data-driven economy, 6–21
  business strategies in, 10
  for digital advertising, 24
  in health sector, 19–20
  implementation of, 19
  John Deere, 17–18
  legal protections for, 44–46
business user's data, 31
  access and transfer rights for, 215–222
  under Digital Markets Act, 242–243
business-to-business (B2B) relationships, 233

capital goods, in data-driven economies, 157–158
Charter of Fundamental Rights, 154
  access and transfer rights under, 217
Cicilline, David, 12, 33–34
civil law traditions, access and transfer rights in, 158–159
CJEU. *See* Court of Justice of the European Union
Clinton, Bill, 3–4, 95–96
cloud services
  by Amazon, 55
  cloud switching, 52–53
  data distribution to, 1
  in data-driven economy, 6, 51–56
    Infrastructure as a Service, 52–53
    Platform as a Service, 52–53
    Software as a Service, 52–53
CMA. *See* Competition and Markets Authority
common data spaces, 147–149
common law traditions, access and transfer rights in, 158–159
commons, data-driven economy and, 23
Competition and Markets Authority (CMA)
  on data collection, 29
  Facebook and, 8
  Google and, 8–9, 13, 15–17
competition laws. *See also specific acts; specific laws*
  abuse of dominance and, 73–86
    application programming interfaces and, 75–76
    in CJEU cases, 74–75
    leverage theory and, 76–77
    Magill case, 74
    Public Sector Bodies and, 73
  Amazon and, 78–79
    German Competition Authority investigation of, 81–82

anticompetitive agreements and, 86–92
collaborations and, 87–88
data pools and, 89–92
research and development projects, 86–88
Technology Transfer Guidelines in, 90
Apple and, 82–83
in Brazil, 84–86
in CJEU cases, 68, 73
abuse of dominance issues, 75
Magill case, 74
data access and transfer under, 93–94
in data driven economies, 93
data portability and, 73
Digital Markets Act, 72, 88
German influences on, 72–76
in ECJ cases, 34
ecosystem agreements and, 168
EU Commission data on, 69–92
in EU member states, 166
exceptional circumstance doctrine, 74–75
Facebook and, 83–84
French Competition Authority and, 77
general, 68–73
sector-specific rules for, 71
standard tools of, 71
German Competition Act, 31–33
German Competition Authority and, 80–82
Amazon and, 81–82
Facebook and, 83–84
Google and, 80–81
Google and, 77–78
German Competition Authority investigation of, 80–81
imbalances in market power and, 69–92
Industrial Internet and, 68–69
insufficient customer performance and, 73
intellectual property law and, 65–66
Internet of Things and, 68–71
market power advantages, 70
market power leverage restrictions, 72–73
methodological approach to, 3
network neutrality and, 77
nowcasting and, 69
procedural challenges under, 92–93
essential facility doctrine, 93
exceptional circumstances doctrine, 93
public interest in, 1
quality parity clauses, 81–82
self-favouring issues, 72–73
Spotify and, 82
under TFEU, 68–69, 73, 88–91
third party data under, barriers to entry influenced by, 72–73
consent, in General Data Protection Regulation, 142
continuous data transfers, 46–47
copyright law, Charter of Fundamental Rights and, 154
copyright protections, under intellectual property law, 176–190
for application programming interfaces, 45, 176–180, 182
copyright-protected databases and, 180–184
Digital Rights Management tools, 176–180, 195
in European Union, 182
sui generis database protections, 184–190, 203, 216
technical protection measures and, 176–180
Court of Justice of the European Union (CJEU)
abuse of dominance cases, 74–75
competition laws in, 68, 73
abuse of dominance issues, 75
Magill case, 74

data. *See also* access and transfer rights; *specific topics*
application programming interfaces and, 59–60
big data, 31–32
business users, 31
access and transfer rights for, 215–222
under Digital Markets Act, 242–243
continuous transfers, 46–47
under Data Act, 44–46
under Database Directive, 39–42
definition of, 32, 38–44
under Digital Markets Act, 42–46, 67
EU Commission on, 41
on free flow of data, 39
regulatory initiatives, 41
on rights to data, 40
under General Data Protection Regulation, 57–59, 61
independent, 42, 214
information compared to, 38–39
copyright protections of, 39
semantic, 39
legal protections for, 44–46
metadata, 211
methodological approach to, 1–5
nowcasting for, 33
under Open Data Directive, 39–40, 43–44
Personal Information Management Systems and, 48
under Public Sector Information Directive, 39–40
rights to, 39–40
EU Commission on, 40

data. (cont.)
under Software Directive, 45–46
application programming interfaces and, 47–48
syntactic, 213
technical protection measures for, 45, 49, 57–58
technology restrictions on, 46–51
on application programming interfaces, 46–48
for block chain technology, 48–51
third party, 72–73
under Trade Secrets Protection Directive, 40
data access, 144–150
common data spaces, 147–149
under competition laws, 93–94
under Data Act, 149–150
under Data Governance Act, 130–131, 146, 149–150
in data-driven economies, 147–150
under Digital Markets Act, 145–147, 149–150
under Digital Services Act, 135, 137
under Directive on Direct Payment Services II, 146, 149–150
EU Commission on, 147–148
under General Data Protection Regulation, 150
government-to-platform and, 149
under Open Data Directive, 128–130, 146–147
preamble for, 130
public sector information and, 128–130
public-sector bodies and, 128–130
regulating platforms for, 127–130
Data Act (Proposal for a Regulation of the European Parliament and of the Council on harmonised rules on fair access to and use of data), EU (2022), 2, 44–46, 102–108
access and transfer rights and, 171, 212, 220, 222, 234–236, 245–247
application programming interfaces, 106–107
data access under, 149–150
data transfer under, 149–150
data-driven economies under, 156
intellectual property law under, 169–171, 204–205
data access tools, 174–175
data holders under, 194–196
data-mining regulations in, 196
Internet of Things and, 244–246
data brokers, General Data Protection Regulation and, 143–144
data collection
access and transfer rights and, 56
by Amazon, 11–12, 29, 240–241
EU Commission findings on, 11–33
privacy policies for, 11
US House Antitrust Committee oversight of, 12, 33–34
anticommons and, 29–30
Competition and Markets Authority on, 29
EU Commission on, use of, 21
data collection by Amazon, 11–33
by Facebook, 7–11, 29, 240–241
advertising revenues from, 12–14
Federal Trade Commission and, 17
under General Data Protection Regulation, restrictions on, 20
by Google, 7–11, 29, 240–241
advertising revenues from, 12–14
DoubleClick ID and, 14–15
personal, restrictions on, 20
pooling of, 20
transparency in, 30
Data Free Flow initiatives, 99–102
Data Free Flow Regulation, 2, 206–227
Data Governance Act, EU, 130–134
access and transfer rights under, 234
data access under, 130–131
data sharing services, 131–134
data transfer access under, 146, 149–150
data transfer under, 146, 149–150
public-sector bodies, 130–131
data leakage, on pornography websites, 13
data points, access and transfer rights and, 160, 211
data pools, anticompetitive agreements and, 89–92
data portability, competition laws and, 73
data sharing, under Data Governance Act, 131–134
data transfer, 144–150
common data spaces, 147–149
under competition laws, 93–94
under Data Act, 149–150
under Data Governance Act, 146, 149–150
in data-driven economies, 147–150
under Digital Markets Act, 145–147, 149–150
under Directive on Direct Payment Services II, 146, 149–150
EU Commission on, 147–148
under General Data Protection Regulation, 150
government-to-platform and, 149
under Open Data Directive, 146–147
Database Directive, 39–42, 183–185, 188
access and transfer rights under, 208–223, 236–238
databases, copyright protections for, 180–184
sui generis database protections, 184–190, 203, 216
data-driven economies. *See also* access and transfer rights; application programming interface
access and transfer rights in, 56–67
data collection and, 56
distribution through property regimes, 62

entitlements and, 61
intellectual property rights, 62–64
anticommons, market failures and, 22–34
data collection and, 29–30
definition of, 23
Internet of Things and, 23–24
tragedy of, 30–31
antivirus software, 6
application programming interfaces in, under Software Directive, 47–48
business models, 6–21
business strategies in, 10
for digital advertising, 24
in health sector, 19–20
implementation of, 19
John Deere, 17–18
legal protections for, 44–46
business users' data and, 31
capital goods in, 157–158
Charter of Fundamental Rights and, 154
cloud services in, 6, 51–56
Infrastructure as a Service, 52–53
Platform as a Service, 52–53
Software as a Service, 52–53
commons and, 23
competition laws in, 93
conceptual approaches to, 151–158
consumer access to digital services in, 6
data access in, 147–150
under Data Act, 156
data transfer in, 147–150
datasets in
control of, 27–28
EU Commission strategy for, 28
interoperability issues, 27
monopolies from concentration of, 27–28
under Digital Markets Act, 156
economics for, 34–38
for Internet of Things, 37–38
platform services, 34–37
European Economic Constitution and, 153–154
framework for establishment of, 158
freedoms in, 152–153
intellectual property rights in
as access and transfer right, 62–64
markets created by, 65
Internet of Things and, 6
anticommons and, 23–24
contracts for, 51–56
economy of, 37–38
laissez-faire economic approach to, 151
legal disciplines of market law and, 154–156
navigation software, 6
in Nordic legal traditions, 154–155
objectives of, 155–156
platform services in, 51–56
platform-to-business regulations, 52
property rights in, 152–157
under Software Directive, 47–48
streaming services, 6
technology restrictions in, 46–51
on application programming interfaces, 46–48
for block chain technology, 48–51
Treaty on the Functioning of the European Union and, 153
data-holding platforms, 98–140
as competition tool, 123–127
under Data Act, 102–108, 194–196
APIs under, 106–107
technical protection measures and, 106–107
Data Free Flow initiatives, 99–102
under Data Governance Act, 130–134
data access under, 130–131
data sharing services, 131–134
public-sector bodies, 130–131
under Digital Markets Act, 108–123, 194–196
core platform services, 109–110
cumulative criteria for, 111
data portability under, 117–118
gatekeeper requirements under, 95–123
price parity clauses under, 112–113
prohibitions under, 111–118
Digital Services Act, 134–140
application programming interfaces under, 138
data access in, 135, 137
national access points in, 134–135
repair and maintenance information, 135
Directive on Payment Services II, 134–140
eCall Directive, 136–137
intellectual property law and, 194–196
Nordic Competition Authorities and, 126
platform-to-business regulations and, 98–102
Data Free Flow Regulation, 101–102
transparency in, 101
Swedish Competition Authority and, 29
data-mining
under Data Act, 196
under Digital Markets Act, 196
intellectual property law and, 196
regulations on, 45–46
text and data mining, 175–176
datasets, in data-driven economy
control of datasets, 27–28
EU Commission strategy for, 28
interoperability issues, 27
monopolies from concentration of, 27–28

digital advertising, 24
digital agricultural operations (ATPs), 17
Digital Markets Act (DMA) (Proposal for a Regulation of the European Parliament and of the Council on contestable and fair markets in the digital sector), EU (2020), 2, 42–46, 67
  access and transfer rights under, 209, 212, 214–216, 220, 222, 225–226, 234–236
  competition laws and, 72, 88
    German influences on, 72–76
  data access under, 145–147, 149–150
  data transfer under, 145–147, 149–150
  data-driven economies under, 156
  as data-holding platform, 108–123
    as competition tool, 123–127
    core platform services, 109–110
    cumulative criteria for, 111
    data portability under, 117–118
    gatekeeper requirements under, 95–123
    price parity clauses under, 112–113
    prohibitions under, 111–118
  in Germany, 124–125
    competition laws and, 72–76
  intellectual property law and, 169–171, 179, 186, 193
    data access tools, 174–175
    data holders under, 194–196
    data-mining regulations in, 196
Digital Rights Management (DRM) tools, 176–180, 195
Digital Services Act (Proposal for a Regulation of the European Parliament and of the Council on a Single Market for Digital Services), EU (2020), 2, 134–140
  access and transfer rights under, 230–231
  application programming interfaces under, 138
  data access in, 135, 137
  national access points in, 134–135
  repair and maintenance information, 135
direct network effects, for platform services, 36
Directive on Direct Payment Services II, 146, 149–150
Directive on Payment Services (PSD), 2, 234. *See also* revisions to Directive on Payment Services
Directive on Payment Services II, 134–140
DMA. *See* Digital Markets Act
DRM tools. *See* Digital Rights Management tools

eCall Directive, 2, 136–137
ECJ. *See* European Court of Justice
economic regulation, structural changes to, 26
economic rights, access and transfer rights as, 159, 218–219
ecosystem agreements
  competition laws and, 168
  intellectual property law and, 167–168
EEA. *See* European Economic Area
Electricity Directive, 213
entitlements, access and transfer rights and, 61
Esayas, Samson Yoseph, 141
essential facility doctrine, 93
EU. *See* European Union
EU Charter, access and transfer rights under, 161
EU Commission
  access and transfer rights and, 162–163, 231
  on competition laws, 69–92
  on data, 41
    on free flow of, 39
    regulatory initiatives, 41
    on rights to data, 40
  on data access, 147–148
  on data collection, use of, 21
    by Amazon, 11–33
  on data transfer, 147–148
  digital agricultural operations and, investigation of, 17
  Directive on Payment Services, 2
  network neutrality and, guidelines for, 97–99, 108–109
  revision to Directive on Payment Services, 2
European Convention for the Protection of Human Rights and Fundamental Freedoms, 164
European Court of Justice (ECJ)
  access and transfer rights cases, 161–164
  competition law cases, 34
  exhaustion doctrine and, 197–202
European Economic Area (EEA), 81
European Economic Constitution
  access and transfer rights and, 161–162
  data-driven economies and, 153–154
European Parliament. *See also* Data Act; Digital Markets Act; Digital Services Act
  eCall Regulation, 2, 136–137
European Union (EU). *See also* Data Act; Digital Markets Act; Digital Services Act; EU Commission; *specific topics*
  Charter of Fundamental Rights, 154
    access and transfer rights under, 217
  copyright protections in, 182
  Data Governance Act, 130–134
    data access under, 130–131
    data sharing services, 131–134
    public-sector bodies, 130–131

EU Charter, 161
General Data Protection Regulation, 57–59, 61
government regulations in, in member states, 165–166
competition law and, 166
network neutrality in, 96
EU Commission guidelines, 97–99, 108–109
Open Internet Regulation, 96–97
Open Data Directive, 2, 39–40, 43–44, 128–130, 186–187
access and transfer rights and, 212–213, 224–226, 234
data access under, 241–242
preamble for, 130
public sector information and, 128–130
public-sector bodies and, 128–130
Trade Secret Act, 190
European Union Intellectual Property Office (EUIPO), 166
exceptional circumstances doctrine, 74–75, 93
exhaustion doctrine, 196–205
in ECJ cases, 197–202
Internet and, 196–203
Internet of Things and, 203–205
New Copyright Directive and, 199
under TFEU, 197–198

Facebook
application programming interfaces and, 59–60
Competition and Markets Authority and, 8
competition laws and, 83–84
data collection by, 7–11, 29, 240–241
advertising revenues from, 12–14
General Data Protection Regulation and, 140
walled gardens and, 8, 17
website tags, 9
Federal Trade Commission (FTC), U.S., 17
freedom of information, 162
French Competition Authority, 77
Friedman, Milton, 153
FTC. *See* Federal Trade Commission

G2P. *See* government-to-platform
gatekeepers, requirements for, under Digital Markets Act, 95–123
GDPR. *See* General Data Protection Regulation
general access and transfer rights, 234–238
general competition laws, 68–73
sector-specific rules for, 71
standard tools of, 71
General Data Protection Regulation (GDPR), EU, 57–59, 61, 140–144, 243
access and transfer rights under, 4, 164, 216–219, 235
consent in, 142
data access under, 150
data brokers and, 143–144
data transfer under, 150
Facebook and, 140
German Competition Authority and, 140
under German Competition Law, 140
intellectual property law and, 190–194
mosaic theory and, 142
personal data collection and, restrictions on, 20
platform database size, 142–143
requirements for, 141
processing in, 140–141
purpose limitation principle, 141
quantitative privacy and, 142
German Competition Act (ARC), 31–33
General Data Protection Regulation and, 140
German Competition Authority
competition laws and, 80–82
Amazon and, 81–82
Facebook and, 83–84
Google and, 80–81
General Data Protection Regulation and, 140
Germany
access and transfer rights in, 206–207
Competition Act, 31–33
Digital Markets Act in, 124–125
German Competition Act, 31–33
Goldfarb, Avi, 87
Google
Competition and Markets Authority and, 8–9, 13, 15–17
competition laws and, 77–78
German Competition Authority investigation of, 80–81
data collection by, 7–11, 29, 240–241
advertising revenues from, 12–14
DoubleClick ID and, 14–15
in European Economic Area, 81
as monopoly platform service, 36
walled gardens and, 8, 14, 17
Yellow Book, 24
Google v Oracle, 7
government-to-platform (G2P), 149

hacking, 45
health sector, business models for, in data-driven economy, 19–20
Henrichsen, Jennifer, 8–9

IaaS. *See* Infrastructure as a Service
incentive systems, access and transfer rights and, 223–227
independent access and transfer rights, 214

independent data, 42, 214
indirect network effects, for platform services, 36
Industrial Internet, 22
  competition laws and, 68–69
information, data compared to, 38–39
  copyright protections of information, 39
  semantic, 39
Infrastructure as a Service (IaaS), 52–53, 102
intellectual property. *See also* intellectual property rights
  under European Union Intellectual Property Office, 166
  public interest in, 1
  under Treaty on the Functioning of the European Union, 165–166
intellectual property law
  competition laws and, 65–66
  conceptual approach to, 167–172
  copyright protections, 176–190
    for application programming interfaces, 176–180, 182
    copyright-protected databases and, 180–184
    Digital Rights Management tools, 176–180, 195
    in European Union, 182
    sui generis database protections, 184–190, 203
    technical protection measures and, 176–180
  under Data Act, 169–171, 204–205
    data access tools, 174–175
    data holders under, 194–196
    data-mining regulations in, 196
  for data architecture, 168
  under Database Directive, 183–185, 188
  data-mining rights and, 170–171
  under Digital Markets Act, 169–171, 179, 186, 193
    data access tools, 174–175
    data holders under, 194–196
    data-mining regulations in, 196
  ecosystem agreements and, 167–168
  under European Union Intellectual Property Office, 166
  exemptions in digital economy and, 172–196
    New Copyright Directive, 172–176
  exhaustion doctrine and, 196–205
    in ECJ cases, 197–202
    Internet and, 196–203
    Internet of Things and, 203–205
    New Copyright Directive and, 199
    under TFEU, 197–198
  General Data Protection Regulation, 190–194
  historical development of, 25–26
  Internet of Things and, 168–169, 188–189
    exhaustion doctrine and, 203–205
  New Copyright Directive
    exemptions under, 172–176
    exhaustion doctrine and, 199–200
    technical protection measures, 176
    text and data mining, 175–176
  New Software Directive, 170, 174–175, 179–180
    UsedSoft case, 185, 200–203
  Open Data Directive, 186–187
  platform providers and, 169
  Rental and Lending Rights Directive, 198–199
  research and development and, 168–169
  in Spain, 173
  spin-off doctrine and, 187–188
  in Sweden, 190
  technical protection measures and, 170, 176
  Trade Secret Act, 190
  Trade Secret Directive, 190–194
    preamble, 192
intellectual property rights (IPRs)
  access and transfer rights and, 62–64
  in data-driven economy
    as access and transfer right, 62–64
    markets created by, 65
  under European Union Intellectual Property Office, 166
  platform services and, 35
  purpose of, 247–248
  under Treaty on the Functioning of the European Union, 165–166
Internet. *See also* network neutrality
  exhaustion doctrine and, 196–203
  Industrial Internet, 22
    competition laws and, 68–69
  Internet service providers, 248
  Open Internet Regulation, 96–97
Internet of Things (IoT), 22, 31, 243–244
  access and transfer rights and, for complex IoT systems, 227–234
  anticommons and, 23–24
  competition laws and, 68–71
  data access, use, and portability and, 17–18
  Data Act and, 244–246
  in data-driven economies, 6
    anticommons and, 23–24
    contracts for, 51–56
    economy of, 37–38
  exhaustion doctrine and, 203–205
  intellectual property law and, 168–169, 188–189
    exhaustion doctrine and, 203–205
  methodological approach to, 3
  public interest in, 1
Internet service providers (ISPs), 248
IoT. *See* Internet of Things

IPRs. *See* intellectual property rights
ISPs. *See* Internet service providers

Japan, access and transfer rights in, 207
John Deere, 17–19, 243–244
  Smart Farming, 17

laissez-faire economies, data-driven economies and, 151
Leads, James, 59–60
Leerssen, Paddy, 137
legal disciplines of market law, 154–156
Lesner, Mathias, 186–187
leverage theory, 76–77
Libert, Timothy, 8–9
Liberty Principle, 26
Locke, John, 26

Magaziner, Ira, 3–4, 95–96
Magill case, 74
Maris, Elena, 8–9
metadata, 211
Microsoft, 29
monopoly platform services, 36. *See also* Amazon; Apple; Google
mosaic theory, 142

national access points (NAP), 134–135
navigation software, 6
network neutrality (net neutrality), 95–98
  competition laws and, 77
  under Directive on Payment Services II, 134–140
  in EU, 96
    EU Commission guidelines, 97–99, 108–109
    Open Internet Regulation, 96–97
  non-interventionist approaches with, 97
  platform-to-business regulations, 98–102
New Copyright Directive
  exemptions under, 172–176
  exhaustion doctrine and, 199–200
  technical protection measures, 176
  text and data mining, 175–176
New Software Directive, 170, 174–175, 179–180
  UsedSoft case, 185, 200–203
Nintendo and Others v PC Box, 178
Nordic Competition Authority, 126
Nordic legal traditions, data-driven economies in, 154–155
nowcasting, 33
  competition laws and, 69
Nozick, Robert, 26

Oettinger, Günther, 207
Open Data Directive, EU (2019), 2, 39–40, 43–44, 128–130, 186–187
  access and transfer rights and, 212–213, 224–226, 234
  data access under, 241–242
  preamble for, 130
  public sector information and, 128–130
  public-sector bodies and, 128–130
Open Internet Regulation, 96–97

P2B regulations. *See* platform-to-business regulations
PaaS. *See* Platform as a Service
Personal Information Management Systems (PIMS), 48
Platform as a Service (PaaS), 52–53
platform services and providers. *See also specific services*
  application programming interface and, 35
  in data-driven economy, 51–56
    platform-to-business regulations, 52
  under Digital Markets Act, 109–110
  direct network effects and, 36
  indirect network effects and, 36
  intellectual property law and, 169
  intellectual property rights and, 35
  monopoly, 36
platform-to-business (P2B) regulations, 2, 52
  network neutrality and, 98–102
pornography websites, data leakage on, 13
porting rights, 209–210
price parity clauses, 112–113
privacy regulations. *See also* quantitative privacy
  for data collection, by Amazon, 11
  public interest in, 1
property rights, 153, 248. *See also* access and transfer rights
  in data-driven economies, 152–157
property rules, in access and transfer rights, 226
property systems, access and transfer rights and, 224–227
Proposal for a Regulation of the European Parliament and of the Council on a Single Market for Digital Services. *See* Digital Services Act
Proposal for a Regulation of the European Parliament and of the Council on contestable and fair markets in the digital sector. *See* Digital Markets Act
Proposal for a Regulation of the European Parliament and of the Council on harmonised rules on fair access to and use of data. *See* Data Act

PSBs. *See* public-sector bodies
PSD. *See* Directive on Payment Services
PSD2. *See* revisions to Directive on Payment Services
public sector information (PSI), 128–130
Public Sector Information Directive, 39–40, 212–213, 224
public-sector bodies (PSBs), 73
  Data Governance Act and, 130–131
  Open Data Directive and, 128–130
purpose limitation principle, 141

quality parity clauses, 81–82
quantitative privacy, 142

Rawls, John, 26
R&D. *See* research and development
regulating platforms, 98–140. *See also* access and transfer rights; data-driven economies; *specific topics*
  for data access, 127–130
Rental and Lending Rights Directive, 198–199
research and development (R&D)
  anticompetitive agreements and, 86–88
  definition of, 87–88
  intellectual property law and, 168–169
revisions to Directive on Payment Services (PSD2), 2, 139

SaaS. *See* Software as a Service
Savin, Andrej, 95–96
semantic data, 39
Smart Farming, 17
Software as a Service (SaaS), 52–53, 102
Software Directive, 45–46
  application programming interfaces and, 47–48
  data-driven economy under, 47–48
Spain, intellectual property law in, 173
spin-off doctrine, 187–188
Spotify, 82
streaming services, 6
sui generis database protections, 184–190, 203, 216
Sweden
  intellectual property law in, 190
  Trade Secret Act, 190
Swedish Competition Authority, 29
syntactic data, 213

TDM. *See* text and data mining
technical protection measures (TPMs), 45, 49, 57–58
  copyright protections and, 176–180
  data-holding platforms and, 106
  intellectual property law and, 170, 176
technology restrictions
  on data, 46–51
    on application programming interfaces, 46–48
    for block chain technology, 48–51
  in data-driven economy, 46–51
    on application programming interfaces, 46–48
    for block chain technology, 48–51
Technology Transfer Guidelines (TTG), 90
text and data mining (TDM), 175–176
TFEU. *See* Treaty on the Functioning of the European Union
TPMs. *See* technical protection measures
Trade Secret Act, EU, 190
Trade Secret Directive, 190–194
  preamble, 192
Trade Secrets Protection Directive, 40, 122–123
  access and transfer rights and, 231
tragedy of anticommons, 30–31
Treaty on the Functioning of the European Union (TFEU)
  access and transfer rights under, 161
  competition laws and, 68–69, 73, 88–91
  data-driven economies and, 153
  exhaustion doctrine under, 197–198
  intellectual property rights under, 165–166
TTG. *See* Technology Transfer Guidelines

United States (US)
  Federal Trade Commission, 17
  US House Antitrust Committee, oversight of Amazon by, 12, 33–34
UsedSoft case, 185, 200–203

vehicles, access and transfer rights for, 230–234
Vestager, Margrethe, 89

Wahl, Nils, 163–164
walled gardens, in APIs, 7–8, 21, 239–241
  Facebook and, 8, 17
  Google and, 8, 17
Wiebe, Andreas, 19

Yellow Book, 24

Zech, Herbert, 207
Zweig, Stefan, 22

Printed in the USA
CPSIA information can be obtained
at www.ICGtesting.com
CBHW061317080624
9773CB00004B/46

9 781009 335164